PRINCIPLES OF INDONESIAN CRIMINAL LAW

This authoritative new work sets out the key tenets of the principles and process of criminal law in Indonesia. Focusing on substantive criminal law, starting from its definition, history, principles, and interpretation, it goes on to explore a criminal offence and its elements, criminal fault and liability, causation, and other issues. The author is a leading scholar, experienced both in practice and teaching in the field. Comparative criminal lawyers will welcome this important new work.

Volume 21 in the series Studies in International and Comparative Criminal Law

Studies in International and Comparative Criminal Law

General Editor: Michael Bohlander

Criminal law had long been regarded as the preserve of national legal systems, and comparative research in criminal law for a long time had something of an academic ivory tower quality. However, in the past 15 years it has been transformed into an increasingly, and moreover practically, relevant subject of study for international and comparative lawyers. This can be attributed to numerous factors, such as the establishment of ad hoc international criminal tribunals and the International Criminal Court, as well as to developments within the EU, the UN and other international organisations. There is a myriad of initiatives related to tackling terrorism, money laundering, organised crime, people trafficking and the drugs trade, and the international 'war' on terror. Criminal law is being used to address global or regional problems, often across the borders of fundamentally different legal systems, only one of which is the traditional divide between common and civil law approaches. It is therefore no longer solely a matter for domestic lawyers. The need exists for a global approach which encompasses comparative and international law.

Responding to this development this new series will include books on a wide range of topics, including studies of international law, EU law, the work of specific international tribunals, and comparative studies of national systems of criminal law. Given that the different systems to a large extent operate based on the idiosyncracies of the peoples and states that have created them, the series will also welcome pertinent historical, criminological and socio-legal research into these issues.

Recent titles in this series:

Principles of German Criminal Procedure, Second Edition
Michael Bohlander

Principles of Chinese Criminal Procedure
Liling Yue

Principles of Indonesian Criminal Law
Topo Santoso

Principles of Indonesian Criminal Law

Topo Santoso

•HART•
OXFORD • LONDON • NEW YORK • NEW DELHI • SYDNEY

HART PUBLISHING

Bloomsbury Publishing Plc

Kemp House, Chawley Park, Cumnor Hill, Oxford, OX2 9PH, UK

1385 Broadway, New York, NY 10018, USA

29 Earlsfort Terrace, Dublin 2, Ireland

HART PUBLISHING, the Hart/Stag logo, BLOOMSBURY and the Diana logo are trademarks of Bloomsbury Publishing Plc

First published in Great Britain 2023

A catalogue record for this book is available from the British Library.

A catalogue record for this book is available from the Library of Congress.

Library of Congress Control Number: 2022949827

ISBN: HB: 978-1-50995-092-8
ePDF: 978-1-50995-094-2
ePub: 978-1-50995-093-5

Typeset by Compuscript Ltd, Shannon

ACKNOWLEDGEMENTS

The author would like to acknowledge the support from the Dean and Vice Deans and all members of the Criminal Law Department of the Faculty of Law, Universitas Indonesia, the input and corrections from K Walton, Mira, E Gustinelly, S Fitriasih, and the support and correction from FM Nelson and other colleagues in Indonesia. The author would like to acknowledge Professor Michael Bohlander who has given me the opportunity to write and publish this book and to Hart Publishing. Finally, I would like to express special thanks to my wife Yuliani and my children, Naufal, Nayla, and Nadia who always gave me support during the research and writing of this book.

CONTENTS

GLOSSARY

Afdoening Buiten Proces	Settlement of criminal matter outside the criminal process
AVAS (Afwezigheid Van Alle Schuld)	No Fault is Found at All
Azas/ Asas	Principle
Bestanddeel (Plural: Bestanddelen)	Written Element in The Formulation of a Criminal Offence
Culpa	Negligence
Dader	Offender/ Perpetrator
Delict/ Delicten	Crime/ Criminal Offence
Dolus/ Opzet	Intention
DPR	House of People Representatives
DPRD	District People's Representative Council (in District/ Municipal/ Provincial level)
FATF	The Financial Action Task Force on Money Laundering
Hoge Raad	The Supreme Court (in the Netherlands)
Hukum	Law
Hukum Pidana	Criminal Law
IDR	Indonesian Rupiah (the name of Indonesian Currency)
Ius Poenale	Criminal Law
Ius Poeniendi	The right (of the state) to punish
ICC	The Rome Statute of The International Criminal Court
ICCPR	The International Covenant on Civil and Political Rights

Jinayah	Criminal Law/ Criminal Offence (in Arabic language)
KPK (Komisi Pemberantasan Korupsi)	Indonesia's Corruption Eradication Commission
KUHP (Kitab Undang-Undang Hukum Pidana)	Criminal Code
Kuliah	Lecture
KUHAP (Kitab Undang-Undang Hukum Acara Pidana)	Criminal Procedure Code
KUH Perdata	The Civil Code
Kutaramanawadharmasastra	The Law Book during Majapahit Kingdom
Lex Scripta	Criminal Law Must Be Written
Lex Certa	Criminal Law Must Have Certainty
Lex Stricta	Criminal Law Must Be Strict
Mahkamah Agung	Supreme Court
Mahkamah Konstitusi	Constitutional Court
Medeplegen	Co-Perpetratorship
Minderjarig	Underage Person
Misdrijven	Crime/ More Serious Offences
MRP (Majelis Rakyat Papua)	Papua People Assembly
MvT (Memorie Van Toelichting)	Explanatory Memorandum of The Dutch Criminal Code
Nalaten	Not Doing Something/ Omission
NICA	The Netherlands Indies Civil Administration
Noodtoestand	State Of Necessity
Nullum Delictum Nulla Poena Sine Praevia Lege Poenali	No Crime, No Punishment, Without Previous Criminal Law

Nullum Crimen Sine Lege Stricta	Criminal Provisions Do Not Exist Unless They Are Narrowly/Strictly Formulated in The Legislation
Opzettelijk	Intentionally
Overmacht	Under Duress
Overtredingen	Violation/ Less Serious Offences
Osamu Serei	Law/ Act/ Statute (during the Japan Occupation in Indonesia)
Passief Nationaliteitsbeginsel/ Beschermingsbeginsel	The Principle of Passive Nationality/ Protection
Penal Mediation	Settlement of criminal matters by way of mediation; same with Restorative Justice
PERDA (Peraturan Daerah)	Regional (Local) Regulation in District/ Municipality/ Provincial Level
PERDASUS (Peraturan Daerah Khusus)	Special Regional (Local) Regulation in District/ Municipality/ Provincial Level (particularly in Papua Provinces)
PERPU (Peraturan Pemerintah Pengganti Undang-Undang)	Government Regulations In Lieu of Laws
Personaliteitsbeginsel/Actief Nationaliteitsbeginsel	The Principle of Personality/Active Nationality
Pid.Sus (Pidana Khusus)	Special Criminal Law
PNPS (Penetapan Presiden)	Presidential Decree
Poging	Attempt
Post Factum	Conditions Reconstructed After the Incident
PUU (Pengujian Undang-Undang)	Judicial Review of an Act/ Statute/Law
Qanun	Regional (Local) Regulation in District/ Municipality/ Provincial Level (particularly in Aceh Special Province)

RHS (Rechtshoogeschool)	Higher Legal Education Institution in Batavia (Jakarta) during the colonial era
RI (Republik Indonesia)	The Republic of Indonesia
RIS (Republik Indonesia Serikat)	The United States of Indonesia
RUU KUHP (Rancangan Kitab Undang-Undang Hukum Pidana)	New Criminal Code Bill
Schuld	Fault
Schulduitsluitingsgrond	Excusatory Defences
Societas Delinquere Non Potest	Legal Entities / Associations Cannot Commit Criminal Offences
Straf	Punishment/ Penal
Strafrecht	Criminal Law
Strafuitsluitingsgronden	Grounds For Exclusion of Criminal Punishment
SV (Strafvordering)	Dutch Criminal Procedure Code
Universaliteitsbeginsel	The Principle of Universality
Territorialiteitsbeginsel	The Principle of Territoriality
The Heeren Zeventien	The Directors of The VOC In the Netherlands
Tindak Pidana	Criminal Offence
TPE (Tindak Pidana Ekonomi)	Economic Crimes based on Emergency Law No 7 of 1955 concerning Investigation, Prosecution, and Trial of Economic Crimes
TPPU	Money Laundering Crimes based on Law No 8 of 2010 Concerning The Prevention and Eradication of The Crime of Money Laundering ('The Money Laundering Law)
TPK/ Tipikor	Corruption Crimes based on Law No 31 of 1999 and Law No 21 of 2001 Concerning Eradication of Criminal Acts of Corruption
Nederlandsch-Indie	The Dutch East Indies

UDHR	The Universal Declaration Of Human Rights
UNCAC	United Nations Convention Against Corruption
UUD 1945	Indonesian 1945 Constitution
UU (Undang-Undang)	Law/ Act/ Statute
UU ITE	Electronic Transactions And Information Law
Ultimum Remedium	Criminal Punishment as the Last Resort
VOC (Vereenigde Oostindische Compagnie)	Dutch East India Company
Wederrechtelijk	Illegality
Wettelijk Strafbepaling	Criminal Law
WvS (Wetboek Van Strafrecht)	Criminal Code

1

A Brief Overview of Indonesian Criminal Law

I. Definition

In this book, many of the terms, concepts, cases, and teachings or theories used refer to Dutch law. This is because Indonesia was a Dutch colony for over 125 years as the Dutch East Indies, with the Dutch Criminal Code (*Wetboek van Strafrecht*) of 1881 being transcribed into the Dutch East Indies Criminal Code in 1915. The code remains in effect today.[1] Further, influential legal lectures were delivered by several Dutch criminal law experts in the then-Dutch East Indies, especially following the establishment of the *Rechtshoogeschool* (RHS) on 28 October 1924, led by a famous professor from the Netherlands, Paul Scholten. A professor of Dutch criminal law, WFC van Hattum, became the head of the RHS and its successor institution, *Fakulteit der Rechsgeleerheid en Sociale Wetenschappen*, which was part of *Nood Universiteit*, which later became *Universiteit van Indonesie* in 1946.[2]

The term for criminal law used in Indonesian (*hukum pidana*) is a translation of the Dutch term *Strafrecht*, which comes from the words *Straf*, meaning punishment, and *Recht*, which can be interpreted to mean law. *Recht* can also mean rights, but in the context of *Strafrecht* the word *Recht* is more accurately interpreted as law.[3] Thus *Strafrecht* literally means the law of punishment (penal law). In *A Handbook of Criminal Law Terms*, criminal law or penal law is defined as 'The body of law defining offenses against the community at large, regulating how suspects are investigated, charged, and tried, and establishing punishments for convicted offenders'.[4] This fairly concise definition defines criminal law with the

[1] A new Criminal Code Bill was drafted in the 1980s, and, in 2020/2021 and 2022 finally discussed and passed in the Indonesian Parliament.

[2] This institution became the Faculty of Law and Social Sciences (FH IPK) of the University of Indonesia in 1950, before finally becoming the Faculty of Law of the University of Indonesia in 1959, separating from the Faculty of Social and Political Sciences. See further: law.ui.ac.id/v3/sejarah-dan-perkembangan.

[3] The term '*hukum pidana*' is more precisely a translation of the Dutch term in an objective sense or *Strafrecht in Objective zin*. See Han Bing Siong, *Hukum Pidana 1 (Capita Selecta) Kuliah Mr. Han Bin Siong 1960–1961* (Jakarta, Faculty of Law and Social Sciences, University of Indonesia, 1961) 1.

[4] Bryan A Garner (ed), *A Handbook of Criminal Law Terms* (St Paul, Minnesota, West Group, 2000) 170.

scope of both substantive criminal law (the law that stipulates criminal offences) and law on criminal procedures (investigation, prosecution, and trial and punishment). Thus, it describes criminal law in a broad sense.

According to Dutch criminal law expert Jan Remmelink, criminal law is used to refer to all provisions that determine what conditions are binding on the state if the state wishes to use criminal law, as well as the rules that define what kinds of punishment are permitted. Criminal law in that sense is the prevailing criminal law or positive criminal law, which is also often called *ius poenale*.[5] With regard to the distinction between *ius poenale* (criminal law in an objective sense) and *ius poeniendi* (criminal law in a subjective sense), the term *ius poeniendi* cannot be translated as criminal law, as '*ius*' in *ius poenale* means 'law', while in *ius poeniendi*, it means 'right'. Thus, *ius poenale* in Dutch is *objectieve strafrecht (strafrecht in objective zin)*, while *ius poeniendi* in Dutch is *subjective strafrecht (strafrecht in subjective zin)*, with both using *ius* or *recht*. Therefore, the term 'criminal law', as used in the legal literature, refers to *ius poenale*.[6]

According to Moeljatno, Professor of Criminal Law at Gadjah Mada University, criminal law is part of the integral law that prevails in a country, which provides the basic rules for: (1) determining which actions are prohibited, accompanied by threats or sanctions through certain forms of punishment for anyone violating the prohibition (criminal act); (2) determining when and in what manner those who have violated the prohibitions may be deemed criminally liable and punished (criminal liability/criminal responsibility); and (3) determining how punishment can be imposed if there are people who are suspected of having violated the prohibition (criminal procedure).[7]

Another Gadjah Mada University Professor of Criminal Law, Eddy OS Hiariej, describes criminal law as 'the legal rules of a sovereign country, containing prohibited acts or ordered actions, accompanied by criminal sanctions for those who violate or do not comply, when and in what manner the criminal sanctions are imposed and how the sanctions are enforced by the state is implemented'.[8]

In my own opinion, criminal law is part of state law and is the basis for:

(a) designating any act, whether carried out by a human or a corporation, as an act that violates a prohibition or order for which the perpetrator is to be punished;
(b) criminal liability and the expansion of criminal liability;

[5] Jan Remmelink, *Hukum Pidana, Komentar atas Pasal-Pasal Terpenting dari Kitab Undang-Undang hukum Pidana Belanda dan Padanannya dalam Kitab Undang-Undang Hukum Pidana Indonesia* (Jakarta, Gramedia Pustaka Utama, 2003) 1.

[6] See Han Bin Siong, *Hukum Pidana 1* (1961) 1–3.

[7] Moeljatno, *Azas-Azas Hukum Pidana* (Jakarta, Rineka Cipta, 2002) 1.

[8] Eddy OS Hiariej, *Prinsip-prinsip Hukum Pidana*, revised edn (Yogyakarta, Cahaya Atma Pustaka, 2016) 16. See also Eddy OS Hiariej, *Pengantar Hukum Pidana Internasional* (Surabaya, Erlangga, 2009) 4.

(c) provisions regarding punishments, sanctions, and actions;
(d) the scope of implementation of the criminal rules, both in terms of time and place;
(e) the elimination of punishment, or for laws regarding aggravation or mitigation of the crime;
(f) provisions regarding the involvement of more than one person in the prohibited act;
(g) the dismissal of the criminal prosecution and the right to execute punishment by the state; and
(h) determining how the state, through its apparatus, conducts preliminary investigations, criminal investigations, prosecutions, trials, sentencing, or acquittal or release of the defendant; provisions on legal appeals against the verdict; the execution of the punishment; and settlement of cases outside the court in certain cases.[9]

My understanding of criminal law includes both substantive criminal law and law on criminal procedure. The scope of substantive criminal law is similar to some of the previous definitions from Dutch and Indonesian criminal law experts; however I define it in more detail and as also applying to corporations, because violations are not only committed by individuals but also by corporations.[10] In the aspect of criminal procedure law, I also include not only the punishment process, but also acquittal and release, as legal decisions can be made in the form of punishment, acquittal, or release from all charges. In addition, I include the settlement of cases outside the court, because criminal law recognises settlement (referred to as *afdoening buiten* in Indonesian and Dutch criminal law), as well as mediation, in cases of economic crime, customs crime, tax crime, and others.

Thus, the scope of criminal law in Indonesia includes all provisions contained in Indonesia's Criminal Code (*Kitab Undang-Undang Hukum Pidana* or KUHP) as well as all laws and regulations that contain human or corporate actions that are prohibited or ordered where there are criminal sanctions if the prohibition or order is violated.

Based on this understanding, when we talk about actions that are prohibited by laws and regulations, but the punishments are administrative or civil sanctions, then we are not talking about criminal law. Not all harmful acts are criminal law matters, after all. For example, if a tenant is late in paying the rent this is not a criminal issue, but rather a civil law issue regarding the relationship between the tenant and the lessor.

[9] Topo Santoso, *Hukum Pidana Suatu Pengantar* (Jakarta, Rajawali Pers, 2021) 12–13.

[10] In the General Elucidation of the Indonesian Criminal Code Bill (September 2020) it is explained that it is possible for criminal liability to be shared by the corporation and its management who have a functional position within the corporation or only the administrators who can be accounted for in criminal law. With the regulation of the criminal liability of the corporation, the criminal liability of the corporation which initially only applies to certain crimes outside this law, also applies generally to other crimes, both inside and outside this law.

Above we have discussed the definition of criminal law, both in the narrow sense that is substantive criminal law, as well as in a broad sense which includes criminal procedure law. From the above formulation, it appears that criminal law clearly involves state institutions or state apparatus in the field of law enforcement, including the police as investigators; attorneys as public prosecutors, as well as investigators for special crimes such as corruption, and executors of court decisions; judges as the officials who examine and decide criminal cases; and correctional institutions, which carry out correctional duties for those sentenced to imprisonment.

Undoubtedly, both substantive criminal law and law on criminal procedure have very important roles in a state. The state determines what actions are prohibited or should be contained in laws and regulations; the state determines the criminal sanctions for violating the criminal provisions in the laws and regulations; and the state also determines all provisions concerning in what manner a person or corporation can be punished, and various rules within the scope of substantive criminal law. In addition, only the state law enforcement apparatus, such as the police, attorneys, or Indonesia's Corruption Eradication Commission (*Komisi Pemberantasan Korupsi* or KPK),[11] may conduct criminal investigations. Only attorneys at the Attorney General's Office of the Republic of Indonesia and KPK attorneys have the authority to prosecute someone before the court.

Thus, it is clear that criminal law is public law. In this case, criminal law involves affairs between the state on the one hand and citizens, residents, or corporations suspected of committing a crime on the other. The state through its apparatus – investigators, public prosecutors, judges, and correctional institutions – is the party who resolves criminal cases that occur, in order to uphold justice, restore the interests of victims, prevent crimes from occurring, and impose penalties or actions on defendants who are found guilty. Therefore, criminal law is regarded as a part of public law, as are constitutional law and state administrative law.[12]

Criminal law determines the sanctions for violating what is prohibited. Sanctions principally consist of the intentional imposition of suffering. In principle, this imposition of suffering is the most important distinction between criminal law and other laws. Executing a sanction is carrying out an action on behalf of the state and, by law, it cannot be carried out by someone else.[13] Most laws regulating most fields include criminal provisions, including laws on, for example, national education, limited liability companies, general elections, banking, traffic, and forestry.

[11] Corruption Eradication Commission has authority to conduct criminal investigation only for corruption and money laundering (in which its predicate crime is corruption).

[12] Also included in public law is public law between countries or public international law.

[13] JM van Bemmelen, *Hukum Pidana 1, Hukum Pidana Material Bagian Umum*, translated by Hasnan (Bandung, Binacipta, 1987) 17.

Criminal law as public law also includes some elements of civil law. For example, 'penal mediation' may be used. Mediation is an alternative dispute resolution mechanism (out of court settlement) that applies in civil law to resolve civil disputes in a way that is more effective and efficient. Certain criminal cases can now be resolved through penal mediation – a settlement process between the party who is the victim of a crime and the party suspected of committing a crime, assisted by a mediator.

Criminal law also uses criminal sanctions as threats to those who violate norms aimed at protecting the interests of the community. For example, in terms of protecting property rights, prohibitions on fraud, theft, and embezzlement were developed. In such cases, as explained above, this sometimes overlaps with norms in other laws, such as civil law or administrative law. However, there are also norms to protect the interests of the community which are clearly different from norms in other laws, such as prohibitions against assault, homicide, or sexual violence. In these cases, it is difficult to say that the criminal sanctions for these acts are in fact to maintain the norms of civil law or state administrative law.

II. Substantive Criminal Law and Law on Criminal Procedure

As mentioned, criminal law can be divided into two: criminal law in a broad sense and criminal law in a narrow sense. Criminal law in a broad sense includes substantive criminal law and criminal procedure; in a narrow sense, it covers substantive criminal law, which is why it is usually referred to simply as criminal law.[14] Thus when we talk about criminal law, generally it is in a narrow sense, as in Moeljatno's definition above, specifically on determining prohibited actions, sanctions, and when and in what cases there is criminal liability.

D Simons, as quoted by Andi Hamzah, shows that substantive criminal law contains instructions and descriptions of offences; regulations regarding the actions for which a person can be convicted (*strafbaarheid*); the appointment of people who can be convicted and provisions regarding the punishment; and stipulations on who can be punished and how that person can be punished.[15] Thus substantive criminal law can be described as the objective regulations which regulate which behaviours must be criminalised as well as the relevant punishments, including what conditions must be met for the imposition or dismissal of punishment.[16]

[14] Han Bin Siong, *Hukum Pidana 1* (1961) 3.
[15] Andi Hamzah, *Asas-Asas Hukum Pidana*, revised edn (Jakarta, Rineka Cipta, 1994) 3.
[16] Han Bin Siong, *Hukum Pidana 1* (1961) 2.

Further, it can also be said that substantive criminal law is:

> part of the state law which is the basis for determining any act, whether of a human being or a corporation as an act that violates a prohibition or order and whose perpetrator is threatened with a punishment, the basis for elimination the punishment, the basis for aggravating or mitigating the punishment, criminal liability and expansion of criminal liability, provisions regarding the involvement of more than one person in the prohibited/ordered act, the basis on the dismissal of the criminal prosecution authority, the scope of application of the criminal rule both in terms of time and place.[17]

The third part of Moeljatno's definition of criminal law is about criminal procedure, which is part of the integral law that provides a basis for determining a punishment is to be imposed if someone is suspected of having violated a prohibition.[18] Meanwhile, according to Simons, law on criminal procedure regulates how the state, through its officials, uses its right to convict.[19] Dutch criminal law expert Jacob Maarten van Bemmelen states that criminal procedure regulates the way in which criminal proceedings should be carried out, and determines the rules that must be observed on that occasion.[20] In more detail, according to Van Bemmelen, criminal procedure observes the regulations created by the state due to allegations of violations of criminal laws where:

(1) the state, through its apparatus, investigates the truth;
(2) to the greatest extent possible, the state carries out an investigation attempting to identify the perpetrator of the act;
(3) the state takes any necessary measures to arrest the alleged perpetrator and if necessary detain that person;
(4) the state collects evidence (*bewijsmateriaal*) that is obtained during the investigation of the truth to be submitted to the judge, and then brings the defendant in front of the judge;
(5) the judge gives a decision on whether the criminal charge is proven against the defendant and if it is proven the judge imposes a punishment or disciplinary action;
(6) it may be possible to bring legal appeals against the decision; and
(7) execution of punishment and disciplinary action takes place.[21]

According to Han Bin Siong, criminal procedure law can be formulated as regulations that determine how a procedure is determined, whether the right to a punishment really exists, and how that right should be exercised.[22] Criminal

[17] Santoso, *Hukum Pidana Suatu Pengantar* (2021) 18.
[18] Moeljatno, *Azas-Azas Hukum Pidana* (2002) 1.
[19] Hamzah, *Asas-Asas Hukum Pidana* (1994) 3.
[20] Van Bemmelen, *Hukum Pidana 1* (1987) 3.
[21] JM van Bemmelen, *Strafvordering* (1950), in AZ Abidin and Andi Hamzah, *Pengantar Dalam Hukum Pidana Indonesia* (Jakarta, Yarsif Watampone, 2010) 4.
[22] Han Bin Siong, *Hukum Pidana 1* (1961) 2.

procedure is thus primarily tasked with seeking and finding the complete truth (including the possibility that a crime has not, in fact, occurred); it is not limited to determining that a criminal act has occurred and that a certain person has committed the crime. This includes situations in which a criminal act has occurred but where criminal procedure involves determining that the suspected perpetrator is not the actual perpetrator and should therefore not be punished.[23]

Thus, the relationship between criminal law and criminal procedure is that criminal procedure is the method by which substantive criminal law is exercised. It contains the principles and procedural proceedings of the criminal justice system, from investigation through to execution of court decisions.[24]

III. Functions of Criminal Law

According to Michael Allen, 'The function of the criminal law is largely to set the parameters within which the criminal justice system operates'.[25] Allen explains that there are two aspects related to this: first, the criminal justice system is a means of social control that includes the authorities, procedures, and sanctions that surround criminal law. Thus, criminal law limits and supervises the use of the powers of the state to investigate criminal acts, prosecute them, and, if guilty, impose punishment on perpetrators. Second, criminal law works as a guide for community members, by outlining what actions are legal or legitimate for them to do and predicting the consequences of violating criminal law.[26]

Thus, there are two functions of criminal law: first, to limit the exercise of the duties of state apparatus incorporated in the criminal justice system in carrying out their authority; second, to provide clear boundaries to the public, which, if violated or ignored, can result in criminal sanctions. The function of criminal law is therefore two-way: upwards to state institutions so that they are careful in carrying out their authority in enforcing the law, and downwards to members of the community so that they do not commit criminal acts.

This means that criminal law must be clear, relatively stable (ie regulations remain in effect for a long period of time), and accessible or knowable in advance (predictable). This is enables people to confidently make rational choices over whether to do or not to do a certain action.[27] On the other hand, if criminal law is unclear, changes often, and is difficult to predict, it can be detrimental to a society, as people are not sure what to do for fear that their actions may be prosecuted by law enforcement as a crime. The principle of legal certainty is thus very important in this context.

[23] Ibid 9.
[24] Hiariej, *Prinsip-prinsip Hukum Pidana* (2016) 19.
[25] Michael Allen, *Textbook on Criminal Law* (New York, Oxford University Press, 2007) 2.
[26] Ibid.
[27] Ibid 2–3.

IV. Types of Criminal Law: General and Special Criminal Law, National and Local Criminal Law

A. General and Special Criminal Law

The distinction between general criminal law and special criminal law differs among both Dutch and Indonesian legal experts. Hamzah describes three main views: (1) Van Poelje's opinion; (2) Pompe and Utrecht's opinion; and (3) Scholten and Mostert's opinion.[28]

According to Van Poelje, general criminal law is all criminal law that is not military criminal law. Thus, criminal law consists of general criminal law and special criminal law (military criminal law). Van Poelje argues that economic criminal law is part of general criminal law because there is nothing that firmly and clearly shows criminal law principles other than those from Book 1 of the Criminal Code.[29]

Meanwhile, according to Pompe and Utrecht, special criminal law is criminal law regulated in a law where there are deviations from the general provisions in the Criminal Code. Under this opinion, economic criminal law is special criminal law. Article 103 of the Criminal Code states 'Rules from the first eight titles to VIII Book 1 of the Criminal Code are also imposed on acts that can be punished according to other laws and regulations if there are no other rules in the law'.[30] Thus, the measure of special criminal law, according to Pompe and Utrecht, is if a law outside the Criminal Code regulates a criminal action differently from the provisions in Book 1, Chapters 1–8 of the Criminal Code.

Finally, according to Scholten and Mostert, the criteria for distinguishing general criminal law and special criminal law are not seen through Article 103 of the Criminal Code. Instead, all generally accepted criminal law is called general criminal law. Special criminal law instead refers to 'non-criminal legislation with criminal sanctions', also known as government criminal law.[31] Thus in Scholten and Mostert's view, criminal law relating to economics, corruption, and politics is not special criminal law but remains general criminal law because it is a generally accepted criminal law.

On the other hand, Hamzah is inclined to use two alternative terms: (1) general criminal legislation and (2) special criminal legislation. According to Hamzah, general criminal legislation is the Criminal Code along with all laws that amend and add to the Criminal Code (eg Law No 1 of 1946, Law No 73 of 1958, and so on). Meanwhile, special criminal legislation is all legislation outside the Criminal

[28] Hamzah, *Asas-Asas Hukum Pidana* (1994) 10–14.
[29] Ibid 10–11.
[30] Ibid 11–12.
[31] Ibid 12.

Code, including both criminal legislation and non-criminal legislation with criminal sanctions.[32]

According to Hiariej, general criminal law is criminal law that applies to everyone as a legal subject, without discriminating against the personal qualities of certain legal subjects. Hiariej also argues that that general criminal law is criminal law in codification. In Indonesia, if it is associated with substantive criminal law and law on criminal procedure, then substantive general criminal law is codified in the Criminal Code (KUHP). Meanwhile, procedural general criminal law is codified in the Criminal Procedure Code (*Kitab Undang-Undang Hukum Acara Pidana* or KUHAP). Hiariej also argues that special criminal law is the provisions of criminal law which are substantively outside the Criminal Code or procedurally outside the Criminal Procedure Code. It can also be said that special criminal law is criminal law outside of codification. Based on these regulations, special criminal law is divided into two parts: (1) special criminal law in criminal legislation and (2) special criminal law outside of criminal legislation.[33]

Meanwhile, according to Satochid Kartanegara,[34] judging by its nature, criminal law is (1) general criminal law (*algemene, ius commune*) – criminal law that applies to everyone; (2) special criminal law (*bezondere, ius speciale*) – military criminal law, which is especially devoted to the military; and (3) fiscal criminal law (*fiscal strafrecht*) – which, among other matters, takes care of matters in taxation. Special criminal law is distinguished from general criminal law because special criminal law is aimed at certain people (*bepaalde personen*), such as the military, who are subject to military criminal law (*wetboek van militeir strafrecht*), which has been in effect since 1923.

Regarding fiscal criminal law, while the Fiscal Criminal Law has been in effect in the Netherlands since 1886,[35] in Indonesia, fiscal criminal law is not a criminal law specifically outside the Criminal Code. Instead, it is an administrative law with criminal provisions, such as through Law No 7 of 1983[36] on Income Taxes as amended by Law No 36 of 2008.[37] In such legislation, there are criminal provisions. Thus, criminal acts in the taxation sector are the same as crimes in other fields, such as education, health, and aviation, contained in non-criminal legislation.

This division of general criminal law and special criminal law is uniquely derived from the Dutch criminal law literature, which was brought to and taught in Indonesia during the colonial period. If we look at the legal dictionary in the Netherlands today, special criminal laws are still known. The term used is

[32] Ibid.

[33] Hiariej, *Prinsip-Prinsip Hukum Pidana* (2016) 23–24.

[34] Satochid Kartanagera was a professor of criminal law at the Faculty of Law and Social Sciences (FH-IPK) University of Indonesia, which later became the Faculty of Law, University of Indonesia (FHUI) in 1959.

[35] Satochid Kartanegara, *Hukum Pidana, Kumpulan Kuliah Prof Satochid Kartanegara* (Jakarta, Balai Lektur Mahasiswa, nd) 5–6.

[36] State Gazette of the Republic of Indonesia of 1983 Number 50.

[37] State Gazette of the Republic of Indonesia of 2008 Number 133.

bijzondere strafrecht, which is defined as '*strafrecht dat wat sancties betreft, afwijkt van het algemene strafrecht. Bijv. Wet op de Economische Delicten of het militaire strafrecht*'[38] ('criminal law that deviates from general criminal law relating to sanctions. For example, the Economic Criminal Law or the Military Criminal Law'). Therefore, general criminal law refers to criminal law set out in the Criminal Code, while special criminal law is criminal law that deviates from the general criminal law relating to sanctions.

According to DC Fokkema, JMJ Chorus, EH Hondius, and E Ch Lisser, general criminal law:

> ... forms the basis of criminal law in all other areas, unless status in these areas expressly departs from it. Substantive general criminal law is set forth in the Penal Code (*Wetboek van Strafrecht*) and the relevant statutes; the general law of criminal procedure is laid down in the Code of Criminal Procedure (*Wetboek van Strafvordering*) and the statutes pertaining to it. The general criminal law also contains special rules for minors punishable under the criminal law. These special rules, substantive as well as procedural, are included in the codes.[39]

Based on the various views above and by looking at the Indonesian context and legal developments, in my view, general criminal law is criminal law in codification. In other words, it includes the Criminal Code for substantive criminal law (but not including the Military Criminal Code) and the Criminal Procedure Code for law on criminal procedure. Also included in general criminal law are all criminal laws that amend the Criminal Code for substantive criminal law and amend the Criminal Procedure Code for law on criminal procedure.[40]

Additionally, it is my view that special criminal law is a criminal law that applies only to military subjects (subject to military law) and criminal law regulated in special criminal legislation outside the Criminal Code and non-criminal legislation. There are also partly regulated criminal procedure laws that differ from the Criminal Procedure Code. This includes all decisions of the Constitutional Court that amend the provisions of substantive criminal law and criminal procedure in criminal law and in non-criminal laws that contain criminal provisions. Based on these arrangements, in my opinion: Special Criminal Law = Military Criminal Law + Special Criminal Law in the Criminal Legislation + Special Criminal Law Outside the Criminal Legislation.[41]

According to Fokkema, Chorus, Hondius, and Lisser, the military criminal code 'is to be found in separate codes of procedural and substantive law. The military law of criminal procedure is entirely independent of civilian law. Substantive military criminal law is contained in the Military Penal Code, which must be

[38] www.juridischwoordenboek.nl/zoek/bijzonder+strafrecht.

[39] DC Fokkema, JMJ Chorus, EH Hondius, and E Ch Lisser (eds), *Introduction to Dutch Law for Foreign Lawyers* (Deventer, Kluwer, 1978) 297.

[40] Santoso, *Hukum Pidana Suatu Pengantar* (2021) 97.

[41] Ibid 98.

considered as a supplement to the Penal Code'.[42] Thus, the Military Criminal Code is a complement to the Criminal Code, while its military criminal procedure law is completely separate from the Criminal Procedure Code.

The definition of military criminal law can be divided into two parts. First, military criminal law in a broad sense, namely substantive military criminal law and procedural military criminal law. Second, military criminal law in a narrow sense, which includes only the substantive criminal law. 'Substantive military criminal law' refers to the rules that stipulate and formulate the actions that can be punished, the rules that contain the conditions to be able to impose a sentence, and the provisions regarding the punishment that applies to the military. 'Procedural military criminal law' refers to the rules that stipulate how the state through the means of its apparatus exercises its right to impose punishment that apply to members of the military.

In military criminal law, what is meant by criminal law in a substantive sense, other than the Criminal Code (which also applies to the military), is the Military Criminal Code as regulated in Law No 39 and 40 of 1947. Meanwhile, military criminal law in a procedural sense is Law No 31 of 1997 concerning military justice, which contains procedures to exercise the right to investigate, prosecute, sentence, and execute of law enforcement officers within the military judiciary, namely military police, military prosecutors, and military judges.

Legal subjects of military criminal law are identified in Article 9 paragraph 1 of Law No 31 of 1997. According to this article, criminal acts that fall under the jurisdiction of the military court are crimes committed by a person who at the time of committing a crime is either: (1) a soldier; (2) a person who by law is equated with a soldier; (3) a member of a group, service or agency where members of that group, service or agency are equal to or considered to be soldiers based on the law; and (4) a person not included in the categories in letter a, letter b, and letter c but who, based on the decision of the Commander in Chief with the approval of the Minister of Justice, must be tried by a court within the military court environment.

Now we will discuss special criminal law in criminal legislation.[43] There are several examples of special criminal law in criminal legislation that exist outside the Criminal Code: Emergency Law No 7 of 1955 concerning Investigation, Prosecution and Trial of Economic Crimes as amended by Emergency Law No 8 of 1958 concerning the Addition of Emergency Law No 7 of 1955 ('Economic Crimes Law'); Law No 31 of 1999 concerning Eradication of Criminal Acts of Corruption as amended by Law No 20 of 2001 ('Corruption Eradication Law'); Law No 15 of 2003 concerning Stipulation of Government Regulation in Lieu of Law No 1 of 2002 concerning Eradication of Criminal Acts of Terrorism to become

[42] Fokkema et al (eds), *Introduction to Dutch Law* (1978) 297.

[43] Hiariej called it 'Internal Special Criminal Law'. Eddy OS Hiariej Paper on the Scientific Discussion on Deferred Prosecution Agreement at the Faculty of Law, University of Indonesia, Depok, 17 February 2020.

Law as amended by Law No 5 of 2018 ('Terrorism Law'); and Law No 21 of 2007 concerning the Eradication of the Crime of Trafficking in Persons ('Trafficking in Persons Law').

The above laws can be referred to as criminal laws because all regulate the provisions of substantive and procedural criminal law regarding certain criminal acts, such as corruption, economic crimes, terrorism, and money laundering. Various aspects and intricacies of these criminal acts are regulated, including the definition, elements, subject of the crime, criminal sanctions, attempt or complicity, and the principle of their application (especially if there are exceptions from the Criminal Code). There are also several procedural criminal provisions (investigation, evidence, prosecution, and examination in court) which partially deviate or differ from the Criminal Procedure Code.[44]

Therefore, criminal legislation is legislation specially made to regulate criminal acts. In legislation like this, the main point is the actions that are categorised as criminal acts themselves and/or the methods of prevention and enforcement or eradication. Criminal legislation has several characteristics. The first is the title of the law, which will generally mention the word criminal or other words that describe an act that is evil in nature and deserves to be punished to reflect that the focus of the law is indeed on criminal rules. The second characteristic is that in legislation like this, the law begins by describing acts that are categorised as criminal.

Meanwhile special criminal law outside of criminal legislation is different from special criminal law in criminal legislation.[45] The latter is regulated in the criminal law, not administrative law containing criminal provisions. Special criminal law outside of criminal legislation is criminal law relating to legislation that regulates various elements of our lives, such as forestry, higher education, health, medicine, narcotics, and the press. This legislation regulates various aspects of administration, duties and authorities, requirements, types, procedures, services, permits, procurement, procurement stages, and other matters that are not criminal matters; however, the legislators deem it necessary to include criminal provisions in order to strengthen norms and compliance. Thus, in almost every piece of non-criminal legislation, at the end there is a chapter on criminal provisions. This chapter regulates substantive crimes as well as procedural aspects which may differ from the Criminal Procedure Code.

Examples of non-criminal legislation that contain criminal provisions are Law No 39 of 2014 concerning Plantations; Law No 12 of 2012 concerning Higher

[44] There was another special criminal law, the Decree of the President of the Republic of Indonesia No 11 of 1963 concerning the Eradication of Subversion Activities, but the law was officially revoked in 1999 based on Law No 26 of 1999.

[45] Hiariej called it 'External Special Criminal Law'. Eddy OS Hiariej, Paper on the Scientific Discussion on Deferred Prosecution Agreement at the Faculty of Law, University of Indonesia, Depok, 17 February 2020.

Education; Law No 36 of 2009 concerning Health; Law No 29 of 2004 concerning Medical Practice; Law No 35 of 2009 concerning Narcotics; Law No 5 of 1997 concerning Psychotropics; Law No 7 of 1992 concerning Banking as amended by Law No 10 of 1998, and Law No 8 of 1995 concerning the Capital Market.

B. National Criminal Law and Local Criminal Law

The distinction here is based on the enforceability of the criminal law. Essentially, there is a unity of national criminal law that applies throughout the territory of Indonesia; this is called the unification of criminal law. This national criminal law includes both substantive criminal law and criminal procedure, for both general and special criminal law. The basis for the enforceability of the national criminal law is the principle of territoriality, with the provisions of criminal law applying to everyone who commits a crime throughout the territory of Indonesia.[46] It can also be said that national criminal law is regulated in legislation (or in government regulations in lieu of law), while local criminal law is that which is regulated in a regional regulation but whose validity is limited to the region itself.[47]

i. National Criminal Law

The national criminal law is the criminal law that applies in a particular country, both nationally and locally. As Indonesia is a unitary state, the prevailing criminal law is criminal law in the national legal system, which is in effect because it is based on the 1945 Constitution. National criminal law in Indonesia also includes national legislation provincial regulations, and district/city regulations.

At the national level, criminal law that applies throughout the territory of the Republic of Indonesia is based on statutory legislation enacted by the House of Representatives (DPR) and the government. At the local level of provinces, districts, and cities, there are many additional local criminal laws, enforceable only within the relevant regions. Provincial regional regulations are statutory regulations established by the Provincial House of Representatives (Provincial DPRD) with the approval of the governor. Meanwhile, district/city regional regulations are statutory regulations established by the District or City House of Representatives (District or City DPRD) with the consent of the district head (sometimes referred to as regent) or mayor.[48]

National criminal law is based on codified criminal law, special criminal law in criminal legislation, and special criminal law outside of criminal legislation. All are valid nationally throughout the territory of the Republic of Indonesia,

[46] Hiariej, *Prinsip-Prinsip Hukum Pidana* (2016) 26.
[47] Including Qanun in Aceh Province and Special Regional Regulation in Papua Province.
[48] Article 1 number 7 of Law No 12 of 2011 concerning the Formulation of Legislation.

in all provinces (currently 38 provinces) and all districts and cities (currently 416 districts, and 98 cities).

ii. Local Criminal Law

Local criminal law is applicable in certain provinces, districts, or cities, and is based on the regulations of those specific regions. One good example of this is the Regional Regulation of the Province of the Special Capital Region of Jakarta No 7 of 2010 concerning Buildings. In this regulation, Article 283 paragraph (1) contains criminal provisions which state that every building owner, building user, or building construction service provider who violates the provisions of Article 24 paragraph (1), Article 42 paragraph (1), Article 51, Article 64, Article 137 paragraph (1), Article 144 paragraph (2), Article 150, Article 151, Article 152. Article 162 paragraph (1), Article 189 paragraph (1), Article 198 paragraph (1), Article 195, Article 206 paragraph (2), Article 219, Article 220, Article 253 paragraph (1), Article 255 paragraph (1), and Article 259 paragraph (1), shall be punished with short-term imprisonment for a maximum of three months or a maximum fine of IDR50,000,000 (approximately US$3,465).

Regional regulations that contain criminal provisions, as well as criminal procedures, can also be found in other areas throughout Indonesia. Of course, criminal provisions and procedures in all regional regulations must refer to higher provisions, especially laws (including the Criminal Code and Criminal Procedure Code). For example, in the context of substantive criminal law, a local regulation must refer to and cannot be in conflict with the Criminal Code when it comes to determining punishment, guilt, criminal liability, attempt, complicity, a combination of criminal acts, and so on. Meanwhile, in the context of the law on criminal procedure, a regional regulation must not regulate itself, because criminal procedure law is already regulated in the Criminal Procedure Code. This is because criminal procedure must be regulated in a *Wet* or law, while substantive criminal law is regulated through criminal legislation, which can be a law or a local regulation.

Regional regulations on criminal provisions must also not conflict with the laws governing the formation of applicable laws and regulations in Indonesia. Specifically, Law No 12 of 2011[49] concerning the Establishment of Legislative Regulations as amended by Law No 15 of 2019.[50] This covers material for the implementation of regional autonomy and assistance tasks, and accommodates special regional conditions and/or further elaboration of higher laws and regulations.[51] This law confirms that regional regulations may indeed contain criminal provisions, stating that criminal provisions can only be contained in laws, provincial

[49] State Gazette of the Republic of Indonesia of 2011 Number 82.
[50] State Gazette of the Republic of Indonesia of 2019 Number 183.
[51] Article 14 of Law No 12 of 2011 concerning the Formulation of Legislation.

regulations, or district/city regulations.[52] There are limits to criminal provisions in regional regulations, namely in the form of maximum short-term imprisonment of six months or a maximum fine of IDR50,000,000.[53] Similar provisions can be seen in Law No 23 of 2014 concerning Regional Government, which states: 'Regional regulation can contain maximum short-term imprisonment of 6 (six) months or a maximum fine of Rp50,000,000 (fifty million rupiahs)'.[54]

There are also some provinces in Indonesia with their own regulations. The most obvious example is that of Nanggroe Aceh Darussalam, whose regulation is based on Law No 11 of 2006 concerning the Government of Aceh.[55] This is because Aceh has special status due to a history of conflict between the Acehnese people and the Dutch and Indonesian governments.[56] Aceh was given special authority in 2006 to regulate and manage its own government affairs and the interests of the local community.[57] Nevertheless, the government of Aceh is a provincial regional government within the system of the Unitary State of the Republic of Indonesia, based on the Constitution of the Republic of Indonesia based on the 1945 Constitution, and carries out government affairs carried out by the Aceh Regional Government and the Aceh Regional People's Representative Council in accordance with their respective functions and authorities.[58]

While other provinces implement regional regulations, Aceh's regulations are known as Qanun. Qanun can be implemented at both the provincial level and the district/city level. Aceh Qanun (provincial level) are statutory regulations similar to provincial regulations that regulate the administration and life of the Acehnese people.[59] Meanwhile, district/city Qanun are statutory regulations similar to a district/city regulations that regulate the administration of government and the life of that specific district/city community.[60] Article 241 paragraph (2) of Law No 11 of 2006 states that the Qanun can contain maximum short-term imprisonment of six months and/or a maximum fine of IDR50,000,000.[61] Qanun may contain criminal sanctions or fines other than those referred to in paragraph (2) in accordance with those stipulated in other laws and regulations.[62] Article 241 paragraph (4) of Law No 11 of 2006 states that Qanun regarding *jinayah* (criminal law) are excluded from the provisions of paragraph (1), paragraph (2), and paragraph (3). This is the reason why in Aceh there are criminal sanctions for acts such as *khalwat* (seclusion with a non-relative to whom you are not married),

[52] Article 15 paragraph (1) of Law No 12 of 2011 concerning the Formulation of Legislation.
[53] Article 15 paragraph (2) of Law No 12 of 2011 concerning the Formulation of Legislation.
[54] Article 238 paragraph (2) of Law No. 23 of 2014 concerning Regional Government.
[55] State Gazette of the Republic of Indonesia Year 2006 Number 62.
[56] Consideration b Law No 11 of 2006 concerning the Government of Aceh.
[57] Article 1 point 2 of Law No 11 of 2006 concerning the Government of Aceh.
[58] Article 1 point 4 of Law No 11 of 2006 concerning the Government of Aceh.
[59] Article 1 point 21 of Law No 11 of 2006 concerning the Government of Aceh.
[60] Article 1 point 22 of Law No 11 of 2006 concerning the Government of Aceh.
[61] Article 141 paragraph (2) of Law No 11 of 2006 concerning the Government of Aceh.
[62] Article 241 paragraph (3) of Law No 11 of 2006 concerning the Government of Aceh.

drinking *khamr* (liquor), and gambling, as well as punishment in the form of public whipping, which is not used in other areas of Indonesia.

In all other provinces in Indonesia, there are religious courts and religious high courts whose authority does not include criminal acts. In Aceh, there is instead what is called the Aceh Syar'iyah Court as well as district/city Syar'iyah Courts. These are the courts which are the authorities of judicial power within the religious judiciary and are part of the national justice system.[63] Based on Islamic law, Syar'iyah Courts have the authority to examine, hear, decide, and resolve cases covering the areas of *ahwal al-syakhsiyah* (family law), *muamalah* (civil law), and *jinayah* (criminal law).[64] Provisions regarding these fields are regulated by Aceh Qanun, as is the procedural law that applies to the Syar'iyah Courts.[65] Syar'iyah Courts consist of district/city Syar'iyah Courts as the court of first instance and the Aceh Syar'iyah Court as the court of appeal.[66] Decisions made by the Aceh Syar'iyah Court can be appealed to the Indonesian Supreme Court.[67]

Special designations are also in place for the provinces of Papua and West Papua, which use Special Regional Regulations (*Perdasus*) and Provincial Regulations (*Perdasi*) as their regional regulations.[68] Provisions regarding *Perdasus* and *Perdasi* are regulated in Law No 21 of 2001 concerning Special Autonomy for the Papua Province, which specifies the certain topics for which special regulations can be made. These topics include provisions regarding membership of the Papuan People's Assembly (MRP), the implementation of the duties and authorities of the MRP, the implementation of the MRP's rights and procedures, and the implementation of the MRP's obligations.[69]

V. Criminal Law as *Ultimum Remedium*

There are several questions which may be asked about the use of criminal law to address social problems due to the severity of punishment and stigma resulting from criminal proceedings. If the impact of the criminal process and sanctions is so great, is it absolutely necessary to use criminal law? Should criminal law with very harsh and even cruel sanctions be used when in fact there are other means available, such as civil law, state administrative law, and constitutional law? Would it be more appropriate to use other rules, such as the rules of decency, religious

[63] Article 15 of Law No 11 of 2006 concerning the Government of Aceh.

[64] Article 128 paragraph (3) of Law No 11 of 2006 concerning the Government of Aceh.

[65] Article 132 paragraph (1) of Law No 11 of 2006 concerning the Government of Aceh.

[66] Article 130 of Law No 11 of 2006 concerning the Government of Aceh.

[67] Article 131 paragraph (1) of Law No 11 of 2006 concerning the Government of Aceh.

[68] Elucidation of Article 7 paragraph (1) point f of Law No 12 of 2011 concerning the Formulation of Legislation.

[69] Wahiduddin Adams, 'Perbandingan dan Hierarki Qanun, Perdasi, Perdasus dan Perda dalam Sistem Hukum Nasional' (2004) 1(2) *Jurnal Legislasi Indonesia* 32–33.

norms, customs, and customary law to overcome social problems? This is why experts and international institutions warn that criminal law is not easy to use, even for states. As a result, criminal law should only be used if there are no other ways to deal with problems in society. In Dutch legal literature, this is referred to as *ultimum remedium*.

In addition, there remain important questions around when to use *ultimum remedium* (criminal law as a last resort) and when to use *primum remedium* (criminal law as a first resort, also known as *optimum remedium*). In some Indonesian laws, it appears that the legislators have arranged for the use of criminal law to be the last resort after other means have been exhausted. An example of this is Law No 32 of 2009 concerning Environmental Protection and Management, which states that the principle used is *ultimum remedium*.[70] Meanwhile, most other laws appears to take a *primum remedium* approach, with criminal law to be used consciously and decisively from the start, perhaps considering the seriousness of the act and its consequences.

Another question is whether *ultimum remedium* is used during the formulation of legislation or the law enforcement process. In the legislation development process, the main focus is on whether it is necessary to criminalise an act. Lawmakers must ask if it is enough that the act is prohibited, with administrative sanctions for those who violate the law. Is it enough that the act is seen as an act against civil law, with violators able to be sued and subject to civil sanctions, such as civil compensation? This is a question that is directly related to the principle of criminal law as *ultimum remedium* or *primum redmium*.

Clearly, the question is whether, during the drafting of legislation, there are harmful actions that need to be controlled or prevented, and whether criminal law should be used. In my opinion, this should be explored during all stages of development: during formulation, discussions with experts, and debates in the House of Representatives. This should be reflected not just in the notes or minutes or meetings, but also in the laws themselves, with articles offering several models of law enforcement which could be used, beginning with civil law, progressing to administrative law, and finally ending with criminal law.

With criminal law, a person's human rights may be violated during the process (arrests, searches, confiscations, detentions) as well as in the sentencing (imprisonment, short-term or 'light' imprisonment, confiscation of property), therefore when criminalising an act or determining that criminal law needs to be used in legislation, legislators must be very careful.

On the other hand, there are, of course, acts that deprive other people of their human rights and fundamental freedoms. Yet these acts are often hard to regulate by other forms of law, so criminal law can be used to protect human rights and fundamental human freedoms. Here, we meet the difficult problem of how to decide whether to use criminal law.

[70] State Gazette of the Republic of Indonesia Year 2009 Number 140.

The principle of *ultimum remedium* is widely discussed in German legal literature. According to Claus Roxin, as quoted by Nils Jareborg, criminal law is not the only appropriate means to protect legitimate values and interests (*rechtsguter*). On the contrary, it must be possible to use all means of orderly law for this purpose, and thus criminal law should be considered as a last resort.[71] Roxin also emphasises that criminal law should only be used when other means, such as civil lawsuits, administrative settlements, and non-criminal sanctions, fail. That is why criminal punishment is called the 'ultimate ratio of social policy', and why the task of criminal law can be called a 'subsidiary' or complementary element to the protection of legitimate values and interests. Criminal law can only protect some of those values and interests, and the protection is sometimes selective rather than general, such as protecting personal property. This is the fragmentary nature of criminal law itself.[72]

Gunther Stratenwerth, as quoted by Nils Jareborg, also states that criminal punishment, as a rule, is state interference with human rights, so it should only be used when other means, especially civil and administrative law, have failed. Therefore, the emphasis is on the fragmentary and subsidiary nature of criminal law.[73] Thus, it is determined that not all interests that are important and need to be protected must be protected by criminal law. If all breaches of contract that resulted in economic harm or loss were to be considered as criminal acts, then the criminal justice system would become so overloaded that it would stop functioning.[74]

Jareborg puts forward six arguments to help determine whether or not to criminalise an act: (1) blameworthiness/penal value [the despicable or evil nature of the act], (2) need, (3) moderation, (4) inefficiency, (5) costs of control, and (6) the victim's interests.[75]

When considering blameworthiness, Jareborg is looking at two aspects. First, the act itself: is it indeed bad or evil? What is its penal value? Then, has the act actually caused harm or resulted in the danger of harm?

The second argument relates to need. Here we ask whether, if certain social problems or conflicts in society cannot be overcome by other means,[76] it is necessary to criminalise an act to provide the means to use criminal law. In order to justify that criminalisation is indeed needed, it requires a belief that equivalent or adequate protection for certain values and interests cannot be achieved by using other means, for example through administrative or civil laws only. In Indonesia, this exploration is conducted through what is referred to as an 'academic text', which is a type of in-depth study of the need for criminalisation that is done prior

[71] Nils Jareborg, 'Criminalization as Last Resort (Ultima Ratio)' (2005) *Ohio State Journal of Criminal Law* 2, 521, 524–25.
[72] Ibid 524–25.
[73] Ibid 525.
[74] Ibid 526.
[75] Ibid 527–30.
[76] Less intrusive (ie does not intrude so much into someone's life) and less expensive.

to the development of a draft regulation. An academic text is the result of research or legal studies on a particular problem that can justify the regulation of the problem in a regulation (at any level) as a solution to community problems and legal needs. In addition, in making changes to the law, there is an obligation to carry out an analysis and evaluation of the implementation of the law.

The third argument is moderation. The purpose of moderation is to reject the use of excessive means to overcome a social problem, even those that are detrimental. If an act is seen as despicable, evil, or bad, is the use of criminal law sufficiently balanced with that level of despicability, evilness, or badness? Is it balanced or proportional enough to justify criminalising an act? Is it excessive to tackle a certain social problem with criminal sanction? Does that act deserve to be criminalised, compared with other acts?

The next argument is inefficiency. Can criminalisation be justified as an efficient way of handling the problem? This is followed by the consideration of the costs of control. That is, are the other means available to overcome the problem very expensive? The cost argument can also be reversed, of course, by arguing how expensive it would be to tackle a certain crime through the criminal justice system if all processes were to be taken seriously.

The last argument is the victim's interest. If a certain act is criminalised, it will be easier for the victim to obtain compensation, as the victim will not have to be personally responsible for investigating the crime or taking legal action. However, there is the argument that sometimes a victim needs to remain anonymous, and thus a criminal case would not be appropriate, but this is more accurately a problem relating to prosecution rather than criminalisation.

These principles should act as obstacles for the formulation of criminal provisions or the use of criminal law to overcome social problems or conflicts. Ultimately, criminal law should not be used by all legislators to solve all problems.

Indonesian criminal law experts have also discussed this *ultimum remedium*, such as Barda Nawawi Arief, Professor of Law at Diponegoro University, Semarang. Nawawi Arief states that, in general, criminal law has limitations as a means of crime prevention because:

(a) the causes of crime are very complex and are beyond the scope of criminal law;
(b) criminal law is only a small part (subsystem) of the means of social control that is unable to solve the problem of crime as a very complex humanitarian and social problem (as a socio-psychological, socio-political, socio-economic, and socio-cultural problem);
(c) the use of criminal law in tackling crime is only *kurieren am symptom* (treatment of symptoms), therefore criminal law does not treat the causes of problems;
(d) criminal law sanctions are *remedium* and contain contradictory/paradoxical properties and contain negative elements and side effects;
(e) the punishment system is fragmentary and individual/personal, not structural/functional;

(f) there are limitations on the types of criminal sanctions and the system for formulating criminal sanctions is rigid and imperative; and
(g) the operation of criminal law requires more and varied supporting facilities and involves high costs.[77]

In legal literature in Indonesia, environmental law is the field which is most often referred to as using the principle of *ultimum remedium*, both in legislation and in practice. Enforcement of environmental law in Indonesia is carried out through state administrative law, civil law, and criminal law, in that order.[78]

Prior to the enactment of Law No 32 of 2009 concerning Environmental Protection and Management, Law No 4 of 1982 concerning Principles of Environmental Management was enacted (and later amended by Law No 23 of 1997 concerning Environmental Management).[79] The earlier two laws used the principle of subsidiarity, in which issues are dealt with at the most immediate (local) level, while in the 2009 law, the principle of subsidiarity was removed and replaced with the principle of *ultimum remedium* (as stated in the law's general explanation). The reason for the abolition of the principle of subsidiarity can be read in the draft law's academic text, which explained that the principle of subsidiarity was one of the main problems in the application of environmental law because of the principle's unclear meaning. Therefore, subsidiarity was removed and replaced with the principle of *ultimum remedium*, with emphasis on the fact that the principle can only be applied to certain formal offences.[80] The Law's general explanation states:

> The enforcement of criminal law in this law introduces the sanction of minimum punishment in addition to the maximum, expansion of evidence, punishment for quality standard violations, integration of criminal law enforcement, and regulation of corporate criminal acts. Enforcement of environmental criminal law still *pays attention to the ultimum remedium principle which requires the application of criminal law enforcement as a last resort* after the implementation of administrative law enforcement is deemed unsuccessful. The application of this *ultimum remedium* principle only applies to criminal acts in certain formal forms, namely the punishment of violations of wastewater quality standards, emissions, and disturbances. (emphasis added)

Currently in Indonesia, there are many laws that reduce and even violate the human rights and constitutional rights of citizens because these laws apply criminal sanctions outside the conception of criminal law as a last resort (*ultimum remedium*), instead positioning criminal law as the first means (*primum remedium*). As a result of this situation, the Indonesian Constitutional Court took a stand through several

[77] Barda Nawawi Arief, *Kapita Selekta Hukum Pidana* (Bandung, Citra Aditya Bakti, 2003) 88.
[78] M Daud Silalahi, *Hukum Lingkungan dalam sistem penegakan hukum lingkungan Indonesia* (Bandung, PT Alumni, 2014) 215.
[79] Syahrul Machmud, *Problematika Penerapan Delik Formil dalam Perspektif Penegakan Hukum Pidana Lingkungan di Indonesia* (Bandung, CV Mandar Maju, 2012) 1.
[80] Machmud, *Problematika Penerapan Delik Formil* (2012) 15.

decisions related to criminal law as *ultimum remedium*, such as Constitutional Court Decision No 12/PUU-VIII/2010,[81] because although the 1945 Constitution itself does not explicitly state the use of the *ultimum remedium* principle, it does regulate human rights, including principles such as equality before the law and legal certainty.

In its legal considerations, the Constitutional Court reconstructed the application of the principle of *primum remedium* in the concept of punishment. This is because there is a tendency for the principle of *primum remedium* to be applied and internalised in legal products, resulting in laws with the potential to violate human rights and citizens' constitutional rights. The Constitutional Court as the protector of human rights and citizens' constitutional rights is obliged to protect citizens from legal products, especially laws that cause constitutional harm (making them contrary to the 1945 Constitution). In its legal considerations, in addition to using the 1945 Constitution as a touchstone, the Constitutional Court also uses three principles that are the objectives of the law: justice, legal certainty, and benefit.

In my opinion, the use of criminal law must be controlled, because more and more laws in Indonesia (both in national legislation and regional regulations) contain criminal sanctions. In fact, every law contains a chapter on criminal provisions, and sanctions have become more severe over time, including more special minimums and the accumulation of imprisonment and fines. Meanwhile, the number of prisoners in correctional institutions is increasing, even to the point of overload.[82] On the other hand, out-of-court settlements remain very loosely regulated. The burden of the state in financing the criminal justice system, from the entrance to the system to its exit, is significant, and there is very little evaluation of the effectiveness of criminal sanctions (especially imprisonment and short-term imprisonment), even though every time there is a change in the law, it seems that criminal sanctions become more severe.

Which are actions that can be mitigated by criminal law, and which are not? In my opinion, the use of criminal law in tackling crime can be divided into two categories. First, it may be used for acts that are classified as *mala per se*, such as fraud, battery, homicide, and rape, where it is appropriate to use the principle of *primum remedium*. Second, for acts that violate administrative laws, criminal law should be used as the *ultimum remedium*. Likewise, for civil violations, such as breaches of contract, civil sanctions should be used, not criminal law. Ultimately, for the hundreds of laws that currently exist in Indonesia, it would be better to evaluate – either through legislative review or judicial review – whether criminal law has been properly used as an *ultimum remedium*.

[81] Titis Anindyajati, Irfan Nur Rachman, and Anak Agung Dian Onita, 'Konstitusionalitas Norma Sanksi Pidana sebagai Ultimum Remedium dalam Pembentukan Perundang-Undangan' (2016) *Jurnal Konstritusi* 12, 4, 884–85.

[82] news.detik.com/berita/d-5374503/ditjen-pas-warga-binaan-252384-orang-kapasitas-lapas-rutan-hanya-135704.

2

The History of Criminal Law in Indonesia

I. Prior to Western Colonisation

Prior to the colonisation by Europeans (especially the Dutch and British), and later the Japanese, most of Indonesia's territory used its own laws. These were generally developed and implemented by the local region's ruling kingdom or sultanate. Long before Europeans arrived in the archipelago, there were several large kingdoms in what is now Indonesia that had their own sources of law. Around the year 1000, King Darmawangsa in East Java ordered the preparation of the *Ciwasana* law book. A few centuries later, the Majapahit kingdom used the *Adigama* law book or the *Kutaramanawadharmasastra* law book, which was handed down from Kanaka (1413–1430), Gajahmada's successor. These law books were all royal law books; most 'ordinary' people lived under unwritten laws that varied from place to place.[1]

Kutaramanawadharmasastra was a kind of criminal code, although at that time there was no clear separation between criminal and civil law. The arrangement was not as systematic as the current system.[2] Other large kingdoms in the archipelago also used their own law books, including in Padjadjaran in West Java, Samudra Pasai in Aceh, Sriwijaya in South Sumatra and the surrounding area, and Kutai in Kalimantan. After the collapse of the great kingdom of Majapahit, the sultanate of Demak stood strong on the island of Java; the sultanate had their own laws and courts that were heavily influenced by Islam. The sultans of Demak were also accompanied by Islamic religious figures known as *wali songo* or the nine guardians.

In addition to the laws of the kingdoms, unwritten customary law was widely applicable – it was acknowledged to exist by customary courts and was used in decision making, including in relation to violations of social norms.[3] In customary law, a violation is a one-sided action which is not justified as a reaction to the actions of the other party (either overtly or covertly). In the legal order of an indigenous community, a violation of the law is any disturbance to social balance or any

[1] Abintoro Prakoso, *Sejarah Hukum* (Yogyakarta, Aswaja Pressindo, 2019) 127.
[2] Topo Santoso, *Hukum Pidana Suatu Pengantar* (Jakarta, Rajawali Pers, 2021) 244.
[3] Santoso, *Hukum Pidana Suatu Pengantar* (2021) 244.

clash of unilateral actions on the necessities of life, both material and immaterial, of an individual or a number of people who are a group, resulting in a 'customary reaction'. With this reaction, the balance can be restored, mostly by way of payment for violations in the form of goods or money.[4] Around the sixteenth century, the customary laws in place across the archipelago – which had until that point been strongly influenced by Hinduism and Buddhism – began to be enriched with Islamic law materials.[5]

II. During the Colonial Period (Dutch, English, and Japanese)

After the arrival of Europeans, and especially following Dutch colonisation, there was a gradual change in Indonesian law, including criminal law, procedural law, and the judiciary. Indonesia's current Criminal Code (and the draft revised code) cannot be separated from its history, notably the Criminal Code that was in effect during the Dutch East Indies era: the *Wetboek van Strafrecht* (WvS) 1915, which itself originated from the Dutch WvS of 1881. Many provisions of the current and proposed revised code are still closely linked with the WvS of the Dutch period.

The Dutch Criminal Code of the colonial period was itself sourced from the *Code Pénal* of France. Following the withdrawal of France (1811–1813), the Netherlands drafted its own *Wetboek van Strafrecht*. On 2 March 1881, the Dutch Criminal Code (*Nederlandse Wetboek van Strafrecht*) was ratified through the Law of the Netherlands dated 2 March 1881, Staatblad 35, and came into force on 1 September 1886.[6]

Thus, the Dutch Criminal Code, which was then enforced in the Dutch East Indies (and later Indonesia), had at least two stages. First, the 1866 version of the Criminal Code (which applied to European peoples) and the 1872 Criminal Code (which applied to East Asian and *Bumiputera* (indigenous) peoples). Second, the Criminal Code that originated from the *Nederlandse Wetboek van Strafrecht*, which was ratified in the Netherlands in 1881 and entered into force in 1886. The Dutch Criminal Code was then brought to and enforced in the Dutch East Indies, replacing the *Wetboek van Strafrecht*, which had come into effect in 1866 and 1872 with the adjustment of conditions in the Dutch East Indies.[7] Thus, in 1915, the *Wetboek van Strafrecht voor Nederlandse Indie* was enacted in the Dutch East Indies, with contents derived from the new Dutch Criminal Code of 1881. However, the 1915 WvS only took effect three years later, in 1918.[8]

[4] B Ter Haar Bzn quoted in Prakoso, *Sejarah Hukum* (2019) 105.
[5] Prakoso, *Sejarah Hukum* (2019) 128.
[6] Santoso, *Hukum Pidana Suatu Pengantar* (2021) 238–39.
[7] JM van Bemmelen, *Hukum Pidana 1, Hukum Pidana Material Bagian Umum*, translated by Hasnan (Bandung, Binacipta, 1987) 17.
[8] Santoso, *Hukum Pidana Suatu Pengantar* (2021) 239.

In 1811–1816, power in the Dutch East Indies fell briefly into the hands of the British, during which time the British Governor-General, Thomas Stamford Raffles, ruled the archipelago. By March 1816, however, power returned to the Dutch, who continued their colonial rule of the Dutch East Indies until 1942, when the Dutch surrendered to the Japanese during World War II. The Japanese ruled the archipelago from 1942 until Indonesia proclaimed independence on 17 August 1945. Despite this proclamation, the Dutch returned in 1945 following the end of the war, and, through military aggression, controlled parts of Indonesia until 1949 with the approval of the Round Table Conference agreement in The Hague and the recognition of Indonesian sovereignty by the Dutch. Thus, in 1949, Indonesia officially became an independent country, with no areas controlled by foreign powers, except the territory of West Papua, which was controlled by the Dutch until it became part of Indonesia in 1963.[9]

Since the beginning of the Dutch colonial period, the law that applied to Dutch people in the archipelago was, as much as possible, equated with the law applied in the Netherlands. This was because it adhered to the Concordance principle (*Concordantie Beginsel*), which was held firmly for as long as the Dutch were in power in Indonesia. An exception was made to the principle of concordance only when the situation in Indonesia was completely different from the situation in the Netherlands. The Vereenigde Oostindische Compagnie[10] (VOC) leaders brought their laws from the Netherlands to regulate the Dutch people who were in VOC territory. Initially, there was a law of ships (*scheepsrecht*) that applied to VOC ships, which consisted of old Dutch law and the principles of Roman law, with the largest section of the law of ships about disciplinary law. After this, the laws of the Netherlands were used in areas that were effectively controlled by the VOC, based on the decision of the *Staaten General* in the Netherlands,[11] at which time the VOC acted as a government agency.[12]

As mentioned above, when the VOC arrived in the region, customary and kingdom/sultanate laws were still applicable throughout most of the archipelago.[13] As the *Wetboek van Strafrecht* (Criminal Code) did not yet exist, in VOC-controlled areas the VOC made regulations with the aim of solving special problems and adapting the legal needs of VOC employees to the circumstances of each region where a VOC trading centre was established. These regulations were made by the central management of the VOC in Banten (and later in Batavia) and by the Directors of the VOC in the Netherlands, the *Heeren Zeventien*, which consisted of 17 VOC leaders.

[9] Ibid 242.

[10] English translation: Dutch East India Company.

[11] *Staaten General* is the highest federative body of the Dutch countries (called the *Provincien*) which together constitute a confederation called *Republiek der Zeven Vereenigde Nederlanden*. See E Utrecht, *Rangkaian Sari Kuliah Hukum Pidana 1* (Surabaya, Pustaka Tinta Mas, 1994) 9.

[12] Utrecht, *Rangkaian Sari Kuliah Hukum Pidana 1* (2000) 8.

[13] Santoso, *Hukum Pidana Suatu Pengantar* (2021) 248–49.

On 27 November 1609, the *Heeren Zeventien* issued an instruction to the first VOC Governor-General, Pieter Both, which was legalized by the *Staaten General.* Articles 3 and 4 of the instruction regarded courts and special provisions regarding criminal law that must be carried out in VOC territories.[14] There were three sources of law used by the VOC at the time: (1) statutory law (which was contained in the *Statuten van Batavia*); (2) old Dutch law; and (3) the principles of Roman law. The prevailing law was statutory law; if a problem could not be resolved with statutory law, then old Dutch law was used. Meanwhile, the principles of Roman law in effect were those relating to the affairs of regulating the legal situation of slaves (slave law or *slavenrecht*).[15] VOC criminal laws thus began to enter into force in its territory, especially for the Dutch.[16]

For native Indonesians and East Asians in areas controlled by the VOC, the applicable law was generally customary law, except in the area around the city of Batavia (known as *Bataviase Ommelanden*). In this region, there was unification, with one law for all national groups. However, in practice, non-Dutch people were still subject to customary law.[17] Thus it can be said that there was no unification of criminal law in the Dutch East Indies at this time.

As discussed in the opening section of this chapter, in the seventeenth and eighteenth centuries, several archipelagic kingdoms and sultanates had their own books of law, including those in Java, Sumatra, Kalimantan, Nusa Tenggara, and Bali.[18] Customary reactions were commonly in place for customary violations, such as compensation for immaterial damages in various forms. For example, forced marriage to her attacker imposed on a girl who has been sexually assaulted; payment of money to the affected person; salvation for victims by cleansing the community of all supernatural impurities; masking for shame; apology; corporal punishment; and social or legal exile.[19]

In this section, we will primarily focus on criminal law during the Herman Willem Daendels era, as it was during this period that important changes occurred in the Dutch East Indies, including changes the criminal system. Daendels was sent to the Dutch East Indies in 1808 with tasks including organising the government (*bestuur*), justice, and the police. In 1810, by order of Daendels, laws and judicial regulations were made, with emphasis given to customary law. For European people – referred to as the European legal group (*rechtsgroup*) – the new *Statute van Batavia* was applied, while for Indonesian peoples – the Indonesian legal group – customary law was applied. However, the Governor-General had the

[14] Utrecht, *Rangkaian Sari Kuliah Hukum Pidana 1* (2020) 9–10.

[15] Ibid 11. Andi Hamzah, *Asas-Asas Hukum Pidana*, Revised Edition (Jakarta, Rineka Cipta, 1994) 15.

[16] Santoso, *Hukum Pidana Suatu Pengantar* (2021) 245.

[17] Utrecht, *Rangkaian Sari Kuliah Hukum Pidana 1* (2020) 11–12.

[18] Prakoso, *Sejarah Hukum* (2019) 78.

[19] Prakoso, *Sejarah Hukum* (2019) 109–10.

right to change customary penitentiary law if: (1) the punishment was deemed inconsistent with the crime committed; (2) customary law could not resolve a case; or (3) customary law did not comply with general orders of high authorities, or violated important principles of law and justice, or where, in major criminal cases, the necessary public security benefits could not be obtained.[20]

During the Daendels era, judges were generally allowed to implement customary law. However, customary law could not be carried out if the principles of general security or the system of equal rights were not met for all residents. Judges, in adjudicating customary criminal cases, were also given great freedom to deviate from the customary law, especially in cases in which customary criminal law was considered contrary to the principles of public security, justice, and propriety.[21] As in the previous period, there was still no codification of criminal law.

After the reign of Governor-General Daendels, a new chapter began with British rule in Indonesia under Thomas Stamford Raffles. Raffles was appointed Lieutenant Governor[22] in 1811 when the British Empire took over the Dutch colonies. Raffles then came to power in Indonesia with the task of regulating the government and boosting trade and security.[23]

The British government made several positive changes to the law. The most significant of these were changes in the law of procedure and the structure of the courts. In Java, a new court structure was established which mirrored the court structure in the British Indies (now India). Meanwhile, for Europeans, substantive law – the Batavia Statute – remained effective, although Raffles did make several minor changes to substantive criminal law, including alleviating criminal punishment, especially for British citizens. The changes included the following: (1) a British citizen may not be sentenced to a more severe punishment than under British law (if committing a similar crime); (2) a criminal conviction against a British citizen may only be executed after being reported to the Lieutenant Governor; (3) capital punishment may only be carried out after reporting to the Lieutenant Governor; and (4) the Lieutenant Governor has the right to grant pardons or partial remissions of punishment. This could be done in cases of non-essential fines, short-term imprisonment, or light corporal punishment.[24] As before, criminal law was still yet to be codified.[25]

When the Dutch again took control of the Dutch East Indies, criminal law in the archipelago remained diverse and without unity across the territory. The main source of law was the Batavian Statute, followed by old Dutch law and the

[20] Utrecht, *Rangkaian Sari Kuliah Hukum Pidana 1* (2020) 18–19.

[21] Ibid 23–24.

[22] The British ruler in Indonesia at that time held the title of Lieutenant Governor, in contrast to the Dutch ruler who had the title of Governor-General.

[23] Santoso, *Hukum Pidana Suatu Pengantar* (2021) 252.

[24] Utrecht, *Rangkaian Sari Kuliah Hukum Pidana 1* (2000) 26–27.

[25] Santoso, *Hukum Pidana Suatu Pengantar* (2021) 253.

principles of Roman law. Finally there was *koloniaal verslag* ('Colonial Report'), which included, among other crimes, criminal offences relating to counterfeiting coins and to participating in the slave trade.[26]

On 10 February 1866, a Criminal Code for the European group was enacted (*Wetboek voor Europeanen*). Coming into effect on 1 January 1867, it was only marginally different to the French Penal Code, which consisted of four books while the Criminal Code for Europeans consisted of only two books (the fourth book in the French Penal Code was not incorporated, and the first three books were condensed into two books).

After the enactment of the Criminal Code for European groups, a copy of the Criminal Code was made for non-European groups in 1872 and declared effective from 1 January 1873. The two codes differed with regards to criminal matters and punishment.[27] With the enactment of this Criminal Code, customary criminal law was no longer to be set by government judges. However, within the judiciary in the kingdoms, autonomous regions,[28] and areas directly under Dutch control but which were allowed to exercise self-government, customary criminal law still applied.[29]

Therefore, by 1873, a Criminal Code was finally in place for all peoples in the Dutch East Indies: the 1866 Criminal Code (valid from 1867 for European groups), and the 1872 Criminal Code (valid from 1873 for non-European groups). There was thus a dualism in criminal codes, alongside a pluralism of criminal law, as the Criminal Code only applied to courts within the government (Netherlands), with customary law still applicable in kingdoms and other regions.[30]

In the Netherlands itself, a new *Wetboek van Strafrecht* had been produced to replace the French Penal Code-derived Criminal Code from the French Penal Code. It was agreed upon in 1881, and took effect on 1 September 1886. Following this, the Dutch colonial government began discussing how to implement the new Code in the Dutch East Indies, as the French-derived code had only been in effect there for a few years. This was a dilemma, because based on the principle of concordance according to Article 75 *Regerings Reglement* and 131 *Indische Staatsregeling*, the Criminal Code in effect in the Netherlands must also be enforced in colonial areas, with adjustments made according to local situations and conditions.[31]

However, it was not until 1915 that the 1881 *Wetboek van Strafetcht* was re-worked for the Dutch East Indies context. The Dutch East Indies government issued a *Koninklijk Besluit* on 15 October 1915 regarding the territory's new Criminal Code, known as the *Wetboek van Strafrecht voor Nederlandsh Indie* (WvSi).

[26] Utrecht, *Rangkaian Sari Kuliah Hukum Pidana 1* (2000) 37–38.
[27] Ibid 43–46.
[28] The autonomous regions, for example, are the Surakarta Sunanate, Yogyakarta Sultanate, and Pontianak Sultanate.
[29] Utrecht, *Rangkaian Sari Kuliah Hukum Pidana 1* (2000) 45–46.
[30] Santoso, *Hukum Pidana Suatu Pengantar* (2021) 256–57.
[31] Ibid 257.

This Criminal Code came into force on 1 January 1918 for all legal groups in Indonesia[32] and was used until the Japanese invasion in early World War II.[33]

The Dutch East Indies government surrendered to the Japanese unconditionally on 8 March 1942, ending Dutch rule in Indonesia.[34] During the Japanese period, WvSi was still enforced by the Japanese Occupation Government based on Law (*Osamu Serei*) Number 1 of 1942, which came into force on 7 March 1942 as a transitional regulation for Java and Madura. Article 3 of *Osamu Serei* stated that all government agencies and their powers, laws, and regulations from the previous government were still recognised as valid for the time being, as long as they did not conflict with the rules of the military government (Japan). Only articles concerning the Dutch government, for example, those mentioning the King/Queen, were no longer valid. Similar regulations were also issued for regions outside Java and Madura.[35]

Thus WvSi remained in effect under the Japanese, after which the spirit of this law was adjusted to the interests and constitutional structure of the Japanese Army. In addition, the Japanese government issued another Code of Criminal Law named *Gunsei Keizi Rei*, applicable during in times of war.[36] Thus, in terms of substantive criminal law, it can be said that very few changes were made during the Japanese period, except for the law on criminal procedure, which underwent several changes due to the unification of procedural law and court structure (through *Osamu Serei* Number 3 of 1942 dated 20 September 1942).[37] This situation remained for about three and a half years until independence was declared in 1945.[38]

III. The Years of 1945–1958

Indonesia proclaimed its independence on Friday, 17 August 1945. The proclamation was read by Soekarno, accompanied by Mohammad Hatta, at 56 Pegangsaan Timur Street, Central Jakarta.[39] The Dutch colonial government, meanwhile, after

[32] Utrecht, *Rangkaian Sari Kuliah Hukum Pidana 1* (2000) 46–50. Originally, it was planned that there would be two Criminal Codes, one for the European group and the other for the indigenous group. With Koninklijk Besluit dated 12 April 1898, the Criminal Code Bill for Europeans was formed. However, the Minister of Dutch Colonialism, Alexander Idenburg believed there should only be one Criminal Code in the Dutch East Indies so that it would be in the form of a codification. See also Hamzah, *Asas-Asas Hukum Pidana* (1994) 19.

[33] Santoso, *Hukum Pidana Suatu Pengantar* (2021) 257–58.

[34] Committee for the 75th Anniversary of Kasman Singodimedjo, *Hidup itu Berjuang, Kasman Singodimedjo 75 Tahun* (Jakarta, Bulan Bintang, 1982) 48.

[35] Hamzah, *Asas-Asas Hukum Pidana* (1994) 20.

[36] Dali Mutiara, *Kitab Undang-Undang Hukum Pidana Republik Indonesia* (Jakarta, Bintang Indonesia, 1948) 4.

[37] Hamzah, *Asas-Asas Hukum Pidana* (1994) 20.

[38] Santoso, *Hukum Pidana Suatu Pengantar* (2021) 261–62.

[39] Frances Gouda, *American visions of the Netherlands East Indies/Indonesia: US foreign policy and Indonesian nationalism, 1920–1949* (Amsterdam, Amsterdam University Press, 2002) 119. Read more in Adam Malik, *Riwayat Proklamasi Kemerdekaan 17 Agustus 1945* (Jakarta, Wijaya, 1962).

being defeated by Japan in 1942, had formed a civil government in Australia, known as the Netherlands Indies Civil Administration (NICA) under the leadership of HJ Van Mook. In September–October 1945, the Dutch returned to Indonesia and occupied Jakarta, then expanded to other areas, while the Government of the Republic of Indonesia, under President Soekarno and Vice President Hatta, moved to Yogyakarta as the new capital of the Republic of Indonesia. Thus, by late 1945, the Dutch controlled some parts of Indonesia while the Republic of Indonesia controlled all other areas. The Government of the Republic of Indonesia in Yogyakarta issued Law No 1 of 1946 dated 26 February 1946, Article 1 of which states 'By deviating as necessary from the Presidential Regulation of the Republic of Indonesia dated October 10, 1945, No. 2, it stipulates that the criminal law regulations currently in force are criminal law regulations that prevails on March 8, 1942.'[40]

In Law No 1 of 1946 concerning Criminal Law Regulations, amendments were made to the Criminal Code, especially regarding terms and designations. For example, Article 3 of this Law states that if, in a criminal law regulation, the words '*Nederlandsch-Indie*' or '*Nederlandsch-Indisch(e) (en)*' appear, then these words must be read as '*Indonesie*' or '*Indonesisch(e) (en)*'. Article 8 stipulates that the word '*Gouverneur-Generaal*' is changed to 'President', '*Inlander*' is replaced with 'Indonesian citizen', '*Indische Staatsregeling*' is changed to 'the Constitution', '*Konings of der Koningin*' is changed to '*van den President en van den Vice President*', and so on.[41]

Law No 1 of 1946 also stipulated that all provisions of criminal law whose contents were colonial or contradict the position of the Republic of Indonesia as an independent state were no longer valid. Article 17 of this stated that it 'applies to the islands of Java and Madura on the day it is announced and for other regions on the day to be determined by the President'. Government Regulation No 8 of 1946 later stated that the law also applied to Sumatra.[42] The Government of the Republic of Indonesia also issued Law No 20 of 1946, which added a new type of principal punishment, namely the 'undisclosed penitentiary' (*Hukuman Tutupan*).[43]

To remedy the power struggle between the Dutch colonial government and the new Republic of Indonesia government, the Round Table Conference was held in The Hague. The conference ended with Dutch parliamentary recognition of the sovereignty of the Republic of Indonesia, with sovereignty officially transferred on 27 December 1949. Initially, the country was called the Republic of the United

[40] Santoso, *Hukum Pidana Suatu Pengantar* (2021) 264.

[41] Ibid 264–65.

[42] Ibid.

[43] Ibid 266. 'Undisclosed penitentiary' (*Hukuman Tutupan*) is an alternative punishment to imprisonment, especially for political criminals who commit criminal acts because they are motivated by intentions that deserve respect. This was carried out in a special place called the Tutupan House which was managed by the Minister of Defence.

States of Indonesia (*Republik Indonesia Serikat* or RIS), with Yogyakarta as one of the states, but after several other states joined the Republic, on 17 August 1950, RIS was dissolved and replaced with the Unitary State of the Republic of Indonesia.[44]

Thus, in the period between 1950–1958, there were two Criminal Codes applicable in Indonesia. First, the Criminal Code in conjunction with Law No 1 of 1946 and, second, *Wetboek van Strafrecht*. This dualism lasted until the issuance of Law No 73 of 1958 – dated 20 September 1958 and in effect from 29 September – which expressly stated that Law No 1 of 1946 concerning Criminal Law Regulations applies to the entire territory of the Republic of Indonesia. Essentially, the effective law was *Wetboek van Strafrecht voor Indonesie* after being transformed by Law No 1 of 1946.[45]

IV. 1958 to Present

Through Law No 73 of 1958, it was confirmed that Law No 1 of 1946 concerning Criminal Law Regulations was applicable for the entire territory of the Republic of Indonesia. Since then, there have been many changes to the Criminal Code, which will be the focus of this section.

Prior to the existence of the Indonesian Constitutional Court, changes to the Criminal Code were only made with changes to laws, namely by mutual agreement between the House of Representatives and the President through a process known as legislative review. However, since the establishment of Constitutional Court in 2003, the Criminal Code has gone through multiple judicial reviews at the Constitutional Court and, subsequently, several changes.

In 2019, there are at least 14 laws or statutory level regulations that amend the Criminal Code, in addition to Law No 1 of 1946 and Law No 20 of 1946.[46] In 1958 there is Law No 73 of 1958. Article I of Law No. 73 of 1958 states: 'Law No. 1 of 1946 of the Republic of Indonesia concerning criminal law regulations is declared to prevail to the entire territory of the Republic of Indonesia.' In addition, Article II states: 'Article XVI of Law No. 1 of 1946 of the Republic of Indonesia concerning criminal law regulations is revoked.'[47]

In 1960, updates were made as Indonesia's population grew, through Law No 1 of 1960 concerning Amendments to the Criminal Code. The law stated that previous legal sanctions against criminal acts of 'causing people to die by accident' (Article 359 of the Criminal Code), 'causing people to be seriously injured

[44] Ibid 267.

[45] R Tresna, *Azas-azas Hukum Pidana Disertai Pembahasan Beberapa Perbuatan Pidana yang Penting* (Yogyakarta, Tiara Wacana, 1959) 211.

[46] Santoso, *Hukum Pidana Suatu Pengantar* (2021) 270.

[47] Article XVI of Law No 1 of 1946 reads: 'Whoever against the Indonesian national flag intentionally carries out an act that can cause feelings of national contempt, is punished with a maximum imprisonment of one year and six months.'

by accident' (Article 360 of the Criminal Code), and 'causing, due to his fault, fire, explosion, or flood' (Article 188 of the Criminal Code) were too light, especially in light of the traffic and housing conditions at the time. The criminal sanction in Article 359 and Article 360 was raised to a maximum of five years, up from one year.[48]

Also in 1960, Government Regulation in Lieu of Law No 16 of 1960 concerning Several Amendments to the Criminal Code was enacted on 14 April. In the consideration section of letter a, that the regulation stated that it was 'deemed necessary to amend articles 364, 373, 379, 384 and 407 paragraph (1) of The Criminal Code relating to the value of the price of the goods referred to in those articles is no longer in accordance with the current situation'. The regulation, just two articles long, altered the sanction of 250 guilders to IDR250.[49]

On the same day, Government Regulation in Lieu of Law No 18 of 1960 concerning Amendments to the Number of Fines in the Criminal Code and in Other Criminal Provisions Issued Before 17 August 1945 was ratified. The regulation explained that the amounts identified as fines in the Criminal Code were no longer commensurate with the nature of the crimes committed, with the fines too small for the 1960 financial situation. This Government Regulation in Lieu of Law states that each fine specified in the Criminal Code should instead be read in rupiah and multiplied by 15.[50]

Shortly thereafter, Government Regulation in Lieu of Law No 24 of 1960 concerning the Investigation, Prosecution, and Examination of Corruption was stipulated on 9 June 1960. In its elucidation, the regulation stated that in order to prevent the possibility of widespread acts of corruption, Article 1 sub c also includes the crimes mentioned in Article 415, 416, 417, 423, 425, and 435 of the Criminal Code as criminal acts of corruption with all their consequences. In addition, to make it easier for public prosecutors and judges to obtain necessary evidence, provisions regarding investigations, prosecutions, and examinations were made which deviate from ordinary criminal procedures.[51]

In the closing provisions of Government Regulation in Lieu of Law No 24 of 1960, it is stated that:

(1) The sanction of imprisonment and fines as stated in Articles 209, 210, 415 to 420, 423, 425 and 435 of the Criminal Code is changed to a maximum imprisonment sentence of twelve years and/or a fine of a maximum of one million rupiah.[52]

[48] Santoso, *Hukum Pidana Suatu Pengantar* (2021) 274.
[49] Ibid 276–77.
[50] Ibid 277–78.
[51] Ibid 278–79.
[52] Before being amended, crimes regulated by Article 209 were punishable by a maximum imprisonment of 2 years and 8 months; Article 210 – imprisonment for a maximum of 7 years; Article 415 – imprisonment for a maximum of 7 years; Article 420 – imprisonment for a maximum of 9 years; Article 423 – imprisonment for a maximum of 6 years; Article 425 – imprisonment for a maximum of 7 years; and Article 435 – imprisonment for a maximum of 9 months.

(2) In the articles of the Criminal Code referred to in paragraph (1) with '*ambtenaar*', shall be equated with one who receives a salary or wages from the state or regional finance, or who receives salary or wages from an agency that receives assistance from state or regional finance or other legal entities that use capital from concessions from the state or society.

Five years later, Presidential Decree No 1 of 1965 concerning Prevention of Abuse and/or Blasphemy of Religion was stipulated on 27 January 1965. In Article 4, the decree stated that a new article is to be issued for the Criminal Code, reading as follows: Article 156a: 'Punishable with a sentence of a maximum imprisonment of five years whoever deliberately publicly express feelings or commits an act: a. which are essentially hostile, abusive or defamatory towards a religion professed in Indonesia; b. with the intention that people do not adhere to any religion, which is based on the Almighty God.'[53]

In 1971, Law No 3 of 1971 concerning the Eradication of Criminal Acts of Corruption was ratified on 29 March 1971. Through this law, Government Regulation in Lieu of Law No 24 of 1960 was repealed. In consideration of this Law, it is stated that acts of corruption are very detrimental to state economy and hinder national development, and Government Regulation in Lieu of Law No 24 of 1960 concerning the investigation, prosecution, and examination of corruption could not achieve the desired result and hence the need to be replaced.[54]

There are two provisions in Law No 3 of 1971 that are directly related to the Criminal Code. First, the General Provisions Article 1 paragraph (1) persons who are punishable for a criminal act of corruption, which reads at letter c 'Whoever commits a crime is listed in Articles 209, 210, 387, 488, 415, 416, 417, 418, 419, 420, 423, and 435 of the Criminal Code', while letter e reads 'Whoever without a reasonable reason, within the shortest possible time after receiving a gift or promise given to him as referred to in Articles 418, 419 and 420 of the Criminal Code does not report the gift or promise to the authorities'. Second, Article 32 reads 'Violations of Article 220, 231, 421, 422, 429 and Article 430 of the Criminal Code in corruption cases are sanctioned with imprisonment for a maximum of 6 (six) years and/or a maximum fine of 4 (four) million rupiah'.[55]

Then in 1974, Law No 7 of 1974 concerning the Control of Gambling was enacted on 6 November 1974. The law stated that the sanctions for gambling in the articles of the Criminal Code were deemed irrelevant, so it was necessary to make changes to make sanctions heavier. In the General Elucidation, the law explained that gambling in all its forms was still widely practised in society, with negative and detrimental impacts on the morals and mentality of the community, especially

[53] Santoso, *Hukum Pidana Suatu Pengantar* (2021) 279–80.

[54] Ibid 281–82.

[55] If it is not in the context of a corruption case, then in the Criminal Code the criminal sanctions are as follows: Article 422 – punishable by imprisonment of 4 years, Article 429 – punishable by imprisonment of 1 year and 4 months and Article 430 – punishable by imprisonment of 2 years and 8 months.

the younger generation. The government wished to take steps and efforts to restore order and re-regulate gambling, limiting it to the smallest possible environment, leading eventually to its complete elimination from the entire territory of Indonesia.[56] Article 1 states that all gambling is a crime.[57] Article 2 paragraph (1) of Law No 7 of 1974 amends the sanction of punishment in Article 303 paragraph (1) of the Criminal Code, from a maximum imprisonment of two years or a maximum fine of IDR90,000 to a maximum imprisonment of 10 years or a maximum fine of IDR25,000,000.[58]

Also in Law No 7 of 1974, Article 2 paragraph (2) amended the sanction in Article 542 paragraph (1) of the Criminal Code from a maximum imprisonment of one month or a maximum fine of IDR4,500, to a maximum imprisonment of four years or a maximum fine of IDR10,000,000. Article 2 paragraph (3) changed the sanction of punishment in Article 542 paragraph (2) of the Criminal Code, from a maximum imprisonment of three months or a maximum fine of IDR7,500 to a maximum imprisonment of six years or a maximum fine of IDR15,000,000. As a consequence of changing the type of criminal act – from violation to offence – the designation of Article 542 becomes Article 303 bis.[59] Thus, in my opinion, Article 542 which is in Book 3 of the Criminal Code becomes Article 303 bis and its location is in Book 2 of the Criminal Code.[60]

Two years later, Law No 4 of 1976 concerning Amendments and Additions to Several Articles in the Criminal Code relating to the Expansion of the Applicability of Provisions for Criminal Laws, Aviation Crimes, and Crimes against Aviation Facilities/Infrastructure, was enacted on 27 April 1976. The basis for consideration of the enactment of this Law was that the provisions of criminal legislation had not yet been applied to Indonesian aircraft. Unlawful control of aircraft and all actions that interfere with flight security and flight facilities/infrastructure are obviously detrimental to national aviation in general, so it is necessary to enact regulations to prevent unlawful acts and ensure the safety and security of passengers, aircraft crew, and cargo, as well as the protection of aviation facilities and infrastructure.[61] This law was prepared by amending and adding provisions to the Criminal Code, primarily by expanding the scope of application of Articles 3 and 4 of Book 1 and adding to Book 1 Chapter IX Articles 95a, 95b, and 95c and in Book 2 Chapter XXIX A concerning Aviation Crimes and Crimes Against Aviation Facilities/Infrastructure. Crimes against aviation facilities/infrastructure as regulated in Article 479a to Article 479d of this Law are different in nature to

[56] See General Elucidation of Law of the Republic of Indonesia No 7 of 1974 concerning Gambling Control.

[57] Previously, some gambling conducts were classified as felonies (as regulated in Book 2 of the Criminal Code) and some were classified as violations (as regulated in Book 3 of the Criminal Code).

[58] Santoso, *Hukum Pidana Suatu Pengantar* (2021) 283.

[59] Article 2 paragraph (4) of Law No 7 of 1974.

[60] Santoso, *Hukum Pidana Suatu Pengantar* (2021) 282–83.

[61] See the consideration of Considering in Law No 4 of 1976.

violations as stated in Article 15 paragraph (1) e of Law No 83 of 1958 concerning Aviation. Thus, in this Law, the articles already contained in the Criminal Code were expanded in scope so that the definition of criminal jurisdiction of the Republic of Indonesia includes Indonesian aircraft. In addition, new provisions were added in line with aviation developments and the obligations of the Republic of Indonesia as a participant in international conventions.[62]

In 1997, Law No 3 of 1997 concerning the Juvenile Court was enacted on 3 January 1997. In the Law's consideration, it was stated that in order to provide protection for children, support needed to be expanded, with both institutions and legal instruments that were firmer and more adequate as well as special treatment provisions for juvenile offenders going through the court system. This is because, based on the elucidation of Article 10 of Law No 14 of 1970 concerning the Basic Provisions of Judicial Authority and the explanation of Article 8 of Law No 2 of 1986 concerning General Courts, the specialisation of juvenile courts lies within the General Courts.[63]

In the interest of the growth and mental development of children, it is necessary to determine the difference in treatment in the procedural law and the sanction of punishment. In this regard, according to the exemption provisions regulated in Law No 8 of 1981 concerning the Criminal Procedure Code, the length of detention is determined with the interests of minors in mind, with the sentence for minors to be half of the maximum criminal sanction that can be enacted on adult perpetrators. The imposition of capital punishment and life imprisonment is not applicable to minors. The difference in treatment and sanctions is intended to better protect and rehabilitate the child so that the child can better face their future.[64]

In addition, the special treatment provided by the Law is intended to provide opportunities for children so that through nurturing, they will be able to become independent, responsible, and useful human beings for themselves, their families, communities, nations, and countries. Specifically, regarding sanctions imposed on child perpetrators, the Law states that sanctions are to be determined based on the child's age. For children aged eight to 12 years old, they are only subject to actions such as being returned to their parents, placed in social care, or handed over to the state, while children between the ages of 12 and 18 can be subject to punishment. The difference in treatment is based on the child's physical, mental, and social growth and development.[65] In view of the characteristics and traits that are unique to children and for the protection of children, the juvenile offenders must be tried in the Juvenile Court, which sits within the General Court. Thus, in cases of juvenile offenders, the whole judicial process – from the time they are arrested

[62] See the General Elucidation and Consideration to Law No 4 of 1976.
[63] See the Consideration to Law No 3 of 1997 concerning Juvenile Court.
[64] See General Elucidation of Law No 3 of 1997 concerning Juvenile Court.
[65] See General Elucidation of Law No 3 of 1997 concerning Juvenile Court.

and detained through to trial and rehabilitation – must be carried out by special officials who have a deep understanding of juvenile issues.[66]

Law No 3 of 1997 also identifies the age limit for juvenile offenders.[67] They must be at least 12 years old[68] but have not yet reached the age of 18 and have never been married. If a child commits a crime within these age limits and is submitted to a court hearing after the child has turned 18 but while the child is not yet 21, the case is still to be submitted to the Juvenile Court.[69]

Meanwhile, according to Article 5 of the Law, if a child has not reached the age of 12 years,[70] but commits or is suspected of committing a criminal act, then the child can be examined by an investigator. If, according to the results of the examination, the investigator is of the opinion that the child can be rehabilitated by their parents, guardians, or foster parents, the investigator shall return the child to them. If according to the results of the examination, the investigator is of the opinion that the child can no longer be rehabilitated by their parents, guardians, or foster parents, the investigator shall hand over the child to the Ministry of Social Affairs after hearing the considerations of the social adviser.[71]

The criminal arrangements and actions in Law No 3 of 1997 are different from the provisions in the Criminal Code. According to Article 23, either basic or additional punishments can be imposed upon juvenile offenders. The basic punishments that can be imposed on a juvenile offender are imprisonment, light (ie short-term) imprisonment, fines, or supervision, while additional punishment may also be imposed in the form of confiscation of certain goods and/or payment of restitution.[72] In addition, juvenile offenders can be returned to their parents, guardians, or foster parents; given to the state to participate in education, rehabilitation, and work training; or handed over to the Ministry of Social Affairs, or civil society organisations engaged in education, rehabilitation, and work training. Such actions may be accompanied by warnings and additional conditions determined by the judge.[73]

As mentioned above, imprisonment for juvenile offenders is a maximum of one half of the maximum imprisonment possible for adults, according to Article 26 of the Law. If a juvenile offender commits a crime which is punishable by death or life imprisonment, a maximum of 10 years' imprisonment can be imposed. If the juvenile offender was under the age of 12 when the crime was committed, and if

[66] See General Elucidation of Law No 3 of 1997 concerning Juvenile Court.

[67] According to Article 1 number 2, juvenile offenders are: (a) a minor who commits a crime; or (b) a minor who commits an act that is declared forbidden for a minor, either according to the laws and regulations or according to other legal regulations that live and apply in the community concerned.

[68] Previously 'at least eight years old', but it then changed to 'at least 12 (twelve) years old' based on the Constitutional Court Decision No 1/PUU-VIII/2010 dated 24 February 2011.

[69] Santoso, *Hukum Pidana Suatu Pengantar* (2021) 287.

[70] Based on the Constitutional Court Decision No 1/PUU-VIII/2010 dated 24 February 2011: 'Children have not reached the age of 12 (twelve) years old.'

[71] Santoso, *Hukum Pidana Suatu Pengantar* (2021) 288.

[72] Ibid.

[73] Ibid.

that crime is punishable by death penalty, life imprisonment, or another sanction, then the offender can only be given 'action' punishments, including being handed over to the state for care.[74] Fines for juvenile offenders are also half the maximum adult fine, according to Article 28. If the fine cannot be paid, it is to be replaced with mandatory work training, to be carried out for no longer than 90 working days for a maximum of four hours a day, and is not to be conducted at night.[75]

In the Law's closing provisions, particularly in Article 67, it is emphasised that when this Law came into force, Article 45, Article 46, and Article 47 of the Criminal Code were declared no longer valid. Thus, the provisions regarding children who commit crimes in Law No 3 of 1997 shall apply and Article 45, Article 46 and Article 47 of the Criminal Code have been declared no longer valid.[76]

In 2012, however, Law No 3 of 1997 was declared invalid following the enactment of Law No 11 of 2012 concerning the Juvenile Criminal Justice System 30 July 2012.[77] This law comprehensively regulates the juvenile criminal justice system and concerns all children who face the law, whether they are children in conflict with the law (juveniles who are 12 years old but not yet 18 years old and who are suspected of committing a crime), children who are victims of crimes (juvenile victims, who are not yet 18 years old and who experience physical, mental, and/or economic losses caused by criminal acts), and children who are witnesses of criminal acts (juvenile witnesses, who are children under the age of 18 years who can provide information for the purposes of investigation, prosecution, and examination in court regarding a criminal case, that they heard, saw, or experienced themselves).[78] Thus, the term 'juvenile offender' was removed and replaced with 'children facing the law'. The new law was developed because Law No 3 of 1997 was seen as no longer in accordance with the development and legal needs of the community because it had not comprehensively provided protection to children facing the law.[79]

Law No 27 of 1999 concerning Amendments to the Criminal Code on Crimes Against State Security was enacted on 19 May 1999. This is a law that was enacted during the *Reformasi* (Reform) period, after the fall of President Soeharto, during which new President BJ Habibie issued many laws that responded to demands for reform from the wider community, including changes to the Criminal Code.[80]

[74] Ibid 288–89.
[75] Ibid 289.
[76] Ibid 289.
[77] See Article 106 of Law No 11 of 2012 concerning the Juvenile Criminal Justice System. This Law is a replacement for Law No 3 of 1997 concerning Juvenile Court, which was carried out with the aim of realising a court that truly guarantees the protection of the best interests of children who are in conflict with the law. See General Elucidation of Law No 11 of 2012 concerning the Juvenile Criminal Justice System.
[78] Article 1 points 1-5 of Law No. 11 of 2012 concerning the Juvenile Criminal Justice System.
[79] See the Considerations on Law No 11 of 2012 concerning the Juvenile Criminal Justice System.
[80] Santoso, *Hukum Pidana Suatu Pengantar* (2021) 291.

In the consideration of Law No 27 of 1999, it is stated that the Criminal Code, especially provisions concerning crimes against state security, has not provided a strong legal basis in an effort to defend the Unitary State of the Republic of Indonesia, which is based on the principles of Pancasila as the basis of the state. In addition, it is also stated that the understanding and teachings of Communism / Marxism / Leninism in the practice of political and state life manifest themselves in activities that are contrary to the principles of the Indonesian people who are godly and religious, and that those teachings have been proven to endanger the survival of the Indonesian nation.[81] Thus it is stated that it is necessary to make changes to the Criminal Code by adding articles relating to crimes against state security.[82] The Law adds six new provisions between Article 107 and Article 108 Chapter 1 Book 2 of the Criminal Code, all concerning Crimes Against State Security, which are contained into five articles on Communism / Marxism / Leninism (Article 107a, Article 107b, Article 107c, Article 107d, Article 107e) and one article on sabotage (Article 107f).[83]

As with Law No 27 of 1999 above, Law No. 31 of 1999 concerning the Eradication of Criminal Acts of Corruption was born in the context of *Reformasi* and the fall of President Soeharto, after which President Habibie immediately formed a legal reform team. This law was passed on 16 August 1999. In its consideration, it was stated that Law No 3 of 1971 concerning the Eradication of Criminal Acts of Corruption was no longer in accordance with the development of legal needs in society, and therefore it needs to be replaced with a new law to be more effective in preventing and eradicating corruption.[84]

In accordance with Article 5 to Article 12 of Law No 31 of 1999, the criminal acts as referred to in Article 209, Article 210, Article 387, Article 388, Article 415, Article 416, Article 417, Article 418, Article 419, Article 420, Article 423, Article 425, and Article 435 of the Criminal Code are criminal acts of corruption. The criminal sanctions of both imprisonment and fines in the articles of the Criminal Code were amended and made more severe in accordance, with minimum sanctions being identified and the formulation of criminal sanctions becoming cumulative.[85]

Originally, Article 419 of the Criminal Code was punishable by a maximum imprisonment of five years; Article 420 of the Criminal Code carried a maximum imprisonment of nine years; Article 423 of the Criminal Code carried a maximum imprisonment of six years; Article 425 of the Criminal Code carried a maximum imprisonment of seven years; and Article 435 of the Criminal Code carried a maximum imprisonment of nine months. With this change, all the

[81] Ibid 291.

[82] See General Elucidation of Law No 27 of 1999 concerning Amendments to the Criminal Code relating to Crimes Against State Security.

[83] Santoso, *Hukum Pidana Suatu Pengantar* (2021) 291–92.

[84] Ibid 292–93.

[85] Ibid 293.

aforementioned crimes are punishable by life imprisonment or imprisonment for a minimum of four years and a maximum of 20 years. Thus, there is an extraordinary increase in criminal sanctions. This can be understood in the context of the reforms at that time, where people were fighting corruption because it was widespread and causing a great crisis.[86]

Only two years after the promulgation of Law No 31 of 1999, amendments were made to the Law, through the issuance of Law No 20 of 2001 concerning Amendments to Law No 31 of 1999 concerning the Eradication of Corruption Crimes. This law was passed on 21 November 2001.[87] With regards to the Criminal Code, Article 43A of Law No 20 of 2001 states that in Chapter VII before Article 44, a new article is added (Article 43 B). This new Article 43 B which states that at the time the Law comes into force, Article 209, Article 210, Article 387, Article 388, Article 415, Article 416, Article 417, Article 419, Article 420, Article 423, Article 425, and Article 435 of the Criminal Code are declared invalid. What now apply are articles with the same substance in Law No 20 of 2001. This means that the substance of the articles in the Criminal Code has been fully taken up in Law No 20 of 2001. Criminal sanctions have been adjusted – generally becoming more severe – there is a minimum punishment for imprisonment and fines, and the criminal sanction is cumulative (for both imprisonment and fines).[88]

In 2007, Law No 21 of 2007 concerning the Eradication of the Crime of Trafficking in Persons was enacted on 19 April 2007. Another law – specifically Article 83 of Law No 23 of 2002 concerning Child Protection – already stipulated the prohibition of trafficking, selling, or kidnapping children for one's self or for sale. However, the provisions of the Criminal Code and the Child Protection Act do not formulate a strict legal definition of trafficking in persons. In addition, Article 297 of the Criminal Code provides sanctions that are too light and not commensurate with the impact suffered by the victim. Therefore, it is necessary to have a special law concerning the criminal act of trafficking in persons that can provide both a material and formal legal basis. For this purpose, this special law anticipates and captures all types of actions in the process, methods, and all forms of exploitation that may occur in the practice of trafficking in persons, whether carried out between regions within the country or between countries, and both by individual perpetrators and corporations.[89] Thus, with these provisions, Article 297 and Article 324 of the Criminal Code are declared no longer valid because Law No 21 of 2007 has comprehensively regulated various criminal acts including the crime of trafficking in persons.[90]

[86] Ibid 293.
[87] Ibid 294.
[88] Ibid 295.
[89] See General Elucidation of Law No 21 of 2007 concerning Eradication of the Crime of Trafficking in Persons.
[90] Santoso, *Hukum Pidana Suatu Pengantar* (2021) 297.

In 2012, the Supreme Court issued Supreme Court Regulation No 2 of 2012 concerning Settlement of Minor Crime Limits and Number of Fines in the Criminal Code. In essence, this Supreme Court Regulation was intended to complete the interpretation of the value of money in minor crimes in the Criminal Code. For example, any suspect of theft in which the item is valued less than IDR2,500,000 cannot be detained. In Supreme Court Regulation No 2 of 2012 Article 1, it is explained that the words 'two hundred and fifty rupiah' in Articles 364, 373, 379, 384, 407 and 482 of the Criminal Code should be read as IDR2,500,000. Then, in Article 2 paragraph (2) and paragraph (3) it is explained, if the value of the goods or money is not more than IDR2,500,000, the Chief of the Court shall immediately appoint a sole judge to examine, hear and decide on the case using a quick examination procedure which is regulated in Articles 205 to 210 of the Criminal Procedure Code; the Chief of the Court does not need to stipulate detention or extension of detention. Regarding fines, Article 3 states that each maximum fine sanctioned in the Criminal Code, except Article 303 paragraphs 1 and 2, 303 bis paragraphs 1 and 2, is multiplied by 1000.[91]

V. The New Criminal Code (Law No 1 of 2023)

The National Criminal Code (*Kitab Undang-Undang Hukum Pidana*) is a criminal law reform effort that is directed towards a primary mission: the decolonisation of the Indonesian Criminal Code through recodification. Additionally, as the development situation has changed over the course of the nation's history, the revision effort also aims to respond to national and international developments. The second mission of the reform is to democratise criminal law, while the third mission is to consolidate criminal law – a critical effort because of the wide-ranging and multiple developments within criminal law since Indonesian independence in 1945, with elements currently located both inside and outside the framework of the Criminal Code and thus needing to be reorganised within the framework of the criminal law principles that are regulated in Book 1 of the Criminal Code. The efforts also have a fourth mission, which is the adaptation and harmonisation of various legal developments that have occurred both as a result of developments in the field of criminal law and the development of values, standards, and norms recognised by the civilised nations in the international world.[92]

[91] www.pn-palopo.go.id/index.php/berita/berita-terkini/106-mahkamah-agung-ri-menerbitkan-perma-no-2-tahun-2012.

[92] Second paragraph of the General Elucidation of the National Criminal Code.

It is explained in the General Elucidation of the Criminal Code that the missions mentioned above are placed within the framework of legal politics, as compiling this Law in the form of codification and unification will create and enforce consistency, justice, truth, order, benefit, and legal certainty by taking into account the balance between national interests, public interests, and individual interests in the Unitary State of the Republic of Indonesia.[93]

The drafters of the National Criminal Code Bill began work in 1981–82, with the burden being placed on what is now the Ministry of Law and Human Rights.[94] The team has standardised several theoretical agreements (doctrines), which were developed in the scientific world of criminal law (especially in Indonesia), so they can be more easily used as guides by legal experts in practice. Some of these points of view are, among others: (a) the elimination of the distinction between felony (*misdrijven*) and violation (*overtredingen*); (b) the term 'criminal act' is used for *strafbaar feit*;[95] (c) although it still recognises the principle of legality, the applicable customary (criminal) law must be given a place; (d) the meaning of the forms of error (*schuld*) in intentional (*opzet*) and negligence (*culpa*) is confirmed; (e) corporate liability is listed; (f) diminished responsibility (*verminderde toerekeningsvatbaarheid*) is included; (g) justification defences that are outside the law (*buitenwettijke strafuitsluttingsgrond*) need to be regulated; (h) the criminal system and types of punishments that reflect the state ideology of Pancasila must be reflected (capital punishment or death penalty, imprisonment, fines and actions, in other words a double-track system); (i) additional penalties to include payment of restitution and fulfillment of customary obligations; and (j) the need for provisions of the purpose of punishment which can serve as guidelines for judges (*straftoemetingsleidraad*).[96]

Regarding Book 1 of the New Criminal Code, it is explained that Book 1 contains general rules as guidelines for the implementation of Book 2 as well as other Laws, Provincial Regulations, and District/City Regional Regulations, unless otherwise stipulated by a Law. Thus Book 1 also forms the basis for laws outside the Criminal Code. The definition of the terms in Book 1 is placed in Chapter V because the meaning of the term does not only apply to the Criminal Code but also applies to laws that are *lex specialis*, unless otherwise stipulated by a Law. Thus Book 1 contains the substance on, among others, the scope of application of criminal law, criminal acts and criminal liability, sentencing, crime, diversion to out of court settlement for juvenile cases, as well as the objectives and guidelines for sentencing, mitigating factors, aggravating factors in sentencing, concurrent

[93] Third paragraph of the General Elucidation of the National Criminal Code.

[94] Until 1988/1989 the drafting team worked at the National Legal Development Agency and after that in the Directorate General of Law and Legislation. Both institutions are in the Ministry of Justice (currently the Ministry of Law and Human Rights of the Republic of Indonesia).

[95] Different translations for *strafbarfeit* have been used, including criminal acts, criminal behaviour, criminalised behaviour, criminal events, and offences.

[96] Mardjono Reksodiputro, *Sistem Peradilan Pidana* (Jakarta, Rajagrafindo Persada, 2020) 389–90.

sentences, grounds for dismissal of criminal prosecution and implementation of punishment, definition of terms, and closing rules.[97]

The more humane character of *daad-dader strafrecht* (Crime-Offender Criminal Law) systemically characterises the New Criminal Code. This is also expressed and implied by the existence of arrangements that try to maintain a balance between objective and subjective elements or factors. This is also reflected, among others, in regulations regarding the purpose of punishment, terms of punishment, pairs of sanctions in the form of punishment and action, development of short-term alternatives for deprivation of liberty, guidelines or punishment rules, capital punishment (which is a special punishment and a final alternative to life imprisonment or 20 years), as well as setting the minimum age for criminal liability, punishment, and action for children facing the law.[98]

Due to the progress that has occurred in the fields of finance, economy, and trade, especially in the era of globalisation and the development of organised criminal acts, both domestic and transnational, the subject of criminal law cannot be limited only to humans (natural persons), but also includes corporations as organised collections of people and/or assets, whether they are legal entities or non-legal entities. In this case, a corporation can be used to commit a crime and it can also benefit from a crime. With the adoption of the notion that corporations are the subject of criminal acts, it means that corporations are considered capable of committing crimes and can be held liable by Indonesian criminal law.[99]

In the New Criminal Code, the types of punishment are regulated in the form of basic punishment, additional punishment, and special punishment (capital punishment/death penalty) for certain crimes as stipulated in the Law. The types of basic punishment consist of imprisonment; *tutupan* (undisclosed penitentiary);supervision; fines; and community service.Of these, supervision and community service are new options for punishment.[100] Supervision, fines, and community service orders need to be developed as alternatives to short-term deprivation of liberty, because by implementing these three types of punishments, convicts can be helped to cope with guilt. Likewise, the community can interact and actively participate in helping the convicted person to contribute back to society.

The death penalty is not listed as a basic type of punishment in the New Criminal Code. The death penalty is explicitly determined in a separate article; this is done to show that this type of punishment is truly special in nature, to be implemented only as a last resort to protect the community. The death penalty is

[97] Sixth Paragraph point 1 of the General Elucidation of the National Criminal Code.

[98] Sixth Paragraph point 3 of the General Elucidation of the National Criminal Code.

[99] Sixth Paragraph point 5 of the General Elucidation of the National Criminal Code.

[100] The order of the types of basic punishment determines the severity of the crime. Judges may decide the type of punishment to be imposed among the five types of punishment, although in Book Two of this Law only three types of punishment are formulated, namely imprisonment, fines, and capital punishment/death penalty. Undisclosed penitentiary, supervision punishment, and social community service punishment are essentially methods of punishment as an alternative to imprisonment.

the most severe punishment and must always have an alternative sanction of life imprisonment or a maximum imprisonment of 20 years. The death penalty can only be imposed conditionally by granting probation. Within the probationary period, the convicted person is expected to be able to improve himself so that the death penalty does not need to be implemented and can be replaced with imprisonment.[101]

Indonesia has long aimed to have its own National Criminal Code. In fact, the idea goes as far back as 1946, when the Government of the Republic of Indonesia in Yogyakarta enacted Law No 1 of 1946 on the Criminal Code. The Law stated that the Criminal Code of 1915 came into force with various changes, and at the end of the Law, it stated that a new Criminal Code would soon be drafted.[102] The contents of the Criminal Code Bill originate from and are influenced by a variety of sources. Some come from community input, gathered through discussions, seminars, research, conferences, workshops, and so on. Other content comes from the results of comparisons with provisions in other countries' criminal laws which are considered good and appropriate to use in Indonesia.[103]

[101] Sixth Paragraph point 7 of the General Elucidation of the National Criminal Code.

[102] This description and subsequent descriptions of the National Criminal Code are partly based on an article written by the author entitled 'Menjadi Negeri Tanpa KUHP Sendiri' published in Media Indonesia, 23 September 2019.

[103] Santoso, *Hukum Pidana Suatu Pengantar* (2021) 308.

3

Sources of Criminal Law in Indonesia

I. Definition

The term 'source of law' can be interpreted in several ways. First, it can be understood as a legal principle – as something that is the beginning of law, such as the will of God, human reason, or the soul of the nation. Second, as a reference to previous law(s), which contributed to the substance of the current law, such as French law or Roman law. Third, as a source of enforcement with the power to implement and enforce regulations, such as rulers or communities. Fourth, as a source from which we study the law, such as documents, laws, papyrus, and inscribed stones. Finally, as a source of the occurrence of law, that is, the source that gives rise to the law.[1]

Sudikno Mertokusumo uses another, more concise division from K Van Algra, dividing sources of law into two: substantive sources of law and formal sources of law. A substantive source of law is the origin from which legal material is taken and is a factor that helps the formation of law. Substantive sources include social relations, political power relations, socio-economic situation, traditions (religious views and morality), results of scientific research, international developments, and geographical conditions. A formal source of law is the origin or source from which a regulation obtains legal force. This relates to the form or manner that causes legal regulations to be formally in effect. Formal sources of law include laws, treaties between countries, jurisprudence, and customs.[2]

Referring to the definition above, in this chapter the discussion is limited to statutory law only. This is because criminal law is very closely related to the principle of legality, which includes the existence of *lex scripta* (criminal law must be written), *lex certa* (criminal law must have certainty), and *lex stricta* (criminal law must be strict). Thus, we will not discuss other sources of law, such as customs, jurisprudence, and treaties (agreements between countries).[3]

Nevertheless, treaties are very important in law, including criminal law. Key examples are extradition treaties and agreements that provide mutual legal assistance. However, treaties between countries cannot be used to bring an alleged

[1] Zevenbergen in Sudikno Mertokusumo, *Mengenal Hukum: Suatu Pengantar* (Yogyakarta, Liberty, 1999) 76.

[2] Mertokusumo, *Mengenal Hukum: Suatu Pengantar* (1999) 76–77.

[3] Topo Santoso, *Hukum Pidana Suatu Pengantar* (Jakarta, Rajawali Pers, 2021) 199.

perpetrator to court or become the basis for imposing a sentence. Therefore, criminal provisions, according to the principle of legality, are only contained in statutory law. Thus, in the following discussion, only the statutory law will be discussed.

One example of an international treaty ratified in Indonesia is the 2003 United Nations Convention Against Corruption (UNCAC), which was ratified by Indonesia through the development of Law No 7 of 2006 concerning Ratification of the 2003 United Nations Convention Against Corruption. Even though it has been ratified, there are several provisions in UNCAC that have not been included in criminal legislation in Indonesia. This is because these provisions are only recommendations, rather than obligations. This includes areas such as illicit enrichment, bribery in the private sector, and trading in influence. Crucially, the criminal provisions contained in UNCAC cannot be used in prosecution in Indonesia because there is no legal basis in the form of national criminal legislation. This is because criminal provisions contained in international treaties are not self-executing and so do not apply automatically. According to Damos Dumoli Agusman, in order to enable the implementation of a provision, implementing legislation is required. If the agreement provides norms but is in accordance with 'the respective constitutional law' (the constitutional law of each country) those norms only apply if regulated by legislation, such as provisions on criminal acts.[4]

The term 'the law' has two quite different meanings: the law in the substantive sense, and the law in the formal sense. In the formal sense, 'the law' means a decision or decree by the authorities, and is determined by its contents, its title, and its universal application to all citizens and/or residents. Accordingly, the law in the formal sense is nothing but a ruling by the authorities which obtains the title 'law' because of the way it is formed.[5]

Perhaps it can be more easily understood if formal law is instead called 'statutory legislation'. In Indonesia, the creation and implementation of law has been regulated by the 1945 Constitution and Law No 12 of 2011 concerning the Establishment of Legislation. Article 1 point 2 of Law No 12 of 2011 states that laws and regulations contain legally binding norms and are formed or determined by state institutions or authorised officials through the procedures set out in laws and regulations. Thus, statutory law can be in the form of laws, government regulations, presidential regulations, provincial regulations, district/city regulations, governor regulations, and district head/mayor regulations.[6]

Article 20 of the 1945 Constitution also regulates the process for the formation of a law. According to this article, the House of Representatives has the power to make laws.[7] Each bill is discussed by the House of Representatives and the

[4] Damos Dumoli Agusman, 'Self-Executing and Non-Self Executing Treaties: What Does it Mean' (2014) 11 *Jurnal Hukum Internasional* 320–44.

[5] Mertokusumo, *Mengenal Hukum: Suatu Pengantar* (1999) 79.

[6] Santoso, *Hukum Pidana Suatu Pengantar* (2021) 200–01.

[7] Article 20 Paragraph (1) of the Constitution of the Republic of Indonesia.

President for mutual approval,[8] with the President then enacting the agreed-upon bill to become law.[9] This process was reaffirmed by Article 1 point 3 of Law No 12 of 2011, which states that a law is statutory legislation established by the House of Representatives with the mutual approval of the President.

In this discussion, the sources of criminal law will be limited to the sense defined by Sudikno Mertokusumo above, namely 'where we can find or explore the law'.[10] In other words, this is the origin or source from which a regulation obtains legal force.[11] Thus this chapter will discuss the sources of law where provisions regarding criminal law can be found, including provisions on the principle of legality; the application of criminal law according to place and person; criminal acts and their elements; criminal sanctions; attempted criminal acts; complicity in criminal acts; concurrence of criminal acts; the basis for aggravating the punishment; the basis for mitigating the punishment; the basis for elimination of punishment; and the dismissal of the criminal prosecution authority.

Literature on criminal law generally presents three sources of criminal law: (1) the Criminal Code and the laws that amend it; (2) Special Criminal Laws outside the Criminal Code; and (3) Non-Criminal Laws which contain criminal provisions. Section II will look at Indonesia's Criminal Code.

II. Criminal Code

A code of law is a collection or compendium. It is a complete positive legal system, scientifically regulated, and declared by legislative authorities. A body of law is drawn up by a legislative authority, and is intended to establish, in a general and systematic form, the principles of all laws, whether written or unwritten, positive or customary, derived from law (enactment) or from a previous decision (precedent). A code of law must be distinguished from a digest, which is generally a report from a court decision, while a code of law consists of the orderly collection and classification of existing state or nation statutes, and is promulgated as a new law covering all fields of jurisprudence.[12]

A Criminal Code can be defined as (1) the aggregate of statutory enactments pertaining to criminal offences, and (2) a systematic and integrated statement of rules and principles pertaining to criminal offences.[13] In Indonesia, the Criminal Code[14] is also referred to as *Kitab Undang-Undang Hukum Pidana* (KUHP) or

[8] Article 20 Paragraph (2) of the Constitution of the Republic of Indonesia.
[9] Article 20 Paragraph (4) of the Constitution of the Republic of Indonesia.
[10] Mertokusumo, *Mengenal Hukum: Suatu Pengantar* (1999) 76.
[11] Ibid 76–77.
[12] thelawdictionary.org/code.
[13] www.dictionary.com/browse/criminal-code.
[14] The term 'Criminal Code' was first recorded in the period 1780–1790. See www.collinsdictionary.com/dictionary/english/criminal-code.

Wetboek van Strafrecht (WvS). The Criminal Code which is currently in force, and which will be replaced by a new National Criminal Code when ratified, is identical to *Wetboek van Strafrecht voor Nederland Indie*, which was derived from the Dutch East Indies Criminal Code 1915 and has been in effect since 1918. The Code was amended by Law No 1 of 1946. Hereafter, we will refer to this as the Criminal Code or WvS. The Criminal Code consists of three books: Book 1 contains General Provisions and is divided into nine chapters; Book 2 contains Articles on Felonies and is divided into 31 chapters; and Book 3 contains Articles on Violations and is divided into 10 chapters.[15]

Confusingly, despite the separate books on felonies and violations, there is no standard that determines which crimes constitute felonies and which violations. Legislators are free to determine whether a prohibited act is an felony or a violation. Thus, any acts contained in legal regulations outside the Criminal Code must be determined separately to establish whether they are felonies or violations.[16] It is only for lower-level legislators (called provincial and district/city lawmakers) that there is certainty: according to Article 27 *Invoeringsverordening Strafwetboek* (Stb 1917 No 497), all acts punishable by law through local regulations (*locale verordening*) are considered violations.

Book 1 of Indonesia's Criminal Code is entitled *Algemeene Bepalingen* (General Rules), and consists of nine chapters. Book 1 begins with Chapter I, *Omvang van werking der wettelijke strafbepalingen* (on the application of criminal rules in the law), and ends with Chapter IX, *Beteekenis van sommige in het wetboek voorkomende uitdrukkingen* (the meaning of some expressions in this law book). The nine chapters of Book 1 of the Criminal Code are as follows:

- Chapter I Concerning the application of criminal rules in the law (Article 1 to Article 9);
- Chapter II Punishment (Article 10 to Article 43);
- Chapter III Exceptions, reductions and additions to punishment (Article 44 to Article 52);
- Chapter IV Attempt (Article 53 and Article 54);
- Chapter V Complicity in committing a crime (Article 55 to Article 62);
- Chapter VI Combined crimes (Article 63 to Article 71);
- Chapter VII Advancing and withdrawing complaints in criminal cases that can only be prosecuted on complaints (Article 72 to Article 75);

[15] Santoso, *Hukum Pidana Suatu Pengantar* (2021) 207.

[16] R Tresna, *Azas-azas Hukum Pidana Disertai Pembahasan Beberapa Perbuatan Pidana yang Penting* (Yogyakarta, Tiara Wacana, 1959) 214. This will change when the National Criminal Code comes into force, as this does not distinguish between offences and violations, and refers only to criminal acts. This means that there will no longer be a separate Book 2 and Book 3, only Book 1 on General Provisions and Book 2 on Criminal Acts. This will have consequences for the reference of offences and violations of legislations outside the Criminal Code.

- Chapter VIII The elimination of the right to prosecute and carry out a punishment (Article 76 to Article 85);
- Chapter IX The definition of a number of terms in this law book (Article 86 to Article 102; Article 103 on Closing Provisions).

Book 2 of the Criminal Code is entitled *Misdrijven* (Felonies) and discusses all criminal acts classified as felonies. Book 2 consists of 31 chapters which are as follows:

- Chapter I Crimes against state security (Article 104 to Article 129);
- Chapter II Crimes against the dignity of the head of state (Article 130 to Article 139);
- Chapter III Crimes against friendly countries and heads of friendly countries (Article 140 to Article 14);
- Chapter IV Crimes regarding carrying out state obligations (Article 146 to Article 153);
- Chapter V Crimes against public order are regulated (Article 154 to Article 181);
- Chapter VI One-on-one fights (Article 182 to Article 186);
- Chapter VII Crimes harmful to the general welfare of people and property (Articles 187 to 206);
- Chapter VIII Crimes against public power (Articles 207 to 241);
- Chapter IX Perjury and false statements (Article 242 and Article 243);
- Chapter X Counterfeiting of money, state banknotes and bank notes (Article 244 to Article 252);
- Chapter XI Falsifying stamps (seals) and signs (brands) (Article 253 to Article 262);
- Chapter XII Forged letters (Article 263 to Article 276);
- Chapter XIII Crimes against the condition (origin) of people (Article 277 to Article 280);
- Chapter XIV Crimes against decency (Article 281 to Article 303);
- Chapter XV Leaving people who need help (Article 304 to Article 309);
- Chapter XVI Insults (Article 310 to Article 321);
- Chapter XVII Disclosing secrets (Article 322 and Article 323);
- Chapter XVIII Crimes against the liberty of persons (Article 324 to Article 337);
- Chapter XIX Crimes against human life (Article 338 to Article 350);
- Chapter XX Battery (Article 351 to Article 358);
- Chapter XXI Causing people to die or be injured due to negligence (Articles 359 to 361);
- Chapter XXII Theft (Article 362 to Article 367);

- Chapter XXIII Extortion and threats (Article 368 to Article 371);
- Chapter XXIV Embezzlement (Article 372 to Article 377);
- Chapter XXV Fraud (Article 378 to Article 395);
- Chapter XXVI Harming people who are owed or are entitled (Article 396 to Article 405);
- Chapter XXVII Destroying or damaging goods (Article 406 to Article 412);
- Chapter XXVIII Crimes of office (Article 413 to Article 437);
- Chapter XXIX Crimes against shipping (Article 438 to Article 479);
- Chapter XXIXA Aviation crimes and crimes against aviation facilities/infrastructure (Article 479 a to Article 479 r);
- Chapter XXX Assisting with malicious intent (Article 480 to Article 485);
- Chapter XXXI Rules regarding repetition of criminal acts (Article 486 to Article 488).

Finally, Book 3 of the Criminal Code is entitled *Overtredingen* (Violations) and is entirely about criminal acts defined as violations. Book 3 consists of 10 chapters, which are as follows:

- Chapter I Violations of public safety for people and goods and for public health (Article 489 to Article 502);
- Chapter II Violations of public order (Article 503 to Article 520);
- Chapter III Violations of public powers (Article 521 to Article 528);
- Chapter IV Violations of the position according to civil law (Article 529 to Article 530);
- Chapter V Violations against people who need help (Article 531);
- Chapter VI Violations of decency (Article 532 to Article 547);
- Chapter VII Violations against regional police (Article 548 to Article 551);
- Chapter VIII Violations of office (Article 552 to Article 559);
- Chapter IX Violations of shipping (Article 560 to Article 569);
- Chapter X Violations of state security (Article 570).

III. Special Criminal Law

As explained in chapter two, Indonesia also uses special criminal law. Special criminal law includes military criminal law, special criminal law in criminal legislation, and special criminal law outside of criminal legislation. As military criminal law was discussed earlier, in this sub-chapter we will focus on special criminal law in criminal legislation.

Indonesia has many criminal laws outside the Criminal Code. They include:[17]

- Emergency Law No 12 of 1951 '*Ordonnantietijdelijke Bijzondere Strafbepalingen*' (Stbl 1948 Number 17) and Law No 8 of 1948 concerning Firearms;
- Emergency Law No 7 of 1955 concerning Investigation, Prosecution and Judiciary of Economic Crimes as amended by Emergency Law No 8 of 1958 regarding the Addition of Emergency Law No 7 of 1955 ('TPE Law');
- Law No 11 of 1980 concerning the Crime of Bribery ('Bribery Act');
- Law No 31 of 1999 concerning the Eradication of Criminal Acts of Corruption as amended by Law No 20 of 2001 ('Law on Eradication of Corruption');
- Law No 15 of 2003 concerning Stipulation of Government Regulations in Lieu of Law No 1 of 2002 concerning Eradication Criminal Acts of Terrorism become Law as amended by Law No 5 of 2018 ('Law on Eradication of Criminal Acts of Terrorism');
- Law No 21 of 2007 concerning Eradication of Criminal Acts of Trafficking in Persons ('Criminal Act of Trafficking in Persons');
- Law No 8 of 2010 concerning Prevention and Eradication of the Money Laundering Crime ('Money Laundering Law');
- Law No 9 of 2013 concerning the Prevention and Eradication of the Financing of Terrorism.

A. Emergency Law No 12 of 1951 and Law No 8 of 1948

If we look at Law No 8 of 1948 concerning the Registration and Granting of Permits for the Use of Firearms,[18] it initially appears that this Law is an administrative law, not a criminal law. However, it does contain criminal provisions, specifically in Part IV concerning Punishment. Accordingly, Law No 8 of 1949 can be described as criminal law contained in non-criminal law. The Law's criminal provisions are covered in Article 14 paragraphs 1 to 4, which can be imposed if the obligations specified in Article 2, Article 9, and/or Article 12 are not fulfilled, or if the prohibitions in Article 3 and/or Article 4 are violated.[19] The other Articles (1 to 13) of Law No 8 of 1948 regulate the registration of firearms and permits required to use firearms.

[17] Santoso, *Hukum Pidana Suatu Pengantar* (2021) 213.

[18] The Law was enacted in Yogyakarta on 31 March 1948, by President Soekarno. At this time the capital of the Republic of Indonesia was still in Yogyakarta, but the Netherlands had not yet recognised the sovereignty of the Republic of Indonesia.

[19] See more in Article 14 of Law No 8 of 1948.

In contrast to Law No 8 of 1948, Emergency Law No 12 of 1951[20] can be referred to as a criminal law, not an administrative law with criminal provisions. The reason is that this Law does in its entirety regulate a criminal act; in this case, the crime of firearms. Articles 1 and 2 of this Law regulate criminal acts which are clearly defined as felonies:[21]

> Article 1
>
> (1) Whoever, without the right to import into Indonesia makes, receives, tries to obtain, delivers, or tries to deliver, controls, carries, has stock with him or has in his possession, keeps, transports, hides, uses, or removes from Indonesia any firearm, ammunition, or any explosive material, is punishable by death or life imprisonment or a maximum temporary prison sentence of twenty years.
>
> Article 2
>
> (1) Whoever, without right to import into Indonesia, manufactures, receives, tries to obtain it, delivers, or tries to deliver, controls, carries, has stock with him or has in his possession, keeps, transports, hides, uses or removes from Indonesia any blunt weapon, slashing weapon, or stabbing weapon (*slag-*, *steek-*, *of stootwapen*), is punishable by a maximum imprisonment of ten years.

It is interesting that the Law mentions corporations as perpetrators of criminal acts, although prosecution and punishment are still to be imposed on the corporation's management or their local representatives rather than the corporation itself. Article 4 paragraph (1) states:

> If an act punishable according to this Emergency Law is committed by or under the authority of a legal entity, prosecution can be carried out and punishment may be imposed on the management or on his local representative.[22]

B. Emergency Law No 7 of 1955

Emergency Law No 7 of 1955 is often referred to as the TPE Law, but its full title is Emergency Law No 7 of 1955 concerning Investigation, Prosecution, and Trial of Economic Crimes[23] as amended by Emergency Law No 8 of 1958 concerning Addition of Emergency Law No 7 of 1955.[24] After that, the Government Regulation in Lieu of Law of the Republic of Indonesia No 1 of 1960 (I/1960) was issued regarding the addition of Emergency Law No 7 of 1955.[25]

[20] Emergency Law No 12 of 1951 was enacted in Jakarta on 1 September 1951, by President Soekarno and promulgated in the State Gazette of the Republic of Indonesia of 1951 Number 78.

[21] See Article 3 of Emergency Law No 12 of 1951.

[22] Santoso, *Hukum Pidana Suatu Pengantar* (2021) 215.

[23] State Gazette of 1955 Number 27.

[24] State Gazette of 1958 Number 156.

[25] Santoso, *Hukum Pidana Suatu Pengantar* (2021) 215.

Economic crimes in the TPE Law cover three groups of crimes: (1) violations that have existed in several previous regulations;[26] (2) new criminal acts in this Law (that is, in Articles 26, 32, and 33); and (3) criminal acts in the future law (after the enactment of the Emergency Law No 7 of 1955) which mention violations of the law as economic crimes (in Article 1).

In addition to imprisonment, short-term imprisonment, and fines, this Emergency Law lists additional punishments, including revocation of rights, closure of companies, confiscation of goods, and announcement of judge's decisions. In addition, there are disciplinary actions that can be imposed, including payment of bail and mandatory rehabilitation.[27]

As with Emergency Law No 12 of 1951, Emergency Law No 7 of 1955 also includes corporations as the possible perpetrator of criminal acts. The term used is not 'corporation' but 'a legal entity, company, association of people, or foundation'. The provisions in this Law regarding the legal subject of corporations are very different from the Criminal Code, which does not address corporations; in the Criminal Code, only natural persons (*personnen*) can carry out criminal acts.[28]

Article 15 of this Emergency Law reads as follows:

(1) If an economic crime committed by or on behalf of a legal entity, a corporation, an association of people or a foundation, then criminal charges are made and criminal sanction as well as disciplinary action imposed, either against the legal entity, company, association or foundation, either against those who gave the order to commit the economic crime or who acted as the leader in the act or omission, or against both.

(2) An economic crime is also committed by or on behalf of a legal entity, a company, an association of people or a foundation, if the act is committed by people who, either on the basis of employment or based on other relationships, act within the environment of a legal entity, a company, an association or a foundation, it does not matter whether these individuals individually commit the economic crime or there are elements of the crime together with them.

(3) If a criminal charge is made against a legal entity, a company, an association of people or a foundation, the legal entity, company, association, or foundation at the time of the prosecution is represented by a manager or, if there are more than one management, by one of them. Representatives can be represented by other people.
The judge can order a manager to appear in person in court and can also order that the administrator be brought before the judge.

(4) If a criminal charge is made against a legal entity, a company, an association of people or a foundation, then all summons to appear before and all submissions of summons will be addressed to the head of the management or the domicile of the head of management or the place where the management convenes or their office.

This Law also regulates some procedural laws that differ from the provisions in Indonesia's Criminal Procedure Code. Provisions on how to investigate economic

[26] Violations contained in *Ordonnantie Gecontroleerde Goederen* 1948, *Prijsbeheersing Ordonnantie* 1948, Hoarding Goods Act 1952, *Rijsterdonnantie* 1948, Rice Milling Obligation Emergency Act 1952, and *Deviezen Ordonnantie* 1950.

[27] See Articles 5 to 16 of Emergency Law No 7 of 1955 concerning the Investigation, Prosecution and Trial of Economic Crimes.

[28] Santoso, *Hukum Pidana Suatu Pengantar* (2021) 216.

crimes are regulated in Articles 17 to 26, while Articles 40 to 48 cover arrangements for examination before courts of first instance, appeal, and cassation. In addition, this Law regulates the power and composition of the courts, determining that in each district court there is one or more judges assisted by one or more clerks, and one or more prosecutors who are solely assigned the respective duties of adjudicating and prosecuting economic criminal cases. This court is referred to as the Economic Court.[29]

C. Law No 11 of 1980

Law No 11 of 1980 concerning the Crime of Bribery was enacted in Jakarta on 27 October 1980 and promulgated in State Gazette of 1980 Number 58. The reason for the enactment of this law was acts of bribery beyond what was already regulated in the existing laws and regulations, as acts of bribery are essentially contrary to the decency and morals of Pancasila and endanger the lives of the people and the nation.[30]

Article 1 of this Law states that, in this Law, what is meant by the crime of bribery is a criminal act of bribery outside the provisions of the existing laws and regulations. Article 2 states:

> Anyone who gives or promises something to someone with the intention of persuading that person to do something or not to do something in his duties, which is contrary to his authority or obligation that concerns the public interest, shall be punished for giving bribes with a maximum imprisonment of 5 (five) years and a maximum fine of IDR 15,000,000 (fifteen million rupiahs).

Article 3 states:

> Anyone who receives something or a promise, while he knows or can reasonably suspect that the gift of something or a promise is intended so that he does something or does not do something in his duties, which is contrary to his authority or obligation that concerns the public interest, accept bribes with a maximum imprisonment of 3 (three) years or a maximum fine of IDR 15,000,000 (fifteen million rupiah).

Article 4 regulates the validity of this Law: 'If the criminal acts referred to in Article 2 and Article 3 are committed outside the territory of the Republic of Indonesia, then the provisions of this law shall also apply to them'. Meanwhile, Article 5 confirms the type of offence, by asserting: 'Criminal acts in this law constitute an offence'.

D. Law No 31 of 1999 and Law No 20 of 2001

Law No. 31 of 1999's full title is Law No 31 of 1999 concerning Eradication of Criminal Acts of Corruption as amended by Law No 20 of 2001 ('Corruption

[29] See Articles 35 to 38 of Emergency Law No 7 of 1955 concerning the Investigation, Prosecution and Trial of Economic Crimes.

[30] See the consideration of Law No 11 of 1980 concerning the Crime of Bribery.

Eradication Law'). This Law was enacted on 16 August 1999, as it was considered that Law No 3 of 1971 concerning the Eradication of the Criminal Acts of Corruption was no longer in accordance with the development of legal needs in society and therefore needed to be replaced with a new law. It was hoped that the new Corruption Eradication Law would be more effective in preventing and eradicating corruption. The Law was amended two years later, on 21 November 2001, through Law No 20 of 2001 concerning Amendments to Law No 31 of 1999 concerning the Eradication of Criminal Acts of Corruption.

Criminal acts of corruption are regulated in Chapter II, starting with Article 2 and Article 3, which cover criminal acts of corruption concerning financial or economic losses to the state. Articles 5 to 12 cover criminal acts of corruption and refer to relevant articles in the Criminal Code (Articles 209, 210, 387, 415, 416, 417, 418, 419, 420, 423, 425, and 435 of the Criminal Code) but provide more severe criminal sanctions than in the Criminal Code. In addition, this Law states that anyone who violates the provisions of the law (which expressly states any violation of the provisions of the law is a criminal act of corruption) is to have the provisions stipulated in this law applied to them.[31] It also regulates a number of acts called 'Other crimes related to corruption crimes' in Articles 21 to 24.

Provisions that clearly indicate that this Law is a special criminal law can be seen in Article 15. It states that 'Everyone who conducts attempt, aiding, or conspiracy to commit a criminal act of corruption, shall be punished with the same punishment as referred to in Article 2, Article 3, Article 5 to Article 14'. With this Article, this becomes a specific provision when compared to the general provisions regarding attempt and complicity (as outlined in Article 53, Article 55 and so on in the Criminal Code). For example, an attempted criminal act under Article 53 of the Criminal Code carries a punishment of one third of a completed crime, while in this Law, the punishment is the same as for a completed crime. Likewise, aiding in the commitment of a crime in Articles 56 and 57 of the Criminal Code is punishable by a third of the punishment dealt to the perpetrators; in the Corruption Eradication Law, the punishment is the same.[32]

Other differences from the Criminal Code are additional punishments as regulated in Article 18 of this Law, including confiscation of goods used or obtained from criminal acts of corruption; payment of replacement money up to a maximum amount equal to any wealth obtained from the criminal act of corruption; closure of all or part of the company for a maximum of one year; and revocation of all or part of certain rights or elimination of all or part of certain profits.[33]

Regarding the subject of criminal acts, the Corruption Eradication Law also recognises corporations as the subject of criminal acts. In Article 20 paragraph (1) it is stated that 'In the case of a criminal act of corruption by or on behalf of a corporation, criminal charges and sentences may be made against the corporation

[31] Article 14 of Law No 31 of 1999 concerning the Eradication of Criminal Acts of Corruption.
[32] Santoso, *Hukum Pidana Suatu Pengantar* (2021) 220.
[33] Ibid 220.

or its management'. This provision is similar to the provisions concerning legal entities in the Emergency Law No 12 of 1951, as discussed above. However, the rules here are more detailed, such as regarding what is corruption committed by corporations and how to prosecute the management.[34]

Likewise, the provisions of the procedural law concerning investigation, prosecution, and examination in court proceedings are regulated from Article 25 to Article 40, with some differences to the Criminal Procedure Code.[35]

Due to some shortcomings in Law No 31 of 1999,[36] as well as the need for a new formulation on 'reverse burden of proof', revisions to the formulation of criminal sanctions, and other points that need to be added, several amendments were made to the Law in 2001. This was done through Law No 20 of 2001 concerning Amendments to Law No 31 of 1999 concerning the Eradication of Criminal Acts of Corruption. In addition, Law No 20 of 2001 added new articles in the form of Article 12A, Article 12B, and Article 12C relating to gratification and Article 26A regarding real evidence. Additional Articles 37 A, 38 A, 38 B, 38 C were also included to regulate procedural law.

E. Law No 15 of 2003, Law No 16 of 2003, and Law No 5 of 2018

The legal basis for countering terrorism in Indonesia is Law No 15 of 2003 concerning Stipulation of Government Regulation in Lieu of Law No 1 of 2002 concerning Eradication of Criminal Acts of Terrorism into Law as amended by Law No 5 of 2018 ('Law on the Eradication of Criminal Acts of Terrorism'). This Law was passed on 4 April 2003 and consists of just two articles. Article 1 states that the Government Regulation in Lieu of Law No 1 of 2002 concerning the Eradication of Criminal Acts of Terrorism is enacted into law.

Among the considerations taken for the issuance of this Law were a series of bombings that occurred in Indonesia which resulted in loss of life and caused widespread public fear and damage to property, and resulted in a broad impact on social life, economics, politics, and international relations. The Law states that terrorism is a transnational crime, is organised, and has a wide network that threatens national and international peace and security. In order to restore an orderly and safe community life and provide a strong legal basis and legal certainty in overcoming urgent problems in eradicating terrorism, with reference to international

[34] See Article 20 of Law No 31 of 1999 concerning the Eradication of Criminal Acts of Corruption.

[35] Santoso, *Hukum Pidana Suatu Pengantar* (2021) 220–21.

[36] Various interpretations developed in the community, especially regarding the application of the law to instances of corruption that occurred before Law No 31 of 1999 was enacted. This is because Article 44 of the Law states that Law No 3 of 1971 concerning the Eradication of Criminal Acts of Corruption was declared null and void as of the enactment of Law No 31 of 1999, leading to an assumption that there was a legal vacuum.

conventions and national laws and regulations relating to terrorism, the President of the Republic of Indonesia stipulated Government Regulation in Lieu of Law No 1 of 2002 concerning Eradication of Criminal Acts of Terrorism.[37]

This Government Regulation f cannot be separated from the context of the 2002 Bali bomb attack. On 12 October 2002, the worst terrorism incident in Indonesian history occurred on the island of Bali, with a series of three bomb explosions that devastated the area at the heart of Indonesian tourism at night. The first two explosions occurred at Paddy's Club and Sari Club on Legian Street, Kuta, with the third at the United States Consulate. The attack resulted in 202 deaths and 209 injuries, mostly foreign tourists at the two popular clubs.[38]

This Government Regulation in Lieu of Law was enacted on 18 October 2002, just six days after the attacks. In connection with the immediate need to respond to the incident, the President of the Republic of Indonesia (pursuant to Article 22 paragraph (1) of the 1945 Constitution as amended by the Fourth Amendment to the 1945 Constitution) decided that it was necessary to stipulate a Government Regulation in Lieu of Law.[39] Article 1 Government Regulation in Lieu of Law No 2 of 2002 states that 'The provisions in the Government Regulation in Lieu of Law No 1 of 2002 concerning the Eradication of Criminal Acts of Terrorism are declared to apply to the bombing incident that occurred in Bali on October 12, 2002'. It was applied retroactively in order to cover the prosecution of the alleged bombers during criminal proceedings.[40] Article 3 and Article 4 of Government Regulation in Lieu of Law No 1 of 2002 regulates both subjects and locations. It applies to every person who commits or intends to commit a criminal act of terrorism in the territory of the Republic of Indonesia and/or another country that also has jurisdiction and states their intention to prosecute the perpetrator.[41] Another state has jurisdiction if the crime is committed by a citizen of the state concerned; the crime is committed against a citizen of the state concerned; the crime is also committed in the state concerned; the crime is committed against a state or government facilities of the state concerned abroad, including representatives of foreign countries or the residence of diplomatic or consular officials of the state concerned; the crime is committed with violence or threat of violence that forces the state concerned to do something or not to do something; a crime is committed against an aircraft operated by the government of the state concerned; or the crime is committed on a ship with the flag of the state concerned or an aircraft registered under the laws of the state concerned at the time the crime is committed.[42]

[37] Refer to the preamble in Law No 15 of 2003 concerning Stipulation of Government Regulation in Lieu of Law No 1 of 2002 concerning Eradication of Criminal Acts of Terrorism, becoming a Law.

[38] sejarahlengkap.com/indonesia/sejarah-peristiwa-bom-bali.

[39] General Elucidation of Government Regulation in Lieu of Law No 2 of 2002.

[40] Santoso, *Hukum Pidana Suatu Pengantar* (2021) 222–23.

[41] Article 3 paragraph (1) Government Regulation in Lieu of Law No 1 of 2002.

[42] Article 3 paragraph (2) Government Regulation in Lieu of Law No 1 of 2002.

This regulation also applies to crimes of terrorism committed against citizens of the Republic of Indonesia outside the territory of the Republic of Indonesia; to the state facilities of the Republic of Indonesia abroad, including the residence of diplomatic and consular officials of the Republic of Indonesia; by violence or threat of violence that forces the government of the Republic of Indonesia to do something or not to do something; to force international organisations in Indonesia to do something or not to do something; on a ship with the flag of the Republic of Indonesia or an aircraft registered under the laws of the Republic of Indonesia at the time the crime was committed; or by any person who does not have citizenship and resides in the territory of the Republic of Indonesia.[43]

The crime of terrorism itself is regulated in Chapter III, from Article 6 to Article 19. In addition, the regulation identifies other criminal acts which are related to criminal acts of terrorism, regulating them in Articles 20 to 23. Criminal procedure law is regulated in Chapter V concerning Investigation, Prosecution, and Examination in Court Sessions, in 10 articles from Article 25 to Article 35. Several provisions on procedural law in this chapter differ from the provisions in the Criminal Procedure Code.[44]

Fifteen years later, in 2018, Law No 15 of 2003 was amended through Law No 5 of 2018 concerning Amendments to Law No 15 of 2003 concerning Stipulation of Government Regulation Law No 1 of 2002 concerning Eradication of Criminal Acts of Terrorism. This law was passed on 21 June 2018 and was intended to provide a stronger legal basis to ensure protection and legal certainty in eradicating criminal acts of terrorism, as well as to meet legal needs and developments in society.[45]

Several of the most important changes covered by Law No 5 of 2018 include (1) criminalisation of various new modus operandi of terrorist crimes, such as new types of explosives and participating in military/paramilitary/other training, domestically and/or overseas, with the intention of committing a criminal act of terrorism; (2) the aggravating of criminal sanctions against perpetrators of criminal acts of terrorism, whether conspiracy, preparation, attempt, and aiding to commit criminal acts of terrorism; (3) expansion of criminal sanctions against corporations, imposed on founders, leaders, management, or people who direct corporations; (4) specificity in criminal procedure law such as increasing the duration of arrest, detention, and extension of arrest and detention; (5) victim protection as a form of state responsibility; and (6) the prevention of criminal acts of terrorism is carried out by the relevant agencies in accordance with their respective functions and authorities, coordinated by the National Counter-Terrorism Agency.[46]

[43] Article 4 Government Regulation in Lieu of Law No 1 of 2002.
[44] Santoso, *Hukum Pidana Suatu Pengantar* (2021) 225.
[45] See the preamble Considering letter c of Law No 5 of 2018.
[46] See the General Elucidation of Law No 5 of 2018.

F. Law No 21 of 2007

Law No 21 of 2007 concerning the Eradication of the Criminal Act of Trafficking in Persons ('the TIP Law') was enacted on 19 April 2007. In the consideration of this law, it is stated that trafficking in persons, especially women and children, is an act that is contrary to human dignity and violates human rights, therefore it must be eradicated. Trafficking in persons has spread in the form of organised crime networks, both inter-state and domestic, becoming a threat to society, nation, and state, as well as to norms of life based on respect for human rights. The desire to prevent and tackle the crime of trafficking in persons is based on noble values as well as national and international commitments to carry out early prevention efforts, action against perpetrators, victim protection, and improvement of cooperation. It was considered that prior to the TIP Law, laws and regulations relating to trafficking in persons had not provided a comprehensive and integrated legal basis for efforts to eradicate human trafficking.[47]

The law recognises that human trafficking, especially of women and children, has become more widespread and involves not only individuals but also corporations and state administrators who abuse their authority and power. Networks of perpetrators range within countries but also between countries.[48]

The provisions regarding the prohibition of trafficking in persons are essentially already regulated in the Criminal Code. Article 297 of the Criminal Code prohibits the trafficking of women, girls and boys and qualifies the act as an offence. Outside of the Criminal Code, Law No 23 of 2002 concerning Child Protection also stipulates in Article 83 the prohibition of trafficking, selling, or kidnapping children for oneself or for sale. However, neither the Criminal Code nor the Child Protection Law formulate a strict legal definition of human trafficking. In addition, Article 297 of the Criminal Code provides sanctions that are too light and not commensurate with the impact suffered by a victim of trafficking. Therefore, it was deemed necessary to implement a special law concerning the crime of trafficking in persons that can provide both substantive and formal legal bases. For this purpose, this special law anticipates and ensnares all types of actions in the processes, methods, and all forms of exploitation that may occur in the practice of trafficking in persons, whether carried out domestically or between countries, and both by individual actors and corporations.[49]

This Law regulates the protection of witnesses and victims as an important aspect of law enforcement, which is intended to provide them with basic protection. In addition, the Law also pays great attention to the suffering of victims as a result of the crime of trafficking in persons, stating that victims have the right to restitution from perpetrators as monetary rehabilitation. It also regulates the

[47] See the preamble Considering in Law No 21 of 2007 concerning the Eradication of the Crime of Trafficking in Persons.
[48] See General Elucidation of Law No 21 of 2007.
[49] Ibid.

rights of victims to medical and social rehabilitation, repatriation, and reintegration, especially for those who experience physical, psychological, and social suffering as a result of trafficking. The Law states that these rights must be fulfilled by the state.[50]

Prevention and handling of criminal acts of trafficking in persons is the responsibility of the central government, regional governments, communities, and families. To realise comprehensive and integrated steps in the implementation of prevention and treatment, it is necessary to form a task force. As the crime of trafficking in persons is a crime that does not only occur within one country's territory but also between countries, it is necessary to develop international cooperation in the form of mutual assistance agreements in criminal matters and/or other technical cooperation in accordance with the provisions of laws and regulations. The drafting of this law is also a manifestation of Indonesia's commitment to implement the 2000 United Nations Protocol to Prevent, Suppress and Punish Trafficking in Persons, especially Women and Children, also known as the Palermo Protocol, which the Government of Indonesia signed.[51]

The criminal act of trafficking in persons itself is regulated by Articles 2 to 9. Article 10 provides that the attempt or aiding of the criminal act of trafficking in persons shall be punished with the same punishment as referred to in Articles 2, 3, 4, 5, and 6. This provision is different from the provisions in Article 53 and Article 56 of the Criminal Code. Other articles, namely Articles 11 to 18, regulate the basis for punishment aggravations, provisions on corporate liability, and the basis for eliminating punishment, while Articles 19 to 27 regulate other criminal acts related to the crime of trafficking in persons.

G. Law No 8 of 2010

Law No 8 of 2010 concerning the Prevention and Eradication of the Crime of Money Laundering ('the Money Laundering Law') was passed on 22 October 2010. This law replaced Law No 15 of 2002 concerning the Crime of Money Laundering as amended by Law No 25 of 2003.

Money laundering not only threatens economic stability and the integrity of the financial system, but can also endanger the foundations of social, national, and state life, based on Pancasila and the 1945 Constitution of the Republic of Indonesia. The prevention and eradication of money laundering requires a strong legal basis to ensure legal certainty, effective law enforcement, tracing of tassets, and recovery of proceeds of crime. It was considered that the previous money laundering law needed had become inadequate with regard to the developing

[50] Ibid.
[51] Ibid.

needs of law enforcement, practice, and international standards, and therefore it needed to be replaced with a new law.[52]

The 2010 Money Laundering Law clearly states that corporations may be the perpetrators of criminal acts. Article 1 point 9 of this law states that 'Any one is an individual or a corporation. A corporation is an organised collection of people and/or assets, whether they are legal entities or not'. This Law regulates a new institution – the Financial Transaction Reports and Analysis Centre – that is responsible for important tasks related to the prevention of money laundering.[53]

In anti-money laundering efforts, perpetrators and proceeds of crime can be identified through a search, in order for the proceeds of crime to be confiscated for the state or returned to the rightful party. If the proceeds of crime can be confiscated or seized, this can discourage potential future crimes. For this reason, efforts to prevent and eradicate money laundering require a strong legal basis to ensure legal certainty and the effectiveness of law enforcement, as well as the tracing of assets and recovery of the proceeds of crime.[54]

Money laundering has become increasingly complex, crossing jurisdictional boundaries, and using increasingly varied modus operandi, including utilising institutions outside the financial system and penetrating certain sectors. To anticipate this, the Financial Action Task Force (FATF) on Money Laundering issued international standards that became a global measure in the prevention and eradication of money laundering and terrorism financing crimes, known as the Revised Recommendations and Special Recommendations (Revised 40+9) FATF. These include the expansion of reporting parties to include gem, jewellery, and precious metal traders, and also motor vehicle traders. In preventing and eradicating money laundering, it is necessary to carry out regional and international cooperation through bilateral or multilateral forums so that the intensity of criminal acts that result in or involve large volumes of assets can be minimised.[55]

The revisions to how money laundering is handled in Indonesia – witnessed in the amendments and changes to the law between 2002 and 2010 – has shown a positive direction. This is reflected in the increasing awareness of their responsibilities by the parties included in the Money Laundering Law, such as financial service providers in carrying out reporting obligations, the Supervisory and Regulatory Agency in making regulations, the Financial Transaction Reports and Analysis Center in analytical activities, and law enforcement agencies in following up on the results of the analysis with the imposition of criminal sanctions and/or administrative sanctions.[56]

[52] See the preamble Considering in Law No 8 of 2010 concerning Prevention and Eradication of the Crime of Money Laundering.

[53] Article 1 Paragraph 2 Law No 8 of 2010.

[54] General Elucidation of Law No 8 of 2010.

[55] Ibid.

[56] Ibid.

The crime of money laundering itself is regulated in Articles 3 to 10, and other criminal acts related to money laundering are regulated in Articles 11 to 16. This Law also regulates the criminal procedure law in Chapter VIII entitled Investigation, Prosecution, and Examination in Court Sessions, covering Articles 68 to 82.

H. Law No 9 of 2013

Law No 9 of 2013 concerning the Prevention and Eradication of the Financing of Terrorism was enacted on 13 March 2013. The element of funding is one of the main factors in all acts of terrorism, meaning that efforts to combat terrorism must be followed by efforts to prevent and eradicate terrorism financing. Indonesia has ratified the 1999 International Convention for the Suppression of the Financing of Terrorism, which requires states to make or harmonise laws and regulations related to the financing of terrorism in accordance with the provisions stipulated in the convention. Law No 9 of 2013 was developed because the existing laws and regulations relating to the financing of terrorism did not sufficiently regulate the prevention and eradication of financing of terrorism in an appropriate and comprehensive manner.[57]

Efforts to eradicate terrorism have been carried out conventionally; that is, by punishing the perpetrators of terrorism. To be able to prevent and eradicate terrorism optimally, it is necessary to follow up other efforts by using systems and mechanisms for tracing the flow of funds, because it is impossible for terrorism to be carried out without supporting funds. The financing of terrorism is transnational in nature so that prevention and eradication efforts are carried out by involving financial service providers, law enforcement officers, and international cooperation to detect the existence of a flow of funds being used, or suspected as being used, for financing terrorism activities. Prior to the 2013 Law being developed, provisions relating to the prevention and eradication of terrorism financing were regulated by Law No 15 of 2003 concerning Stipulation of Government Regulations in Lieu of Law No 1 of 2002 concerning Eradication of Criminal Acts of Terrorism, and Law No 8 of 2010 concerning Prevention and Eradication of the Crime of Money Laundering.[58] However, it was determined that Law No 15 of 2003, which regulated the financing of terrorism, had several shortcomings. Likewise, efforts to include terrorism as one of the crimes in Law No 8 of 2010 had not been implemented effectively in the prevention and eradication of financing of terrorism.[59]

Financing of terrorism is regulated in Articles 4 to 8 of this Law, while other related crimes are regulated in Articles 9 and 10. This Law also regulates

[57] Preamble Considering in Law No 9 of 2013 concerning the Prevention and Eradication of the Financing of Terrorism.

[58] General Elucidation of Law No 9 of 2013.

[59] Ibid.

the freezing of funds which are directly or indirectly known to be used, or it is reasonably suspected that they are being used or will be used, either in whole or in part, for terrorism.[60] Provisions regarding freezing of funds are regulated in Chapter VI, from Article 22 to Article 26. There are several other provisions also related to the freezing of funds, such as the freezing of funds belonging to individuals or corporations, which are listed in Article 28 to Article 35. As for procedural law, the rules regarding investigation, prosecution, and examination in court are regulated in Article 36 to Article 40.[61]

In conclusion, the above laws can be referred to as criminal laws because all regulate the provisions of substantive and formal criminal offences regarding criminal acts, such as corruption, economic crime, terrorism, money laundering, and the financing of terrorism. For example, economic crimes such as corruption are regulated in their own special law, not in the Criminal Code, with the special law including the relevant definitions, elements, subjects, criminal sanctions, any exceptions from the Criminal Code regarding attempt or complicity or the principle of validity, and so on. The special law contains not only substantive criminal provisions, but also a number of criminal procedure provisions on investigation, evidence, prosecution, and examination in court which differ from the Criminal Procedure Code.[62]

IV. Administrative Law with Criminal Provisions

Special criminal law outside of criminal legislation is different to special criminal law in criminal legislation. In special criminal law, the various specifics of criminal acts (such as corruption) are discussed, with some criminal procedures included. On the other hand, special criminal law outside of criminal legislation regulates topics that are not criminal acts, focusing instead on areas such as administration, duties and authorities, requirements, types, procedures, services, permits, and procurement. Nevertheless, these laws often also include some criminal provisions in order to strengthen norms and compliance with these laws.

In Indonesia, examples of special criminal law outside of criminal legislation covers topics such as plantations, higher education, health, medicine, narcotics, psychotropics, press, broadcasting, sports, banking, capital markets, political parties, elections, transportation, buildings, road traffic, and aviation.[63] If we open and read the relevant legislation on any of these topics, at the end there is a chapter

[60] Article 22 of Law No 9 of 2013.

[61] Santoso, *Hukum Pidana Suatu Pengantar* (2021) 233.

[62] There is another special criminal law, namely Law No 11/PNPS/ 1963 concerning Eradication of Subversion Activities, State Gazette of 1963 Number 101. However, this Law itself was officially revoked in 1999, based on Law No 26/1999 on the revocation of Law No 11/PNPS/1963 concerning the Eradication of Subversion Activities. While this law was in effect, many people were prosecuted and sentenced, so the existence of this law itself was seen as very repressive and used for the interests of the authorities.

[63] Santoso, *Hukum Pidana Suatu Pengantar* (2021) 233.

on criminal provisions. These chapters regulate substantive crimes (criminal acts and their sanctions) but also procedural aspects which may be different to or deviate from the Criminal Procedure Code. The criminal provisions (substantive and procedural) in these various laws are therefore what is meant by the term 'special criminal law outside of criminal legislation'.[64]

There are a vast number of laws across many fields of life that contain criminal provisions, but this chapter will briefly mention only several examples of non-criminal legislations that contain criminal provisions. Some of these are described in Table 3.1.[65]

Table 3.1 Examples of Criminal Provisions in Administrative Laws

No	Law	Date ratified	Criminal Provisions	Procedural Provisions
1	Law No 7 of 2017 concerning the General Election	15 August 2017, by President Joko Widodo, LN 2017 No 182.	Article 488 to Article 554	Article 476 to Article 487
2	Law No 7 of 1992 concerning Banking in conjunction with Law No 10 of 1998	Law No 7 of 1992 was enacted on 25 March 1992 by President Soeharto (LN 1992 No 31) Law No 10 of 1998 by President BJ Habibie (LN 1998 No 182)	Articles 46, 47, 47A, 48, 49, 50, 50A, 51	–
3	Law No 8 of 1995 concerning the Capital Market	10 November 1995, by President Soeharto (LN 1995 No 64)	Article 103 to Article 110	Article 101
4	Law No 35 of 2009 concerning Narcotics	12 October 2009, by President Susilo Bambang Yudhoyono (LN 2009 No 143)	Article 111 to Article 148	Article 73 to Article 103
5	Law No 5 of 1997 concerning Psychotropics	11 March 1997, by President Soeharto (LN 1997 No 10)	Article 59 to Article 72	Article 55 to Article 58
6	Law No 22 of 2009 concerning Road Traffic and Transportation	22 June 2009, by President Susilo Bambang Yudhoyono (LN 2009 No 96)	Article 273 to Article 317	Article 259 to Article 272
7	Law No 44 of 2008 concerning Pornography	26 November 2008, by President Susilo Bambang Yudhoyono (LN 2008 No 181)	Article 29 to Article 38	Article 23 to Article 27

[64] Ibid 234.
[65] Ibid 234–35.

As identified in Table 3.1, one example of a non-criminal law that contains criminal provisions is Law No 44 of 2008 concerning Pornography. The consideration of this law explains that the State of Indonesia is a legal state based on Pancasila by upholding moral values, ethics, noble character, and noble personality of the nation, having faith and fear of God Almighty, respecting diversity in social life, as a nation, and the state, and protect the dignity of every citizen. The Law goes on to explain that the manufacture, distribution, and use of pornography is increasingly widespread in society, that this threatens the life and social order of the Indonesian people, and that it has been determined that the current laws and regulations relating to pornography have not been able to meet the legal needs and development of society.[66]

In regulating pornography, Law No 44 of 2008 includes (1) prohibiting and restricting the manufacture, distribution, and use of pornography; (2) protection of children from the influence of pornography; and (3) prevention of the production, distribution, and use of pornography, including public participation in prevention. This Law explicitly stipulates the forms of punishment for violations of the manufacture, distribution, and use of pornography, which are adjusted to the level of the offence committed – severe, moderate, and light – as well as increasing the punishment if the criminal acts involve children. In addition, increased punishment may be imposed against corporate perpetrators of criminal acts, by doubling the basic punishment and providing additional punishment. To provide protection for victims of pornography, this Law obliges all parties – in this case the state, social institutions, educational institutions, religious institutions, families, and/or the community – to provide guidance, assistance, social recovery, and physical and mental health treatment for every child who is a victim or perpetrator of pornography.[67]

Criminal provisions in this Law are regulated in Articles 29 to 38. Article 29 also states that Articles 29 to 38 of this Law are classified as offences.[68] Article 44 states: 'At the time this Law comes into force, all laws and regulations governing or relating to the crime of pornography are declared to remain in effect as long as they do not conflict with this Law'. There are provisions regarding pornography in the Criminal Code itself, as well as in the Electronic Transactions and Information Law (UU ITE) and the Broadcasting Law.[69]

Thus, we can conclude that the elaboration of criminal law outside of criminal legislation is common in Indonesia, because almost all of the county's laws contain criminal provisions as well as criminal procedures. Some provisions of criminal law also differ from the general provisions in the Criminal Code, hence more specific provisions are used (ie, those contained in the relevant law).

[66] See the preamble in Law No 44 of 2008 concerning Pornography.
[67] See General Elucidation of Law No 44 of 2008.
[68] It means that the type of crime is an offence, and not a violation.
[69] Santoso, *Hukum Pidana Suatu Pengantar* (2021) 236.

Likewise, if there are special procedural provisions in the law that differ from those in the Criminal Procedure Code, then the Law's special provisions apply. For crimes that are not regulated under a specific law, it will be necessary to refer to the general provisions in the Criminal Code and the Criminal Procedure Code.

4

Scope of Application of Criminal Law

This chapter begins with a discussion of the application of criminal law over time, and focuses on discussing the legality principle as reflected in the formulation of *nullum delictum nulla poena sine praevia lege poenali* (no crime, no punishment, without previous criminal law). The four principles contained in the principle of legality are also discussed: *lex scripta* (punishments must be based on written laws); *lex certa* (laws must be formulated in detail and carefully, with the form and severity of punishments clearly determined and distinguished); *lex praevia* (prohibition of retroactive application of criminal law); and *lex stricta* (laws must be strictly formulated). This chapter discusses the scope of the application of criminal law according to the place, person, and character of the crime,[1] focusing on the principles applying criminal law in Indonesia as regulated in Article 2 to Article 9 of the Criminal Code. Articles 2 to 3 of the Criminal Code are based on place, Articles 5 to 8 are based on people, and Articles 4, 5 to 8 are based on the nature of people's actions.[2] This discussion is done while keeping in mind the four key principles when applying criminal law: territoriality; active nationality; passive nationality; and universality.

I. The Legality Principle

Although the expression *nullum delictum nulla poena sine praevia lege poenali* is Latin in origin, this formulation was not known in Ancient Roman law. It came instead from German jurist Paul Johann Anselm Ritter von Feuerbach (1775–1833).[3] If we talk about actions that are prohibited and sanctioned with

[1] According to Utrecht, Articles 2 to 9 of the Criminal Code regulate '*grondgebied*' (based on place) and '*persongebied*' (based on person). See E Utrecht, *Rangkaian Sari Kuliah Hukum Pidana 1* (Surabaya, Pustaka Tinta Mas, 1994) 220. However, other authors also include 'based on the character of the crime', eg Jan Remmelink, *Hukum Pidana, Komentar atas Pasal-Pasal Terpenting dari Kitab Undang-Undang hukum Pidana Belanda dan Padanannya dalam Kitab Undang-Undang Hukum Pidana Indonesia* (Jakarta, Gramedia Pustaka Utama, 2003) 371.

[2] Bambang Poernomo, *Asas-asas Hukum Pidana*, 7th edn (Jakarta, Ghalia Indonesia, 1994) 67.

[3] Remmelink, *Hukum Pidana* (2003) 356.

punishment, then we are talking about criminal acts, where a very important basis is the principle of legality; that is, the determination that an act is not prohibited and sanctioned with punishment if this is not specified in the legislation,[4] or, in Latin, *nullum delictum nulla poena sine praevia lege poenali.*[5]

According to Feuerbach, from the provisions of this legality principle, three rules emerged which in Latin are known as *nulla poena sine lege*, *nulla poena sine crimine*, and *nullum crimen sine poena legali.*[6] *Nulla poena* means that every criminal penalty must be based solely on the law. *Nulla poena sine crimine* means that the imposition of a sentence is only possible if the act that has occurred is punishable by law. Meanwhile, *nullum crimen sine poena legali* means that an act that is punishable by law has a legal consequence, and, by law, there is a punishment for it.[7]

According to Cleiren and Nijboer et al, the principle of legality means that there is no crime without law and no punishment without law. The principle of legality is to protect the rights of citizens from the arbitrariness of authorities, in addition to the state's authority to impose criminal penalties.[8] Thus, in this view, criminal law is written law, and no one can be convicted under customary law as customary law does not define acts which can be punished by law (*strafbaarheid*).[9] In other words, the principle of legality means (1) there are no ambiguous (or elastic) provisions; (2) there is no customary law; and (3) no analogies may be used.

According to Jan Remmelink, the principle of *lex certa* means that legislators must formulate criminal provisions as carefully or with as much detail as possible. The formulation of criminal provisions that are not clear or that are too complicated creates legal uncertainty and hinders the success of prosecution efforts, as defendants can argue that such provisions are not intended as guidelines for behaviour. Unfortunately, legislators are not always able to meet these requirements. Remmelink noted that nowadays the *lex certa* principle is also affected by the freedom of criminal judges who allow the use of teleological and functional interpretation.[10]

[4] Moeljatno, *Asas-Asas Hukum Pidana* (2002) 23.

[5] Bambang Poernomo, in Eddy OS Hiariej, *Asas Legalitas & Penemuan Hukum dalam Hukum Pidana* (Jakarta, Erlangga, 2009) 7.

[6] See Hiariej, *Asas Legalitas & Penemuan Hukum dalam Hukum Pidana* (2009) 7.

[7] AZ Abidin and Andi Hamzah, *Pengantar dalam Hukum Pidana Indonesia* (2010) 57–58.

[8] Cleiren and Nijboer et al in Abidin and Hamzah, *Pengantar dalam Hukum Pidana Indonesia* (2003) 55. This is also the view of Anselm von Feurbach as quoted by D Schaffmeister, N Keizer and E PH Sutorius, *Hukum Pidana* (Yogyakarta, Liberty, 2003) 5.

[9] Cleiren and Nijboer et al in Abidin and Hamzah, *Pengantar dalam Hukum Pidana Indonesia* (2010) 55.

[10] Remmelink, *Hukum Pidana* (2003) 358.

II. Legality in Article 1 of the Criminal Code, 1945 Constitution, Human Rights Law, and New Criminal Code Bill

A. Legality in Article 1 of the Criminal Code

i. The Principle of Legality

In the Criminal Code, the legality principle is contained in Article 1 paragraph (1), which reads '*Geen feit is strafbaar and uit kracht van eene daaran voorafgegane wettelijk strafbepaling*'. Dali Mutiara translates the provision as 'No act may be punished, other than by the force of the criminal code in the law, which was held at the time before the act'.[11] The purpose of this provision is that no *feit* (action) is *strafbaar* (punishable) if *wettelijk strafbepaling* (criminal law) does not precede the act.

According to Moeljatno, the principle of legality as written in Article 1 paragraph (1) contains three elements: (1) there is no prohibited act that is sanctioned with punishment that is not already stated in a statutory regulation; (2) in determining the existence of a criminal act, analogies (*qiyas*) may not be used; and (3) the rules of criminal law are not retroactive.[12]

The term *wettelijk strafbepaling* (criminal legislation) in the clause above refers to criminal law in a broad sense. That is, any legislation with criminal provisions, not just laws in the narrow sense of the word (ie those jointly formed between the government and the House of Representatives (as the people's representatives formed through elections). Thus, the criminal legislation includes provincial and district/city regional regulations, as regional regulations may also contain criminal provisions.[13] In addition, there are other regulations that contain criminal provisions, such as government regulations in lieu of laws (*Perppu*).[14]

Provisions regarding the principle of legality, as regulated in criminal procedural law, differ slightly but must also be based on the law (*Strafwet*). According to Remmelink, the provisions of Article 1 of *Strafvordering* (Sv) (Dutch Criminal Procedure Code) stipulates that only law in a formal sense can provide regulation in the field of court.[15] What is the law in the formal sense? It is a type of legislation

[11] Dali Mutiara, *KUHP, Kitab Undang-Undang Hukum Pidana Republik Indonesia (Wetboek van Strafrecht voor Indonesie jang telah dirobah dan dibaharui)* [Books of Criminal Law of the Republic of Indonesia] (Jakarta, Toko Buku 'Suar', 1951) 12.

[12] Moeljatno in Abidin and Hamzah, *Pengantar dalam Hukum Pidana Indonesia* (2010) 54.

[13] See Abidin and Hamzah, *Pengantar dalam Hukum Pidana Indonesia* (2010) 60.

[14] Topo Santoso, *Hukum Pidana Suatu Pengantar* (Jakarta, Rajawali Pers, 2021) 320–21.

[15] Remmelink, *Hukum Pidana* (2003) 357.

that is made and approved jointly between the House of Representatives and the government; in other words, what we know and generally refer to as 'laws', such as the Law on the Eradication of Criminal Acts of Corruption, the Narcotics Law, or the Road Law. In other countries, this may be called an Act or Statute.

As explained above, according to Moeljatno the principle of legality as written in the Criminal Code contains three meanings. Of the three meanings, the third understanding is that the rules of criminal law are not retroactive.[16] Likewise, for criminal procedural law, MS Groenhuijsen states that one of four meanings in the principle of legality is that legislators may not retroactively apply criminal provisions.[17] Criminal experts Wirjono Prodjodikoro[18] and Sudarto[19] agree, arguing that criminal laws and regulations must exist before the occurrence of a crime.

One of the principles contained in Article 1 paragraph (1) of the Criminal Code is that criminal law regulations must be formulated strictly, with no analogies to be used. In Latin, this is referred to as '*nullum crimen sine lege stricta*', meaning that criminal provisions do not exist unless they are narrowly/strictly formulated in the legislation.[20] An analogy is a similarity or agreement between two different objects or things, where an equivalence between forms of language provides the basis for the occurrence of other forms.[21]

In criminal law, the use of analogies is not permitted, especially when determining whether an act is a criminal act, due to concerns about violations of individual rights. If an analogy is used in imposing punishment for an act that is similar to acts regulated in criminal legislation, but which itself is not regulated as a prohibited act, then a person will be prosecuted for something that is not a crime. This will happen despite there being no basis for prosecution nor punishment, with the act only being prosecuted because it resembles a crime that can be punished. Of course, this will cause harm to the individual, as well as creating legal uncertainty for the broader community.[22]

Article 1 of the Criminal Code does not explicitly state the prohibition of analogy. However, criminal law experts argue that it contains an element which is a prohibition on the use of analogies. This is a consequence of the principles *lex scripta*, *lex certa*, and *lex stricta* in Article 1 of the Criminal Code.[23]

[16] Moeljatno in Abidin and Hamzah, *Pengantar dalam Hukum Pidana Indonesia* (2010) 54.

[17] Groenhuijsen as quoted by Komariah Emong Sapardjaja, *Ajaran Sifat Melawan Hukum Materiil dalam Hukum Pidana Indonesia* (Studi Kasus tentang Penerapan dan Perkembangannya dalam Yurisprudensi) (Bandung, Alumni, 2002) 5–6.

[18] Wirjono Prodjodikoro, *Asas-Asas Hukum Pidana di Indonesia* (Bandung, Refika Aditama, 2004) 42.

[19] Sudarto, *Hukum Pidana I* (Semarang, Sudarto Foundation, 1990) 22–24.

[20] Remmelink, *Hukum Pidana* (2003) 359. See also Eddy OS Hiariej, *Prinsip-prinsip Hukum Pidana*, Revised Edition (Yogyakarta, Cahaya Atma Pustaka, 2016) 108.

[21] kbbi.web.id/analogi.

[22] Santoso, *Hukum Pidana Suatu Pengantar* (2021) 342.

[23] Ibid.

Most Indonesian criminal law experts refuse to use analogies in criminal law, including Sudikno Mertokusumo who states that in criminal law analogies are prohibited, although extensive interpretation is allowed. The situation is different for customary criminal law, where the implementation of the analogy of existing provisions is common and necessary. This has been deemed insufficient to justify the use of analogy in general criminal law.[24]

ii. Retroactive Exceptions: Transitional Conditions

Article 1 (2) of the Criminal Code reads 'If there is a change in the legislation after the occurrence of a crime, the most favourable provisions must be applied to the defendant'. This confirms that if law enacted after the crime was found to be more favourable for the defendant, then its retroactive enforcement is permitted.[25] Prodjodikoro states that this is a deviation from the retroactive prohibition of criminal law.[26]

Thus, regarding Article 1 paragraph (2) of the Criminal Code, we must ask, what is the meaning of the amendment to the legislation? And what does the 'more favourable' provision mean for the defendant?

On the first question, the answer is that there is no collective understanding on the matter. There are formal teachings, limited substantive teachings, and unlimited substantive teachings. But which is more accepted by the court? If the change reduces sanctions from imprisonment to short-term imprisonment or a fine, or the article is completely revoked, then there is no dispute of opinion, as there has been a clear change in legislation. However, if, for example, there is a change in an article in the Civil Code (*KUH Perdata*) regarding the age limit – such as lowering the definition of maturity from 21 years to 20 years – this would give rise to problems on Article 293 of the Criminal Code, which can punish a person who violates the law by committing a crime of (in)decency against an underage person (*minderjarig*). If, at the time of the crime, the victim was 20 years and 6 months old – that is, underage – but then the age limit is lowered to 20 years, how is the law to be interpreted?[27] According to the unamended Civil Code, the victim is not yet an adult, so the defendant can be prosecuted because their actions were committed against a minor. Meanwhile, according to the amended Civil Code, the victim is an adult because maturity is defined as 20 years old. If changes in the Civil Code are seen as 'changes to legislation' under Article 1 paragraph (2) of the Criminal Code, then the new provisions must be used. On the other hand, if the changes in the Civil Code are not considered as 'changes in legislation', then there is absolutely no change, and the perpetrator is still punished for committing an act against a minor under Article 293 of the Criminal Code.[28]

[24] Sudikno Mertokusumo, *Mengenal Hukum: Suatu Pengantar* (Yogyakarta, Liberty, 2002) 164.
[25] Santoso, *Hukum Pidana Suatu Pengantar* (2021) 334.
[26] Prodjodikoro, *Asas-Asas Hukum Pidana di Indonesia* (2004) 44.
[27] Ibid 46.
[28] Santoso, *Hukum Pidana Suatu Pengantar* (2021) 335.

What constitutes 'changes in legislation' differs between teachings. According to formal teaching, what is meant by 'changes to legislation', as written in Article 1 (2) of the Criminal Code, is changes to criminal legislation. If changes occur in other laws, such as the Civil Code in the example above, then this does not fall within the meaning of Article 1 (2). Thus, in this example, it is considered that there is no change to the legislation, and the perpetrator can still be punished.[29]

Substantive teaching takes the opposite viewpoint, arguing that changes do not have to occur in criminal legislation, but can occur in other laws. The changes apply as long as they affect the implementation of criminal legislation. Thus, in the case above, it is deemed that there has been a change in the legislation, making the victim an adult (over 20 years old) and meaning the perpetrator cannot be convicted, because Article 293 of the Criminal Code is not fulfilled, especially the element 'against minors'. According to WFC van Hattum, the Dutch *Hoge Raad* (Supreme Court) adheres to the substantive view.[30]

Substantive teaching on changes to legislation in the context of Article 1 (2) of the Criminal Code is further divided into two areas: limited substantive teaching and unlimited substantive teaching. According to unlimited substantive teaching, what is meant by 'changes to legislation' in Article 1 (2) of the Criminal Code includes all legislative change, both in criminal legislation and non-criminal legislation relating to criminal law. Meanwhile, according to limited substantive teaching, not all changes in non-criminal legislation that affect criminal law can be included in the meaning of 'change in legislation' under Article 1 (2) of the Criminal Code. Rather, it is only if there is a change in the 'legal belief' of the legislator that there is deemed to be a change in the legislation. For example, if there is a temporary law in place only for a certain period (for example, one year or until a condition exists), after that period has ended, the regulation will be revoked or declared invalid. According to limited substantive teaching, such an incident is included in the formulation of 'change in legislation', while according to unlimited substantive teaching, it is not 'change in legislation', because it changes due to time, not because of a change in the legal beliefs of the lawmakers.[31]

The second issue concerns the meaning of the 'more favourable' provisions for the defendant. What changes are seen as favourable for the defendant? There are many, including changes in the types of criminal acts from ordinary offences to complaint-based offences, or from felonies to violations; changes in the types of criminal sanctions from imprisonment to fines or short-term imprisonment, from imprisonment to undisclosed penitentiary, from fines to supervision, and so on; and changes in the elements of criminal acts, especially from fewer criminal elements to more. If there are more criminal elements, of course, the burden

[29] Prodjodikoro, *Asas-Asas Hukum Pidana di Indonesia* (2004) 46.
[30] Ibid 46.
[31] Ibid 46.

of proof on the prosecutor to prosecute the defendant becomes heavier, making the situation more favourable for the defendant.[32]

Questions that arise in this context are often difficult to answer. What if the type of crime or type of punishment becomes more detrimental – for example, it changes from a violation to a crime – yet, from the criminal's perspective, it becomes more favourable – for example, a decrease of length of imprisonment from one year to five months? Thus it can be hard to determine which provisions – new or old – are more favourable to the perpetrator. In my opinion, law enforcers, especially judges, must work on a case-by-case basis to see which provisions should be applied, as 'more favourable' cannot be generalised to all cases.[33]

B. Legality in the Constitution and Human Rights Law

The principle of legality has been regulated in several international declarations and conventions. Originally regulated in the 1789 Declaration on the Rights of Man and the Citizen following the French revolution, the principle is also contained in the 1950 European Convention on Human Rights, the International Covenant on Civil and Political Rights (ICCPR), and the Statute of the International Criminal Court.

The Universal Declaration of Human Rights (UDHR) also contains this fundamental principle. Article 11 paragraph (2) states that:

> No one shall be held guilty of any penal offence on account of any act or omission which did not constitute a penal offence, under national or international law, at the time when it was committed. Nor shall a heavier penalty be imposed than the one that was applicable at the time the penal offence was committed.

This clearly contains the principle of legality. The provisions are very similar to the provisions in Article 1 paragraph (1) of the Criminal Code in Indonesia.

The ICCPR also recognises this principle. Article 15 (1) states that:

> No one shall be held guilty of any criminal offence on account of any act or omission which did not constitute a criminal offence, under national or international law, at the time when it was committed. No shall a heavier penalty be imposed than the one that was applicable at the time when the criminal offence was committed. If, subsequent to the commission of the offence, provision is made by law for the imposition of the lighter penalty, the offender shall benefit thereby.

Article 15(1) of the ICCPR has the same substance as Article 11 of the UDHR, as both state that no one may be found guilty of a criminal offence due to an act or omission which was not a criminal offence, under national or international law,

[32] Santoso, *Hukum Pidana Suatu Pengantar* (2021) 337.
[33] Ibid 338.

when the deed was done, and no more severe punishment shall be imposed than the punishment in force when the crime was committed. This provision is in line with Article 1 paragraph (1) of the Criminal Code.[34] As the ICCPR also emphasises favourable conditions for defendants ('if, after a crime has been committed, provisions are made by law for the imposition of a lighter sentence, the perpetrator will benefit from it') these are also in line with Article 1 paragraph (2) of the Criminal Code.

Article 15 paragraph (2) of the ICCPR contains an exception from Article 15 paragraph (1). Article 15 paragraph (2) of the ICCPR states:

> Nothing in this article shall prejudice the trial and punishment of any person for any act or omission which, at the time when it was committed, was criminal according to the *general principles of law recognised by the community of nation.* [emphasis added]

From this provision, it appears that, although there is no written regulation, if the act is already a criminal act according to the 'general principles of law' recognised by the community of nations, the perpetrators can be tried and punished.

The Geneva Convention also defines the principle of legality. Rule 101 states that:

> No one may be accused or convicted of a criminal offence on account of any act or omission which did not constitute a criminal offence under national or international law at the time it was committed; nor may a heavier penalty be imposed than that which was applicable at the time the criminal offence was committed.

The principle of legality is also applied in the Rome Statute of the International Criminal Court (the ICC Statute), which entered into force in 2002, in particular in Article 22(1), Article 23, and Article 24(1). Article 22, located in Section 3 on General Principles of Criminal Law, entitled *Nullum crimen sine lege*. Article 22(1) states 'A person shall not be criminally responsible under this statute unless the conduct in question constitutes, at the time it takes place, a crime within the jurisdiction of the Court', while Article 22(2) reads 'The definition of a crime shall be strictly construed and shall not be extended by analogy. In case of ambiguity, the definition shall be interpreted in favour of the person being investigated, prosecuted or convicted'. The essence of these provisions is that the definition of a criminal act must be understood strictly and should not be expanded by using analogies. In the event of ambiguity or uncertainty, the meaning must be interpreted in favour of the suspect or defendant. This is therefore a provision regarding *lex stricta*.[35]

In Indonesia, the law which regulates courts for human rights violations is Law No 26 of 2000 concerning Human Rights Courts.[36] Article 43 paragraph (1)

[34] Ibid 348–49.
[35] Ibid 350.
[36] State Gazette of the Republic of Indonesia Year 2000 Number 208.

of this Law states that: 'Gross violations of human rights[37] that occurred *prior to the promulgation of this* Law shall be examined and decided by ad hoc human rights court' (emphasis added). Meanwhile, Article 43 paragraph (2) states that the ad hoc Human Rights Court referred to in paragraph (1) is to be established at the suggestion of the House of Representatives based on certain events and by Presidential Decree. Article 43 paragraph (3) adds that the court will be located in the General Court environment.

The explanation for Article 43 paragraph (2) of Law No 26 of 2000 states:

> In the event that the Indonesian House of Representatives proposes the establishment of an ad hoc Human Rights Court, the Indonesian House of Representatives is based on allegations that serious human rights violations have occurred which are limited to certain *locus* and *tempus delicti* that occurred before the promulgation of this law.

Retroactive law enforcement has happened previously in Indonesia. One prominent case was the Bali terrorism attack that killed 204 people and injured hundreds of others on 12 October 2002. In response to the attack, just six days later, the government issued two Government Regulations in Lieu of Law: Government Regulation in Lieu of Law No 1 of 2002 on Combating Terrorism[38] and Government Regulation in Lieu of Law No 2 of 2002[39] on the Implementation of Government Regulation No 1 of 2002 on the Bali bombings.[40] Article 46 of Government Regulation in Lieu of Law No 1 of 2002 statest:

> The provisions in this Government Regulation in Lieu of Law can be applied retroactively to legal actions or certain cases prior to the entry into force of this Government Regulation in Lieu of Law, the application of which is stipulated by a separate Law or Government Regulation in Lieu of Law.

Government Regulation in Lieu of Law No 2 of 2002 then retroactively enforced Government Regulation in Lieu of Law No 1 of 2002 to ensure it could be applied to the Bali bombings.

Government Regulation in Lieu of Law No 1 of 2002 was later enacted into Law No 15 of 2003,[41] while Government Regulation in Lieu of Law No 2 of 2002 was later ratified into Law No 16 of 2003.[42] But even prior to this, the two Government Regulations in Lieu of Law were used when investigating, prosecuting, trying, and

[37] According to Article 7 of Law No 43 of 2000, gross human rights violations include genocide and crimes against humanity.

[38] State Gazette of the Republic of Indonesia of 2002 Number 106.

[39] State Gazette of the Republic of Indonesia of 2002 Number 107.

[40] Article 1 of Government Regulation in Lieu of Law No 2 of 2002 states: 'Provisions in Government Regulation in Lieu of Law Number 1 of 2002 concerning The Eradication of Criminal Acts of Terrorism is declared to apply to the bombing that occurred in Bali on October 12, 2002.' Meanwhile, in the general explanation of this Government Regulation in Lieu of Law it is stated that: 'In connection with the occurrence of criminal acts of terrorism in Bali on October 12, 2002 and the existence of a very urgent need to overcome this problem …'

[41] State Gazette of the Republic of Indonesia of 2003 Number 45.

[42] State Gazette of the Republic of Indonesia of 2003 Number 45.

imposing criminal charges on the perpetrators of the Bali bombings. The public seemed to understand and accept this situation because they were badly shaken by the incident so that the retroactive implementation of the regulations remained in effect without significant community pushback.

Law No 16 of 2003 was later submitted to the Constitutional Court for judicial review. In its decision, the Constitutional Court (Decision No. 013/PUU-I/2003 dated 23 July 2004) essentially decided that Law No 16 of 2003 concerning the stipulation of Government Regulation in Lieu of Law No 2 of 2002 into law was contrary to the Constitution and had no binding legal force, because its enactment is contrary to the prohibition of retroactive implementation of criminal law, as stated in the 1945 Constitution, which, in Chapter XA, Article 28 paragraph (1), states:[43]

> The right to life, the right not to be tortured, the right to freedom of thought and conscience, the right to religion, the right not to be enslaved, the right to be recognized as a person before the law, and *the right not to be prosecuted on the basis of retroactive law* is a human right that cannot be reduced under any circumstances. [emphasis added]

It should be emphasised that what the Court revoked was Government Regulation in Lieu of Law No 2 of 2002 (which was later ratified as Law No 16 of 2003), while Government Regulation in Lieu of Law No 1 of 2002 on the Eradication of Criminal Acts of Terrorism (later enacted into law through Law No 15 of 2003) remained in effect.[44] The principle is reaffirmed in Article 18 paragraph (2) of Law No 39 of 1999 concerning Human Rights, which states 'Every person may not be prosecuted or sentenced to a crime, except based on a statutory regulation that existed before the crime was committed'.[45] Meanwhile, Article 18 paragraph (3) of this Law states 'Every time there is a change in the legislation, the provisions that are most favourable to the suspect shall apply'. These provisions are very similar to the provisions in Article 1 paragraph (1) and paragraph (2) of the Criminal Code.

C. Legality in the New Criminal Code

As mentioned in previous chapters, Indonesia is looking to replace the current Criminal Code with a new code that is a better fit with contemporary developments. In Article 1 paragraph (1) of the new Criminal Code,[46] legality is formulated as 'There is no single act that can be subject to criminal sanctions and/or actions except for the strength of the criminal regulations in the laws and regulations that

[43] Santoso, *Hukum Pidana Suatu Pengantar* (2021) 330–31.
[44] Ibid 331.
[45] State Gazette of the Republic of Indonesia Year 1999 Number 165.
[46] The last discussion between the Government and the House of Representatives on 24 November 2022.

existed before the act was done'. This formulation is very similar to that of Article 1 paragraph (1) of the current Criminal Code, except for the addition of 'that can be subject to criminal sanctions and/or actions'. The Elucidation for Article 1 explains that:

> This provision contains the principle of legality which determines that an act is a criminal offence if it is determined by or based on laws and regulations. The laws and regulations in this provision are Laws and Regional Regulations. The principle of legality is a basic principle in criminal law. Therefore, laws and regulations containing criminal sanctions must exist before a crime is committed. This means that criminal provisions must not be retroactive.

The issue of *lex scripta* above is a serious issue for discussion in this context, considering provisions in upcoming criminal law, as seen in the formulation of Article 2 paragraph (1) of the Criminal Code:

> The provisions as referred to in Article 1 paragraph (1) do not reduce the validity of the *living law in a society* that determines that a person deserves to be punished *even though the act is not regulated in this law*. (emphasis added)

Meanwhile, Article 2 paragraph (2) of the Criminal Code states:

> The living law in society as referred to in paragraph (1) applies in the place where the law lives and as long as it is not regulated in this Law and is in accordance with the values contained in Pancasila, the 1945 Constitution of the Republic of Indonesia, human rights, and general legal principles recognized by civilised society.

What is meant by 'law that lives in society' is explained in the Elucidation of Article 2 paragraph (1) of the Criminal Code:

> What is meant by 'living law in society which determines that a person deserves to be sentenced' is customary criminal law. The living law in society in this article is related to the law that is still valid and developing in community lives in Indonesia. In certain areas in Indonesia, there are still unwritten legal provisions that live in the community and apply as law in the area, which determines that a person deserves to be punished. To provide a legal basis regarding the application of criminal law (customary offences), it is necessary to be affirmed and compiled by the government derived from the Regional Regulations of each place where customary law applies. This compilation contains the law that lives in the community which is qualified as a customary crime. This situation will not rule out and will still guarantee the implementation of the legality principle and the prohibition of analogies adopted in this Law.

Elucidation of Article 2 paragraph (2) of the Draft Criminal Code states:

> In this provision what is meant by 'applicable in the place where the law lives' is applicable to everyone who commits customary crimes in the area. This paragraph contains guidelines in determining customary criminal law which validity is recognised by this Law.

In the future, if the New Criminal Code is applied, including Article 2, then the customary law which also contains criminal matters can be accepted and can be tried in court – not by customary courts, but by district courts. This is clearly an exception to the principle of legality as regulated in Article 1 paragraph (1) of the Criminal Code and Article 1 of the Criminal Code.[47]

In contrast to the concise provisions in Article 1 paragraph (2) of the Criminal Code, the problem of transition due to changes in legislation is regulated in more detail in Article 3 of the Criminal Code as follows:

(1) In the event of changes to laws and regulations after the act has occurred, a new statutory regulation is enacted, except if the old statutory provisions are favourable to the perpetrators and assistants of the crime.
(2) In the event that the act that occurs is no longer a criminal offence according to the new laws and regulations, the legal process against the suspect or defendant must be terminated by law.
(3) In the event that the provisions as referred to in paragraph (2) are applied to a suspect or defendant who is in custody, the suspect or defendant is released by the competent authority in accordance with the level of examination.
(4) In the event that after the sentencing decision has permanent legal force and the act that occurred is no longer a criminal offence according to the new laws and regulations, the execution of the sentencing decision will be abolished.
(5) In the event that the sentencing decision has permanent legal force as referred to in paragraph (4), the agency or official carrying out the release is an authorised agency or official.
(6) The release as referred to in paragraphs (3) and (5) does not give rise to the right of the suspect, defendant, or convict to demand compensation.
(7) In the event that after the sentencing decision has permanent legal force and the action that occurred is threatened with a lighter sentence according to the new laws and regulations, the implementation of the sentencing decision is adjusted to the criminal limit according to the new laws and regulations.

III. Articles 2 to 9 of the Criminal Code

This section will discuss the four principles of criminal procedural law in the context of Articles 2 to 9 of the Criminal Code and other relevant legislation. As mentioned in the introduction above, there are four principles when it comes to applying criminal law: the principle of territoriality (*territorialiteitsbeginsel*); the principle of personality / active nationality (*personaliteitsbeginsel / actief nationaliteitsbeginsel*); the principle of passive nationality/protection (*passief nationaliteitsbeginsel / beschermingsbeginsel*); and the principle of universality (*universaliteitsbeginsel*).[48]

[47] Santoso, *Hukum Pidana Suatu Pengantar* (2021) 325.
[48] See eg Poernomo, *Asas-asas Hukum Pidana* (1994) 58. See also Utrecht, *Rangkaian Sari Kuliah Hukum Pidana* (1994) 231.

A. Principle of Territoriality

i. Crimes Committed in the Territory of Indonesia

According to Satochid Kartanegara, the principle of territoriality is the main principle of the four. The other three principles are secondary.[49] Bambang Poernomo agrees, arguing that the principle of territoriality for the enactment of the criminal law is the main basis for the rule of law, while other principles are seen as exceptions/ extension.[50] The word 'territorial' is defined as 'relating to a territory'.[51] It can also be interpreted as 'pertaining to, associated with, or restricted to a particular territory or district'.

The formulation of the principle of territoriality is regulated in Article 2 of the Criminal Code, which reads 'The criminal rules in the laws of the Republic of Indonesia apply to everyone who within the territory of the Republic of Indonesia commits an act that can be punished'. To reaffirm this, Law No 73 of 1958 later declared that the Criminal Code was valid throughout Indonesia.

The enactment of Indonesian criminal law therefore depends on where the crime was committed. If the crime is committed in the territory of Indonesia, then Indonesian criminal law applies. The nationality of the perpetrator of the crime is not a concern.[52]

Thus, for every criminal act committed in the territory of Indonesia, regardless of the perpetrator's identity, then Indonesian criminal law applies to the crime. According to AZ Abidin and Andi Hamzah, the territoriality principle is the oldest legal principle, and is a logical principle because, of course, the legal provisions of a country apply in its own territory.[53] Moeljatno states that this first principle is commonly used by most countries, including Indonesia.[54]

This is also a form of Indonesian legal sovereignty in Indonesia's own territory. It would be inappropriate if the crime occured in Indonesia but the criminal law of other countries applied. This would not be in accordance with Indonesia's sovereignty. It is the obligation of a state to enforce the law and maintain law and order in its own territory.[55]

Returning to Article 2 of the Criminal Code, which states that 'The criminal law in the laws of the Republic of Indonesia applies to everyone who within the territory of the Republic of Indonesia commits an act that is punishable'. The mention of 'territory' is decisive. Regardless of the nationality of the perpetrator of the crime and regardless of interests. Even in customary law, the principle of

[49] Satochid Kartanegara, *Hukum Pidana, Kumpulan Kuliah Prof Satochid Kartanegara, SH dan Pendapat-Pendapat Para Ahli Hukum Terkemuka* (Jakarta, Balai Lektur Mahasiswa, nd) 162.

[50] Poernomo, *Asas-asas Hukum Pidana* (1994) 58–59.

[51] www.merriam-webster.com/dictionary/territorial.

[52] Moeljatno, *Asas-Asas Hukum Pidana* (1993) 38.

[53] Abidin and Hamzah, *Pengantar dalam Hukum Pidana Indonesia* (2010) 83.

[54] Moeljatno, *Asas-Asas Hukum Pidana* (1993) 38.

[55] Abidin and Hamzah, *Pengantar dalam Hukum Pidana Indonesia* (2010) 84. See also Kartanegara, *Kumpulan Kuliah* (nd) 163.

territoriality is known. As stated by Abidin and Hamzah, according to customary law in South Sulawesi based on Lontara, the principle of territory applies, enshrined in the customary proverb 'where the fire burns, there it is extinguished', which means that the offence will be judged based on the customs prevailing in the area where it is committed.[56]

The principle of territoriality shows that anyone who commits a crime in the territory of the country where the criminal law applies, is subject to the relevant criminal law. This includes the situation where the person who commits the crime is not physically present in Indonesia, but the crime occurred in the territory of Indonesia.[57] In other words, the enactment of the Indonesian criminal law is focused on the place of the act, not the location of the perpetrator; it is enough that the perpetrator committed a criminal act that 'occurred' within the territory of the Indonesian state. According to Bambang Poernomo, this can be understood to deal with the possibility that someone who is on the other side of the territorial border uses certain methods or tools to commit a crime in Indonesia, and thus allows prosecution under Indonesian criminal law.[58]

ii. Crimes Committed on Indonesian Ships and Aircrafts

Article 3 of the Criminal Code expands the application of the principle of territoriality by recognising Indonesian ships as a place where Indonesian criminal law applies. However, it does not expand Indonesian territory.[59] In other words, Article 3 of the Criminal Code expands the operation of Article 2.[60] This can be seen from the affirmation that the Criminal Code can be applied to those who commit criminal acts on board ships of the Republic of Indonesia.[61] Article 3 reads:

> The criminal rules in the laws of the Republic of Indonesia apply to anyone outside the territory of the Republic of Indonesia, on ships or boats of the Republic of Indonesia who commits an act that is punishable by law.[62]

The Dutch term in *Wetboek van Strafrecht* (WvS) for marine vehicles is *vaartuig* and not *schip* (ship).[63] However, in Article 95 of the Criminal Code,[64]

[56] According to Van Vollenhoven as cited by Abidin dan Hamzah, in the Dutch East Indies there were 19 customary law regions. Abidin and Hamzah, *Pengantar dalam Hukum Pidana Indonesia* (2010) 83.

[57] Abidin and Hamzah, *Pengantar dalam Hukum Pidana Indonesia* (2010) 84.

[58] Poernomo, *Asas-asas Hukum Pidana* (1994) 58. See also Utrecht, *Rangkaian Sari Kuliah Hukum Pidana* (1994) 233. Utrecht says that what becomes the measurement in Article 2 is the place where the criminal act (and not the perpetrator) is located.

[59] Abidin and Hamzah, *Pengantar dalam Hukum Pidana Indonesia* (2010) 85. See also Utrecht, *Rangkaian Sari Kuliah Hukum Pidana I* (1994) 239–40.

[60] Moeljatno, *Asas-Asas Hukum Pidana* (1993) 42.

[61] Kartanegara, *Hukum Pidana, Kumpulan Kuliah* (nd) 165.

[62] Mutiara, *KUHP* (1951) 12.

[63] Utrecht interprets this '*vaartuig*' as a sailing tool (in his book, it is called 'student tool' (sic), but the meaning is of course 'sailing tool'). See Utrecht, *Rangkaian Sari Kuliah Hukum Pidana* (1994) 240.

[64] Article 95 is located in Chapter IX of the Criminal Code which contains the meaning of several terms in the Criminal Code. See the explanation in Santoso, *Hukum Pidana Suatu Pengantar* (2021).

what is described is *schip* and not *vaartuig*. The article reads 'Ship of the Republic of Indonesia means a ship (boat) which, according to the general law concerning sea certificates and ship passes in the territory of the Republic of Indonesia, must have a sea certificate or ship pass or permits as a temporary substitute for the sea certificate or passport'.[65]

In Law No 17 of 2008 concerning Shipping, it is explained in Article 1 number 36 that a ship is a water vehicle with a certain shape and type, which is driven by wind power, mechanical power, other energy, towed or suspended, including vehicles that have dynamic support, vehicles under the water surface, as well as floating equipment and floating buildings that do not move.[66]

According to E Utrecht, from the words of Article 95 of the Criminal Code, it can be concluded that *vaartuig* thus has a broad meaning, while *schip* has a specific meaning. According to Pompe, as quoted by Utrecht, *vaartuig* includes anything that can sail; that is, anything that can move on water.[67]

This is not to mean that the territory of the water vehicle is the territory of a country. The general principle which states that 'ships become territory' (*schip is territoir*) has long been deemed invalid.[68] Thus it is not correct to consider that Indonesian boats/ships are part of the territory of the country, and therefore that what happens on those boats/ships is happening within Indonesian territory. This assumption is contrary to the principle of territoriality. The reason is, if the boat/ship is in the territory of another country, other countries also have the right to try the perpetrators of a crime, according to the principle of territoriality of that country. The purpose of Article 3 of the Criminal Code is so that criminal acts that occur on Indonesian ships/boats can be brought to justice.[69] The provisions in Article 3 of the Criminal Code cannot be interpreted as meaning that a boat is a territorial area or an exterritorial legal area.[70]

What about Indonesian aircraft? When the Criminal Code was drafted there were no aircraft, thus Article 3 only includes regulations regarding criminal acts committed onboard *vaartuig* (ships/boats/marine vehicles). However, after the aircraft were invented and began to be widely used, there was a need to include aircraft in the expansion of the territoriality principle in Article 3. Thus, *luchtvaartuig* (aircraft) was included in Article 3 of the WvS in the Netherlands on 16 June 1952,[71] so that the formulation became *vaartuig of luchtvaartuig* (marine vehicle or aircraft).[72]

[65] Mutiara, *KUHP* (1951) 56.
[66] State Gazette of the Republic of Indonesia Year 2008 Number 64.
[67] Utrecht, *Rangkaian Sari Kuliah Hukum Pidana I* (1994) 240.
[68] Ibid.
[69] Moeljatno, *Asas-Asas Hukum Pidana* (1993) 42.
[70] Suringa in Poernomo, *Asas-asas Hukum Pidana* (1994) 60.
[71] The Netherlands Staatblad Year 1952 No 408.
[72] Van Hattum and Pompe in Utrecht, *Rangkaian Sari Kuliah Hukum Pidana I* (1994) 241.

In 1976, Law No 4 of 1976 concerning Amendments and Additions to Several Articles in the Criminal Code relating to the Expansion of the Applicability of Provisions for Criminal Law, Aviation Crimes, and Crimes against Aviation Facilities/Infrastructure was enacted.[73] for the reason for the development of this law was that the provisions of criminal legislation had not yet been applied to Indonesian aircraft. The Law was drafted by amending and adding to the provisions of the Criminal Code, specifically by expanding the scope of application of Articles 3 and 4 of Book 1 and adding to Book 1 Chapter IX the Articles 95a, 95b, and 95c.[74] Thus, the articles already in the Criminal Code were expanded in scope so that the definition of criminal jurisdiction of the Republic of Indonesia includes Indonesian aircraft.[75]

On first reading, it appears this was already regulated in Article 2 and Article 3 of the Criminal Code and its amendments. In fact, this provision also includes new developments relating to criminal acts in the field of information technology or other criminal acts which consequently are experienced or occur in the territory of Indonesia. Thus this provision is far more developed than the provisions of Article 2 and Article 3 of the Criminal Code.

B. Principle of Active Nationality

The principle of active nationality or personality determines that the enactment of the criminal law of a country is based on the citizenship or nationality of a person who commits a crime, not the place where the crime was committed (territoriality).[76] This principle is adhered to in Article 5 of the Criminal Code.[77] Article 5 thus adds principle of nationality to the principle of territoriality contained in Article 2 (and its expansion in Article 3), so the criminal law of the Republic of Indonesia does not exclusively apply to criminal acts that occur in the territory of the Republic of Indonesia only, but also applies to criminal acts

[73] This law was enacted in Jakarta on 27 April 1976 by President Soeharto and published in the State Gazette of the Republic of Indonesia Year 1976 Number 26.

[74] In addition, this Law also adds to Book 2 Chapter XXIX A concerning Aviation Crimes and Crimes Against Aviation Facilities / Infrastructure. Crimes against aviation facilities / infrastructure as regulated in Article 479a to Article 479d of this Law are different in nature to violations as stated in Article 15 paragraph (1) e of Law Number 83 of 1958 concerning Aviation.

[75] In addition, new provisions were added as a result of developments in the world of aviation. These amendments and additions to the Criminal Code are the implementations of the obligations of the Republic of Indonesia as a participant in three conventions (the Tokyo Convention 1963, the Hague Convention 1970, and the Montreal Convention 1971). In addition, the desire to amend the Criminal Code is also encouraged to suit the current situation (at the time this Law was enacted). See General Explanation and Considerations of Law No 4 of 1976. See also Santoso, *Hukum Pidana, Suatu Pengantar* (2021).

[76] Kartanegara, *Hukum Pidana* (nd) 161.

[77] Prodjodikoro, *Asas-Asas Hukum Pidana di Indonesia* (2003) 53. A similar opinion was expressed by Pompe in Poernomo, *Asas-asas Hukum Pidana* (1994) 63.

that occur outside the territory of Indonesia if the person who commits the crime is an Indonesian citizen. This principle is referred to as 'active nationality'.[78]

According to Satochid Kartanegara, the basis of the principle of active nationality is state sovereignty, where every sovereign state can expect its citizens to submit to the laws of their country, wherever they are. In other words, the laws of a sovereign state always follow its citizens.[79]

However, not all criminal acts covered by the criminal law of the Republic of Indonesia apply to Indonesian citizens overseas. Why not? It is because of the need to avoid violating the sovereignty of foreign countries where an Indonesian citizen commits a crime. Therefore, these criminal acts are limited to certain crimes, with violations excluded entirely.[80] The criminal acts are limited to those regulated in Article 5 of the Criminal Code, and can be divided into three groups:

(1) crimes in Chapters I and II of Book 2 of the Criminal Code;
(2) which articles are clearly determined [Article 5 paragraph (1) number 1]; and
(3) which limits are stated yet the article is not mentioned [Article 5 paragraph (1) number 2].[81]

The provisions made in Article 5 paragraph (1) to 1 and 2 are in response to concerns where actions that are punishable by Indonesian criminal provisions are not in fact prohibited or sanctioned with punishment in the state where the act was committed. In this situation, the criminal provisions in the laws of the Republic of Indonesia do not apply to such incidents. For example, acts related to narcotics, abortion, adultery, and others that are prohibited under Indonesian law (and are even felonies rather than merely violations) but that in some countries are not criminal acts. Alternatively, if the act is committed by an Indonesian citizen in another country, and that country considers the act to be a criminal act, yet in Indonesia it is not considered a felony but a violation, Indonesian criminal law does not apply.

If the act committed by an Indonesian citizen in another country is a crime regulated in the Criminal Code, then the Code is clear on how to determine whether the act is a felony or a violation. The indicators are clear: all criminal acts in Book 2 of the Criminal Code are felonies, and all criminal acts in Book 3 are violations.

The application of Article 5 and the principle of active nationality is limited by the provisions of Article 6, specifically relating to criminal acts that are punishable by the death penalty. Article 6 states:

> The application of Article 5 paragraph (1) to 2 is limited by not being allowed to impose the death penalty for acts that are not punishable by death penalty according to the laws of the country where the act was committed.

[78] Prodjodikoro, *Asas-Asas Hukum Pidana di Indonesia* (2003) 54.
[79] Kartanegara, *Hukum Pidana* (nd) 166–67.
[80] Ibid 167–68.
[81] Poernomo referred to it with the sentence: 'The personal principles (actief nationaliteit) contained in Article 5 of the Criminal Code can be divided into three groups of problems …' See Poernomo, *Asas-asas Hukum Pidana* (1994) 62.

So, for example, consider a criminal act committed by an Indonesian citizen ('person B') in Amsterdam in the Netherlands, which is determined to be premeditated murder (Article 340 of the Criminal Code, which is punishable by death). If person B is tried in Indonesia, for example in the District Court of Central Jakarta, then person B cannot be charged with the death penalty because premeditated murder is not punishable by death in the Netherlands. In fact, the Netherlands does not recognise the death penalty for any crime, and neither do other European countries.

It should also be noted that the principle of active nationality as regulated in Article 5 of the Criminal Code also applies even if, at the time of committing the crime, the perpetrator was a foreign citizen but after committing the crime became a citizen of the Republic of Indonesia. This is confirmed in Article 5 paragraph (2): 'The crime referred to in sub 2 may also be prosecuted, if the defendant becomes a citizen of the Republic of Indonesia after committing the act'. This person will not be handed over to the country of origin, because the person has become an Indonesian citizen and Indonesia will not surrender this nationality to another country. The defendant will be prosecuted and tried in Indonesia.[82]

C. Principle of Passive Nationality

The principle of passive nationality comes from the Dutch term *passief nationaliteitsbeginsel*, which in the Dutch legal encyclopedia is defined as the principle that Dutch courts have the competence to act on crimes committed against Dutch people abroad. This principle itself is only maintained sporadically because it violates the sovereignty of foreign countries.

In the Indonesian context, passive nationality refers to the application of Indonesian criminal law outside the territory of Indonesia, for any person, Indonesian citizen, or foreign citizen who violates the legal interests of Indonesia or commits a criminal act that endangers Indonesia's national interests abroad. The emphasis of this principle is aimed at the protection of national interests that are jeopardised by criminal acts committed by someone abroad, so this principle is also known as the principle of protection.[83] Thus, the word 'nationality' here is not aimed at the position of a citizen, but rather against the legal interests of a country that adheres to this principle. Therefore, it is called 'passive nationality', in contrast to the principle of 'active nationality', which refers to the status of a person who commits a crime as a citizen.[84]

Each sovereign country has the right to protect its legal interests, even if those legal interests are violated by someone who is abroad. Thus, Indonesian criminal

[82] R Tresna, *Azas-azas Hukum Pidana Disertai Pembahasan Beberapa Perbuatan Pidana yang Penting* (Yogyakarta, Tiara Wacana, 1959) 228.
[83] Poernomo, *Asas-asas Hukum Pidana* (1994) 63–64.
[84] Kartanegara, *Hukum Pidana* (nd) 171.

law can be enforced against anyone, both Indonesian citizens and non-Indonesian citizens, who commits a crime against the legal interests of Indonesia anywhere, including abroad. This principle is contained in Book 1 of Article 4 of the Criminal Code, as follows:

> The Indonesian statutory penal provisions are applicable to any person who outside Indonesia is guilty of:
>
> 1st, one of the crimes described in articles 104, 106, 107, 108, 110. 111 bis, under 1st, 127 and 131;
>
> 2nd-ly, any crime with respect to currency or banknote issued by the State or by the Bank, or with respect to stamps issued and marks used by the Indonesian Government;
>
> 3rd-ly, Forgery of debentures of debt certificates changeable to Indonesia, to a region or part of a region, including counterfoils, evidence of dividends and interests belonging to said documents, and certificates issued in lieu of said documents, or the use of such false or forged documents as if it genuine and unfalsified;
>
> 4th-ly, one of the crimes described in articles 438, 444–446, as far as they concern piracy, and those crimes described in article 447 relating to the surrender of a vessel to pirates, and article 479j relating to the unlawful exercises of control of aircraft, article 479i, m, n and o relating to crimes which jeopardize the safety of civil aviation.[85]

The points from Article 4 of the Criminal Code above that contains the principle of passive nationality are: (1) Articles 4 to 1 (committing one of the crimes mentioned in Articles 104, 106, 107 and 108, 110, 111 bis to 1, 127 and 131); (2) Article 4 to 2 (specifically on the phrase 'any crime with respect to … stamps issued and marks used by the Indonesian Government';[86] and (3) Article 4 number 3, on forgery of debentures of debt certificates changeable to Indonesia, to a region or part of a region, including counterfoils, evidence of dividends and interests belonging to said documents, and certificates issued in lieu of said documents, or the use of such false or forged documents as if it genuine and unfalsified.

In (1) above, the reasoning is that the crimes listed there are considered serious crimes because they involve the dignity of the State, the Head of State, the government, State security, and State finances or economy.[87] With regard to stamps and marks, it is logical for the Indonesian government to punish Indonesian citizens abroad who commit crimes, such as counterfeiting Indonesian stamps or marks, which may not be protected by the criminal law of the foreign country.[88]

If a case is related to an Indonesian citizen who commits a crime as stated in Article 4 of the Criminal Code, enforcement is more feasible, although it is still necessary to look at criminal law enforcement in the country where the crime

[85] Mutiara, *KUHP* (1951) 12–13.

[86] Article 4 point 2 regarding the phrase 'committing crimes against currency, state banknotes or banknotes'. This does not include the principle of passive nationality but is included in the principle of universality. See Andi Hamzah, *Asas-Asas Hukum Pidana*, Revised Edition (Jakarta, Rineka Cipta, 1994) 69–70.

[87] Poernomo, *Asas-asas Hukum Pidana* (1994) 64.

[88] Hamzah, *Asas-Asas Hukum Pidana* (1994) 70.

was committed. So, if an Indonesian citizen returns to Indonesia, or, based on mutual legal agreement between Indonesia and another country, can be brought back to Indonesia, then the Indonesian citizen can be tried in Indonesia and the Indonesian criminal law applies. However, what if the perpetrator is a citizen of the country where the crime was committed? This is a more difficult situation, because no country is willing to give up its citizens to be tried in another country. However, in the context of substantive criminal law, criminal provisions in Indonesian law may apply to such acts.

D. Articles Containing Mixed Principles

Some situations may involve multiple principles. For example, according to JM van Bemmelen, the crime of counterfeiting currency committed by anyone, anywhere, and involving any country's currency invokes the principle of protection (passive nationality) and the principle of universality. Likewise, the crime of piracy at sea is a mixture of protection and universality.[89]

The principles of active nationality and passive nationality are both adopted in Article 7 of the Criminal Code which reads 'The criminal law in Indonesian legislation applies to every civil servant outside Indonesia who commits one of the criminal acts mentioned in Chapter XXVIII of Book Two'. In fact, Chapter XXVIII of Book 2 in *WvS voor Ned-Indie* was entitled *Ambtsmisdrijven* ('Crime of Position'), covering Articles 413 to 437. According to van Bemmelen, the provisions concerning officials (*ambtenaar*) who commit crimes abroad (as regulated in the Article 7) contain the principle of active nationality. However, in this case, there is also the principle of protection (passive nationality), because it is in the interests of the country itself that government officials do not commit crimes abroad.[90] Hamzah agrees, stating that the provisions are mixed, covering both active and passive nationality. In addition, according to HB Vos, it can also be said that, according to its content, Article 7 of the Criminal Code 'expands' Article 5 of the Criminal Code (which contains the principle of active nationality) because of crimes committed by public officers.[91]

E. Principle of Universality

The principle of universality also implies protection, but its protection is broader than the principle of passive nationality, which protects national interests regardless

[89] JM van Bemmelen, *Hukum Pidana 1, Hukum Pidana Material Bagian Umum*, translated by Hasnan (Bandung, Binacipta, 1987) 86.
[90] Ibid 88.
[91] Poernomo, *Asas-asas Hukum Pidana* (1994) 64.

of the perpetrator's nationality and the place where the crime was committed.[92] The universality principle also does not pay attention to the nationality of the perpetrator. However, it instead centres on the protection of the interests of all countries, not just one country. The universality principle tries to protect the 'interests of the world'.[93] Through this universality principle, a country declares that its criminal law applies to a particular crime, wherever or by whomever it is committed.[94]

In English, the term 'universality' means 'the quality or state of being universal'.[95] This is more or less the same as the Indonesian language definition. Meanwhile, as a legal principle, in Dutch this is referred to as '*universaliteitsbeginsel*', or '*beginsel dat Nederland het recht heeft bepaalde, door buitenlanders in het buitenland gepleegde strafbare feiten, alhier te vervolgen*' ('the principle that the Netherlands has the right to prosecute certain crimes committed by foreigners abroad').[96]

This principle sees that criminal law is generally accepted, beyond the boundaries of the territory of the state and its citizens. What is protected here is the interest of the world. Types of crimes that are punishable by law according to this principle are very dangerous, not only from the perspective of Indonesia's interests. Universally, this type of crime is deemed necessary to be prevented and eradicated. Here, the power of the judiciary becomes absolute, because the jurisdiction of the court no longer depends on location, nationality, or domicile.[97] According to this principle, the criminal law of a country that adheres to universality can be applied to anyone who violates the legal interests of the whole world.[98]

This principle is regulated in Article 4 to 2 of the Criminal Code, especially in the phrase 'any crime with respect to currency or banknote issued by the State or by the Bank'. According to Utrecht, citing JE Jonkers, initially, the formulation in *WvS voor Ned-Indie* was 'currency, state banknotes, or banknotes valid in the Dutch East Indies'. However, the Netherlands became a party to the Geneva Convention in 1929, which seeks to eradicate counterfeiting or making counterfeit money. Based on the Netherlands' participation, the words 'lawfully applicable in the Dutch East Indies' were removed. Therefore, with this formulation, the Criminal Code provisions regarding counterfeiting money applies anywhere and to anyone. For example, a German citizen who counterfeits French money in England can be punished in Indonesia according to the Indonesian Criminal Code. Thus, it shows that Article 4 to 2 contains the principle of universality.[99]

[92] According to Moeljatno, the principle of protecting interests (*beschermingsprincipe or schutzprincipe*) can be distinguished between protecting national interests (passive nationality principle) and protecting international interests (universal principle). See Moeljatno, *Asas-Asas Hukum Pidana* (1993) 40.

[93] Utrecht, *Rangkaian Sari Kuliah Hukum Pidana* (1994) 247–48.

[94] Bemmelen, *Hukum Pidana 1* (1987) 88.

[95] dictionary.cambridge.org/dictionary/english/universality.

[96] www.juridischwoordenboek.nl/zoek/universaliteitsbeginsel.

[97] Hazewinkel-Suringa in Hamzah, *Asas-Asas Hukum Pidana* (1994) 73.

[98] Kartanegara, *Hukum Pidana* (nd) 162.

[99] Utrecht, *Rangkaian Sari Kuliah Hukum Pidana* (1993) 44.

The universality principle is also found in Article 4 point 4 of the Criminal Code, which states 'committing one of the crimes mentioned in articles 438, 444–446 concerning piracy and those mentioned in article 447 concerning surrendering ships to pirate powers'. A person who hijacks a foreign ship outside Indonesian territory, if caught by Indonesian law enforcement, can thus be tried in Indonesia under the Criminal Code.[100] To also cover aircraft, Article 4 point 4 has been amended to read 'one of the crimes referred to in Articles 438, 444–446 regarding pirates and those referred to in Article 447 concerning surrendering ships to pirates and Article 479 letter j concerning unlawful control of aircraft, Article 479 letters l, m, n, and o concerning crimes that threaten the safety of civil aviation'. This addition is based on Article 1 of Law No 4 of 1976.[101]

F. Exceptions Applicable in International Law

Briefly, Article 9 of the Criminal Code states that 'The applicability of Articles 2–5, 7 and 8 is limited by the exceptions, which are recognised in international law'. According to Satochid Kartanegara, those who are granted the right to immunity are diplomatic envoys or representatives of foreign countries residing in Indonesia. This group includes ambassadors, envoys, their security staff, and their families.[102] The criminal law of the country of origin applies to people belonging to this group, as well as any foreign head of state in Indonesian territory with the approval of the Indonesian government. However, if a foreign head of state enters the country by himself (incognito), these provisions do not apply to him.[103]

Diplomatic representatives are different from the consul representatives. The consul is not a diplomatic representative and the Criminal Code of the country in which the consul is stationed may apply. Consuls generally represent their country in trade and commerce matters. Meanwhile, the consul general may be exempted from the application of the criminal law legislation of the country in which the consul general is stationed if there is an agreement between the country where the consul general is assigned and the country of origin, if the consul general is considered to be a diplomatic representative. The right of extraterritoriality only applies to the person and not to the place of residence. This means that if a crime occurs at the Indonesian residence of an ambassador of a foreign country, Indonesian law enforcement officials have the right to conduct an inspection at that place. However, they must first ask permission from the ambassador of the foreign country concerned.[104]

[100] Moeljatno, *Asas-Asas Hukum Pidana* (1993) 44.

[101] Hamzah, *Asas-Asas Hukum Pidana* (1994) 73. See also Utrecht, *Rangkaian Sari Kuliah Hukum Pidana* (1994) 248.

[102] Regarding this family, there are differing views from experts: some consider that it is included in the exemption, but some do not agree. See Kartanegara, *Hukum Pidana* (nd) 176–77.

[103] Kartanegara, *Hukum Pidana* (nd) 176.

[104] Ibid 177.

In line with this, Derkje Hazewinkel-Suringa states that exterritoriality means that the law of a country does not apply to certain people from foreign countries and is intended for ambassadors of foreign countries, consuls (according to agreement), foreign heads of state, and their families. It is called the right of immunity because it provides immunity against the laws of foreign countries.[105] In addition, the territory of a foreign country that is within a country, such as foreign warships including their crews and foreign troops based in a country by agreement is also exterritorial.[106]

IV. Scope of Application of Criminal Law in the New Criminal Code

How is the principle of territoriality set in the new Criminal Code?[107] The Code does regulate the principle of territoriality. In the first book of the Code, the application of criminal law according to place is expressly stated in Paragraph 1 on Territorial Principles. Article 4 stipulates:

> Criminal provisions in the Law apply to Everyone who commits: a. Any criminal act within the territory of the Unitary State of the Republic of Indonesia; b. Any criminal act that takes place on Indonesian Ships or on Indonesian Aircraft; or c. Any criminal acts in the field of information technology or other Crimes whose consequences are experienced or occur in the territory of the Unitary State of the Republic of Indonesia or on Indonesian Ships and on Indonesian Aircraft.

Active nationality is also expressly addressed in the Criminal Code. Book 1, Article 8, Paragraph 4, states:

> (1) Criminal provisions in the Law apply to every Indonesian citizen that commits a crime outside the territory of the State Unitary Republic of Indonesia.
> (2) The provisions as referred to in paragraph (1) shall apply if the act is also a crime in the country where the crime is committed.
> (3) The provisions as referred to in paragraph (1) do not apply to Crimes that are only subject to category III fine.
> (4) Prosecution of the crime as referred to in paragraph (1) is carried out even though the suspect is an Indonesian citizen after the crime is committed as long as the act is a crime in the country where the crime was committed.
> (5) Indonesian citizens outside the territory of the Unitary State of the Republic of Indonesia who commit the crime as referred to in paragraph (1) cannot be sentenced to death if the crime according to the law of the country where the crime is committed, is not punishable by the death penalty.

[105] Poernomo, *Asas-asas Hukum Pidana* (1994) 67–68.
[106] Ibid.
[107] The New Criminal Code Bill was enacted on 2 January 2023.

The provisions in Article 8 of the New Code expressly state the principle of active nationality. These provisions are almost identical to the provisions in Article 5 of the prevailing Criminal Code, but are regulated in a simpler but wider scope. Article 5 of the current Criminal Code specifically determines the criminal acts in certain chapters and certain articles, while Article 8 of the New Criminal Code applies to all criminal acts (except for criminal acts that are only subject to a category III fine). Thus it is easier to implement the provisions, because there is no need to find out which articles use the principle of active nationality for crimes committed outside Indonesia. Another difference is that there is no longer a category as regulated in Article 5 paragraph (1) point 2 of the prevailing Criminal Code, where it is determined that the act must constitute a crime according to Indonesian criminal law. The new Article 8 of the New Criminal Code mentions only 'crimes' in general. This is because the Criminal Code does not differentiate between felonies and violations, and instead calls them all criminal acts.

How is the principle of passive nationality set in the new Criminal Code? In Book 1, Paragraph 2 expressly mentions the principles of protection and passive nationality. In Article 5, it is stated that the criminal provisions in the law apply to everyone outside the territory of the Republic of Indonesia who commits a crime against the interests of the Republic of Indonesia, relating to:

(a) state security or the process of state administration;
(b) the dignity of the President, Vice President, and/or Indonesian officials outside the country;
(c) currency, seals, state stamps, stamp duty, or securities issued by the Government of Indonesia, or credit cards issued by Indonesian banks;
(d) the Indonesian economy, trade, and banking;
(e) safety or security of shipping and aviation;
(f) safety or security of buildings, equipment, and national assets or the state of Indonesia;
(g) safety or security of electronic communication systems;
(h) Indonesia's national interest as stipulated in the Constitution; or
(i) Indonesian citizens based on international agreement with the country where the crime occurred.

How is the principle of universality used in the new Criminal Code? Paragraph 3 is entitled 'Universal Principle', and in Article 6, it is stated that the criminal provisions in the law apply to everyone outside the territory of the Republic of Indonesia who commits a crime according to international law which has been stipulated as a crime in the law. The Elucidation of Article 6 explains that this provision contains a universal principle that protects the legal interests of Indonesia and/or the legal interests of other countries. The basis for this arrangement is contained in international conventions that have been ratified by Indonesia, for example: international conventions on counterfeit money; international conventions on the high seas and the law of the sea which regulates the crime of sea piracy; international conventions concerning aviation crimes and crimes against aviation facilities or

infrastructure; or international conventions on traffic and circulation of narcotics and psychotropic substances.

The principle of universality is also found in Article 7. It states that the criminal provisions in the law apply to everyone who commits a crime outside the territory of the Republic of Indonesia whose prosecution is taken over by the Government of Indonesia on the basis of an international agreement which authorises the Government of Indonesia to carry out criminal prosecutions. The Elucidation of Article 7 states that this provision is intended to anticipate the development of an agreement between Indonesia and another country that allows citizens from other countries to be tried by Indonesia for committing certain criminal acts. In the new Criminal Code, the provision in Article 9 of the current Criminal Code remains. It now states: 'The application of the provisions as referred to in Articles 4 to 8 is limited by things that are excluded according to ratified international law'.

5

Criminal Offences

I. Definition

A criminal offence (called *tindak pidana* in Indonesian) is an act for which the perpetrator can be held liable according to criminal law.[1] WFC van Hattum[2] states that the Dutch term, *strafbaar feit*, refers to a *feit* (act) that causes someone (the perpetrator) to be punished, or, at least, for which the perpetrator could be punished.[3] According to Van Hattum, acts[4] and perpetrators are totally inseparable.[5] In considering whether punishment is to be imposed for an act, the key principle is that 'a person can only be convicted for a *feit* that he himself did'. According to Van Hattum, whether unlawful behaviour (*wederrechtelijk*) occurred can often only be determined after understanding the circumstances in which the perpetrator was placed. Thus, *feit* and its perpetrator cannot be separated.[6] Some experts, though, do not provide a definition of a crime; for example, Derkje Hazewinkel-Suringa explains the elements of a *strafbaar feit* and states that from these elements, one can conclude what the criminal act was.[7]

Experts differ when it comes to defining criminal offences. Experts who take a monistic view believe that crime includes actions as well as culpability/responsibility. On the other hand, experts with a dualistic view separate the criminal behaviour (the criminal act itself, known as *actus reus*) and the culpability/responsibility (*mens rea*, the 'criminal intent' or malicious mental attitude). The dualistic view exists in common law countries.[8] The same idea has been expressed by Loebby Loqman, who states that the separation of criminal acts and criminal

[1] Wirjono Prodjodikoro, *Asas-asas Hukum Pidana di Indonesia* (Bandung, Refika Aditama, 2003) 59.

[2] Dutch criminal law expert who was a professor and chairman of the *Rechsthogeschool* (law school), a law school that was established during the Dutch colonial period in Indonesia (1924–1942) which later became the Faculteit de *Rechgelerheid en Sociale Wetenschappen* (Faculty of Law and Social Sciences) Nood Universiteit van Indonesie (1946). This school later became the Faculty of Law, University of Indonesia (law.ui.ac.id/profil/sejarah-dan-perkembangan).

[3] E Utrecht, *Rangkaian Sari Kuliah Hukum Pidana I* (Surabaya, Pustaka Tinta Mas, 1994) 254.

[4] Utrecht uses the term 'event'. See Utrecht, *Rangkaian Sari Kuliah Hukum Pidana I* (1994) 254.

[5] *de feit en persoon in het strafrecht onafscheidnenlijk zijn.*

[6] Utrecht, *Rangkaian Sari Kuliah Hukum Pidana I* (1994) 254.

[7] Ibid 253.

[8] See Sudarto, *Hukum Pidana I*, Revised Edn (Semarang, Sudarto Foundation, 2013) 73.

responsibility is not recognised in the continental European legal system, but does occur in countries which use the Anglo-Saxon criminal law concept.[9]

However, others disagree. The opinion that the common law system separates criminal offences and criminal responsibility is not supported by Chairul Huda. According to Huda, the system does make a distinction between offences and liability, but in fact 'unifies' *actus reus* and *mens rea* into one concept: crime.[10] Thus, in the common law system, the issue of criminal acts and criminal responsibility is always associated with the Latin maxim '*actus non facit, nisi mens sit rea*' ('an act does not render a man guilty of a crime unless his mind is equally guilty'). It is understood that criminal offence consists of *actus reus* and *mens rea*. According to LB Curzon, as quoted by Chairul Huda, 'the maxim draws attention to two essential elements of a crime: the physical element (actus reus) and the mental element (mens rea)'.[11]

Thus, in common law systems, an act is not a crime if it is not accompanied by malicious thoughts of the perpetrator. It is not a crime if there is no *mens rea*.[12] However, this construction is not accepted by all parties, even in common law systems, as there are several statutory offences (criminal offence based on legislation) that are formulated without any mental element. Therefore, *mens rea* is not always an absolute element of a crime.[13]

Experts from the monistic view put forward the definition of a crime as follows. Dutch legal expert D Simons defines it as: '*Strafbaar feit is een strafbaar gestelde onrechmatige (wederrechtelijk), metschuld in verband staande handeling van een toerekeningsvatbaar person*' ('An action that is punishable by law, which is against the law related to fault and is carried out by people who are capable of being responsible').[14] Another Dutch criminal law expert, GA Van Hamel, argues that *strafbaar feit* is a human behaviour that is formulated in statutes, is unlawful, deserves to be punished, and is committed with fault.[15] There are also German jurists who hold the same view, such as E Mezger, who states that a criminal offence is the entire prerequisite for the imposition of punishment. Thus, the elements of a criminal offence are: acts, unlawful nature, accountability (a perpetrator can be identified), and the threat of punishment.[16] Another German legal expert, J Bauman, states that a criminal offence is an act that fulfills the

[9] Loebby Loqman in Chairul Huda, *Dari 'Tiada Pidana Tanpa Kesalahan' Menuju Kepada Tiada Pertanggungjawaban Pidana Tanpa Kesalahan – Tinjauan Kritis Terhadap Teori Pemisahan Tindak Pidana dan Pertanggungjawaban Pidana*, 6th edn (Jakarta, Kencana, 2015) 9.

[10] Huda, *Dari 'Tiada Pidana Tanpa Kesalahan'* (2015) 9.

[11] Ibid 23.

[12] Ibid.

[13] Ibid.

[14] Simons as quoted by AZ Abidin and Andi Hamzah, *Pengantar Dalam Hukum Pidana Indonesia* (Jakarta, Yarsif Watampone, 2010) 117. So here there is an objective element, namely an act and against the law, and there is a subjective element, namely a fault and a person who can take responsibility. Compare with the explanation from Sudarto, in Sudarto, *Hukum Pidana I* (2013) 68.

[15] Abidin and Hamzah, *Pengantar Dalam Hukum Pidana Indonesia* (2010) 117.

[16] Mezger in Sudarto, *Hukum Pidana I* (2013) 69.

formulation of an offence, is unlawful, and is committed with fault.[17] Meanwhile, an Indonesian legal expert, R Soesilo, argues that a criminal offence is an act that violates or is contrary to the law and is carried out by fault by people who can be accounted for.[18]

In contrast to these experts, the Dutch legal expert HB Vos states that *strafbaar feit* is human behaviour (*menselijke gedraging*) which is punishable by legislation; therefore, in his view, a criminal act is a human behaviour that is generally prohibited and threatened with punishment.[19] This human behaviour is not separated from the individual who perpetrates the behaviour. In other words, human behaviour that violates the law is not always a crime; only behaviour that is prohibited and threatened with punishment constitutes a criminal offence.[20]

Moeljatno is an Indonesian legal expert who clearly adheres to a dualistic view in terms of defining criminal acts. Moeljatno consistently uses the term 'criminal act', not 'criminal offence', and states that a criminal act is an act that is prohibited by a legal rule, and this prohibition is accompanied by threats (sanctions) in the form of certain punishment for anyone who violates the relevant prohibition. According to Moeljatno, it can also be said that criminal acts are those that are prohibited by a legal rule and are punishable by sanctions, with the key element being that the prohibition is aimed at an act (ie a situation or event caused by the behaviour of a person), while the threat of sanctions is directed at the person who causes the incident to happen.[21]

The Dutch jurist WPJ Pompe offers two views. First, theoretically, *strafbaar feit* is a norm of violation of rules (*normovertreding*),[22] deemed as such because of the offender's fault,[23] and which must be punished (*strafbaar*). Here it appears that, theoretically, this falls into the monistic view. Meanwhile, Pompe also states that according to positive law, *strafbaar feit* is merely a *feit* that is punishable by criminal law in the provisions of the law.[24] German legal expert Herman Kantorowicz in his 1933 book *Tat und Schuld* states that a criminal offence is an act that fulfills the formulation of the law and which is not justified, and, if it is done with a fault, then there is no reason to eliminate the punishment of the person who did it.[25] This dualistic teaching removes the element of fault from the action and incorporates it into the aspect of the offender.[26]

[17] Bauman in Sudarto, *Hukum Pidana I* (2013) 69–70.
[18] R Soesilo, *Pokok-Pokok Hukum Pidana Peraturan Umum dan Delik-Delik Khusus* (Bogor, Polietia, 1984) 26.
[19] Vos in Utrecht, *Rangkaian Sari Kuliah Hukum Pidana I* (1994) 251–52.
[20] Utrecht, *Rangkaian Sari Kuliah Hukum Pidana I* (1994) 252.
[21] Moeljatno, *Asas-Asas Hukum Pidana* (Jakarta, Rineka Cipta, 1993) 54.
[22] An act that is contrary to (against) the law (*onrechtmatig* or *wederrechtelijk*). See Utrecht, *Rangkaian Sari Kuliah Hukum Pidana I* (1994) 252.
[23] *Aan schuld van de overtreder te wijten*. See Utrecht, *Rangkaian Sari Kuliah Hukum Pidana I* (1994) 252.
[24] Sudarto, *Hukum Pidana I* (2013) 71.
[25] Ibid 73–74.
[26] Ibid 74.

According to Sudarto, there is no need to separate the two types of offence formulation (monistic and dualistic), because both are, in fact, the same. However, it remains important for the public prosecutor because the core part of the offence, the *actus reus*, must be included in the indictment and must be proven. If it is not proven, then the perpetrator cannot be found guilty of criminal charges. While criminal liability (the existence of fault) does not need to be indicted and does not need to be proven by the public prosecutor, if the defendant or legal counsel can prove that there is no fault, then the perpetrator is acquitted from all criminal charges.[27]

Sudarto also argues that there are no principal differences in determining the existence of a crime. However, if a person adheres to one theoretical position, they should hold that position consistently to avoid confusion. So, when using the term 'criminal offence', it must be clearly understood what is meant; that is, according to a monistic or dualistic view. For people who take a monistic view, if someone commits a crime this is sufficient for them to be punished, while for dualistic view holders, this is not at all sufficient because the act must also be accompanied by the conditions establishing the criminal responsibility of the perpetrator.[28]

In my opinion, a criminal offence is an act or series of actions, or failure to commit an act, committed by an individual or a corporation, which is against the law and which can be carried out under certain circumstances or accompanied by certain results, and the act or series of actions, or failure to commit the act, is sanctioned with punishment and/or actions according to laws and regulations.

This understanding includes a broader subject, covering not only humans but also corporations. A criminal offence is always against the law. I state 'an act or a series of actions' here considering that a crime can be carried out through one action or through a series of actions. To emphasise that an offence can consist of not only an act (active) but also negligence (*nalaten*/omission), I also state that a criminal offence can also be committed by the failure to commit an act. Additionally, sometimes what is formulated in the law is not the action itself (formal offence), but the result of an action (substantive offence), therefore that result is also listed here. To distinguish this from violations in other legal fields, I emphasise that the act or series of actions is threatened with punishment and/or action according to laws and regulations.

This definition is in line with the tendency of Indonesia's new Criminal Code Bill to hold that every criminal offence is no longer reliant on fault (especially *opzet*/intention), but rather that every criminal act is considered to be have been conducted intentionally. In other words, only acts that are carried out intentionally are prohibited in the Criminal Code Bill, therefore there is no need to include this element in every criminal offence. Whether the person/corporation that commits

[27] Abidin and Hamzah, *Pengantar Dalam Hukum Pidana Indonesia* (2010) 120.
[28] Sudarto, *Hukum Pidana I* (2013) 75.

the crime can be punished is a matter of criminal responsibility. Therefore, criminal offences are separated from criminal responsibility. The exception to this is certain punishable criminal offences which are committed as the result of negligence or omission, for which the element of negligence/omission must be clearly stated in the formulation of the crime.

II. Types of Criminal Offence

In the current Indonesian Criminal Code, criminal offences can be divided into two types: felony (regulated in Book 2 of the Criminal Code) and violation (Book 3). Special criminal laws outside the Criminal Code, as well as non-criminal laws containing criminal provisions, also sometimes contain criminal offences (both felonies and violations). Outside the Criminal Code, most laws specify which articles constitute a felony and which constitute a violation. However, there are also some laws that do not clearly define the distinction between felony and violation, raising problems in law enforcement because this distinction has implications for the implementation of criminal law. This is discussed particularly on the principle of an active nationality (Article 5 of the Criminal Code). To overcome this issue, in the new Criminal Code Bill, the distinction between felony and violation has been abolished; they have been combined and are referred to as 'criminal offences'. Thus, although in the current Code there are three books, the new Criminal Code Bill contains only Book 1 on General Provisions and Book 2 on Criminal Offences.

A. Types of Criminal Offence

In criminal legal studies, experts often divide criminal offences into several types, such as felony and violation. Some of the most important types of criminal offence in Indonesia are discussed below.[29]

i. Misdrijven *and* Overtredingan *(Felony and Violation Offences)*

According to the *Memorie van Toelichting* (MvT) or Explanatory Memorandum of the Dutch Criminal Code, a felony offence is an offence that, prior to the enactment of the law that considers that act as a form of misconduct, was already unjust,

[29] For further details on the types or divisions of these offences, see Eddy OS Hiariej, *Prinsip-Prinsip Hukum Pidana*, Revised Edn (Yogyakarta, Cahaya Atma Pustaka, 2016) 134–50; Abidin and Hamzah, *Pengantar Dalam Hukum Pidana Indonesia* (2010) 126–35; Satochid Kartanegara, *Hukum Pidana, Kumpulan Kuliah Prof Satochid Kartanegara* (Jakarta, Balai Lektur Mahasiswa, nd) 91–130; Moeljatno, *Asas-Asas Hukum Pidana* (1993) 71–77; and PAF Lamintang and Fransiscus Theojunior Lamintang, *Dasar-Dasar Hukum Pidana di Indonesia* (Jakarta, Sinar Grafika, 2019) 207–25.

and should be prohibited and threatened with punishment, even though the act had not in fact been prohibited nor threatened with punishment by law (ie *recht-delicten*). So, if even though the act is not prohibited by law, the act deserves to be punished.[30] According to Hazewinkel-Suringa, in Indonesia's current Criminal Code there is no qualitative difference, only a quantitative difference: (a) the punishment for a felony is generally more severe than for violations, such as capital punishment, imprisonment, short-term imprisonment, undisclosed penitentiary, and/or fines; (b) attempting to commit a felony can be punished (Article 53 of the Criminal Code); (c) assisting a felony can be punished (Article 56 of the Criminal Code); (d) the statute of limitation for a felony is longer (Article 78 of the Criminal Code); (e) a complaint-based offence is a felony offence; (f) the provisions on combined criminal charges for a different felony are different from violations (aggravation, not pure accumulation); and (g) the application of criminal law outside Indonesia (principle of active nationality), as in Article 5 of the Criminal Code, which states that if an Indonesian citizen commits a felony in another country where it is a criminal offence, then Indonesian law may apply.[31] Examples of these felony offences are Article 338 of the Criminal Code (homicide), Article 362 of the Criminal Code (theft), Article 365 of the Criminal Code (robbery with violence), and Article 351 of the Criminal Code (battery).

Meanwhile, according to the MvT, for a violation offence, before there was a law prohibiting the act, it was not considered to involve injustice or as misconduct. Considering the act a form of misconduct only emerged after the law came into existence. The act is considered an offence if it has been prohibited by law (ie *wet delicten*).[32] Differences to felony offences are as follows: (a) the punishment for a violation is generally lighter than a felony (only short-term imprisonment or a fine); (b) an attempted violation cannot be prosecuted (Article 54 of the Criminal Code); (c) assisting a violation cannot be prosecuted (Article 60 of the Criminal Code); (d) the statute of limitation for a violation is shorter than the statute of limitation for a felony (Article 78 of the Criminal Code); (e) there are no complaint-based offences that are considered violations; (f) rules regarding combined criminal charges are different from combinations of a felony (pure cumulation is applicable);[33] and (g) in relation to the application of criminal law outside Indonesia (active nationality principle), Article 5 of the Criminal Code states if an Indonesian citizen commits a violation in another country,

[30] See full explanation in Kartanegara, *Hukum Pidana Kumpulan Kuliah* (nd) 94–117. My explanation for *delicten recht* in everyday language is 'it has been bad from the beginning'. Serious crimes such as theft, murder, and abuse have since the 'beginning' of time been considered evil, even though Articles 362, 338, and 351 of the Criminal Code did not yet exist. Sometimes this is called *mala per se* or *mala in se*, with 'mala' meaning 'evil'. See Hiariej, *Prinsip-Prinsip Hukum Pidana* (2016) 134–36.

[31] See the explanation of the application of criminal law (principle of active nationality etc) in ch 4.

[32] This is sometimes called *mala prohibita*. The implication is that an individual is bad because the act is prohibited by law. Hiariej, *Prinsip-Prinsip Hukum Pidana* (2016) 34–136.

[33] See full explanation in Kartanegara, *Hukum Pidana Kumpulan Kuliah* (nd) 94–117.

then Indonesian law cannot apply.[34] Examples of violations are Article 503 of the Criminal Code (violations of public order) and Article 504 of the Criminal Code (soliciting in public).

ii. Opzettelijk Delicten / Doluse Delicten *and* Culpose Delicten *(Intentional Offences and Negligence Offences)*

An intentional offence is a crime committed intentionally or a crime that contains an element of *opzet* (intention). For example, phrases such as 'intention', 'with intent', 'deliberately', or 'what he knows' are involved. For example, Article 338 of the Criminal Code (homicide), Article 310 of the Criminal Code (defamation), Article 368 of the Criminal Code (extortion), Article 354 of the Criminal Code (with intent to severely harm another person), Article 187 of the Criminal Code (arson), and Article 232 (2) of the Criminal Code (deliberately damaging the seal guarding an article which has been confiscated).

A negligence offence is a crime committed through negligence or an offence that contains elements of *culpa* (omission/negligence). For example, phrases such as 'because of negligence', 'because of his mistake', 'because of omission', 'what he should have known', and 'should have known' are involved. For example, Article 205 of the Criminal Code (negligence regarding dangerous goods), Article 359 of the Criminal Code (negligence leads to death), Article 189 of the Criminal Code (due to negligence causing a fire), and Article 231 (4) of the Criminal Code (negligence causing the release of goods in confiscation).

Aside from *dolus* (intentional) offences and *culpa* (negligence) offences, there are also *proparte dolus proparte culpa* (intentional and negligence offences). *Proparte dolus proparte culpa* are criminal offences which in their formulation includes elements of intent as well as elements of negligence. For example, Article 287 of the Criminal Code ('it is known or should be presumed that he is not yet 15 years old'), and Article 480 of the Criminal Code (receipt of stolen property).

iii. Formeel Delict *and* Materieel Delict *(Formal Offences and Substantive Offences)*

Formal offences are criminal offences in which the form of action (*handeling*) is formulated in the law, not the results. These criminal offences are said to be completed with the act (eg taking something) and do not wait for the results. This crime is also called a crime with a formal formulation.[35] For example,

[34] See the explanation of the application of criminal law (principle of active nationality etc) in ch 4.
[35] *Delict met formele omschrijving.*

Article 263 of the Criminal Code (document forgery), Article 362 of the Criminal Code (theft), and Article 242 of the Criminal Code (perjury).

Substantive offences are offences in which the law formulates the result (*gevolg*), not the act. The offence completes with the occurrence of results (eg loss of life, inflicting damage). This criminal offence is also called a crime with a substantive formulation.[36] Examples are Article 338 of the Criminal Code (homicide), Article 368 of the Criminal Code (extortion), and Article 187 of the Criminal Code (deliberately committing arson, or causing an explosion or a flood).

iv. Delicta Commissiones / Commisie Delicten *and* Delicta Omissiones / Ommisie Delicten *(Commission Offences and Omission Offences)*

A commission offence is a criminal offence that violates a prohibition with an active act, or violates an act that is prohibited by law. This crime can be formulated formally (as a formal offence), such as theft, or formulated substantially (as a substantive offence), such as homicide. Examples include Article 338 of the Criminal Code (homicide), Article 362 of the Criminal Code (theft), Article 368 of the Criminal Code (extortion), and Article 378 of the Criminal Code (fraud).

An omission offence (pure) is a criminal offence in which a person commits a criminal act by passive action or violates an order by not acting. Examples include Article 164 of the Criminal Code (knowing there is a conspiracy but not reporting it to the official), and Article 224 of the Criminal Code (a person is summoned as a witness, expert, or interpreter but does not present themselves).

In addition, there is also what is called the *commissionis per omissionem commissa*[37] (omission offences [impure]). This is where a person commits an offence through a passive action or by violating a prohibition by not acting. The prohibition here, for example, is causing death, such as in Article 194 of the Criminal Code (intentionally causing a public traffic hazard on trains), by, for example, by not ringing the warning bell or closing the railroad crossing gate. Another example is Article 195 of the Criminal Code, which is similar to Article 194 but with negligence instead of intent. It is also possible that this crime has occurred in the case of homicide (Article 338 of the Criminal Code) which was carried out by deliberately letting a child die, for example by not breastfeeding a child for long enough. In other words, Article 338 of the Criminal Code can be carried out with active actions (commission offences), but it can also be passive actions (impure omission offences).

[36] *Delict met materieele omschrijving.*

[37] This is called the *Oneiggenlijk Commissie Delicten.*

v. Gewone Delict *and* Klacht Delict *(Ordinary/Report-based Offences and Complaint-based Offences)*

An ordinary offence is a criminal offence where the prosecution does not require a complaint to be made. It is sufficient to have a report from someone who saw or knows about the crime, and does not require a complaint from a victim or other involved person. For example, Article 285 of the Criminal Code (rape) and Article 340 of the Criminal Code (premeditated murder). A report is a notification submitted by a person, either independently or due to an obligation under the law, to an authorised official about a criminal event that has occurred or is occurring or it is suspected will occur (Article 1 point 24 of the Criminal Procedure Code).

Complaint-based offences are criminal offences where the prosecution requires a complaint to be made. There must be a complaint from the victim or another certain person stipulated by the law. Examples of this are Article 310 of the Criminal Code (defamation) and Article 284 of the Criminal Code (adultery). Complaints for this absolute complaint offence must be addressed to all offenders, and cannot be divided. Complaints are different to reports. A complaint is a notification accompanied by a request by an interested party to an authorised official to take legal action against a person who has committed a criminal offence that harms the victim (Article 1 point 25 of the Criminal Procedure Code).

There is also what is called a relative complaint-based offence. This is a criminal offence which is essentially an ordinary offence (not a complaint offence), but because there is a certain relationship between the offender and the victim, the type changes to a complaint offence. One example of this is Article 367 paragraph (2) of the Criminal Code (theft in the family). Complaints for this relative complaint offence do not have to be addressed to all offenders, and can be divided. For example, there are two burglars at the home of A. One perpetrator is A's child (B) and the other is B's friend (C). A is permitted to complain to the police about C without also reporting B.

vi. Eenvoudige Delicten, Gequalificeerde Delicten, *and* Geprevilegeerde Delicten *(Basic/Simple Offences, Qualified Offences, and Privileged Offences)*

A simple offence is a criminal offence that in its formulation includes the main elements that determine the punishment or, in short, the offence in the basic form. For example, Article 362 of the Criminal Code (theft), whose elements are: (1) whoever; (2) takes; (3) goods which are wholly or partly owned by another person; (4) with an intent; (5) to possess unlawfully. A qualified offence is a criminal offence that has the same elements as the main offence plus an element that aggravates the sentence or an offence. Examples are Article 363 of the Criminal Code (qualified theft), Article 365 paragraph (4) of the Criminal Code (theft with violence resulting in serious injury), and Article 351 paragraph (2) of the Criminal Code (battery resulting in serious injury). Meanwhile, a privileged offence is a criminal offence that has the same elements as the main offence plus elements that mitigate the crime. Examples are Article 308 of the Criminal Code (a fearful mother who leaves her child to release the child from her care) and Article 364 of the Criminal Code (petty theft).

B. General

Not all of the types of criminal offences above are often used in practice. In the law-making process, the topics that are most frequently discussed relate to the division of criminal offences into felony offences, *dolus-culpa* offences, ordinary complaint-based offences, omissions-commissions crimes, and formal-substantive offences. Unfortunately, during discussions in the House of Representatives or Regional House of Representatives, sometimes lawmakers do not realise the importance of the division of these types of criminal offences, except for the distinction between a felony and a violation. This is despite the fact that the division of other types of criminal offences is also important, such as the difference between formal and substantive offences, in order to determine when a criminal offence has been committed and when it has not.

In some situations, a criminal offence may fall into more than one type of criminal offence. For example, homicide by means of shooting the victim is included in a variety of forms: as a felony offence in Book 2 of the Criminal Code regulating felonies; as a commission offence because the act violates a prohibition (ie eliminating the life of another person) with an active act; as a substantive offence because Article 338/340 of the Criminal Code which regulates the criminal offence is formulated in a substantive manner (ie the result is the main element of the offence; as a simple offence because it contains the basic elements of a criminal offence (not a qualified offence); as a *dolus* offence because Article 338/340 of the Criminal Code contains elements of intention (not negligence); as a communal offence because it can be committed by anyone; not a *propia* offence (offence committed by certain categories of perpetrator), and so on.

The types of criminal offences detailed above are the divisions according to criminal legal studies doctrines. Meanwhile, according to the current Criminal Code, the distribution is established according to the legal interests that are jeopardised by a criminal offence or according to the characteristics of the criminal offence. Thus, the division can be seen in the chapter titles of Books 2 and 3 of the Criminal Code. For example, in Book 2 of the Criminal Code, there are: felony against state security (Chapter I); felony against the dignity of the president and vice president (Chapter II); felony against friendly countries and against heads of friendly countries and their representatives (Chapter III); felony against the carrying out of state obligations and rights (Chapter IV); felony against public order (Chapter V); felony against endangering public safety for people or goods

(Chapter VII); felony against public authorities (Chapter VIII); felony against forgery of documents (Chapter XII); felony against morality (Chapter XIV); felony against life (Chapter XIX); felony of theft (Chapter XXII); and felony by a public officer (Chapter XXVIII).

III. Elements of a Criminal Offence

Every criminal offence contained in the current Criminal Code can generally be described as involving two kinds of elements: objective elements and subjective elements. Objective elements are elements that exist outside of human beings, in the form of action / conduct / behaviour, certain results, or the circumstances (*omstandigheid*) in which the action or conduct is carried out.[38] Examples of objective elements are elements of the perpetrator's actions (eg taking goods, forging letters, using fake documents, driving vehicles, polluting the environment); results (eg loss of life, damage to an object, burning of a house); unlawful elements of an act (eg taking goods 'unlawfully' (*wederrechtelijkheid*), doing something 'without rights'); as well as elements of circumstances attached to the act (eg theft committed 'in a house'; theft 'at night'; theft 'at a time of disaster'; insults 'to a civil servant on duty').

It should be explained that the unlawful element (*wederrechtelijkheid*) must always be considered a requirement in every formulation of a criminal offence, even though the element is not always written down or is not always a description of a criminal offence.[39] This is also contained in Article 12 paragraphs (2) and (3) of the Criminal Code Bill, which states:

> Article 12
>
> (1) Criminal Offences are acts that are punishable by criminal sanctions and/or actions by laws and regulations.
> (2) To be declared a Criminal Offence, an act that is subject to criminal sanctions and/or action by laws and regulations *must be against the law* or contrary to the law that exists in society.
> (3) Every Criminal Offence is *always against the law* unless there is a justification.[40] [emphasis added]

On the other hand, a subjective element is an element that is attached to the offender or related to the offender, including the circumstances of the offender. For example, elements in the form of the capacity of the offender (eg 'a civil servant', 'a mother', 'a captain'); the element 'deliberately' (*dolus* element); the element

[38] Kartanegara, *Hukum Pidana Kumpulan Kuliah* (nd) 75.
[39] See also Lamintang and Lamintang, *Dasar-Dasar Hukum Pidana di Indonesia* (2019) 192.
[40] Ministry of Law and Human Rights of the Republic of Indonesia, Draft Criminal Code, 4 July 2022 manuscript.

'with intent' (*voornemen*); the element 'because of negligence' (*culpa* element); and the elements 'with premeditation' or 'fear of being known to give birth to a child', among others.

It is important to discuss the perpetrator of a criminal offence (ie the one who commits a criminal offence) according to Indonesian criminal law. The problem of the perpetrator of a criminal offence is increasingly important today in criminal law in Indonesia because social, legal, economic, and political developments have led to many criminal offences that can be committed by other entities, not just a natural person.

Corporations are one example. Corporations have not yet been legally defined as the subject (offender) of a criminal offence according to the Criminal Code. This is because in the Netherlands at the time the Code was formulated in the the late 1800s, the drafters accepted the criminal law principle that '*societas delinquere non potest*', meaning that legal entities / associations cannot commit criminal offences.[41] For a long time, according to the Dutch Criminal Code (which, as discussed in chapter one, was later adopted as the Indonesian Criminal Code) criminal offences could only be committed by humans.

That corporations were not considered as perpetrators, and that only people were, can be concluded from the following points:

(1) The formulation/description of a criminal offence which always determines the subject with terms such as 'whoever' (*hij die*), 'Indonesian citizen', 'captain', 'public officer', 'a mother', 'people who are of sufficient age', 'doctors' and so on, which are contained in the articles of criminal offences in Book 2 and Book 3 of the Criminal Code, in addition to the general provisions in Book 1 of the Criminal Code, especially in Article 2 to 9, which also mentions the term 'everyone'.[42] All these terms refer to humans, not corporations or other entities.

(2) Provisions regarding criminal responsibility, as regulated mainly in Articles 44, 45, and 49 of the Criminal Code, among other things require a certain 'mental state' (*verstandelijke vermogen atau geesteljke vermogens*/mental capacity) on the part of the offender.[43]

(3) In criminal law, there is an important principle regarding criminal responsibility which in Dutch is known as '*geen straft zonder schuld*', in German as '*keine straf ohne schuld*', and in Latin as '*nulla poena sine culpa*'. All refer to the same thing: that there is no crime without fault. Only humans as natural persons can have that fault, whether it is a fault as an element of a criminal

[41] According to Kanter and Sianturi, this is a teaching from Von Savigny and Feurbach. See EY Kanter and SR Sianturi, *Asas-Asas Hukum Pidana di Indonesia dan Penerapannya* (Jakarta, Storia Grafika, 2018) 218.

[42] See Kanter and Sianturi, *Asas-Asas Hukum Pidana di Indonesia dan Penerapannya* (2018) 218. See also Sutan Remy Sjahdeini, *Ajaran Pemidanaan: Tindak Pidana Korporasi & Seluk-Beluknya* (Jakarta, Kencana, 2017) 19–20.

[43] Kanter and Sianturi, *Asas-Asas Hukum Pidana di Indonesia dan Penerapannya* (2018) 218.

offence (*opzet*/intentionally or *culpa*/negligence) or a fault in the sense of 'to be held accountable' or 'the action can be blamed on him'. In Latin there is an adage: '*actus non facit reum, nisi mens sit rea*' ('an act does not make a person guilty unless the mind is guilty'). This, of course, also refers only to humans, who can have a guilty mind.

(4) Provisions regarding criminal offences regulated in Article 10 of the Criminal Code include capital punishment, imprisonment, light imprisonment, and undisclosed penitentiary. All refer to forms of punishment that can only be imposed on humans.

In addition, Article 59 of the Criminal Code states:

> In cases whereby reason of misdemeanour punishment is imposed upon directors, members of a board of management, or commissioners, no punishment shall be pronounced against the director or commissioner who evidently does not take any part in the commission of the misdemeanour.

According to Article 59 of the Criminal Code, if the manager of a corporation commits a crime in the context of representing the corporation, or the crime is carried out for and on behalf of the corporation led by that manager, then criminal responsibility is imposed only on the manager who commits the criminal offence. Corporations are not burdened with criminal responsibility.[44]

From the description above, it is clear that humans are the perpetrators of criminal offences. This is still adhered to in the Indonesian Criminal Code to this day, as it has not been revised since ratification. However, there has been rapid development in special criminal laws outside the Criminal Code and in non-criminal (administrative) legislation which contains criminal provisions that already recognise that there may be other perpetrators / offenders besides humans, particularly corporations. Likewise, in the Criminal Code Bill, which will replace the current Code when finalised and ratified, corporations are included as the possible perpetrator of a criminal offence.

The development of the subject of criminal offence outside the Criminal Code was initially related to various criminal offences such as economic crimes (in the narrow sense, regulated in Emergency Law No 7 of 1955),[45] crimes relating to customs (eg smuggling), taxation, banking, and capital markets, then developed more recently into emerging fields of concern, such as corruption, terrorism, and others.

Article 15 of Emergency Law No 7 of 1955 states, among other points, that if an economic crime is committed by or on behalf of a legal entity, an association of people, or a foundation, then the offender can face criminal charges and penalties, as well as disciplinary actions, can be imposed on the legal entity, company,

[44] Sjahdeini, *Ajaran Pemidanaan* (2017) 19.

[45] Emergency Law Number 7 of 1955 concerning Investigation, Prosecution and Trial of Economic Crimes. State Gazette 1950 Number 27, Supplement to State Gazette Number 801.

association, or foundation, either against those who gave the order to commit the economic crime, or those who acted as leaders in the act or negligence, or against both.

More recently, laws have clearly made it possible that corporations are included among those who may commit criminal offences. This is seen in the usage of terms such as 'whoever' or 'everyone' in several laws. For example, Article 1 point 3 of Law No 31 of 1999 concerning the Eradication of Corruption Crimes[46] as amended by Law No 20 of 2001, states that 'anyone' includes individuals and corporations. In Article 1 number 1, a corporation is defined as 'an organized collection of people and/or assets, whether they are legal entities or not'. In the general elucidation of the law, it is stated that: 'The new developments regulated in this law are corporations as the perpetrator of the crime of corruption which can be subject to sanctions. This is not regulated in Law No. 3 of 1971'. Several other laws also regulate corporations in a similar matter, for example Law No 5 of 1997 concerning Psychotropics and Law No 22 of 1997 concerning Narcotics.

Based on the elaboration above, the criminal offences in Indonesia today may be committed by humans (*naturlijke personen*) and corporations. For criminal offences regulated in the Criminal Code, only humans are included because the Criminal Code does not recognise corporations as the subject of a criminal offence, while for some special criminal laws and non-criminal laws that contain criminal provisions, corporations are the subject of criminal offences. In the future, when the Criminal Code Bill is ratified, the Criminal Code will also recognise corporations as the subject of criminal offences.

When formulating a criminal offence, there are two basic elements that must be considered: (1) the objective part, which is the act itself (referred to in Dutch as *een doen* [active action] or *een nalaten/een niet doen* [inaction / passive action]) and / or the results (it depends on what is contained in the article whether it covers the act or the results). Carrying out the act or causing the results is either contrary to positive law or is prohibited in the laws and regulations, making it an unlawful act; and (2) the subjective part, which relates to the element of fault in the offence.[47]

According to LJ Van Apeldoorn, the elements of a criminal offence consist of an objective element in the form of behaviour that is contrary to the law (*onrechmatig/wederrechtelijk*) and a subjective element in the form of an offender (*dader*) who is able to be responsible or can be held liable (*toerekeningsvatbaarheid*) for the behaviour that is contrary to the law.[48]

HB Vos provides us with another explanation about the elements of a criminal offence. Vos states that in a *strafbaar feit* it is possible to have several elements: (1) actions or behaviour of people, in terms of action (*een doen*) or inaction (*een nalaten*); (2) the results of the action in the offence is completed; (3) fault,

[46] State Gazette of 1999 Number 140, Supplement to State Gazette Number 3874.
[47] See also Bambang Poernomo, *Asas-Asas Hukum Pidana* (Jakarta, Ghalia Indonesia, 1992) 103.
[48] Van Apeldorn in Poernomo, *Asas-Asas Hukum Pidana* (1992) 103.

which is manifested by intention (*opzet*) or negligence (*culpa*); (4) against the law (*wederrechtelijkheid*); and (5) other elements according to the formulation/description of a criminal offence in the law. These elements are distinguished from an objective point of view (eg 'in public') and a subjective aspect (eg 'by premeditation').[49]

Meanwhile, according to Hazewinkel-Suringa, the elements of *strafbaar feit* are (1) people's behaviour (either in the form of action or inaction); (2) the result, which is determined in the formulation of a criminal offence (especially in substantive offences, in which what is formulated is the result of an act); (3) mental elements such as *oogmerk*/with intent, *opzet*/deliberately, *nalatigheid*/by negligence; (4) objective elements that accompany the circumstances of a criminal act such as 'in public'; (5) additional conditions for the conviction of an act (*bijkomende voorwaarde van strafbaarheid*); and (6) being against the law (*wederrechtelijkheid*).[50]

According to Jacob Maarten Van Bemmelen, elements of *strafbaar feit* can be divided into two: (1) *elementen voor de strafbaarheid van het feit* (elements that can be convicted of *feit*/actions) which is objective because it involves behaviour that violates the law, including in this context the elements which are against the law as well as the cause of that behaviour (although this causality is not included in the formulation of the criminal offence); and (2) *elementen voor de strafbaarheid van de dader* (the element that can be punished by the *dader*/offender) which is subjective because it involves the mental state of those who violate the law, through either intention or negligence.[51]

Bestanddeel (plural: *bestanddelen*) is a written element in the formulation of a criminal offence. According to Van Bemmelen, *bestanddeel/bestanddelen* means the core written part of the formulation of a criminal offence in the article of law. Only this core part is included in the indictment and proven before the court.[52] Meanwhile, any other elements are not included in the core formulation of the article, and thus they are not proven by the public prosecutor. However, these elements must nevertheless be met/fulfilled for the conviction of the defendant because this forms part of criminal responsibility.

This requirement comes from the general section of the Criminal Code and the general legal principles: (1) the act can be accounted for by the offender or the offender is capable of being responsible for the act; (2 the offender can be held liable for the act; and (3) the act is carried out against the law.[53] The phrase 'against the law' is key. If this phrase is included in the formulation of a criminal offence in an article of criminal legislation – for example, Article 362 of the Criminal Code, which reads 'whoever takes goods which partly or wholly belongs to another person shall be punished for theft', where 'against the law' is the *bestanddeel*

[49] Vos in Poernomo, *Asas-Asas Hukum Pidana* (1992) 104.
[50] Poernomo, *Asas-Asas Hukum Pidana* (1992) 104.
[51] See JM van Bemmelen, *Hukum Pidana 1, Hukum Pidana Material Bagian Umum*, translated by Hasnan (Bandung, Binacipta, 1987) 108–11. See also Poernomo, *Asas-Asas Hukum Pidana* (1992) 103.
[52] Hiariej, *Prinsip-Prinsip Hukum Pidana* (2016) 129.
[53] Bemmelen, *Hukum Pidana 1* (1987) 99.

(core part) of a criminal offence – it must be included in the arraignment and the core part must be proven before the court. If it is not proven to be against the law, then the verdict is not guilty (*vrijspraak*).[54]

In Indonesian literature as well as in legal documents such as arraignments, indictments, or defences, this is often only referred to as 'element', but sometimes the distinction between *bestanddeel* and element is explained. For simplicity, we can refer to *bestanddeel* as an element of a criminal offence that is written in the definition of a criminal offence (written in the text of an article) and an element as an unwritten element. Or, we can also say that there are two kinds of elements, written and unwritten, in the formulation of a criminal offence.

Not all of the core parts of the offence – for example, the acts or results – are formulated in every description of a criminal act. In a formal offence that is formulated as an act, there is no element of result in the criminal offence. For example, Article 362 of the Criminal Code concerning theft reads, 'Whoever takes goods which partly or wholly belong to another person'. Here there is an element of action, but there is no element of result. Thus, the elements of the act must be included in the arraignment, while the results are not included in the arraignment.

In the elements of criminal offences where, in the formulation of the offence, especially those that are objective in nature, there is an element of action / behaviour, there are two Dutch terms in use: '*handeling*' and '*gedraging*'. *Handeling* includes both active actions (*een doen*) and passive actions/negligence (*een nalaten/een niet doen*). According to Satochid Kartanegara, it is more appropriate to use the term '*gedraging*', meaning an attitude that is '*een gesteldheit*' (a state).[55] If a person who does not do something (*een nalaten/een niet doen*) even though he is required to do that act by law, then this person has committed a crime.[56] What are some examples of that obligation? They include the obligation to report (Article 164 of the Criminal Code), the obligation to be a witness (Article 522 of the Criminal Code), and the obligation to help people who are in danger of putting their lives at risk (Article 531 of the Criminal Code). Obligations can also arise from a person's job and position, such as the keeper of the railroad crossing gate, or doctors and midwives in a hospital. The obligation can also arise because of an agreement made by the person who has committed the offence.[57]

There are also criminal offences which, in the formulation of the offence, use the word 'or', for example, 'with violence or threats of violence' in Article 285 of the Criminal Code. Here, 'or' means 'alternatively', thus it is enough to fulfill either element. For example, if an act is committed 'with violence' or 'with the threat of violence', then either of these is sufficient and there is no need to fulfill both. The case is different if it is formulated cumulatively, with the word 'and'. Then,

[54] Ibid.
[55] Kartanegara, *Hukum Pidana Kumpulan Kuliah* (nd) 66.
[56] Ibid 67.
[57] Ibid 68.

both elements must be fulfilled. What if it is formulated with the element 'with A and/or B'? In this case, both elements can be fulfilled or just one element.

A. Additional Conditions Required for Conviction

Additional conditions are elements that add onto the main elements of a criminal offence and become additional requirements for a person to be convicted. Not all criminal offences have additional requirements. One example is Article 123 of the Criminal Code, which reads:

> An Indonesian citizen who voluntarily joins the army of a foreign country even though he knows that the country is at war with Indonesia, or will face war with Indonesia, in the latter case *if war breaks out* with Indonesia, is punishable with imprisonment for a maximum of 15 years. [emphasis added]

The additional requirement for being convicted in Article 123 of the Criminal Code is 'in the latter case if war breaks out with Indonesia'. Thus, if the person in question joins a foreign army even though he knows that country may go to war with Indonesia, he can only be convicted if a war indeed does break out between that country and Indonesia. If that country does not go to war with Indonesia, then he will not be punished.

An example of another additional requirement is Article 164 of the Criminal Code, which reads as follows:

> Whoever knows that there is a conspiracy to commit a felony based on articles 104, 106, 107, and 108, 113, 115, 124, 187 or 187 bis, while there is still time to prevent the felony, and with the intent not to immediately notify the judicial or police officials or the person threatened by the felony, is punishable by law *if the crime is indeed committed*, with a maximum imprisonment of one year and four months or a maximum fine of three hundred rupiahs. [emphasis added]

In the criminal offence above, the criminal sanction is intended for anyone who knows there is a conspiracy to commit one of the felonies mentioned above and where there is still time to prevent the felony, but who deliberately does not notify an official. However, with the additional requirement of 'if the crime is indeed committed', the individual can only be convicted if the felony is committed. If the felony has not occurred, then a person who knows of the conspiracy but does not seek to prevent or report it will not be punished.

B. Additional Conditions to be Prosecuted

Some laws also have additional requirements that are necessary for prosecution. For example, in complaint-based offences, the offence can only be prosecuted if a complaint is made. If there is no complaint, then the offence cannot be prosecuted. An example of this can be seen in Article 319 of the Criminal Code, which reads 'Insults which are punishable by law according to this chapter, are not prosecuted if there is no complaint from the person affected by the crime, except in this case Article 316'. Thus the offence can only be prosecuted if there is a complaint by the victim.

IV. Causality

A. Definition and Application to Result-based Offences

When discussing criminal offences, we encounter some criminal offences that contain elements of results. For example, substantive crimes. Here we need an explanation of what is the cause of the emergence of that result. We know this as 'causality', which is 'the principle that there is a cause for everything that happens'[58] or 'the relation between a cause and its effect or between regularly correlated events or phenomena'.[59] In Dutch, the equivalent term, *causaliteit*, is defined as '*verband tussen oorzaak en gevolg*' ('reationship between cause and effect').[60] Another term used is '*oorzakelijkheid*'.

In the context of criminal law, *causalitet* exists when '*… is er sprake van causaliteit wanneer de verdachte een bepaald feit heeft veroorzaakt en daarvoor verantwoor …*' ('… the suspect has caused a certain act and is responsible for it …').[61] Thus, this understanding of causality can be in a general context, but it can also be used in a specific context, for example, in criminal law where causality is associated with someone's actions that cause certain things (*gevolg* / results) and that person can be held accountable for it. Thus, in the end, after knowing the cause, we can talk about the criminal responsibility of the person who caused the result.

Historically, the issue of causality has been limited only to homicide. Now, it has expanded to other crimes. The teaching of causality was considered new until the nineteenth century. At the time, people only adhered to one idea regarding the cause of death: that every act of injuring the body of another must be considered as the cause of the death of the injured person. It was only then that another understanding emerged, which stated that only the act of injuring another's body could be considered as the cause of death is; in other words, if the characteristics of the wound that has been inflicted can indeed cause the death of another person.[62]

In some criminal offences, namely those formulated in a formal manner, we are not faced with the question of what causes a result to occur. For example, in the case of theft, there is no 'result' element in the description of the criminal offence.

[58] dictionary.cambridge.org/dictionary/english/causality.
[59] www.merriam-webster.com/dictionary/causality.
[60] www.woorden.org/woord/causaliteit.
[61] Ibid.
[62] Van Hamel in Lamintang and Lamintang, *Dasar-Dasar Hukum Pidana di Indonesia* (2019) 236–37.

Thus, there is no need to look for the cause of the result that has arisen. This is in contrast to homicide, battery that results in death, or theft carried out with violence resulting in the death of a person. In such cases, the cause of this result must be examined.

Moeljatno states that in a substantially formulated offence, certain conditions are prohibited. For example, homicide requires the presence of a dead person (A). To be able to prosecute someone (B) for A's death, it must be proven that it was because of B's behaviour that the death of A occurred, or that the behaviour of B was the cause of A's death. There must be a causal relation between the death of A and the behaviour of B. If the causal relation can be determined, then it can also be determined that the death of A is due to the behaviour of B, therefore B can be prosecuted and held accountable for A's death. In other words, it can be said that B's behaviour was the cause of A's death.[63]

In criminal offences that sanction acts that have results – such as loss of life (Article 338 of the Criminal Code) or arson (Article 187 of the Criminal Code), as well as criminal offences with additional elements of aggravating circumstances, such as causing death in the act of arson, causing an explosion or causing flooding (Article 187 number 3 of the Criminal Code), battery resulting in death (Article 351 paragraph 3 of the Criminal Code), and intentionally causing the death of a foetus in a woman's womb (Article 347 of the Criminal Code) – then the issue of causality arises. The question 'what is the cause of the result?' must be answered.

There are also other types of criminal offences that cause a result not due to active actions, but by inaction / passive actions. In homicide and negligence causing death, criminal law provides sanctions for criminal offences that result in the death of a person. However, criminal law does not specify what are the prohibited actions that could result in the death of the person. Criminal law generally punishes someone who commits an act that causes death, but criminal law also punishes someone who fails to prevent an act that results in the death of a person.[64] Causing death by inaction is called an omission offence, or, more specifically, an impure omission offence. This impure omission violates a prohibition with passive actions or inaction.

Impute omission offences are differentiated from pure omission offences. The latter are when an order is violated by inaction or passive action, such as an order to appear as a witness to a court, an order to report a birth, or an order to report taxes. According to Pompe, Vos, JE Jonkers, Hazewinkel-Suringa, Van Bemmelen, and Van Hattum, the results very likely occur because of the perpetrator 'not doing something' or *nalaten*.[65]

In my opinion, a pure omission offence (violating an order) does not require the teaching of causality because a crime here occurs when an order is violated

[63] Moeljatno, *Asas-Asas Hukum Pidana* (1993) 88.
[64] Arthur Leavens, 'A Causation Approach to Criminal Omissions' (1988) *California Law Review* 1.
[65] Hiariej, *Prinsip-Prinsip Hukum Pidana* (2016) 209–10.

(eg reporting taxes, appearing as a witness in court, etc) where there is no element of the result in the criminal offence, so there is no urgency to seek the cause. Meanwhile, if the offence is an impure omission (violating a prohibition by not acting), there is a result that is an element of a criminal offence, for example, due to negligence causing death (eg neglecting to close a railroad crossing gate), or intentionally killing a baby by inaction (eg not giving milk to the baby for some time until the baby dies). In cases like this where the type of offence is an impure omission, there are results that become the elements of criminal offences, thus it is necessary to find the cause of that result and therefore the teaching / theory of causality is required.

Thus, we can conclude that causality teachings are needed when we encounter criminal offences which are: (1) substantive offences (offences with substantive formulation); (2) qualifying offences (especially those qualified with results); or (3) omission offences (criminal offence that occurs by passive actions/inaction), especially impure omissions (violating a prohibition by inaction, for example, the prohibition of killing by inaction).

B. Theories of Causality

Causality theories try to explain what is meant by the cause of the occurrence of a result. Several causality theories provide different explanations of what causes the result to occur. Thus, there may be different causes depending on which theory is used. According to Jonkers, it is complicated because there may be several factors/causes leading to an event, thus it is not just one cause/factor that influences the occurrence of the result. Rather, several conditions must be in place for the result to occur. If these conditions are not present, a question of whether the result will occur remains.[66]

Van Hamel states that the difficulty in solving the problem of causality is primarily because almost every real situation is essentially the result of several factors working together, or what John Stuart Mill called the result of the working 'whole of the antecedents', where no single factor can be eliminated without negating the result itself.[67]

The following are causality theories that we encounter in the criminal law literature.[68]

(1) *Conditio sine qua non* (*bedingungstheorie*/equivalence). Former Chief Justice of the German Supreme Court, Maximilian Von Buri, states that a cause is every condition that cannot be eliminated for a result to arise. The occurrence

[66] JE Jonkers, *Buku Pedoman Hukum Pidana Hindia Belanda* [*Handboek Van Het Nederlandsch-Indische Strafrecht*], translated by Tim Penerjemah Bina Aksara (Jakarta, PT Bina Aksara, 1987) 113.

[67] See Lamintang and Lamintang, *Dasar-Dasar Hukum Pidana di Indonesia* (2019) 236.

[68] See Hiariej, *Prinsip-Prinsip Hukum Pidana* (2016) 210–20; Moeljatno, *Asas-Asas Hukum Pidana* (1993) 88–28.

of a situation is not due to causes alone, but because of a series of causes, the number of which is impossible to determine.[69] This theory is difficult to use in determining criminal liability because it is very broad. Indeed, what this theory explains is what causes the results to arise. This theory is also called equivalence because each condition is equal in value (equivalent). It is also known as *bedingungstheorie* because there is no difference between condition (*bedingung*) and cause.[70]

(2) The limitation of the *conditio sine qua non* with the teachings of fault by Dutch criminal law expert Van Hamel. This theory limits the too broad *conditio sine qua non* theory. For this theory to be perfect, it needs to be limited by the teachings of fault (*dolus/culpa*)[71] so that it can be used in determining criminal responsibility.

(3) Generalisation theory. Here, we must look for limitations in general or in an abstract way, so they are not tied to a particular case, and therefore take a stand at the time before the result arises (*ante factum*).[72] The question posed by generalisation theory is: 'Is there any particular act which in general can (perhaps) lead to prohibited results?' If the answer is 'Yes', then the action is the cause of the effect.[73] This generalisation theory includes several theories, one of which is the subjective generalising theory, particularly the Adequate theory from German mathematician Johannes von Kries. According to this theory, the cause of an event is a condition which, in general, according to the course of normal events, can or is capable of causing the result or event.[74]

(4) The generalisation theory of Simons, a professor of Dutch criminal law. According to Simons, the cause is every behaviour where, according to the general lines of human experience, there could be a possibility that, because of the behaviour itself, there can be a result. There is no need to *personlijk* (personally) know about it, nor is there a need to know or to be able to reasonably guess.[75] Thus, what it is important to take into account are: things that can generally be known, and, given what can be understood from experience, whether these results can be predicted or are expected to arise from that behaviour. If the result also happens because of things that are unexpected and are not related to behaviour, then there is no causal relation between behaviour and result.[76]

(5) The objective generalisation theory (objective forecast), namely the adequacy theory (*objectif nachtragliche prognose*) from Gustav Rumelin. The adequacy theory is based on objective forecasting, namely by remembering the

[69] Moeljatno, *Asas-Asas Hukum Pidana* (1993) 91.
[70] Ibid 92–94.
[71] See ibid 92–94.
[72] See ibid 94–99.
[73] Ibid 94.
[74] Ibid.
[75] Ibid 97.
[76] Ibid.

circumstances after the occurrence of the result.[77] In determining whether a behaviour is the cause of a prohibited result, what must be answered is: 'whether that result, taking into account all the objective conditions that existed at the time after the occurrence of the result, will predictably arise from the behaviour?' With this explanation, especially from the phrase 'after the effect', means seeing it as *post factum*. Some refer to Rumelin's theory as a group of individualising theories.

(6) Next, after generalisation theories, there is another group called individualising theory. These theories hold specific limitations, do not review in general and abstract, but see concrete results based on certain events. Each event is reviewed individually to determine the cause of the result. Therefore, this stance can only be taken after the result (*post factum*). One theory is from Birkmeyer and is based on the *condition sine qua non*. In a series of conditions that cannot be eliminated without the result also disappearing, it is sought which conditions, under certain circumstances, are the most helpful for the occurrence of a result.[78]

(7) Kohler's individualising theory. According to Kohler, a cause is a condition that by its nature has a result. Here the question is not which condition has the strongest effect (as in Birkmeyer's theory), but which condition, by its nature (ie according to its "meaning") is the most important for the result.[79]

(8) The individualising theory of Karl Binding. According to Binding, a cause is a condition that provides provisions for positive terms to exceed negative terms. According to Binding, all conditions that help an effect to arise are causes, not just one condition.[80]

(9) Finally, there is the relevance theory from GE Langemeijer and E Mezger. This theory does not begin by distinguishing between 'cause' and 'conditions' but begins by interpreting the formulation of the offence. From the formulation of the offence, which only contains the prohibited results, it is determined what behaviours were addressed when making the prohibition.[81] According to Langemeijer, when the law uses terms that contain the assumption of a causal relation, those terms refer not only to a causal relation but also to other conditions for holding people accountable for the results.[82]

The description above explains the existence of several known theories related to the teaching of causality, the first of which is Von Buri's theory of *conditio sine qua non*. Moeljatno, a professor of Indonesian criminal law, rejects Von Buri's *conditio sine qua non* theory because he considers that this theory is too broad and cannot be used in practice. In addition, the value of each cause and condition cannot

[77] Ibid 110–11.
[78] Ibid 100.
[79] Ibid.
[80] Ibid 101.
[81] Ibid 113.
[82] Ibid 114.

be generalised. This is contrary to the general view in social interaction which distinguishes between conditions and causes.[83]

As Von Buri's theory is considered too broad to be used in criminal law, several experts limit Von Buri's theory, including Van Hamel. Moeljatno also rejects the limitation of the *condition sine qua non* theory by Van Hamel with the doctrine of fault because the issue of causality lies in the matter of 'criminal offence', while 'fault' lies in the mind of the offender. According to Moeljatno, the two are separate. Causality determines whether the defendant committed the prohibited act or not. Thus, it is not about the defendant's fault.[84]

Other theories also limit the overly broad theory of *conditio sine qua non*, such as individualising theories and generalising theories. Moeljatno disagrees with the generalisation theory because it seeks boundaries between conditions and causes, and thinks abstractly or in general terms, and by doing so, it leaves behind concrete, specific matters, and consideration of what solution is actually expected from the determination of these limits.[85]

The Criminal Code does not provide guidelines or instructions on how to determine the cause of a result. It is not explicitly determined in doctrine and jurisprudence in Indonesia how a judge must use the doctrine of causality to determine the cause of the occurrence of a result, and thus all theories or teachings of causality can be used. Thus, causality remains in the doctrines (the opinion of the jurists). The doctrines of causality in Indonesian criminal law were greatly influenced by the thoughts of Dutch and German jurists.[86]

The Criminal Code does not explicitly refer to any of the existing teachings. This can be concluded from the history of the formation of the Criminal Code as well as from the articles in the Criminal Code.[87] According to Jan Remmelink, the teaching of relevance is the closest basis for understanding causality in the Criminal Code in both the Netherlands and Indonesia. In contrast to Remmelink, Wirjono Prodjodikoro argues that the Criminal Code does not adhere to a certain theory of causality. Prosecutors and judges are given the freedom to choose between known causality theories.[88]

Problematically, courts in Indonesia apply the teachings of causality from experts in different ways and do not consistently or continuously use one type of causality theory. In Ahmad Sofian's research, it was concluded that the teaching of causality was not used consistently by prosecutors and judges, although some understood that one of the important elements in determining substantive offences was the existence of a causal relation as an element. However, other court decisions do not mention the element of a causal relation in determining the criminal responsibility of the offender. In looking for this causal relation,

[83] Ibid 92–94.
[84] See ibid 92–94.
[85] See ibid 94–99.
[86] Ahmad Sofian, *Ajaran Kausalitas Hukum Pidana* (Jakarta, Kencana, 2020) 333–34.
[87] Kartanegara, *Hukum Pidana Kumpulan Kuliah* (nd) 200.
[88] Wirjono Prodjodikoro, *Asas-asas Hukum Pidana di Indonesia* (Bandung, Eresco, 1969) 48.

for example in a homicide case, the court relies on evidence, including expert testimony. In determining or looking for this causal relation, not all courts take it from doctrine but find it for themselves by reacting to the facts found in the court. The court provides space for the use of the teaching of causality in a criminal offence that causes death, but judges do not conduct an in-depth exploration of the doctrine of causality in cases whose causes are complex and branching, meaning that their decisions do not have a strong enough basis for the doctrine of causality.[89]

V. Criminal Offences in the New Criminal Code

Unlike the current Criminal Code, which does not specifically discuss criminal offence in any of the chapters in Book 1 of the Criminal Code, the new Criminal Code specifically regulates criminal offences in Chapter II of Book 1, with the title Criminal Offence and Criminal Responsibility. There are two parts to this chapter. The first part discusses criminal offences and the second part discusses criminal responsibility. Article 12 states:

(1) A Criminal Offence is an act which by law is punishable with criminal sanctions and/or action.
(2) To be declared a Criminal Offence, an act that is subject to criminal sanctions and/ or action by laws and regulations must be against the law or contrary to the law that exists in society.
(3) Every Criminal Offence is always against the law unless there is a justification.

The most important reform of substantive criminal law in the New Criminal Code [90] is that it no longer distinguishes between felony and violation. For both, the term 'criminal offence' is used. Thus, this proposed Code only consists of two books: Book 1 on General Rules and Book 2 on Criminal Offence. The original Book 3 on Violations in *Wetboek van Strafrecht* has been removed, with its substance selectively accommodated in the new Book 2.

The reason for the abolition is because, conceptually, the difference between felony as *rechtsdelict* and violation as *wetsdelict* turned out to be untenable. This is because during its development, several *rechtsdelicts* have been qualified as violations, while on the other hand, some acts that should constitute *wetsdelict* are formulated as felonies because the criminal sanctions are aggravated. In fact, it is evident that the issue of the severity of the quality and impact of felonies and violations is relative, and thus qualitative criteria of this kind can no longer be consistently maintained.

[89] Sofian, *Ajaran Kausalitas Hukum Pidana* (2020) 334–35.

[90] All points in this section refer to the General Elucidation of Criminal Code Bill, as on 18 October 2021.

In the Criminal Code, it is also recognised that there may be a criminal offence based on a law that exists in society (customary crimes). This is done to better fulfil the sense of justice that lives in society. In fact, in some areas of the country, there are still unwritten legal provisions that exist and are recognised as law in the area concerned and which determine that violations of that unwritten law deserve to be punished. In this case, the judge can determine sanctions in the form of fulfilling local customary obligations to be carried out by the offender. This means that the standards of values and norms that live in the local community are protected. Such a situation will not hinder justice and will still guarantee the implementation of the legality principle and the prohibition of analogy adhered to in this Law.

Additionally, in the New Criminal Code, several criminal offences that were originally developed outside the Criminal Code – including, among others, criminal offences related to aims such as the prevention and eradication of money laundering, the eradication of terrorism, the eradication of corruption, the eradication of trafficking in persons, human rights violation, the protection and management of the environment and cultural heritage – are also incorporated.

Anticipatively and proactively, it also includes regulations covering the criminal offences of pornography; crimes against informatics and electronics, the environment, and aviation; crimes against organs, body tissues, and human blood; and crimes against the judicial process. In addition, Criminal Code has also adopted several international conventions, both ratified and not ratified, including Law No 5 of 1998 on the Ratification of the Convention Against Torture and Other Cruel, Inhuman or Degrading Treatment or Punishment.

With the criminal offence formulation system above, the criminal offences of gross violations against human rights, terrorism, corruption, money laundering, and narcotics are grouped into one separate chapter on Special Criminal Offences. Placement in this separate chapter is based on the following specific characteristics:

(a) the impact on victims is large;
(b) the crime is often transnationally organised;
(c) the arrangement of the criminal procedure is special;
(d) the formulation of the criminal offence often deviates from the general principles of substantive criminal law;
(e) the existence of special law enforcement supporting institutions with special powers;
(f) supported by international conventions; and
(g) the crime is a heinous and despicable act and is highly condemned by society.

The formation of this Criminal Code also takes into account the results of the decisions of the Constitutional Court relating to the judicial review of the Criminal Code, including, among others, the criminal offences of insulting the president, blasphemy, and decency.

In line with the process of globalisation, the pace of development, and social development accompanied by rapid social mobility, as well as advances in science and technology, it is estimated that new types of criminal offences will continue to emerge in the future. Therefore, for new types of criminal offences that will appear and have not been regulated in this Law, arrangements can still be made through amendments to the new Code or through regulation in a separate law.

The division of criminal offences in the Criminal Code among other are as follows: criminal offences against state security (Chapter I); criminal offences against the dignity of the president and vice president (Chapter II); criminal offences against friendly countries (Chapter III); criminal offences against the holding of legislative meetings and against government agencies (Chapter IV); criminal offences against public order (Chapter V); criminal offences against the judicial process (Chapter VI); criminal offences against religion and religious life (Chapter VII); criminal offences that endanger the safety of people, health, goods, and the environment (Chapter VIII); criminal offences against public powers and state institutions (Chapter IX); false statement under oath (Chapter X); criminal offences of forgery of money (Chapter XI); criminal offences of forgery of stamp, country stamp (Chapter XII); criminal offences of forgery of letters (Chapter XIII); criminal offences of morality (Chapter XV); criminal offences of defamation (Chapter XVII); people smuggling (Chapter XX); criminal offences against life and the foetus (Chapter XXI); and criminal offences against the body (Chapter XXII).

6

Culpability and Criminal Liability

I. Definition

In criminal law literature in Indonesia, the definition of fault generally refers to the opinion of Dutch legal experts, such as Jacob Maarten van Bemmelen and Jan Remmelink. According to Van Bemmelen, 'fault' has four primary types:[1]

(1) Faults contained in the formulation of the offence as *Bestandelen* (part of the core of the offence), used in a narrow sense (*culpa* or omission).
(2) Faults that are not contained in the formulation or description of the offence. These are defined as 'reproachable' but fall within the context of 'no fault at all' or AVAS (*afwezigheid van alle schuld*).
(3) Faults in the sense of a compilation of *dolus* (intentional) and *culpa* (omission/negligence).
(4) Faults in the sense of 'have committed'.[2]

Remmelink holds a similar opinion on the existence of four *schuld* (faults) as Van Bemmelen.[3]

Indonesian criminal law expert Satochid Kartanegara argues that there are three meanings of 'fault'.[4] They are:

(1) *Schuld* (fault) in a social-ethical sense. This context refers to the relationship between the mental state of a person who commits an act with that person's action or the results of that person's action. The relationship of the

[1] JM van Bemmelen, *Hukum Pidana 1, Hukum Pidana Material Bagian Umum*, translated by Hasnan (Bandung, Binacipta, 1987) 142–43.

[2] This can be found in Articles 2 to 7 WvS (KUHP), especially if we look at the original language, Dutch. In those articles, we find the word '*Schuldig*' (which means 'has committed'), for example in Article 2: 'Criminal rules in Indonesian legislation apply to everyone who *commits a* criminal act within Indonesia' (emphasis added). In the Dutch WvS (and also the Dutch East Indies WvS), the words 'doing the deed' are written as '*schuldig*'. The word *schuldig* is also found in Articles 3 to 7. In addition, this word also appears in Article 189 WvS (KUHP) of the Netherlands (or Article 221 of the Indonesian Criminal Code), which reads: ('whoever intentionally hide people who have *committed crimes* or …'). The word *schuldig* in the sense of 'has done' is also found in the Dutch WvSv (Code of Criminal Procedure).

[3] Jan Remmelink, *Hukum Pidana, Komentar atas Pasal-Pasal Terpenting dari Kitab Undang-Undang hukum Pidana Belanda dan Padanannya dalam Kitab Undang-Undang Hukum Pidana Indonesia* (Jakarta, Gramedia Pustaka Utama, 2003) 150–51.

[4] Satochid Kartanegara, *Hukum Pidana Kumpulan Kuliah Prof Satochid Kartanegara dan Pendapat-Pendapat Para Ahli Hukum Terkemuka* (Jakarta, Balai Lektur Mahasiswa, nd) 244–45.

person's mental state and the act or results is such that, due to the person's mental state, the act or results can be blamed on that person (reproachable/ *verwijtbaarheid*).

(2) *Schuld* viewed from a criminal law point of view (*in strafrechtelijk zin*), namely *schuld* in the sense of *dolus* (intentional) and *culpa* (omission/negligence).

(3) *Schuld* in a narrow sense covering *culpa* only.

Sudarto agrees with Kartanegara's definitions of fault.[5]

Meanwhile, in the opinions of D Schaffmeister, N Keijzer, and E PH Sutorius, faults are always about inappropriate action: that is, doing something that should not be done, or not doing something that should be done. Furthermore, fault views the relationship between an improper act and the offender in such a way that the act (in the actual sense) is the offender's act. This person's actions are not only objectively inappropriate but also reprehensible. In other words, 'fault' is objectively inappropriate behaviour for which the actor can be blamed.[6] Thus, for sentencing, it is not only required that someone has done something wrong in the objective sense, but also that the improper conduct can be blamed on that person.[7]

Fault can be considered to exist, or the requirement for fault fulfilled (but not yet proven by the public prosecutor), unless an 'excuse defence' is presented by the defendant. If an excuse defence is presented (which would relieve the fault inherent in the defendant), then it is necessary to prove whether the fault in this sense is fulfilled. If no faults are found in this sense, it is said to be AVAS (*Afwezigheid Van Alle Schuld*), or no fault is found at all. If this is accepted by the judge, the defendant's fault is forgiven and the judge renders the decision 'acquitted from all criminal charges' or '*onslag van rechtvervolging*'.

As stated above, *schuld* refers to the relationship between the mental state of the person who commits the act and his actions, or the relationship of the mental state of the offender and the results of his actions. Thus the mental state of the person is such that the act or the results of his actions can be blamed on him. This is in line with D Simons' statement that fault is present in the sense of '*sociaal-ethisch*' and is the basis for liability in criminal law. In other words, in a psychological sense, the offender can be reproached for his actions.[8]

E Mezger takes a similar line, stating that fault is the whole condition that provides the basis for personal reproach against the perpetrators of a criminal offence.[9] Karni adds that the term 'fault' itself has the meaning of 'reproach'. Fault (in Karni's usage, 'sinful fault') is present if the act can be accounted for by the offender; the offender must be reproached for his actions; the act must contain a

[5] Sudarto, *Hukum Pidana I*, Revised Edn (Semarang, Sudarto Foundation, 2013) 152–53.

[6] D Schaffmeister, N Keijzer, and E PH Sutorius, *Hukum Pidana* (Bandung, Citra Aditya Bakti, 2007) 79.

[7] Ibid 79–80.

[8] Sudarto, *Hukum Pidana I* (2013) 149.

[9] Ibid 149.

conflict of rights (against the law); and the act was done either intentionally or by mistake (negligence).[10]

Meanwhile, according to Roeslan Saleh, a fault can be blamed on the perpetrator of a crime, because from the perspective of society, that person could do something else rather than carrying out the act. Chairul Huda further explains that the definition is composed of three main components: it is (1) reproachable; (2) viewed from the perspective of society; and (3) the offender can do otherwise.[11]

Regarding the first component, according to Chairul Huda, 'reproachable' has two meanings: first, can be held liable in criminal law, and second, can be sentenced to punishment. The first meaning relates to the preventive function of criminal law, with the word 'can' here indicating that criminal liability is no longer relevant if there is a reason to relieve the fault.[12] The second meaning here relates to the repressive function of criminal law, with the word 'can' indicating that reproach or criminal imposition does not always have to be done by a judge. Thus even if the act is proven and the requirement for fault fulfilled, the judge can only impose an action or grant a pardon. This is known as or 'judicial pardon' in some countries, such as in the Netherlands ('*rechterlijke pardon*').[13]

This concept has been accommodated in Indonesia's new Criminal Code Bill (as of 4 July 2022), specifically in Article 54 paragraph (2), which states:

> The lightness of the act, the personal circumstances of the offender, or the circumstances at the time the crime was committed as well as what happens then can be used as a basis for consideration *not to impose a punishment or not to take action* by taking into account the aspects of justice and humanity.' [emphasis added]

In this formulation, it is clear that although it has been determined that the criminal offences were committed by the offenders, several issues prevent the judge from imposing a sentence or taking action. So, in such a case, the judge can state in the decision that a person is proven to have committed a crime but that a punishment (or action) will not be imposed.[14] For instance, if the defendant commits a crime, but the act is minor or the defendant is a very poor person and the act is committed because of poverty, the judge may use this kind of provision.

Regarding the second component of Huda's definition of fault, 'from the perspective of society', according to Saleh this is an affirmation of the normative assessment of faults. In regard to humans as the subject of law, whether there is a fault is not determined by the condition of the defendant's mind but rather on

[10] Karni, *Ringkasan tentang Hukum Pidana* (Jakarta, Balai Buku Indonesia, 1950) 41–42.

[11] Chairul Huda, *Dari 'Tiada Pidana Tanpa Kesalahan' Menuju Kepada Tiada Pertanggungjawaban Pidana Tanpa Kesalahan, Tinjauan Kritis Terhadap Teori Pemisahan Tindak Pidana dan Pertanggungjawaban Pidana* (Jakarta, Kencana, 2015) 77.

[12] In my opinion, 'excuse of fault' here is the same as 'reason for forgiveness'.

[13] Huda, *Dari 'Tiada Pidana Tanpa Kesalahan'* (2015) 78.

[14] Ibid.

the legal assessment of the defendant's mental state (whether he is judged to be at fault or not).[15] Although fault is understood in a normative sense, specifically for human subjects, it does not mean that it is completely separated from the mental state of the person committing the crime nor the relationship between that mental state and the crime. The normative judgment here is aimed at the act, its perpetrator, and the relationship between the two. In humans, the relationship between the act and the offender is more focused on the relationship between the offender's inner state and the criminal act. From this, it can be concluded that 'from the perspective of society', the offender 'can be reproached' for having committed a crime.[16]

On the third component of fault, in which 'the offender can do something else' if he does not want to commit a crime, this means that it is always possible for the offender to avoid the occurrence of the crime. Therefore, that person can be reproached because he could, in fact, have done something else and not committed a crime, but nevertheless went ahead and still committed the crime. On the other hand, if there was no possibility for the offender to do anything other than commit the crime, this will cause the offender to be released from fault.[17] This is a logical conclusion, as offenders cannot be blamed if they have no possibility or option of doing otherwise.

II. Categories of Culpability

A. Intentionality (*Opzet*) and its Types

In the Dutch Criminal Code (WvS), *Memorie van Toelichting* (Explanatory Memorandum) states that it is important to assess where the *dolus* (*opzet* in Dutch) or intentional element is placed in the formulation or description of a criminal offence. The placement of this element will affect the understanding and scope of the element. What is affected by the intentional element? Anything that follows the word 'intentionally' will be affected by that word. Thus, *dolus* can be associated with actions/deeds, results, and elements of other criminal offences.[18] Of course, conversely, anything that is written before the word 'intentionally' is not influenced by intention.

According to Remmelink, *dolus* does not need to be aimed at the forbidden nature of the act. The law does not even require the existence of 'intentional malice' (*dolus malus*).[19] For example, Article 134 of the Criminal Code reads 'Intentional

[15] Roeslan Saleh, *Perbuatan Pidana dan Pertanggungjawaban Pidana: Dua Pengertian Dasar dalam Hukum Pidana* (Jakarta, Aksara Baru, 1983) 77. See also Huda, *Dari 'Tiada Pidana Tanpa Kesalahan'* (2015) 78.

[16] Huda, *Dari 'Tiada Pidana Tanpa Kesalahan'* (2015) 78–79.

[17] Ibid 79.

[18] Remmelink, *Hukum Pidana* (2003) 151–52.

[19] Ibid 152.

insult to the President or Vice President …'. Here the intentional element covers other elements behind the intentional element, including that the offender must know that the person insulted was the president or the vice president. If the offender does not know that that person is the president or vice president, then he is not subject to Article 134 of this Criminal Code. Another article relating to insult may be imposed instead.[20] Deliberate actions are always *willens* (willed) and *wetens* (realised or known). This kind of opinion, according to Remmelink citing Hans-Heinrich Jescheck,[21] also exists in criminal law in Austria, Switzerland, France, and Belgium. Jescheck calls this the *Wissen und Wollen*.[22]

In the explanation of the MvT of the Dutch Criminal Code, it is firmly stated that the government only accepts as correct the definition that is written in the 1809 law: 'Intentional is the will/wish to commit or not to commit acts that are prohibited or required by law.' In debate in the Dutch Parliament, it was found that sometimes 'intentionally' is not merely about 'willing' but in certain circumstances it is also necessary to 'know' or 'know about' the existence of such a situation. Thus, both knowledge and will are important.[23]

i. Willens *(Willed)*

What exactly is meant by *willens* (willed)? Willing or wishing is more than wanting or hoping. For example, in order to fulfill Article 406 of the Criminal Code regarding the destruction of goods, there must be a will to damage. People who accidentally or due to carelessness break an item cannot be punished by Article 406.[24]

This is true for commission offences as well as omission offences. For example, a person who is required to be present as a witness in court but forgot to attend (rather than intentionally not attending) cannot be punished under Article 224 of the Criminal Code ('Anyone who is summoned by law to be a witness, expert, or interpreter, intentionally does not carry out their obligations …').[25]

However, *dolus* and *culpa* have no effect if we talk about a crime whose type is a violation. For example, Article 224 is a felony, not a violation. It is different if the person does not appear when summoned under Article 522 of the Criminal Code ('Anyone who does not appear if summoned by law to be a witness, become an expert or interpreter …'), as this is classed as a violation.[26] As another example, if we forget to carry vehicle documents such as a driver's licence, if there is a police

[20] Article 134 of the Criminal Code has been declared invalid based on the Constitutional Court Decision Number 013-022/PUU-IV/2006 because it was declared contrary to the 1945 Constitution. However, in the Criminal Code Bill (4 July 2022) as well as in the discussion of the government team regarding the Criminal Code Bill as of December 2021, there is an article on the crime of insulting the president with changes to the formulation and type of criminal offence (to be a complaint offence).

[21] Hans-Heinrich Jescheck was a professor of law at the University of Freiburg (Germany) and was Director of the Max Planck Institute.

[22] Remmelink, *Hukum Pidana* (2003) 152.

[23] Van Bemmelen, *Hukum Pidana 1* (1987) 113.

[24] Remmelink, *Hukum Pidana* (2003) 152–53.

[25] Ibid.

[26] Ibid.

inspection, we can still be charged with a sanction even if this is an accidental error, because the offence is a violation, not a felony.

ii. Wettens *(Known)*

'Knowing' here is the same as recognising, understanding, being aware, or realising something. Thus, any person can fulfill this requirement, as we do not necessarily have to have knowledge as befits a legal expert, for example regarding legal concepts. Everyday knowledge of laypeople is considered sufficient. In Dutch, *dolus/opzet* is always used in a neutral and nuanced way (*kleurloos*). Therefore, *opzet* does not always connote or mean that the act was committed intentionally or with malicious intentions.[27]

Sometimes it is not easy for the judge to determine with certainty whether the offender 'knows' a certain situation (ie whether the offender acted on purpose), or whether the offender should suspect that the situation is a certain way (common sense). To determine whether the defendant knew or was acquainted with certain circumstances, judges often drew conclusions not only from the defendant's testimony but also from certain circumstances.[28] In my opinion, this particular situation could be in the form of educational or occupational background or the defendant's experience in a particular field.

Kartanegara argues that *opzet* is most relevant to the act (*opzet is gericht op de handling*). Quoting Simons, Kartanegara states that an act committed intentionally by a person is stated as the embodiment of that person's will (*uiting van de wil van iemand*). The question is what the will (*wil*) is aimed at. To answer this, we must look at the formulation of a criminal offence, which consists of objective elements (eg actions, results, circumstances attached to the act) and subjective elements (eg *dolus*, *culpa*, circumstances attached to the subject). By looking at the elements of a criminal offence, we can see that the will can relate to prohibited acts, to results that are prohibited by law, and to conditions that are elements of a criminal offence. The *opzet* of prohibited acts is called formal intent (*formeel opzet*), while the *opzet* of prohibited results and circumstances which constitute elements of a criminal offence is called substantive intent (*matereel opzet*).[29]

An example of formal intent is Article 406 of the Criminal Code on the damaging of other people's property (vandalism). The intentionality in this criminal offence is aimed at the act, that is, the damaging. In addition to 'damaging' which is an element of action, there is also an element of circumstance, namely that what is damaged is property owned by someone else. Thus, intention here refers to the act (damaging) as well as the circumstance (other people's property).[30]

What, then, about results? Results are also elements of offences, especially substantive offences. Is 'will' also relevant to the results of an act? This is where

[27] Ibid 153.
[28] Van Bemmelen, *Hukum Pidana 1* (1987) 116.
[29] Kartanegara, *Hukum Pidana Kumpulan Kuliah* (nd) 247–48.
[30] Ibid 248–49.

the differences between will theory and imagining theory emerge. According to will theory, which holds the view that *opzet is de wil*, will is aimed at both actions and results. Adherents of imagining theory (*vorstelling theory*) do not agree, arguing that 'results' and 'conditions' cannot be desired and can only be imagined or wished.[31] By imagining the arising of that result, the offender then adjusts his actions to the result that he imagines.[32] This imagining theory focuses on what the offender knows or imagines about what will happen when he acts. The theory of imagining was adopted by Reinhard Frank, while the theory of will was adopted by Simons and Willem Zevenbergen.[33]

According to Kartanegara, in fact there is no principal difference between the two theories. For adherents of will theory, if a person does an action to cause a result, what that person wants is not only his action but also the result of this action, because if the person does not want the result, he will not personally commit the act. In this case, the desired result encourages the offender to carry out the actions.[34] This point is also where imagining theory comes in, arguing that the offender cannot wish for the result – the offender can only imagine the result that might occur, and he will adjust his actions to achieve the result he imagines.

In line with Kartanegara, Moeljatno states that in practice the results of these two theories are the same. This is because if intentionality is seen in relation to the whole, namely acting intentionally, including the results and accompanying circumstances, then in essence, there is no difference. Quoting Van Hattum, Moeljatno says that the difference is not a juridical matter but a psychological one. The results of these two theories are more or less the same, so that in general it appears that merely the terminology is different.[35]

iii. Three Intentionality Categories

In the Criminal Code, there is no division of *opzet*/intentionality into categories. However, in doctrine, intentionality can be divided into several categories. In general, in the literature, there are three agreed-upon categories on intentionality, but some experts also argue for a fourth category. The categories are as follows:[36]

(1) *Opzet als oogmerg* (intentionality with purpose).
(2) *Opzet met zekerheindsbewustzijn / opzet met noodzakelijkbewustzijn* (intentionality with awareness / conviction of certainty).
(3) *Opzet met waarschijnlijkheidsbewustzijn / opzet metwuortzwajndeli/eventzet*[37] (intentionality with awareness / conviction of possibility).

[31] Ibid 247–49.
[32] Wirjono Prodjodikoro, *Asas-Asas Hukum Pidana di Indonesia* (Bandung, Refika Aditama, 2003) 67.
[33] Sudarto, *Hukum Pidana I* (2013) 173.
[34] Kartanegara, *Hukum Pidana Kumpulan Kuliah* (nd) 250.
[35] Moeljatno, *Asas-Asas Hukum Pidana* (Jakarta, Rineka Cipta, 1993) 172–73.
[36] See Moeljatno, *Asas-Asas Hukum Pidana* (1993) 174. See also Prodjodikoro, *Asas-Asas Hukum Pidana di Indonesia* (2003) 66. See also Sudarto, *Hukum Pidana I* (2013) 174.
[37] See Remmelink, *Hukum Pidana* (2003) 154–55.

Some experts separate *dolus eventualis* (conditional intentionality) into an additional fourth category of intentionality, while others include it in the third category. I personally divide intentionally into the three categories stated above. As Moeljatno says, intentionality as a possibility (*opzet bij mogelijkheid bewustzijn*) is usually called *dolus eventualis*,[38] thus I also include *dolus eventualis* in the third category. Experts such as HB Vos, Derkje Hazewinkel-Suringa, JE Jonkers, Simons, Kartanegara, and Moeljatno also hold this view. In my opinion, there is no clear difference between conviction/awareness of possibility and *dolus eventualis*.[39]

Meanwhile, experts who separate *dolus eventualis* from intentionality with conviction / awareness of possibility include Remmelink, D Schaffmeister, Keijzer, Sutorius, and Hiariej.[40]

iv. Intentionality as an Intent/Purpose

Also known as *dolus directus*: to achieve the (immediate) goal. Intentionality here is the usual and simple form of intentionality. It is also the most common. A person carries out an act with the aim of causing the prohibited result. If that result would not happen (exist), then that person would not commit the act. The offender wants the action *and* its result.[41]

v. Intentionality with Conviction / Awareness of Certainty

In this case, the action has two results: (1) the result that is intended by the offender (this can be a separate offence, or it may not be an offence); and (2) an undesirable result that is nonetheless a pre-requisite to achieve the purpose (the former). Both results must occur.[42]

A clear example of this kind of wilful conviction / awareness of certainty is the case of Thomas of Bremerhaven, Germany, which occurred in 1875. In this case, Alexander Keith (Thomas) shipped one crate of dynamite from Bremerhaven to New York with a device set to explode in eight days. The plan was as follows: at Bremerhaven, the crate would be loaded on the ship, then in Southampton, England, Thomas would insure the ship with a high value. In the middle of the ocean between Bremerhaven and New York, the crate would explode. Thomas' objective was to make a large insurance claim. However, due to carelessness, the crate fell as it was about to be loaded in Bremerhaven and exploded. As a result, 83 people died and 50 were injured (including six who later died and 20 who were injured on board). In this case, the result – that is, the death and injury of dozens of

[38] Moeljatno, *Asas-Asas Hukum Pidana* (1993) 174.

[39] See Eddy OS Hiariej, *Prinsip-Prinsip Hukum Pidana*, revised edition (Yogyakarta, Cahaya Atma Pustaka, 2016) 174.

[40] Ibid.

[41] Sudarto, *Hukum Pidana I* (2013) 174–75.

[42] Ibid 175.

people – was not Thomas' purpose. Nevertheless, people were killed and injured, even though this was not his intention (which was to lodge an insurance claim). Thus, Thomas was charged with intentional murder, with 'intentional' here not meaning intent but rather intentionality with conviction / awareness of certainty.[43]

vi. Intentionality with Conviction / Awareness of Possibility

In this third category of intentionality, there are certain circumstances (results) that *may* occur that are not the purpose/intention of the offender. To achieve his real purpose (either a criminal or non-criminal offence), the offender continues to carry out the actions even though they may have unintended results. For example, a person intends to take action X (criminal or non-criminal offence) that has the possible result of Y, where Y is a criminal offence. Although achieving Y was not the purpose of the offender, the offender continued to take action X, resulting in a criminal offence.

A clear example of this type of intentionality with conviction / awareness of possibility or *dolus eventualis* is the case of a tart cake from the City of Hoorn, the Netherlands. This case is found in the decision of the Amsterdam Court on 9 March 1911 (decision W 9154), and at the appeal level by the Dutch Supreme Court on 19 June 19 1911 (decision W 9203). The offender (A) bought a tart on 28 September 1910, and filled it with poison. He sent the tart from Amsterdam with the intention of killing the Market Orderly (B) in Hoorn City. A would have known that there was a possibility that B's wife (C), who had no problem with A, would also eat the tart he sent and might also become ill or die. Even though A knew about the unintended possibility (C's death), he did not do anything about it or alter his course of action. What actually happened was that B did not eat the tart but his wife (C) did, on 30 September 1910. As a result, C died. A's intention was to kill B, but it didn't work, because B didn't eat the cake, thus the category of intentionality was as purpose / intention. In other words, the offender intentionally attempted premeditated murder on B. Meanwhile, for the death of C, the offender was convicted of intentionally committing premeditated murder on C, even though he had, in fact, sent the poisoned cake not to kill C but to kill B. In the death of C, the category of A's intentional act was not intentional in the sense of intention, but intentional with conviction / awareness of possibility.[44]

Another example occurred in North Jakarta in 1994. The case, known as the 'deathly Metromini case' was decided by the North Jakarta District Court on 27 April 1995,[45] affirmed by an appellate court judgment at the Jakarta High Court on 6 July 1995,[46] and affirmed by the cassation judgment in the Supreme Court of

[43] Ibid 175–76. See also Hiariej, *Prinsip-Prinsip Hukum Pidana* (2016) 173.

[44] Sudarto, *Hukum Pidana I* (2013) 177–78. See also Moeljatno, *Asas-Asas Hukum Pidana* (1993) 176–77. See also Hiariej, *Prinsip-Prinsip Hukum Pidana* (2016) 174–75.

[45] Decision Number 03/PID/B/1995/PN.JKT UT.

[46] Decision Number 59/PID/1995/PT.DKI.

the Republic of Indonesia on 30 January 1996.[47] In this case, a Metromini public transport driver named Ramses drove his vehicle exceedingly fast (80km/hour) with 46 passengers aboard, even though the maximum permitted capacity was only 15 passengers, swerving to avoid potholes. Ramses had already received a warning from the bus assistant and passengers not to drive fast so but he reportedly did not care. The Metromini then hit a hole, hit the curb, and jumped over a ditch and into the Sunter River. As a result, 33 people died and 13 were injured. In this case, Ramses was sentenced to 15 years in prison under Article 338 of the Criminal Code, which is intentional manslaughter, and not Article 359, relating to negligence causing death. Thus, the case falls under intentionality with conviction / awareness of possibility (*dolus eventualis*). The judge used the theory of Kauf Nehmen (the concept/theory 'approves them'), because with his actions, the driver could predict the results that would arise, such as the vehicle overturning and falling into the river on the side of the road. However, the driver did not care and was willing to take this risk, therefore his attitude was considered to be in accordance with the concept/ theory 'approves them' – that is, knowing that a result may occur, but regardless, he continued to take actions to achieve his goals.[48]

vii. 'What Else' Theory

As I mentioned above, to explain the existence of intentionality with conviction/awareness of possibility, it is also possible to use the Kauf Nehmen theory. This theory is also known as the *Op de Koop Toe Nemen Theorie*. In Indonesian, Moeljatno and Sudarto call it the 'what else' theory – as in, what else did the offender expect to happen?[49]

This theory explains that the perpetrator is aware of the potential unwanted/ undesired result. However, to achieve what is intended, the risk of other results or circumstances arising (besides the purpose/objective being achieved) is accepted. If something that is a known risk will actually occur, what else could the offender do but dare to take the risk? Thus, according to this theory, two conditions are needed for intentionality.[50] (1) The person is aware of possible results or circumstances that constitute an offence. This can be proven by, among other methods, the person's own words around the act or by showing that the person did not make any effort to prevent the undesired results.[51] (2) The person's attitude towards the possibility of the undesired result is that, if it does arise, what else could he have done? The person decides he can accept the risk then dares to take that risk. That the defendant knows that the possible result constitutes a criminal act can be

[47] Decision Number 1530.K/PID/1995.
[48] See Law Magazine, Varia Peradilan [Court Miscellany] No 131 Year XI, August 1996.
[49] See Moeljatno, *Asas-Asas Hukum Pidana* (1993) 175. See also Sudarto, *Hukum Pidana I* (2013) 180.
[50] Moeljatno, *Asas-Asas Hukum Pidana* (1993) 175–76.
[51] Ibid 175.

proven by the person's experience, education, or the strata of society in which he lives.[52]

According to Remmelink, the judge can conclude that an act was intentional by relying on external conditions (data) that were collected and selected with the guidance of human experience in general, reason, and a sense of responsibility, through conditions reconstructed after the incident (*post factum*). This refers to the decision of the Dutch Supreme Court dated 1 December 1970, NJ 1971, 139. Looking at the existing conditions and based on how one person hit another, it can be concluded that the act was done intentionally. Even if a person is intoxicated with alcohol, the court will assume, as long as it is proven that there is still a minimum level of awareness, that intentionality exists. Remmelink said, of course, the factors of reason or propriety in law are taken into account. Thus, we can say that regarding purpose there is a process of objectification or inference about related norms.[53] Sudarto calls this 'objective intentionality'.[54]

B. Negligence (*Culpa*) and its Types

What is the meaning of *culpa*? In general, people recognize *culpa* as a type of fault that is less serious than *dolus*; likewise, the criminal penalty for *culpa* offences is lighter than the criminal penalty for *dolus* offences (although some are not differentiated in Indonesian law). Therefore, in the Criminal Code, criminal offences with an element of *opzet* (intentionality) are sanctioned with more severe punishment, while criminal offences with an element of *culpa* are sanctioned more lightly.[55] For example, the criminal penalty for homicide with an intentional element – that is, murder – is a maximum imprisonment of 15 years in prison (Article 338 of the Criminal Code). If the case is more severe, for example not only intentional but also planned, the offence is punishable by capital punishment, life imprisonment, or imprisonment for a maximum of 20 years (Article 340 of the Criminal Code). Meanwhile, negligent homicide (homicide with the element of *culpa*) is sanctioned with imprisonment for a maximum of five years (Article 359 of the Criminal Code). Likewise, intentionally severely injuring another person is punishable by a maximum of eight years of imprisonment (Article 354 paragraph (1) of the Criminal Code), while negligence causing serious injury may result in a maximum of five years' imprisonment (Article 360 paragraph (1) Criminal Code). There are also criminal offences in which there is only an element of *opzet* without a counterpart in the form of a crime with an element of *culpa*. Examples are some decency crimes, such as rape (Article 285 of the Criminal Code).[56]

[52] Ibid 176.
[53] Remmelink, *Hukum Pidana* (2003) 157–58.
[54] See the explanation of this objective intention in Sudarto, *Hukum Pidana I* (2013) 181–82.
[55] E Utrecht, *Rangkaian Sari Kuliah Hukum Pidana I* (Surabaya, Pustaka Tinta Mas, 1994) 326.
[56] Ibid 326.

So, what exactly is the meaning of *culpa*? In contrast to *dolus* where the will of the defendant is manifested as an act against a prohibition/order and the existing criminal penalty, in the case of *culpa*, it is the circumstances/results that are prohibited and punishable by the law because they pose a danger to the public. This danger to the public is related to the safety of people and loss of goods, so the law must also act against acts committed carelessly or negligently.[57]

As with the definition of intentionality, the definition of negligence is not provided in the Criminal Code. However, as I have explained above, from the explanation of the Dutch Criminal Code we can obtain a basic understanding that *culpa* that is omission or negligence is both the opposite of intentionality and the opposite of coincidence.[58] This explanation is quite helpful, although it does not discuss the elements of omission or negligence themselves.

In criminal law literature, it is often said that negligence is the opposite of intentionality. Intentionality emerges in an act by wanting the result of the act, while in negligence, offender does not want the result of the act, but it is the offender *not* acting that causes the outcome.[59] This is clear when *culpa* is compared to the first category of *opzet* (intentionality as intent/purpose), as well as if *culpa* is contrasted with the second category of *opzet* (intentionality with awareness of certainty) and the third category of *opzet* (intentionality with awareness of possibility / conditional intentionality). In the case of the second or third category of intentionality, even though the result is not the intent of the offender, this person still commits the act even if he knows that the result will occur. Meanwhile for *culpa*, if the person knew the result was happening, he would not have done the act. This demonstrates the difference between *dolus* and *culpa*.

According to R Tresna, lack of care or recklessness in doing or allowing something, sometimes exists to such an extent that it is clear that the offender has no sense of responsibility for other people's interests or the public interest.[60] Meanwhile, according to Vos, there are two elements of *culpa*: (1) the offender suspects the existence of results (*voorzienbaarheid*); and (2) the offender is not careful with what he does or does not do (*onvoorzictigheid*).[61] Both elements must be met.[62] For the first element, there is a relationship between the defendant's inner being and the results that arise (fault). Even the causal relationship (cause-effect) between the defendant's actions and the prohibited results must be sought (criminal act). Meanwhile, for the second element Vos explains that fulfilment requires two things: (1) the offender does not act carefully as he should; and (2) the offender has acted with care, but the offender's actions in principle are not allowed to be done.[63]

[57] Bambang Poernomo, *Asas-Asas Hukum Pidana*, 7th edn (Jakarta, Ghalia Indonesia, 1994) 171–72.

[58] PAF Lamintang and Fransiscus Theojunior Lamintang, *Dasar-Dasar Hukum Pidana di Indonesia* (Jakarta, Sinar Grafika, 2019) 339. See also R Tresna, *Azas-Azas Hukum Pidana* (Jakarta, Tiara, 1959) 65.

[59] Ibid. See also Poernomo, *Asas-Asas Hukum Pidana* (1994) 172.

[60] Tresna, *Azas-Azas Hukum Pidana* (1959) 65.

[61] Poernomo, *Asas-Asas Hukum Pidana* (1994) 174.

[62] Ibid.

[63] Ibid 175.

According to Karni, in essence, negligence contains less carefulness and less prudence.[64] Caution can only be expressed if you are able to anticipate results, or in other words, if you can anticipate what will happen because of your actions and therefore you realise you must avoid these actions. Thus, negligence involves both a lack of caution and a lack of calculation of probabilities. In other words, the individual should carry out the act in another way, or not act, but does not have the prudence to do so.[65]

According to Van Bemmelen, negligence is a normative notion and not a fact-based notion. The question we can ask is: would a sane and prudent person do the same in a particular situation? If the question is answered with 'no', then it can be objectively said that the person has committed a mistake or has been negligent. In this case, it should be noted that people who are usually sane and careful may sometimes do things with less attention and care, leading to an unintended result. Of course, it is very difficult to draw the line between accidents and carelessness. Sometimes the situation is so complicated that it is not easy to prove the existence of negligence, for example in cases of traffic accidents.[66]

According to Tresna, who says cases of intentionality are 'colourless', the same can be said for omission/negligence. That is, those who commit the omission do not need to know that their actions are against the law. Here we also encounter the thinking that everyone is presumed to know the law, once the law has been ratified.[67] So it is not necessary in every criminal case with an element of omission/negligence for the public prosecutor to prove that the defendant knew that his act was against the law.

i. Types of Culpa

After discussing the term and meaning of culpa, we now discuss the types of *culpa* as known in the doctrine or criminal legal studies. There are two distinctions of *culpa* that are well known in the criminal law literature, namely: (1) *culpa levis/levissima* and *culpa lata*; (2) *bewuste schuld* and *onbewuste schuld*. We will discuss them one by one to distinguish between them.

a. *Culpa Levis / Levissima* and *Culpa Lata*

On *culpa levis* or *culpa levissima* (mild negligence) is not a felony, goes unnoticed, or is not sanctioned with criminal punishment.[68] This is the case for offences defined as violations. The purpose is to impose a penalty on the defendant in the

[64] The meaning of 'prudent' here is not prudent as opposed to extravagant, but prudent in the sense of 'thought' or 'opinion'. See kbbi.web.id/hemat-3.

[65] Karni, *Ringkasan tentang Hukum Pidana* (1950) 68–69.

[66] See more about this in Van Bemmelen, *Hukum Pidana 1*(1987) 134–35.

[67] Tresna, *Azas-Azas Hukum Pidana* (1959) 70.

[68] Poernomo, *Asas-Asas Hukum Pidana* (1994) 173.

case of a criminal offence whose type of violation indicates a measure of mild negligence or omission.[69]

In *culpa lata* (severe negligence), negligence is seen as present in the type of felony and is to be sanctioned with criminal punishment.[70] In a crime that is a felony with an element of omission or negligence, then a severe level of omission / negligence is determined to exist.[71]

b. *Bewuste Culpa* and *Onbewuste Culpa*

In *bewuste culpa* (conscious *culpa*), the offender has realised or imagined the possible results, but believes he could still do the deed while avoiding those consequences. This is similar to *voorwardelijk opzet* (the third category of intentionality – intentionally with awareness of possibility). The difference is, in intentionality with awareness of possibility, the offender still commits the act, despite knowing that the result (which the offender does not want) may or will occur. In conscious negligence, the offender has tried to keep the result from happening. Had he known that the result would occur, he would not have done the deed.[72]

In conscious negligence, the negligent person can imagine the possible results, but does not believe that the results will occur. Maybe the person believed too much in his dexterity or his experience, or maybe he risked everything based on his previous good fortune so that he believed there would be no consequence. Here lies the fault: his overconfidence in himself, or because he is too confident in his good fortune.[73] An example of conscious negligence is told by Jonkers, as quoted by Bambang Poernomo: someone is having a party with a lot of candles near flammable materials. Although fire extinguishers have been prepared for safety, if an unwanted fire occurs, it is considered to be conscious negligence because the person was aware of the danger.[74]

In *onbewuste culpa* (unconscious *culpa*), the offender in committing the act does not imagine the potential results that arise, even though he should have been aware.[75] For the unconscious *culpa*, if the person who commits the act is completely unaware of the results of his actions then his fault lies in negligence or lack of proper thinking.[76] An example of unconscious negligence, also narrated by Jonkers, is as follows: if a person throws things away outside the building without thinking about the possibility that others will pass by, then his negligence is due

[69] Tresna, *Azas-Azas Hukum Pidana* (1959) 70.
[70] Poernomo, *Asas-Asas Hukum Pidana* (1994) 173.
[71] Tresna, *Azas-Azas Hukum Pidana* (1959) 70.
[72] AZ Abidin and Andi Hamzah, *Pengantar Dalam Hukum Pidana Indonesia* (Jakarta, Yarsif Watampone, 2010) 160–61. See also Poernomo, *Asas-Asas Hukum Pidana* (1994) 173.
[73] Tresna, *Azas-Azas Hukum Pidana* (1959) 68.
[74] Poernomo, *Asas-Asas Hukum Pidana* (1994) 173–74.
[75] Ibid 173.
[76] Tresna, *Azas-Azas Hukum Pidana* (1959) 68.

to a lack of concern for unforeseen events, the possibility of which he should have been aware.[77]

ii. Proving Culpa

As mentioned above, if omission/negligence is a written element of a criminal offence (being the core part of offence formulation / *bestandelen*), then the omission /negligence must be included in the indictment and must be proven in court. If not proven, then the defendant must be acquitted. According to Schaffmeister, Keijzer, and Sutorius, the essence of *culpa* is to cause the results. In the Criminal Code, this can be seen in Article 199 ('… because negligence causes a boat to sink …'), Article 409 ('… because negligence causes a building to be damage or destroyed …'), and others.[78] Thus, we must first find the cause. If it turns out that the cause is someone doing or not doing something, the problem is the fault of the person who caused the result. This fault may be intentional, or due to recklessness, inattention, indifference, or lack of forward thinking. If proven, the offence is a *culpa* offence.[79]

Let us take the case of a bus accident. A bus collided into another bus, injuring passengers of both buses in Haastrecht, the Netherlands (Decision of the Hoge Raad of 4 December 1939, NJ 1940, no 272, NJ 273). Van Bemmelen describes several elements which illustrate elements of *culpa* in the defendant: driving the bus very recklessly, carelessly, and very unguardedly. The verdict explained:

> … the defendant drove the vehicle carelessly, did not pay enough attention to the multiple-unit train in front of him, did not see at the right time when the vehicle in front of him braked when there was a bus from the opposite direction, so he braked so hard and the rear wheel was caught, the bus slipped and collided with another bus coming from the front.

As a result, the defendant could be blamed for his negligent actions.[80]

III. Criminal Liability

What is criminal liability? Criminal liability leads to the conviction of a person if that person has committed a crime and fulfilled its legal elements.[81] According to Huda, criminal liability is the responsibility of a person for a criminal offence

[77] Poernomo, *Asas-Asas Hukum Pidana* (1994) 174.

[78] Other examples, for example, are clear in Article 395 of the Criminal Code '… because negligence causes the death of another person' or Article 360 of the Criminal Code '… because negligence causes another person to be seriously injured'.

[79] See Van Bemmelen, *Hukum Pidana 1* (1987) 131. See also Schaffmeister, Keijzer, and Sutorius, *Hukum Pidana* (2007) 105–06.

[80] Van Bemmelen, *Hukum Pidana 1* (1987) 132.

[81] EY Kanter and SR Sianturi, *Asas-Asas Hukum Pidana di Indonesia dan Penerapannya* (Jakarta, Storia Grafika, 2018) 249.

committed. The criminal liability of the offender is related to the public's rejection of the act he committed. The public (through the state) condemns the act, which is manifested in the criminal sanction for the act prohibited or required by legislation. Therefore, anyone who commits that act will be reproached. The offender is reproached if while committing the act he was able to do something else (ie it was possible for him to not commit the act). Thus, the reproach is directed at the offender for the crime he committed.[82]

Therefore, Saleh is correct in arguing that the aim of criminal liability is to impose reproach on the offender for his actions that are in breach of a prohibition or inflict a prohibited situation. Criminal liability is thus a process of shifting the blame from the crime to the offender.[83]

As stated by Simons above, the fault in the social-ethical sense or the mental state of the offender is the basis of the offender's criminal liability. So, a person is not convicted only where the written elements (*bestandelen*) of the criminal offence are proven; fault must also be fulfilled. 'Fulfilled' here does not require fault to be proven, as it is already assumed to be fulfilled. The exception is if the defendant presents an excuse defence that eliminates his fault, in which case his actions remain against the law, but their fault is relieved.

Similarly, GA Van Hamel argues that fault in a criminal offence is a psychological understanding, which connects between the state of mind of the offender and the realisation of the elements of the crime due to his actions. A fault is thus a liability in law. Similarly, above we have discussed Karni's opinion, which states that it is a fault if the offender can be held accountable for the action; the offender must be reproached for his action; the action must contain resistance to rights (unlawful nature); and the action must be committed either intentionally, or by mistake (negligence).

What is the relationship between criminal offence and fault, in terms of criminal liability? First, we can look at the academic manuscript for the new draft Criminal Code Bill, which refers to the views of Sauer and Herbert L Packer. It is explained that there are three main issues of criminal law: (1) criminal offences (*strafbaarfeit* / *actus reus*); (2) fault (*schuld* / *mens rea*) or criminal liability; and (3) punishment (*straf* / *poena*). Sauer calls these three main issues the Trias of Criminal Law (unlawful nature, fault, and punishment) while Packer calls them the three concepts or the three basic problems (offence, guilt, and punishment).[84] So, if we talk about fault then we are also talking about criminal liability – distinguishing the fault / criminal liability from a criminal offence. In the Bill, criminal offences cannot be separated from legality – they are, by definition, against the law. Meanwhile for criminal liability, the principle is that of culpability (*geen straf*

[82] Huda, *Dari 'Tiada Pidana Tanpa Kesalahan'* (2015) 70–71.

[83] Saleh, *Perbuatan Pidana dan Pertanggungjawaban Pidana* (1983) 75. Previously in the 2000 Criminal Code Bill, the formulation of criminal liability as known in this doctrine was introduced in Article 34. However, later in the discussion in the House of Representatives, this formulation was abolished because it was deemed too theoretical, and it was considered sufficient to allow it to remain in doctrine, rather than including it in the Criminal Code Bill.

[84] Draft of Academic Paper on the Criminal Code Bill (KUHP) from The National Legal Development Agency of the Ministry of Law and Human Rights of the Republic of Indonesia (March 2015) 19.

zonder schuld), although in the later stages of drafting, exceptions were made (see the discussion on the sub-chapter of the fault and criminal liability in the New Criminal Code).

What are the conditions for a person to be found guilty? According to Sudarto, several conditions must be met: (1) the offender's ability to be responsible (*schuldfahighkeit* or *zurechnungsfahigkeit*), meaning that the state of mind of the offender must be 'normal'; (2) the inner relationship between the offender and his deeds, that is, whether they were intentional (*dolus*) or negligent (*culpa*); (3) and the offender has no reason to be excused from fault.[85]

Of course, before the offender is found to be at fault (liable), it must first be declared that his actions are against the law. If the action is not against the law (or the nature of being against the law can be eliminated, for example on the grounds of justification), then there is no need to determine the fault of the offender. On the other hand, a person who commits an act that is against the law is not at fault, so he cannot automatically be blamed for his action. Therefore, argues Sudarto, we must always be aware of the existence of a pair of conditions for conviction: (1) punishable deed (*strafbaarheid van het feit*) and (2) punishable person or offender (*strafbaarheid van de persoon*).[86]

In criminal law, criminal liability is generally formulated negatively, setting out the circumstances that can render the offender unaccountable.[87] Thus, what is regulated are the circumstances that can lead to the offender to be forgiven and not punished (*strafuitsluitingsgronden*). Criminal liability is considered to exist unless there is a reason for the excuse of fault. A similar model is adopted by Indonesia's current Criminal Code, where criminal liability is not formulated positively, but negatively. In the context of practice, a defendant is held responsible for his crime if he cannot prove that he has grounds to be excused from the fault of committing the crime.[88] In contrast to the above, the Criminal Code Bill used a mixed approach (both negative and positive): in addition to the reasons that make a person unable to be held liable, there are also certain circumstances that must exist for a person or corporation to be able to be held liable.[89]

IV. Criminal Liability and Competency

For the existence of criminal liability, it is required that the offender has 'competence' (*toerekeningsvatbaarheid*). It is not possible for a person to be held accountable when that person is not competent to be held accountable.

In what sense is a person said to be able to be responsible? What is the measure of competency? As mentioned previously, according to Simons, competency can be

[85] Sudarto, *Hukum Pidana I* (2013) 155.
[86] Ibid.
[87] Andi Zainal Abidin, *Hukum Pidana I* (Jakarta, Sinar Grafika, 1883) 260.
[88] Huda, *Dari 'Tiada Pidana Tanpa Kesalahan'* (2015) 64.
[89] Ibid 66–67.

defined as a psychological state that justifies the application of a criminal effort, both from a public point of view and the offender's point of view. How is an offender's state of mind measured? Essentially, a person can be responsible if his mental state is healthy, that is, if: (1) he is able to know or be aware that his actions are against the law; and (2) he can determine his will in accordance with that awareness.[90]

Van Hamel gives a slightly different meaning and a little more measure. He argues that competency is a state of psychological normality and maturity (intelligence) that carries three abilities: (1) the ability to understand the value of the results of his own actions; (2) being able to realise that his actions in the eyes of the public are not allowed; and (3) being able to exercise his will over the acts.[91]

The above definitions explain the meaning of competency in a positive way. In contrast, the *Memorie van Toelichting* of the Dutch Criminal Code (WvS) was formulated negatively. It is stated therein that there is no competency and therefore no accountability if: (1) the person has no freedom to choose between doing and not doing what is prohibited or ordered by law; and (2) the person is in such a state that he cannot realise that his actions are against the law and cannot determine the results of his actions.[92]

Therefore, we can conclude that, first, a person is able to be responsible if he is able to realise or know his actions are against the law, he is able to understand the value of the results of his actions, and realise that his actions are prohibited or ordered by law, and he is able to exercise his will over the act. Second, a person is not competent when he does not have the freedom to choose between doing and not doing what is prohibited or ordered by law, and he is unable to realise that his actions are against the law and unable to determine the results of his actions or unable to understand the value of the results of his actions.

In addition to not providing positive regulations on criminal liability, the Criminal Code does not provide a definition or formulation of competency. However, the Criminal Code does contain a provision in a negative way, in the sense that the person who fulfills the formulation can be declared legally incompetent. The provision is Article 44 paragraph (1), which reads: '*Niet strafbaar is hij, die een feit begaat, dat hem wegens de gebrekkige ontwikkeling of ziekelijke storing zijner verstandelijke vermogens niet kan worden toegerekend*'. This text is translated by Moeljatno as 'Whoever commits an act which cannot be held liable to him, due to his mental state being defective in growth (*gebrekkige ontwikkeling*) or disturbed by disease (*ziekelijke storing*), is not punished'.[93]

Examples of people who cannot be held responsible ('less than perfect in mind'), according to R Soesilo, include people who are mentally impaired, deaf-mute, and/or blind since birth. Soesilo argues that such individuals are not ill, but rather have under-developed minds (child-like) or disabilities.[94] Soesilo combines the

[90] Sudarto, *Hukum Pidana I* (2013) 157–58.

[91] Ibid 158.

[92] Ibid 158–59.

[93] Moeljatno, *KUHP-Kitab Undang-Undang Hukum Pidana* (2016) 21–22.

[94] R Soesilo, *Kitab Undang-Undang Hukum Pidana (KUHP) Serta Komentar-Komentarnya Lengkap Pasal demi Pasal* (Bogor, Politeia, 1995) 61.

categories of mental impairment with disabilities such as deafness, muteness, and blindness, when in fact they are different. This is perhaps related to Sudarto's view that 'intellectually disabled, deaf, and blind person [are included] if this affects the state of his psyche'.[95] According to Sudarto, social disabilities, such as a low level of education or being in a state of destitution, are not included in the formulation of 'less than perfect in mind' in Article 44 of the Criminal Code.[96] Meanwhile, those who fall into the definition of 'disturbed by disease' (*ziekelijke storing zijner verstandelijke vermogens*), include people experiencing insanity, mania, hysteria, epilepsy, melancholy, and various other mental illnesses.[97]

The Criminal Code's lawmakers, in their formulation of Article 44, use the assumption that everyone is able to be responsible for their actions, because it is considered that everyone has a healthy state of mind. That is why what is formulated in Article 44 centres on incompetence. Thus, to find out who is capable of being responsible, reverse interpretation (*a contrario*) is used. If a person who cannot be held responsible is defined as a person who has a learning disability or has a mental illness, then, on the other hand, a person who *can* be held responsible is a person who does not have the conditions noted in Article 44.[98]

If the defendant (or his lawyer) argues that the defendant cannot be punished as he is not competent, who should determine whether the defendant is capable of being held liable? It is the judge who decides this. However, judges are not experts on mental illness, so require assistance from experts (in the form of certificates) or psychiatrists (giving testimony in court). The expert can provide testimony on whether the defendant has a mental state as specified in Article 44 of the Criminal Code as well as the level/degree of this mental state. In addition, a diagnosis of the level of responsibility of the defendant can be provided. The judge may or may not believe the expert's testimony.[99]

V. Culpability and Criminal Liability in the New Criminal Code

In Book 1 of the new Criminal Code,[100] two main issues in criminal law are discussed: criminal offences (Part One) and criminal liability (Part Two). The section on criminal liability covers the general discussion, excuse defences,

[95] Sudarto, *Hukum Pidana I* (2013) 162.
[96] Ibid.
[97] Soesilo, *Kitab Undang-Undang Hukum Pidana* (1995) 61.
[98] The reverse interpretation of Article 44 of the Criminal Code to determine who is capable of being responsible is not always correct, for example, related to the competency of children under a certain age (formerly in Articles 45–46 of the Criminal Code, now in the Juvenile Criminal Justice System Law) and other circumstances. See further in Kanter and Sianturi, *Asas-Asas Hukum Pidana di Indonesia dan Penerapannya* (2018) 257.
[99] Kanter and Sianturi, *Asas-Asas Hukum Pidana di Indonesia dan Penerapannya* (2018) 260.
[100] Chapter I.

and corporate liability. There are no specific definitions of criminal liability. As mentioned above, what is provided is a regulation on what can render an offender not competent to being held liable under Article 44 (regulated negatively).

More specifically, Article 36 of the New Criminal Code states:

> (1) Every person can only be held liable for a criminal offence committed *intentionally or due to negligence*;
> (2) acts that can be punished are criminal offences committed *intentionally*, while criminal offences committed due to negligence can be punished if explicitly specified in the legislation. [emphasis added]

Article 37 of the New Criminal Code states:

> In the case determined by law, every person may:
> a. be punished solely for having fulfilled the elements of the criminal offence *without regard to the fault*; or
> b. be held liable for criminal offences *committed by others*. [emphasis added]

Article 38 of the New Criminal Code states:

> Any person who at the time of committing a crime suffers from a mental disability and/or intellectual disability, his punishment may be reduced and/or subject to action.

This is a new provision that does not exist in the current Criminal Code.

Article 39 of the New Criminal Code itself states:

> Any person who at the time of the crime suffers from a mental disability that is in a state of acute relapse and is accompanied by a description of psychotic and/or intellectual disability of moderate or severe degree cannot be convicted but an action can be imposed on him.

This formulation is quite different from the formulation of Article 44 of the current Criminal Code, which reads: 'Whoever commits an act which cannot be held liable to him, due to his mental state being defective in growth (lack of intellect) or disturbed by disease (mental illness), is not punished.' The term used by the New Criminal Code refers to the world of medicine, especially mental illness: the New Code uses the term 'suffering from mental disability' as well as the degree of its 'acute relapse state' and 'psychotic picture'. The New Criminal Code not only refers to mental disability but also 'intellectual disability', of moderate or severe degree. Both points mean an offender cannot be prosecuted, although other actions may be taken.

In the new Criminal Code, criminal liability based on fault is mainly limited to acts committed intentionally (*dolus*). The conviction of *culpa* offences are exceptions; that is, when it is strictly determined by law. Liability for certain results of a criminal act, which by law is aggravated by its criminal sanction, is only imposed when the offender should have been able to anticipate the possibility of the result if negligent. Thus, the orientation remains on the basis of fault. In the event of fault, either a fault of fact (*error facti*) or a fault of law (*error iuris*), in principle, the offender cannot be held liable and therefore is not to be punished.

However, if the fault is due to the offender's mistaken conviction and should therefore still be blamed on him, the offender can still be punished.[101]

This is different from *error in persona* which is a *dwalling* (misunderstanding or confusion) of the defendant regarding the person targeted. For example, a misunderstanding of the object of the deed, such as if A wants to kill B by firearm. A shoots a person whom he believes to be B, and that person dies. A thinks that he has succeeded in killing B, but in fact, it is not B who was killed, but C. In this situation, A can still be punished for committing murder. The *error in persona* here does not make A go unpunished. However, it is different if the quality of the object becomes an element of the criminal offence. For example, A insults B, whom A believes to be the Head of State or the head of a friendly State, whereas in fact B is an ordinary person. Here A cannot be punished for insulting the Head of State or insulting the head of a friendly State but can be punished for ordinary insult.[102]

[101] Draft of Academic Paper on the Criminal Code Bill (KUHP) from The National Legal Development Agency of the Ministry of Law and Human Rights of the Republic of Indonesia (March 2015) 181.

[102] Moeljatno, *Asas-Asas Hukum Pidana* (1993) 193–94.

7

Justificatory Defences

I. Definition

Grounds for excluding criminal punishment (*Strafuitsluitingsgronden*) are discussed in Chapter III of the Dutch and Indonesian Criminal Codes on Grounds for Excluding, Aggravating, and Mitigating Criminal Sanctions. According to Satochid Kartanegara, *Strafuitsluitingsgronden* is any circumstance that can result in a person, who has committed an act which is expressly prohibited and sanctioned with punishment by law (ie has committed a criminal act/offence), cannot be punished.[1] Why are grounds to exclude criminal punishment needed in the Criminal Code? In relation to this question, I cite the view of E Utrecht, who states that, due to the general nature of criminal law, it is possible for a person to be given an unjust sentence. So, there is a possibility that someone who is not guilty will still be sentenced for a crime if they commit an act that aligns with the description of a prohibited act, yet that person had absolutely no intention of violating the law. It could also be that the person had no intention of committing the forbidden act, but nevertheless committed the prohibited act due to an external force or reason, such as *overmacht* (duress) or necessity.[2]

In my opinion, *Strafuitsluitingsgronden* (grounds for exclusion of criminal punishment) can be divided into several categories:

(1) *Location of the grounds*. Grounds for exclusion of criminal punishment are found (a) in the law (especially in the Criminal Code), as well as (b) outside the law.
(2) *Validity*. There are (a) general grounds for the exclusion of criminal punishment, and (b) special grounds for exclusion.[3]
(3) *Nature*. There are (a) justificatory defences (*rechtvaardigingsgronden*) and (b) excusatory defences (*schulduitsluitingsgronden*).[4]

The differences between these types of grounds for excluding criminal punishment are discussed below.

[1] Satochid Kartanegara, *Hukum Pidana Kumpulan Kuliah Prof Satochid Kartanegara dan Pendapat Para Ahli Hukum Terkemuka*, Part One (Jakarta, Balai Lektur Mahasiswa, nd) 366.
[2] E Utrecht, *Rangkaian Sari Kuliah Hukum Pidana I* (Surabaya, Pustaka Tinta Mas, 1994) 343.
[3] Kartanegara, *Hukum Pidana* (nd) 368.
[4] Ibid 372.

In the law, grounds for the exclusion of criminal punishment are formulated by legislators. In addition to the Criminal Code, there are also grounds for excluding criminal punishment contained in other pieces of legislation which apply specifically to criminal acts regulated in the law. There are also grounds which are not formulated in the law; these can be referred to as grounds for the exclusion of criminal punishment for unwritten crimes. Unwritten laws are those contained in customary law, norms of public decency, and other rules that are not stated in the law.[5]

Grounds for excluding criminal punishment are contained in Articles 44, 48, 49, 50, and 51 of the Criminal Code. Several other articles outside Chapter III also formulate grounds for exclusion, including Article 166 and Article 221 (2). Article 166 is a special ground for exclusion of criminal punishment, and only applies to criminal acts in Article 164 and 165 of the Criminal Code. Article 221 paragraph (2) is a special ground for exclusion of criminal punishment for criminal acts contained in Article 221 paragraphs (1) point 1 and point 2. Therefore, these grounds for exclusion cannot be applied to other criminal acts, either within or outside the Criminal Code.

For unwritten crimes, grounds for exclusion of criminal punishment include: (1) the rights of parents, guardians, and teachers to supervise and educate their children and students; (2) the rights of doctors, nurses, midwives, and biological researchers due to their profession; (3) the consent or approval of the person affected by the act; and (4) when representing the affairs of others.

In addition to the above grounds, there are also various grounds for exclusion of criminal punishment related to actions (ie no material unlawful nature was found) and the faults of the person in question (ie no blame at all). With regards to actions, the grounds for the exclusion of criminal punishment take the form of 'no finding of an unlawful nature in a material sense'. Here, the nature of being against the law in a material sense can be used as a ground for exclusion (ie to negate criminal punishment), not positively (ie to convict).

On the other hand, if it is related to the fault of the person who committed the act, grounds for exclusion of criminal punishment for unwritten criminal acts are found in the form of AVAS (*afwezigheid van alle schuld*), meaning no fault is found in the offender. In this case, the act is prohibited and sanctioned with punishment by the law (and remains against the law), but the fault of the person who commits the act is negated. Thus, the offender is not convicted. This can also be described as 'without despicable nature' or an 'excusable error'.[6]

In terms of nature, grounds for exclusion of criminal punishment are distinguished into two forms: justificatory defences and excusatory defences.

[5] See Utrecht quoting Van Hattum's opinion: Utrecht, *Rangkaian Sari Kuliah Hukum Pidana I* (1994) 345.

[6] D Schaffmeister, N Keijzer and E PH Sutorius, *Hukum Pidana* (2007) 68.

This distinction is the type most commonly discussed by criminal law experts in both the Netherlands and Indonesia. The justificatory defences are: Article 48 on state of necessity (*Noodtoestand*);[7] Article 49 (1) on self-defence (*Noodweer / Noodzakelijke Verdediging*); Article 50 on acting on the basis of a statutory provision (*Wettelijk Voorschrift*); and Article 51 (1) on acting on the basis of an official order (*Ambtelijk Bevel*). These justificatory defences function to negate *wedderechtelijkheid* (unlawful nature) from a criminal act, meaning the act committed is no longer a criminal act. This determination applies to everyone involved in the criminal act. If it can be proven that there is justification, then the unlawful nature of the crime is negated, hence the act becomes legal or no longer against the law. Thus, those involved cannot be held criminally responsible.

II. *Noodtoestand*/Necessity (Article 48 of the Criminal Code)

What is the legal basis for necessity? If we review Article 48 of the Criminal Code, the word *noodtoestand* (necessity) does not appear at all. In its original formation, this article reads: '*Niet strafbaar is hij die een feit begaat waartoe hij door overmacht is gedrongen*.' This formulation is the same as Article 40 of the current Dutch Criminal Code, although Articles 40 to 48 of the Dutch Criminal Code only contain the word *overmacht* (under duress) and not the word *noodtoestand* (necessity). The translation of the above formulation is therefore: 'A person who commits an act because he is forced to do so by a force that cannot be resisted, cannot be punished.'

So how does Article 48 of the Criminal Code explain that necessity can be used as a ground for the exclusion of criminal responsibility? Initially, Article 48 was only the basis for *overmacht* (under duress), which was the ground for excusatory defences. According to Derkje Hazewinkel-Suringa and C Bronkhorst, as quoted by E Utrecht, *overmacht* was defined narrowly until 1923, when its meaning became broader due to the decision of the Dutch Supreme Court dated 15 October 1923. The decision is known as the Optician's Decision (described further below). After that, jurisprudence in both the Netherlands and the Dutch East Indies/Indonesia accepted *noodtoestand* (a state of necessity) as a type of *overmacht* which could exempt perpetrators from criminal conviction.[8] In addition to jurisprudence, doctrine also states that Article 48 of the Criminal Code, in addition to containing *overmacht*, also contains *noodtoestand*.

[7] Here *noodtoestand* (state of necessity) is included in the justificatory defence, as it is in the opinion of many criminal law experts, including Simons, Noyon, Langemeijer, and others. Vos and Utrecht have different opinions, stating that a state of necessity could be a justificatory defence and a excusatory defence. See the description in the next section.

[8] Utrecht, *Rangkaian Sari Kuliah Hukum Pidana I* (1994) 355.

Thus, we cannot directly search for the word *noodtoestand* (state of necessity) in Chapter III of the Criminal Code. But by following the jurisprudence and doctrine, *noodtoestand* can be said to be contained in Article 48 of the Criminal Code. Thus, necessity is a type of duress that forces people to commit criminal acts.[9]

Criminal law doctrine distinguishes between duress in the form of under duress (*overmacht*) and state of necessity (*noodtoestand*). D Simons, as quoted by Utrecht, states that *overmacht* is divided into psychological duress (*psychische drang*, also called *overmacht in engere zin*) and *noodtoestand* (state of necessity). He adds that *overmacht* is an excusatory defence, while necessity is a justificatory defence.[10] The subject of under duress will be discussed further below when discussing excusatory defences (*schulduitsluitingsgrond*).

A. Terminology and Definition of Necessity

The term *noodtoestand* has been translated by almost all Indonesian legal experts as 'necessity'. This includes Utrecht,[11] Kartanegara,[12] Andi Zainal Abidin and Andi Hamzah,[13] R Soesilo,[14] and many others.

In a legal sense, necessity means that a perpetrator commits a criminal act because he is motivated by external duress. The perpetrator is forced to choose between two 'bad' things or outcomes, and ultimately chooses to commit an offence rather than experience the negative outcomes. Therefore, it is the perpetrator himself who chooses to commit the crime, even though the choice is caused by the situation he faces. This is different from being under duress, where the choice to commit a crime is made by the person who forces the perpetrator to carry out the act.[15] There is also another difference found in the literature regarding duress: in a situation of being under duress, the duress on the perpetrator comes from

[9] I adapt this description from the opinions of Utrecht and Sudarto, which divide coercion into two: (1) absolute coercion (*vis absoluta*) and (2) relative coercion (*vis compulsiva*), the latter of which is divided into *overmacht* (under duress) and *noodtoestand* (necessity). See Utrecht, *Rangkaian Sari Kuliah Hukum Pidana I* (1994) 353–54. See also Sudarto, *Hukum Pidana* I (Semarang, Yayasan Sudarto – FH Undip, 2013) 241. In contrast, Jonkers divides *dwang* (coercion) into three types: (1) absolute coercion (*vis absoluta*); (2) relative coercion (*vis compulsiva*), ie *overmacht*; and (3) coercion in the form of *noodtoestand* (necessity). So, according to Jonkers, necessity is not part of *vis compulsiva* but rather a third form of coercion. See JE Jonkers, *Buku Pedoman Hukum Pidana Hindia Belanda* [*Handboek Van Het Nederlandsch-Indische Strafrecht*], translated by Tim Penerjemah Bina Aksara (Jakarta, PT Bina Aksara, 1987) 261–64. See also R Soesilo, *Kitab Undang-Undang Hukum Pidana (KUHP) Serta Komentar-Komentar Lengkap Pasal demi Pasal* (Bogor, Politeia, 1995) 63–64.

[10] Utrecht, *Rangkaian Sari Kuliah Hukum Pidana I* (1994) 352.

[11] Ibid 355.

[12] Kartanegara, *Hukum Pidana* (nd) 380.

[13] AZ Abidin and Andi Hamzah, *Pengantar Dalam Hukum Pidana Indonesia* (Jakarta, Yarsif Watampone, 2010) 191.

[14] Soesilo, *Kitab Undang-Undang Hukum Pidana* (1995) 64.

[15] Utrecht, *Rangkaian Sari Kuliah Hukum Pidana I* (1994) 355.

other people, while in the case of necessity, the duress on the perpetrator does not come from people but from circumstances.[16]

In 1923, an interesting case was decided by the Dutch Supreme Court. An optical shop was about to close for the day because the regulated working hours were almost over, but the optician at the shop did not close on time. This was the optician needed to make glasses for someone who had recently lost his own pair, and who was unable to go home without wearing them. The optician's action was deemed justified by the Dutch Supreme Court through its decision on 15 October 1923, NJ 1923. This decision is known as the Optician's Decision. The situation faced by the optician is an example of necessity (*noodtoestand*).[17] He was faced with two choices: immediately close his shop according to the applicable regulations, because if he continued to serve that person, he would be punished (option 1), or not close immediately and continue to make glasses for the customer because he was afraid that the customer would get hurt without his new glasses (option 2). So, the optician was in a state of necessity and when he chose option 2, his act of violating the rules regarding shop opening hours lost its unlawful nature.

In our daily lives, we can find many examples of such state of necessity. Take, for example, the classic case given by Utrecht in his book. A is being chased by a mad dog and jumps over the fence of B's yard. He therefore steps on someone else's land without that person's permission. There is an element of necessity here, namely that person A, because of the circumstances he faces, must choose between continuing to run, therefore being chased and probably bitten by a mad dog, or jumping over a fence and entering someone else's yard.[18]

In a state of necessity, a perpetrator who commits a prohibited act and is sanctioned with a criminal offence does so because of the duress of circumstances, resulting in having to choose one of the options available to him. What are the conflicting options? In criminal law literature, there are three dilemmatic situations that must result in a choice. Utrecht calls this the existence of three forms or joints of *noodtoestand*.[19] They are:

(1) *Conflicts between different legal interests.* A classic example: two people drifting in the ocean are fighting over a floating wooden block that can hold only one person. The stronger person pushes the other person away, saving only themselves.[20]
(2) *Conflicts between different legal obligations.* For example, a person was summoned as a witness at the Central Jakarta District Court. On the same day

[16] Ibid.

[17] Cultureel Woordenboek, '*noodtoestand*' (see cultureelwoordenboek.nl/wet-en-recht/noodtoestand). See also Utrecht, *Rangkaian Sari Kuliah Hukum Pidana I* (1994) 356–57. The same case is discussed in Kartanegara, *Hukum Pidana* (nd) 387.

[18] Utrecht, *Rangkaian Sari Kuliah Hukum Pidana I* (1994) 355.

[19] Ibid 358. See also Kartanegara, *Hukum Pidana* (nd) 380–82.

[20] Utrecht, *Rangkaian Sari Kuliah Hukum Pidana I* (1994) 359. See also Kartanegara, *Hukum Pidana* (nd) 381.

and time, the same person was also summoned as a witness at the Surabaya District Court. He cannot attend both, and therefore must choose between them.

(3) *Conflicts between legal interests and legal obligations.* The classic example was described earlier: A is chased by a mad dog and, to avoid it, jumps over the fence into B's yard.[21] Another example is the Optician's Case discussed above.[22]

B. Differences between *Noodtoestand* (Necessity) and *Overmacht* (*Under Duress*)

Now we will briefly discuss the difference between necessity and under duress. As explained above, necessity is a justificatory defence (*rechvaardigingsgrond*) while being under duress is an excusatory defence (*schulduitsluitingrond*). The state of necessity negates the unlawful nature of the act, while in the case of duress, the act itself is still against the law but the criminal responsibility of the person who commits the *schuld* (fault) is negated. In both cases, the perpetrator is not convicted. The difference is this: in the case of necessity, the person who commits an act is not punished because that act has lost its unlawful nature (with justificatory defence), while in the case of the duress, the person who committed the act has his fault negated (with the excusatory defence), even though his actions are still against the law.

Additionally, if an act is deemed to have been performed due to necessity, the act is no longer against the law, therefore all those who committed the act are not punished. Meanwhile, if the act was committed under duress, not everyone who committed the act can escape from criminal charges. Only people who have grounds for being under duress are deemed not criminally responsible; other people involved in the crime can still be held liable.

There is another difference between necessity and duress. In the case of necessity, a person commits an act that violates the provisions of the law because of a situation in which he must make a choice. So, the person himself chooses, but he chooses because of a situation that forces him to make that choice. Whereas if a person is under duress, a person commits an act that violates the provisions of the law because he is forced not by circumstances but by other people. So, it is not the person who chooses his action, but instead his choice is determined by the person who forces him. This other person can be punished, while the person who does the criminal act itself is not punished.

[21] See Kartanegara, *Hukum Pidana* (nd) 388.
[22] Utrecht, *Rangkaian Sari Kuliah Hukum Pidana I* (1994) 359.

C. Is Necessity a Justificatory Defence or an Excusatory Defence?

As explained above, as well as by other criminal law books and in teaching, necessity is a justificatory defence. This is reinforced by the provisions in the New Indonesian Criminal Code, where necessity is included in the section that regulates justificatory defences. This is in line with the opinion of Simons, and Noyon and GE Langemeijer.[23] However, there is one Dutch legal expert, HB Vos, who states that necessity can be seen both as *schulduitsluitingsgrond* (excusatory defence) and *rechtvaardigingsgrond* (justificatory defence).[24] This opinion was approved by Utrecht, who states that necessity could indeed be either *schulduitsluitingsgrond* or *rechtvaardigingsgrond*.[25]

Based on this description, we can analyse whether necessity is a justificatory defence or an excusatory defence. The key element is that it must be determined whether the act committed is or is not an act that is 'unacceptable by the community'.[26] If it turns out that the action in question cannot be accepted by the community, then the necessity is an excusatory defence. However, if the necessity is acceptable to the community, then the necessity is a justificatory defence. Of course, this cannot be seen in general terms, so it must be determined on a case-by-case basis.[27] On this issue, I agree with the opinions of Vos and Utrecht, that necessity can be both an excusatory and a justificatory defence. However, in my opinion, in general, necessity is a justificatory defence (thus negating the unlawful nature of the act), but in certain situations and conditions where the necessity of the act cannot be accepted by the community (ie the act remains reproachable) then necessity can be an excusatory defence.

III. Self-Defence (Article 49 (1) of the Criminal Code)

A. Legal Grounds of Self-Defence: Article 49 (1) of the Criminal Code

What are the legal grounds for *noodweer* (self-defence)? In the Criminal Code, Article 49 paragraph (1) states that a person is not to be punished if that person commits an act that he is forced to do or which is required because of an indispensable defence of self or body, or honour or decency in a sexual sense, or property, which may be his own or that of others. With regards to the attack, it should be

[23] Ibid 352.
[24] Vos as quoted by Utrecht, *Rangkaian Sari Kuliah Hukum Pidana I* (1994) 352.
[25] See Utrecht, *Rangkaian Sari Kuliah Hukum Pidana I* (1994) 348–49 and 362–63.
[26] In Dutch: *Maatschappelijk ajkeurens waardig.*
[27] Utrecht, *Rangkaian Sari Kuliah Hukum Pidana I* (1994) 362–64.

against the law and threatened at that moment or feared to happen soon. Regarding the object that needs to be defended, the article mentions honour, which here is referring to sexual dignity, therefore covering attacks in the form of rape or other sexual violence. In this context, honour does not include one's good name, so acts such as insults are not covered, meaning someone who is insulted by another person cannot legally use self-defence (*noodweer*), for example by insulting the person in return or hitting them.[28]

It should be clarified that the last element of Article 49 paragraph (1) – 'there is concern that it will happen immediately' (*onmiddelijke dreigen*) – is not contained in the Dutch Criminal Code, which only states 'threatening at that moment' (*ogenblijkkelijke*).[29] Why is that? WFC Van Hattum, as quoted by Wirjono Projodikoro, states that, in the Explanatory Memorandum of the Dutch Criminal Code, what was meant by *ogenblijkkelijk* (threatening at that moment) also includes *onmiddelijke dreigen* (concern that it will happen immediately). In fact, the Dutch government once suggested that the phrase *onmiddelijke dreigen* be added to Article 41 (1) of the Dutch WvS, but this proposal was rejected by the Dutch Parliament, perhaps fearing that it would be misused.[30]

Meanwhile, in the Dutch East Indies (Indonesian) Criminal Code which took effect on 1 January 1918, the phrase *onmiddelijke dreigen* was added. Regarding this matter, Wirjono Prodjodikoro states that the addition of the words 'it is feared that it will happen immediately' (*onmiddelijke dreigen*) related to special conditions in Indonesia, specifically that several robbers may band together to carry out robberies in a house at night. If in this case the robbers only approached the house they were targeting, and after they had approached the house from afar, the householder shoots the robber, it would be deemed that the robber had already became the perpetrator of the attack, meaning that there was 'a concern that it will happen immediately' (*onmiddelijke dreigen*).[31] According to Moeljatno, people are allowed to carry out a defence when an attack has not yet begun but there is a threat of an attack, so it is permissible to carry out self-defence. This is due to the consideration

[28] See JM van Bemmelen, *Hukum Pidana 1, Hukum Pidana Material Bagian Umum*, translated by Hasnan (Bandung, Binacipta, 1987) 190–91. See also Moeljatno, *Asas-Asas Hukum Pidana* (Jakarta, PT Rineka Cipta, 1993) 146–47.

[29] Article 49 paragraph (1) of the Indonesian Criminal Code comes from the Dutch East Indies WvS. The formula is very similar to Article 41 paragraph (1) of the Dutch WvS which reads: *Niet strafbaar is hij die een feit begaat, geboden door de noodzakelijke verdediging van eigen of eens anders lijf, eerbaarheid of goed tegen ogenblikkelijke, wederrechtelijke aanranding.* The difference is that Article 49 paragraph (1) of the Indonesian Criminal Code includes the phrase 'it is feared that it will happen immediately' (*onmiddelijke dreigen*) while originally (in the Dutch WvS) no such phrase was used.

[30] Wirjono Prodjodikoro, *Asas-Asas Hukum Pidana di Indonesia* (Bandung, Refika Aditama, 2003) 85.

[31] This information was given by A Heyman, teacher in criminal law and director of the Rechtschool in Batavia (Jakarta) where Wirjono Prodjodikoro studied law at the high school level. See Prodjodikoro, *Asas-Asas Hukum Pidana di Indonesia* (2003) 85–86. Rechtschool was founded in 1909 and closed in 1928, because at that time there was also a Rechtshogeschool (RHS) which was established in 1924. Prodjodikoro was one of 189 graduates of Rechtschool, along with other figures such as Soepomo and Kartanegara. See https://law.ui.ac.id/v3/inilah-generasi-pertama-orang-indonesia-lulusan-sekolah-hukum.

that in Indonesia, with very limited state tools, the government should give more freedom to the population to maintain their own safety.[32]

B. Terminology and Definition of Self-Defence

In Article 49 paragraph (1) of the Criminal Code, the term *noodweer* (self-defence) does not appear. Instead, the term *noodzakelijke verdediging* (an indispensable defence) is used. However, in the criminal law literature, the term that is more widely used is *noodweer*. So as Kartanegara said, in contrast to the term *overmacht* which is clearly provided for by law (as stated explicitly in Article 48 of the Criminal Code), the term *noodweer* itself is not explicitly stated in the law (specifically, in Article 49 of the Criminal Code). The term *noodweer* instead comes from legal doctrine.[33]

What does *noodweer* mean? As we have explained, Article 49 paragraph (1) does not provide an understanding of *noodweer*. The article only provides the conditions for *noodweer*. Nevertheless, an explanation can be found from the definition of *noodweer* in the Explanatory Memorandum of the Dutch Criminal Code, which explains the term in a negative way. It is argued that there is no *noodweer* without: (1) unlawful attacks; (2) direct danger to the body, honour, or property of oneself or others; (3) the need to take the action concerned to eliminate the real danger that has been caused by the attack, which cannot be eliminated by other means.[34]

Prodjodikoro gives an example of the absence of issues as regulated in Article 49 paragraph (1) of the Criminal Code. In this example, A hits B with the stick he is carrying. B fends off A's punch by pushing A's hand to the side. Self-defence was performed by B against A's attack, but no elements of the act are covered by Article 49 of the Criminal Code. On the other hand, an element is regulated by the article if the story is as follows: B, who had been beaten by A with a stick, defended himself by using his own stick to hit A, and people came to separate them. A later reported B to the police for battery, when in fact A was the one who started beating B, while B only defended himself.

If we analyse this example against Article 49 paragraph (1) of the Criminal Code, we can note the following. There was an attack that is *wedderrechtelijk* (against the law) by A against B. The attack was faced directly and immediately by B (*ogenblijkkhelijk*) and was aimed at B's body. In this situation, B did not have time to run, so he had was no other option to avoid being hurt, therefore he was required (*geboden*) to defend himself. This defence is indispensable (*noodzakelijk*)

[32] Moeljatno, *Asas-Asas Hukum Pidana* (1993) 145.

[33] Kartanegara, *Hukum Pidana* (nd) 388. See also PAF Lamintang and Fransiscus Theojunior Lamintang, *Dasar-Dasar Hukum Pidana di Indonesia* (Jakarta, Sinar Grafika, 2019) 469.

[34] Abidin and Hamzah, *Pengantar Dalam Hukum Pidana Indonesia* (2010) 469–70.

because if B did not hit back (at A), he would be the one hit (by A). Thus, all elements of *noodweer* as mentioned in Article 49 paragraph (1) are fulfilled. The counterattack by B against A was not *wederrechtelijk* (against the law); rather, it became valid, legal, and lawful, because its otherwise unlawful nature was negated because it was self-defence.[35]

As quoted by Abidin and Hamzah, GA Van Hamel states that *noodweer* itself is not something new. For a long time, people have been forced to defend themselves from attacks. Even some wars are defensive in nature. The same principle is maintained today in criminal law, in addition to being recognised in customary law, religious law, and social life.[36] A person who is being attacked is about to be killed or injured, therefore he can defend himself, and if that defence causes harm to the attacker, it is justified. If a person who sees someone else being attacked (for example, being robbed) by a perpetrator, that person may also defend the victim, for example by hitting or kicking the perpetrator.

In self-defence, if a person's certain legal interests are attacked by another person, and that attack is against the law, then the victim can be justified in making a defence against the attack, even in a way that is detrimental to the legal interests of the attacker. On the other hand, in a situation that cannot be considered self-defence, the person's actions cannot be not justified and are against the law, and can therefore be subject to criminal penalties. As Jacob Maarten van Bemmelen states, *noodweer* is '*de wet staat hier eigen richting toe*' ('self-defence is a special event of under duress'), meaning that *wet* (law) allows people to *eigen richting* (retaliate).[37] The point here may be that the person acted himself against the attack, because of the urgency of the situation meant it was not possible or too late to report it to law enforcement. WPJ Pompe, as quoted by PAF Lamintang and Fransiscus Theojunior Lamintang, says that:

> Under normal circumstances to stop the attack one has to ask for help from the authorities, but in necessity, as referred to in Article 49 paragraph (1) of the Criminal Code, he does not have the opportunity to do so, because of that, he can be justified to stop the attack himself without the help of state apparatus.[38]

According to Van Bemmelen, there is a kind of necessity seen in cases of self-defence,[39] resulting in a conflict of several legal interests. If the legal interest of a person is attacked, in principle that person may defend himself, even if he is forced to violate the legal interests of another person (namely, the attacker) by committing an act which in other circumstances constitutes a criminal act. Van Bemmelen gives the following example: a person who is threatened by another person with a gun or knife, may hit the hand holding the weapon with a stick even though he

[35] Prodjodikoro, *Asas-Asas Hukum Pidana di Indonesia* (2003) 83–84.

[36] See description in Abidin and Hamzah, *Pengantar Dalam Hukum Pidana Indonesia* (2010) 470–71.

[37] Lamintang and Lamintang, *Dasar-Dasar Hukum Pidana di Indonesia* (2019) 471.

[38] Ibid 471–72.

[39] Van Bemmelen, *Hukum Pidana 1* (1987) 180. In the translation of Van Bemmelen's book on page 189, it is stated 'self-defence is a special event of under duress', but in my opinion what is meant is under duress in a broad sense, namely in the sense of 'necessity', not in a narrow sense of under duress.

would hurt that person, thus committing harm. In fact, the person being attacked could justify killing the assailant if his life was threatened.[40]

C. Conditions for Self-Defence

According to Soesilo, there are three conditions for self-defence:

(1) The actor committing the act must be compelled to defend. The defence must be indispensable; ie there is no other way. There must be a balance between defence and attack; for example, one may not kill or injure another person to defend meaningless interests.
(2) The defence must be carried out only against the interests referred to in the legal article: that is, the body, honour (in the sexual sense), or the property of yourself or others; and
(3) There must be an attack that is against the victim's right (against the law) and is happening at that instant or will happen immediately.

As with Kartanegara, Sudarto considers that there are two elements to *noodweer*: (1) there is an attack, and (2) there is a defence that must be performed against the attack. Specifically, attack must meet the following conditions: (1) sudden, (2) directly threatening, (3) against the law, and (4) intentionally directed at the body, decency, or property. Meanwhile the defence must meet the following requirements: (1) the defence must be carried out, and (2) the defence must involve the interests referred to in the law (attacks on bodies, decency, or property).[41]

Based on the description above, therefore, we can see that there must be both an attack and a defence. Not all attacks can be defended, and not all defences meet the requirements of self-defence. Thus, in my opinion, in order to fulfil the definition of self-defence, there are four conditions:

(1) there is an attack, where the attack must threaten at the same time (*ogenblijkkelijke*) or it is feared that it will happen immediately (*onmiddelijke dreigen*);
(2) the attack must be against the law (*wederechtelijk*);
(3) there is a defence that is required (*geboden*) and very necessary/forced (*noodzakelijk*); and
(4) those defended are limited, namely: oneself or other people, the honour (in a sexual sense) of oneself or others, or one's own or other people's property.

The first condition requires that there is an attack, where the attack must be immediately threatening at that point in time (*ogenblijkkelijke*) or it is feared that the attack will happen immediately (*onmiddelijke dreigen*).

What is meant is by 'immediate' (also translated as 'sudden' or 'prompt')? The legislators wished to exclude two events from self-defence: (1) an event where

[40] Ibid 190.
[41] Sudarto, *Hukum Pidana I* (2013) 250–53.

the threat of a new attack will occur in the future; and (2) an event in which the attack was resolved.[42] For example, A threatens to beat his enemy the next day. In this case, there is no 'immediate' attack. Or for the second point, if an attack has already stopped, there can be no self-defence. In other words, if the unlawful attacks have stopped, the victim cannot defend himself by attacking back, as this would be considered revenge. However, Moeljatno states that:

> Regarding the end of the attack, it should not be interpreted that there are no more attacks. If so, if someone sees that his property has been taken by a thief, he is no longer allowed to defend himself even though the thief is still nearby. In practice, a moment after an attack is seen as [though] an attack still exists.[43]

Thus, according to Moeljatno, the measure is not just a matter of time before or after the attack, and the main measure that must be seen is the word 'forced'. That is, the defence must be forced, meaning that there is no other way for the victim of the attack to, at that time, prevent the attack from happening.[44]

We must look at this issue on a case by case basis. This is because courts have confirmed the existence of self-defence in certain cases when the attacks had not yet occurred. For example, in the Decision of Hoge Raad dated 8 February 1932, NJ 1932 (famously known as *Vrees-Arrest* or the Decision on Fright), someone intended to kill his enemy the next day. Here, the person who was threatened took action to prevent an attack on himself. The decision ruled that such actions were permitted, for example laying land mines and traps to prevent others from entering his garden. This decision was noted by Van Bemmelen, who stated that if a person lays a mine or trap, others in the area must be informed, in particular to protect the interests of those who do not intend to carry out an attack.[45] However, in my personal opinion, in a situation such as this, there is a high likelihood of endangering other people. It is also possible that the interests that are sacrificed are greater than those protected, so if there is sufficient time and opportunity, it would be better for the individual threatened to report it to the authorities, who can protect him from the attack.

The second condition for self-defence is that the attack must be against the law (*wederechtelijk*). The attack[46] is an attack that is against the law, either sudden (promptly) or threatening at that time (ie the attack is imminent). As the attack is against the law, it can be concluded that the attack is carried out by a person or persons, either directly or indirectly. An attack from a dog or a monkey, for example, is not an attack against the law because an animal cannot carry out an attack against the law. In other words, if someone is attacked by a dog and he kills the dog, this is not *noodweer*.[47]

[42] See Van Bemmelen, *Hukum Pidana 1* (1987) 192.
[43] Moeljatno, *Asas-Asas Hukum Pidana* (1993) 145.
[44] Ibid.
[45] Van Bemmelen, *Hukum Pidana 1* (1987) 192.
[46] Tresna uses the term 'rape'. Here 'rape' is not only in the sense of forced intercourse as regulated in Article 285 of the Criminal Code, but rape in the sense of assault.
[47] R Tresna, *Azas-Azas Hukum Pidana* (Jakarta, PT Tiara, 1959) 162–64.

It is vital that the attack is against the law. It is only against unlawful attacks that the affected person has the right to defend himself.[48] For example, an arrest made by a legitimate official such as from the police, prosecutor's office, or the Corruption Eradication Commission is not against the law, so the person cannot defend himself by attacking the arresting officer.

Sudarto states that the attack could constitute a criminal act, but this is not necessary as long as it fulfils the requirements mentioned above.[49] This is confusing: on one hand, it is stated that the attack is 'unlawful', but on the other hand, it is stated that the attack 'could' constitute a criminal act but it does not need to be as long as it fulfils the conditions. In my opinion, what is meant by 'attack' here is an attack that is against the law in the sense that the attack is something that is prohibited by criminal law.

Since the attack must be against the law, it is not permissible to defend oneself or others against an 'attack' that is not against the law. What if someone is defending an attack that they believe is an unlawful attack? In other words, they believe they are carrying out self-defence. To illustrate: A was attacked with a sharp weapon by B. A carried out self-defence by seizing the weapon and, with the same weapon, attacking B. At that time, C was passing by and saw that A was swinging a sharp weapon at B. C thought that A was attacking B, even though at that time, A was defending himself against B's attack. C hit A and because he was hit by C, A fell and was injured. Question: Can C be punished for hitting A in a situation where C thought he was defending B (self-defence)? This is called '*poetatief noodweer*'.[50] C must not carry out self-defence in another case of self-defence (ie A carried out self-defence for an attack by B). The defence of A against B is not against the law, so self-defence cannot be carried out by C. However, C was able to avoid criminal responsibility because C thought he was in a state of self-defence. This is excusatory defence rather than a justificatory defence.

The third condition states that the defence is required (*geboden*) and indispensable/forced (*noodzakelijk*). The act that was carried out was ordered or directed by a defence that could not be avoided.[51] In the formulation of Article 49 paragraph (1) of the Criminal Code (or Article 41 paragraph 1 of the Dutch Criminal Code), there is a phrase that reads '*geboden door de noodzakelijke verdediging*', meaning 'which he had to do' or 'which was required because the defence was very necessary'. In other words: 'required for self-defence'. The word '*geboden*' ('required') and the adjective '*noodzakelijk*' ('indispensable' / 'forced') both refer to the principle of subsidiarity. According to Van Bemmelen, this phrase is an excess of useless words, but the lawmakers clearly wished to state that – as in the case of self-defence – the principles of both subsidiarity and proportionality must be considered.[52]

[48] Moeljatno, *Asas-Asas Hukum Pidana* (1993) 147.

[49] Sudarto, *Hukum Pidana I* (2013) 251.

[50] The situation where a person mistakenly believes that he has to defend himself against danger when the danger is imagined: www.juridischwoordenboek.nl/?zoek=putatief%20noodweer.

[51] Tresna, *Azas-Azas Hukum Pidana* (1959) 162–64.

[52] Van Bemmelen, *Hukum Pidana 1* (1987) 190.

Meanwhile, the proportional principle means that the defence is required (*geboden*). This requirement is driven by the attack itself. There must be a balance between the legal interest threatened by the attack and the legal interest violated by the defence. The legal interest being defended must be of greater or equal importance.[53]

In this context, there must be a fair balance between the nature of the unlawful attack and the defence made. One should not kill or injure people in defence of something unimportant. For example, a chicken thief may not be shot dead by the owner of the chicken, even if to defend his property. Meanwhile if a big and strong person is attacked with a bat by a small person, the victim may grab and use the bat but this is enough – the victim cannot stab the attacker with a knife or machete.[54] Other examples include the defence of mango trees, in which the owner or security officer should not shoot and kill mango thieves, or an attack on an adult by a young child with his bare hands, in which the adult should not defend himself by attacking the child with a lethal weapon.

A Decision of Hoge Raad in 1934 examined the imbalance between defence and attack. The case was about a fish trap owner, who, with a rope, connected the fish trap to the trigger of a gun tied nearby, in such a way that if a thief wanted to take the fish in the trap, the gun would fire. A thief was blinded as a result of being shot while attempting to take the fish. The Hoge Raad rejected any self-defence in this case on the basis of Article 49 paragraph (1) of the Criminal Code.[55]

Finally, the fourth condition states that the scope for self-defence is limited. The defence can only be aimed at the interests referred to in the law, as in Article 49 paragraph (1) of the Criminal Code: safety (meaning the safety of life or body) of yourself and others, honour (in the sexual sense) of yourself and others, or your property or property belonging to others. Thus, attacks on honour in a sexual sense such as rape and sexual harassment are included, while honour in the sense of a 'good name' is not included.[56]

IV. Acting on the Basis of a Statutory Provision (Article 50 of the Criminal Code)

A. Legal Ground on Acting on the Basis of a Statutory Provision

The original formulation of Article 50 of the Criminal Code is '*Niet strafbaar is hij die een feit begaat ter uitvoering van een wettelijk voorschrif*.' We can translate this

[53] Ibid. See also Kartanegara, *Hukum Pidana Kumpulan Kuliah* (nd) 393–95.
[54] Tresna, *Azas-Azas Hukum Pidana* (1959) 162–64.
[55] Moeljatno, *Azas-Azas Hukum Pidana* (1993) 146.
[56] Tresna, *Azas-Azas Hukum Pidana* (1959) 162–64.

by looking at the individual elements: '*Niet strafbaar*' means 'cannot be punished'; '*hij die een feit begaat ter uitvoering*' means 'anyone who commits an act'; and '*van een wettelijk voorschrif*' which can be interpreted as 'to carry out the orders of the law'. Dali Mutiara translates the formulation of this article as 'Anyone who commits an act to enforce the law cannot be punished'.[57] Meanwhile, Moeljatno translates it as 'Whoever commits an act to implement the provisions of the law, will not be punished'.[58]

There is an interesting opinion from Hazewinkel-Suringa, who states that the provisions of Article 42 of the Dutch Criminal Code (Article 50 of the Indonesian Criminal Code), as the basis for justificatory defence, are excessive (*overbodig*), because if people carry out the provisions of the law by themselves, this means the act is not against the law. The word '*feit*' in that article refers to an act that fulfils the elements of the offence. How, then, is it possible for someone to carry out the provisions of the law and then be considered to have committed an offence? Every statutory regulation, implemented by the government through its state apparatus in carrying out the provisions of the law, is legal and not against the law, as long as it is carried out honestly and properly.[59]

In my opinion, Hazewinkel-Suringa's view is correct. It is quite clear that people who carry out the law by themselves are not acting against the law and should not be punished. In reality, law enforcement officers (police, prosecutors, and others) do not process (investigate and prosecute) people who commit acts as the implementation of statutory orders. Nevertheless, retaining Article 50 of the Criminal Code is acceptable because it acts as a guarantee for everyone who carries out the provisions of the law, stating that they are not to be investigated, prosecuted, or convicted. After all, there are times when officers' actions can be questioned. For example, the community is guaranteed freedom by the Constitution and other laws to assemble and express their opinions. However, there are times when police officers disperse rallies if they are violating the law (eg continuing past an imposed time limit or entering a prohibited place).

B. Definition of Acting on the Basis of a Statutory Provision

The word 'law' in Article 50 needs to be clarified. This is because it can be interpreted in multiple ways. First, in a broad or substantive sense, meaning all statutory regulations made by bodies/institutions that are authorised to make regulations that are binding for the general public. Thus, regulations are not limited to only laws and regulations in a narrow sense (regulations made jointly between the government and the House of Representatives), but also other regulations such

[57] Dali Mutiara, *KUHP (Wetboek van Strafrecht voor Indonesie yang telah dibaharui dengan penjelasannya)* (Jakarta, Suar Bookstore, 1951) 38.

[58] Moeljatno, *KUHP-Kitab Undang-Undang Hukum Pidana* (Jakarta, Bumi Aksara, 2016) 24.

[59] Abidin and Hamzah, *Pengantar Dalam Hukum Pidana Indonesia* (2010) 201–02.

as government regulations and regional regulations. 'Law' can also be interpreted in a narrow or procedural sense (*wet in formele zin*). This is a form of statutory regulation made by the House of Representatives and the President.[60] For example, the Police Law, Prosecutors Law, Corruption Eradication Commission Law, Narcotics Law, Health Law, and many others. Thus, regulations other than laws are not included in this category, such as government regulations, regional regulations, and gubernatorial regulations.

In Netherlands, initially, the Dutch Hoge Raad (with a decision dated 27 June 1887, W 5447) interpreted 'law' in a narrow (formal) sense. Specifically, regulations made by the king together with the *staten general* (parliament) plus AMvB (*Algemene Maatregel van Bestuur*)[61] and supplementary regulations of the laws as a whole or ordered by law. This view changed with another Hoge Raad Decision (dated 26 June 1899, W 7307), where the Hoge Raad interpreted 'law' as any provision issued by a power that has the authority to issue legislation according to the constitution or laws.[62] Pompe's opinion that 'law' is to be interpreted in a narrow/procedural sense is based on the Memory of the Explanation of the Dutch Criminal Code. This is supported by Noyon and Langemeijer, who state that carrying out the provisions of the law only involves carrying out obligations that come from written laws.[63]

Thus 'law' in Article 50 of the Criminal can be interpreted in either a broad or a narrow sense. So, people who carry out orders from government regulations presidential regulations, or regional regulations, can also use Article 50 as grounds for the exclusion of criminal responsibility.[64] This view was adopted by the Dutch Hoge Raad in a 1899 Decision. The opinion is supported by JE Jonkers and HB Vos. As quoted by Eddy OS Hiariej, Vos states that implementing a statutory regulation is for the public benefit and the public interest.[65] Van Bemmelen also adheres to the opinion that the law is in a broad (substantive) sense, not a narrow sense, and argues that *wettelijk voorschrif* (statutory provisions) here has the meaning of a provision made by a power given the right to make laws in accordance with the authority given to them. In other words, the law in the broadest sense of the term. Lawmakers almost always make laws that apply generally, not only for certain events, and lawmakers are not considered as individuals but as an institution (eg parliament and/or government).[66]

[60] Article 20 paragraph (2) of the 1945 Constitution states: 'Every Bill is discussed by the House of Representatives and the President for mutual approval'. Article 20 paragraph (4) of the 1945 Constitution states 'the President shall ratify a bill that has been mutually agreed upon to become a law'.

[61] Legislative-level regulations formed by *Kroon* (King) and ministers and receiving advice from the *Raad van State* (Council of State).

[62] Abidin and Hamzah, Pengantar Dalam Hukum Pidana Indonesia (2010) 200.

[63] Eddy OS Hiariej, *Prinsip-Prinsip Hukum Pidana*, Revised Edn (Yogyakarta, Cahaya Atma Pustaka, 2016) 279.

[64] Compare this with the explanation from R Soesilo, *Pokok-Pokok Hukum Pidana Peraturan Umum dan Delik-Delik Khusus* (Bogor, Polietia, 1984) 66.

[65] Hiariej, *Prinsip-Prinsip Hukum Pidana* (2016) 279.

[66] Van Bemmelen, *Hukum Pidana 1* (1987) 197.

On *wettelijk voorschrif* (the order of the law), let us use the example of a bailiff who evicts occupiers from a house. The baliff is legally obliged to put the goods from that house on the street. But in many municipalities, local regulations prohibit placing items on the street. Did the bailiff commit a crime by complying with the law? No, because he is following statutory provisions. A person who commits a crime according to the provisions of law is not punished. Of course, the application of this principle is rare, because compliance with the rule of law does not usually result in another crime.[67]

Soesilo states that Article 50 of the Criminal Code lays down a principle that what is required or ordered by law cannot be sanctioned by another law. Thus, implementing the law can mean two things: (1) carrying out an act that is ordered by law; and (2) all acts carried out under the authority granted by law.[68]

C. Subsidiarity and Proportionality

According to EY Kanter and SR Sianturi, the tools used by an authority to carry out an obligation that comes must be balanced, appropriate, and reasonable. For example, it would not be permitted for assistant investigators to take a shortcut through a private, closed field in order to reach the prosecutor's office faster. Likewise, it would be inappropriate for a traffic policeman, who wants to stop a motorcyclist for not using headlights at night, to shoot that person in the back. There must be a balance between the objectives and the tools in the implementation of the provisions of the law.[69]

V. Acting on the Basis of an Official Order (Article 51 (1) of the Criminal Code)

A. Legal Basis for Acting on an Official Order

The original formulation of Article 51 paragraph (1) of the Criminal Code reads: '*Niet strafbaar is hij die een fet begaat ter uitvoering van een ambtelijk bevel, gegeven door het daartoe bevoegde gezaag*.' In English, this can be translated as: 'No person shall be punished who commits an act to carry out an official order given by an authorized official.' Dali Mutiara translates it as: 'A person who commits an act to carry out an official order given by a dignitary who is entitled to it, cannot

[67] Nederlands Encyclopedie, 'Kopie van "Scholieren.com – Documap Recht in het algemeen"', encyclo.nl/lokaal/10586.

[68] Soesilo, *Pokok-Pokok Hukum Pidana* (1984) 66.

[69] EY Kanter and SR Sianturi, *Asas-Asas Hukum Pidana di Indonesia dan Penerapannya* (Jakarta, Storia Grafika, 2018) 294–95.

be punished.'[70] Meanwhile, Moeljatno translates it as: 'Whoever commits an act to carry out the official order given by the competent authority, will not be punished.'[71]

B. Definition of Acting on an Official Order

In contrast to statutory orders (in the broad sense above), or what are commonly called statutory regulations (which are generally accepted provisions), official orders are given by legitimate, authorised officials and are made for a particular event.[72] For example, an order to carry out evictions, an order to vacate a place, an order to arrest or detain an offender, and so on.

The order is by virtue of the position held. Thus between the person who gives the order and the person being ordered, there is a public legal relationship. The person giving the order must have the authority of the official or ruler, in the sense that giving the order must be based on the provisions of public law. However, the relationship does not need to be a direct relationship between superiors and subordinates. For example, if a mayor asks a member of the military for help in solving a problem, that is not a direct relationship between superiors and subordinates.[73] Likewise, in the provisions of Article 525 of the Criminal Code, it is stated:

> Whoever when there is a public danger to people or goods, or when a crime is caught red-handed, is asked for assistance by the public authorities, but refuses it, even though he is able to give it without endangering himself directly, is sanctioned with a fine …

This means that the public authorities can ask anyone for help to overcome a certain situation. This is included in the meaning of an official order, and not in the sense of an order from a superior to his subordinates.

Article 51 paragraph (1) of the Criminal Code does not need to include concrete orders, so it includes general instructions. This was confirmed in the Decision of the Dutch Hoge Raad dated 17 December 1899, W 6603.[74] We can see examples of such official orders in the following cases. A person carrying out an official order from a police officer exercising his discretion should not be penalised. For example, motorcyclist A stopped at an intersection because of a red traffic light. A nearby police officer told him to keep going; this was at the police officer's discretion. Sometime later, A received an electronic ticket and was ordered to pay a fine according to traffic regulations. It turned out that there was a lack of synchronisation of the settings in the electronic ticketing camera with police officers in the field. In such a case, A may request a letter stating that there was an order

[70] Mutiara, *KUHP* (1951) 38–39.
[71] Moeljatno, *KUHP* (2016) 24.
[72] Van Bemmelen, *Hukum Pidana 1* (1987) 197.
[73] Abidin and Hamzah, *Pengantar Dalam Hukum Pidana* (2010) 203.
[74] Ibid.

from a police officer that made A drive through a red light. It cannot be said that A violated the law because he was carrying out an official order. In such cases, there is also a public relationship, but not in the sense of superiors and subordinates. This is different from the provisions in Article 51 paragraph (2) of the Criminal Code, where there must be a superior-subordinate relationship.

VI. Justificatory Defence in the New Criminal Code

In the current Indonesian Criminal Code, justificatory defences and excusatory defences are not separated into different sections or articles. All are regulated in Chapter III of Book 1, namely in Articles 44, 48, 49, 50, and 51. Article 44 contains excusatory defences; Article 48 contains justificatory defences and excusatory defences; Article 49 paragraph (1) contains justificatory defences; Article 49 paragraph (2) contains excusatory defences; Article 50 contains justificatory defences'; Article 51 paragraph (1) contains justificatory defences; and Article 51 paragraph (2) contains excusatory defences. These articles do not expressly state that there are justificatory defences and excusatory defences. The classification is only explained in the doctrine or opinion of jurists.

In contrast to this, the New Criminal Code separately regulates justificatory defences and excusatory defences. This is adjusted to the nature of the two categories: the justification defence negates the unlawful nature of the crime and is located in the discussion section of the crime, while the excusatory defence negates the perpetrator's guilt and is located in the criminal responsibility section. Thus, this arrangement is very synchronous and in accordance with criminal legal studies, making it easier for both in terms of study and practice.

Book 1 Chapter II of the New Criminal Code regulates criminal offences and criminal responsibility. This chapter is divided into two parts: Part One on Criminal Offences and Part Two on Criminal Responsibility. The justificatory defence is regulated in Part One, specifically in paragraph 8. There are five articles which are classified as justificatory defences: Articles 31, 32, 33, 34, and 35. This is different from the existing Criminal Code, which contains just four justificatory defences. The justificatory defences that are new in the New Criminal Code are not regulated in the current Criminal Code, but are contained in doctrine: 'The absence of the unlawful nature of a crime is a justification'.

When compared with the justificatory defences in the current Criminal Code, it will look as shown in Table 7.1. As the table shows, there are no major differences between justificatory defences in the current Criminal Code and the New Criminal Code. The main visible difference is the addition of one justificatory defence, the 'absence of unlawful nature' of the crime. The other defences are almost the same.

Table 7.1 Justificatory Defences in the Current Criminal Code and the New Criminal Code

Justificatory Defence			
No	**Category**	**Current Criminal Code**	**New Criminal Code**
1	Necessity	Article 48 Not punishable shall be the person who commits an act to which he is compelled by duress.	Article 33 Whoever commits a prohibited act will not be not punished if the act is carried out due to necessity.[75]
2	Self defence	Article 49 paragraph (1) Not punishable shall be the person who commits an act necessitated by the defence of his own or another's body, chastity, or property against direct or immediate threatening unlawful assault.	Article 34 Whoever is forced to do a prohibited act is not punished if the act is carried out because of defence against attack or threat of an immediate attack that is unlawful against himself or another person, as well as honour in the sense of decency or his own property or someone else's property.[76]
3	Acting on the basis of a statutory provision	Article 50 Not punishable shall be the person who commits an act for the execution of a statutory provision.	Article 31 Whoever commits a prohibited act is not punished if the act is carried out to execute any statutory provision.
4	Acting on the basis of official order	Article 51 paragraph (1) Not punishable shall be the person who commits an act for the execution of an official order issued by the competent authority.	Article 32 Whoever commits a prohibited act is not punished if the act is carried out to carry out an official order from an authorised official.[77]

(continued)

[75] Elucidation of Article 33 of the New Criminal Code: 'What is meant by "a Necessity", for example: (a) when the ship in the middle of the sea sank, there was a struggle for the buoy between two people which caused one of them to die; (b) the actions of a doctor who faces a situation of pregnant women with high risk, whether the doctor will save the mother at the risk of the baby dying or save the baby at the risk of the mother dying; or (c) firefighters who are faced with a choice between saving nearby houses and tearing down the burning house.'

[76] Elucidation of Article 34 of the New Criminal Code: 'This provision regulates under duress which requires 4 (four) conditions, namely: (a) there must be an immediate attack or threat of unlawful attack; (b) the defence is carried out because there is no other way (subsidiarity) to repel attacks; (c) the defence can only be carried out against interests that are determined in a limited manner, namely the legal interests of oneself or others concerning honour, decency, or property; and (d) balance between defences carried out and attacks received (proportionality).'

[77] Elucidation of Article 32 of the New Criminal Code: 'In this provision, there must be a relationship of a public law nature between the one giving the order and the one carrying it out, this provision does not apply to a civil relationship.'

Table 7.1 ***(Continued)***

Justificatory Defence			
No	**Category**	**Current Criminal Code**	**New Criminal Code**
5	Absence of unlawful nature	Not regulated	Article 35 The absence of the unlawful nature of the crime as referred to in Article 12 paragraph (2) is a justification.[78]

However, the provisions in the New Criminal Code are clearer than in the existing Code. For example, the necessity defence is explicitly stated in Article 33 of the New Criminal Code, whereas Article 48 of the current Criminal Code does not do so. In addition, acting on the basis of a statutory provision, as in Article 50 of the Criminal Code, is formulated more clearly with the phrase 'to execute any statutory provision'. There is thus no need for debate or legislation in a procedural (narrow) or substantive (broad) sense, because it is clear that what is meant is statutory regulations (not just laws).

[78] Article 12 paragraph (2) of the New Criminal Code reads: 'To be declared a criminal offence, an act that is subject to criminal sanctions and/or action by laws and regulations must be against the law or contrary to the law that lives in society.'

8

Excusatory Defences

I. Insanity (Incompetency)

A. Legal Grounds

The legal ground for excluding criminal responsibility is contained in Article 44 of the Criminal Code. This article is related to lack of mental competency (*onto-erekeningsvatbaarheid*).[1] The first paragraph of Article 44 regulates the reasons for excluding criminal responsibility; the second paragraph regulates the judge's decision; and the third paragraph regulates where the provisions of the previous paragraph apply. Article 44 paragraph (1) of the Criminal Code reads: '*Niet strafbaar is hij, die een feit begaat, dat hem wegens de gebrekkige ontwikkeling of ziekelijke storing zijner verstandelijke vermogens niet kan worden toegerekend.*'[2] Moeljatno translates this as 'Whoever commits an act that cannot be accounted for by him, because of defective mental development or disturbed by mental disorder due to illness, will not be held liable.'[3] Meanwhile, R Soesilo translates it as 'Whoever does an act, which cannot be accounted for because of his imperfect mind or because of illness that alters mental capacity, should not be punished.'[4]

Therefore, in Article 44, a defendant cannot be sentenced if he is not accountable for his actions because of his 'defective mental development' or because he is 'disturbed by mental disorder due to illness'. If we compare this with other grounds for excluding criminal responsibility in the Criminal Code, we can see that the ground listed in Article 44 relates to the internal condition of the perpetrator himself, while the other grounds for excluding criminal responsibility are all external factors, such as being under duress (Article 48), state of necessity (Article 48),

[1] AZ Abidin and Andi Hamzah, *Pengantar Dalam Hukum Pidana Indonesia* (Jakarta, Yarsif Watampone, 2010) 182.

[2] The formulation in Article 44 paragraph (1) of the Criminal Code is still very similar to Article 39 of the current Dutch WvS: '*Niet strafbaar is hij die een feit begaat, dat hem wegens de gebrekkige ontwikkeling of ziekelijke stoornis van zijn geestvermogens niet kan worden toegerekend.*' (A person who commits an act that cannot be attributed to him because of a developmental disorder or pathological disorder of mental ability is not to be convicted.) Meanwhile, in the Netherlands paragraphs (2) and (3) are no longer in Article 39, but are regulated in other articles.

[3] Moeljatno, *Kitab Undang-Undang Hukum Pidana (Indonesian Criminal Code)*, new edition (Jakarta, Bumi Aksara, 2016) 21–22.

[4] R Soesilo, *Kitab Undang-Undang Hukum Pidana (KUHP) Serta Komentar-Komentarnya Lengkap Pasal demi Pasal* (Bogor, Politeia, 1995) 60.

self-defence (Article 49), acting on the basis of a statutory provision (Article 50), and acting on the basis of an official order (Article 51).[5]

B. Terms and Definitions

As discussed above, there is no provision in the Criminal Code regarding 'competency'. Article 44 paragraph (1) of the Criminal Code also does not provide an understanding of 'incompetency', but there is a relationship between the ability to be responsible and the formulation of the article. The article does not define or regulate 'responsibility' but rather regulates 'incompetency', which, as mentioned above, is because of defective mental development or a disturbance by mental disorder due to illness. Infancy does not fall within the scope of the regulation of this article, therefore Article 44 cannot be used in such a case.[6]

Since there is a relationship between 'responsibility' and 'incompetency' as regulated in Article 44 paragraph (1) of the Criminal Code, let us discuss in more depth the ability to be responsible, as this is an element of 'fault'. As previously explained, in order to be convicted, fault must exist. To prove the existence of fault, responsibility must also be proven. This is, of course, very difficult, time-consuming, and it is also costly, if in every case evidence of responsibility must be provided. However, in general, the people who become defendants in court are mentally healthy people who are able to be responsible, thus the element of 'responsibility' is deemed inherently present, unless there are signs indicating that the defendant may have an 'abnormal' mind. In such a case, the judge must order a special examination of the mental state of the accused.[7] This can also be requested by the defendant's legal counsel. If the defendant does not ask for an examination, but the judge deems it necessary, the judge can nevertheless order the examination to be carried out. If the results of the examination are indeed 'abnormal', then, according to Article 44 of the Criminal Code, the sentence cannot be imposed.[8]

Jan Remmelink writes that legislators in the Netherlands have not dealt with this incompetency issue in a thorough manner in comparison to, for example, the German Penal Code, which states that:

> Innocents are those who act as a result of an illness that interferes with their mental abilities/consciousness, causes profound disturbances to their mental awareness or because of mental disability or other serious mental aberrations, and are therefore unable to understand the unlawful nature of their actions or make decisions based on that understanding.[9]

[5] JM van Bemmelen, *Hukum Pidana 1, Hukum Pidana Material Bagian Umum*, translated by Hasnan (Bandung, Binacipta, 1987) 209.

[6] Moeljatno, *Asas-Asas Hukum Pidana* (Jakarta, PT Rineka Cipta, 1993) 167.

[7] The examination is carried out by a judicial psychiatrist.

[8] Moeljatno, *Asas-Asas Hukum Pidana* (1993) 168.

[9] In Jan Remmelink, *Hukum Pidana, Komentar atas Pasal-Pasal Terpenting dari Kitab Undang-Undang hukum Pidana Belanda dan Padanannya dalam Kitab Undang-Undang Hukum Pidana Indonesia* (Jakarta, Gramedia Pustaka Utama, 2003) 216–17.

Instead, legislators in the Netherlands have regulated the issue more succinctly, leaving examinations of the defendant's psychological condition to the authority of the judge. Remmelink says that lawmakers are obliged to decide 'incompetency', if, due to a mental illness (disorder of mental abilities), there is no sufficient reason to demand criminal responsibility. In this case, the judge is required to ask for expert assistance (such as a psychiatrist) so that the decisions he makes are more accountable.[10]

The issue of whether there is criminal responsibility is thus also decided by the judge. According to WPJ Pompe, as quoted by AZ Abidin and Andi Hamzah, this is a juridical definition, not a medical one. Responsibility (*toerekenbaarheid*) is linked to fault (*schuld*). If the defendant can be held responsible, it means that the defendant's mental state also determines that he is to be held liable for the act. Responsibility itself is not *bastendelen* (the core part of the offence, or the written element in the formulation of the article) so it does not need to be proven by the public prosecutor. However, incompetency is the reason for excluding criminal responsibility.[11] Thus, as described above, if there is any doubt about the responsibility of the defendant, it is necessary for an expert to examine the defendant and provide information to the judge. The judge then decides whether the defendant can be held liable.

Now, we shall return to the three terms in Article 44 paragraph (1) of the Criminal Code above: (1) *verstandelijke vermogen* (mental capacity/reason); (2) *gebrekkige ontwikkeling* (defects in growth); and (3) *ziekelijke storing* (disturbed by mental disorder due to illness). The phrase '*verstandelijke vermogen*' here means the mental capacity, reasoning, or intelligence of the mind. The original Dutch text in the Dutch East Indies WvS and Indonesian Criminal Code is '*verstandelijke vermogen*' (mental capacity/reason, while the current Dutch Criminal Code uses the term '*geestvermogens*' (psychological abilities) in Article 39.[12] Interestingly, the Dutch Criminal Code also originally used '*verstandelijke vermogen*' but this was altered to '*geestvermogens*' on 2 May 1925, which came in effect on 1 November 1928, and remains in use today.[13]

I am interested in the difference between '*verstandelijke vermogens*' (mental capacity/reason), used in Article 44 of the Indonesian Criminal Code, and '*geestvermogens*' (psychological abilities), used in Article 39 of the Dutch Criminal Code. Why did the Dutch Criminal Code initially use the term *verstandelijke vermogens*, leading to it still being used in the Indonesian Criminal Code? One reason was that at that time when the Code was originally written, there was still a strong belief that an offender could simultaneously have intact reasoning abilities but also possess flawed ethical and social skills, and therefore be unfit to escape criminal

[10] Remmelink, *Hukum Pidana* (2003) 216–17.

[11] Abidin and Hamzah, *Pengantar Dalam Hukum Pidana Indonesia* (2010) 183.

[12] Soesilo, *Kitab Undang-Undang Hukum Pidana* (1995) 60–61. See also EY Kanter and SR Sianturi, *Asas-Asas Hukum Pidana di Indonesia dan Penerapannya* (Jakarta, Storia Grafika, 2018) 258.

[13] Remmelink, *Hukum Pidana* (2003) 220. See also van Bemmelen, *Hukum Pidana 1* (1987) 212.

responsibility. Therefore, at first, the term *verstandelijke vermogen* (mental capacity) was used, as this would not exclude offenders who are morally flawed from criminal responsibility.

Let us now turn to the next term in Article 44 of the Criminal Code: '*gebrekkige ontwikkeling*'. The meaning of this term is 'poor growth' or 'defects in growth'. The combination of the two terms gives the meaning: a soul, mind, or mental capacity that is defective in growth. Moeljatno calls this 'defective mental development'.[14]

EY Kanter and SR Sianturi use very similar terms, namely 'a defective mentality in growth',[15] while Soesilo uses 'imperfect intellect'[16] and Abidin and Hamzah translate the term as 'his common sense is flawed'.[17] This is the first condition in Article 44 paragraph (1) of the Criminal Code. Conditions such as a defective/imperfect mind or reason are referred to as imperfect mental development, or intellectual disabilities caused by delayed mental growth. Soesilo also mentions that the condition, as stated in the Criminal Code, includes congenital physical and other disabilities such as blindness, deafness, and muteness. In his view, these disabilities also impact the individual's mental condition.[18] He argues that what is meant by a mental condition that is disabled due to growth is any person who is an adult but behaves like a child.[19]

It is interesting that Soesilo's opinion that an imperfect intellect includes congenital physical disabilities such as deafness, blindness, and muteness. This seems to be in line with Remmelink's explanation that the lawmakers did not mention disabilities one by one, but rather took into account a number of developmental disorders, challenges, and disabilities. Physical defects, whether present at birth or acquired later in childhood, were – at the time – thought to be the cause of mental imperfections.[20]

Finally, what is meant by '*ziekelijke storing der verstandelijke vermogens*'? We can translate this as 'disturbed by mental disorder due to illness', or, to use Soesilo's term, 'illness that alters mental capacity'. Soesilo explains that this definition includes madness, mania, hysteria, epilepsy, melancholia, and various other mental illnesses.[21]

Disabilities that are present from birth (or since childhood) and those that occur later due to illness are viewed as influencing individuals' psychological state. In this regard, under the Criminal Code, both conditions would be considered

[14] Moeljatno, *Kitab Undang-Undang Hukum Pidana* (2016) 22.

[15] Kanter and Sianturi, *Asas-Asas Hukum Pidana* (2018) 256–57.

[16] Soesilo, *Kitab Undang-Undang Hukum Pidana* (1995) 60. Dali Mutiara has the same opinion as Soesilo. See Dali Mutiara, *KUHP, Kitab Undang2 Hukum Pidana Republik Indonesia* (Jakarta, Toko Buku 'Suar', 1951) 36. Balai Pustaka translates the term in the same way as Soesilo and Dali Mutiara: *Kitab Oendang2 Hoekoeman Bagi Hindia Belanda* (Batavia, Balai Poestaka, 1940) 39.

[17] Abidin and Hamzah, *Pengantar Dalam Hukum Pidana Indonesia* (2010) 182.

[18] Soesilo, *Kitab Undang-Undang Hukum Pidana* (1995) 60–61. See also Kanter and Sianturi, *Asas-Asas Hukum Pidana* (2018) 258. See also Remmelink, *Hukum Pidana* (2003) 221.

[19] Kanter and Sianturi, *Asas-Asas Hukum Pidana* (2018) 258.

[20] Remmelink, *Hukum Pidana* (2003) 221.

[21] Soesilo, *Kitab Undang-Undang Hukum Pidana* (1995) 61.

psychological disorders. Therefore, according to Nieboer as quoted by Remmelink, it can be concluded that the difference between 'defective development' and 'disturbed by mental disorder due to illness' is not clear. From a psychiatric point of view, this distinction is also untenable and juridically useless.[22]

Let us return to Article 44. It should be emphasised that not every person whose mind is deemed defective or of imperfect intellect is automatically incapable of being responsible. The provision of Article 44 of the Criminal Code (or Article 39 of the Dutch Criminal Code) requires serious disability to mean that the perpetrator cannot be held accountable for his actions. If the perpetrator can still be blamed even though he has a mental disorder, he can still be held liable for the action, and at least he will be deemed capable of being subject to criminal sanctions.[23]

We must look at the history of Article 44 in order to understand it better. Historically, the Netherlands was colonised for several years by the French (1811–1813), during which the French Penal Code of 1810 was applied. The Penal Code only recognised severe *etat de démence* (state of dementia)[24] as a basis for not being able to take responsibility. The Dutch Penal Code, which came into force in 1886, accepted a wider range of reasons for incompetency. This can be seen in the formulation of Article 39 of the Dutch Criminal Code, which states that a person cannot be convicted of an act for which he cannot be held liable, because his mental capacity is defective in growth or is disturbed by mental disorder.[25] We have discussed this above.

In terms of determining capacity, a psychiatrist can provide evidence on the severity of the intellectual or mental disability. It is the judge who then decides whether the person can be held responsible. So, there are two important elements that must be investigated: first, is there a causal relationship between the illness (mental disability and mental disorders due to illness) and the actions taken; and, second, can the perpetrator can be held liable for his actions?[26]

This causal relationship needs to be investigated if an individual suffers from a mental disorder. For example, if an individual suffers from delusions of being followed by other people who he thinks threaten him, and he attacks the people around him who he thinks threaten him, then there is a causal relationship between the delusional disorder and his attacks on others. Similarly, someone who suffers from kleptomania cannot be blamed if he commits an act of theft caused by that urge. On the other hand, if an individual who suffers from delusions (such as the man described above who believes those around him are threatening him) commits an act of theft, there is no causal relationship between the perpetrator's

[22] Remmelink, *Hukum Pidana* (2003) 221–22.

[23] Ibid 212.

[24] Dementia is a mental health disorder caused by damage to nerve cells and the connections between nerves in the brain. https://www.dementia.org.au/sites/default/files/helpsheets/Helpsheet-AboutDementia01-WhatIsDementia_indonesian.pdf accessed on 30 April 2022.

[25] van Bemmelen, *Hukum Pidana 1*(1987) 212.

[26] Remmelink, *Hukum Pidana* (2003) 212.

mental disorder and his actions. Similarly, if a person suffering from kleptomania physically assaults another person, there is no relationship between his illness and his actions. In such cases, the person can be held accountable for his actions.[27]

In Indonesia, the New Criminal Code has recognised this and proposes to change the formulation to 'mental disability and/or intellectual disability'. The full text of the draft Article 38 reads: 'Everyone who at the time of committing a crime suffers from a mental disability and/or intellectual disability whose criminal offence can be reduced and subject to action.' What is meant by 'mental disability' is a disturbance in the function of thought, emotion, and behaviour. This includes, among others, psychosocial illnesses such as schizophrenia, bipolar, depression, anxiety, and personality disorders, and developmental disabilities that affect social interaction skills, such as autism and hyperactivity. What is meant by 'intellectual disability' is a disturbance in the function of thought due to a below average level of intelligence. Under the New Criminal Code, offenders who suffer from mental disabilities and/or intellectual disabilities are judged to be incapable of realising the unlawful nature of the actions committed or to act based on awareness that they can be punished. Therefore, they cannot be held liable.[28] This is an improvement on the provisions of Article 44 of the current Criminal Code.

The current Article 44 also appears in the New Criminal Code, specifically in Article 39, which reads:

> Any person who at the time of committing a crime suffers from a mental disability who is in an *acute relapse* and is accompanied by psychotic features and/or moderate or severe intellectual disability cannot be sentenced but may be subject to action. [emphasis added]

II. Duress

A. Legal Grounds

The legal basis of *overmacht* (duress) is Article 48. Most legal scholars argue that duress is an excusatory defence. However, there is a different opinion held by Van Hamel, who argues that duress is a justificatory defence.[29] As discussed previously when discussing state of necessity, Article 48 of the Criminal Code is the key article, as both necessity and duress are contained in this article, even though the drafters initially only referred to duress. The original formula reads: '*Niet strafbaar is hij die een feit begaat waartoe hij door overmacht is gedrongen*.' The translation is: 'A person who commits an act because he is forced by a duress that cannot be resisted cannot be punished.'

[27] Ibid.

[28] Elucidation of Article 38 of the Criminal Code Bill.

[29] See Satochid Kartanegara, *Hukum Pidana Kumpulan Kuliah Prof Satochid Kartanegara dan Pendapat Para Ahli Hukum Terkemuka* (Jakarta, Balai Lektur Mahasiswa, nd) 385.

According to Derkje Hazewinkel-Suringa and C Bronkhorst, *overmacht* (duress) was narrowly defined until 1923 and could not be separated from French jurisprudence regarding *overmacht*, which viewed the term in a narrow sense; that is, only covering psychological coercion and not a state of necessity. Simons, as quoted by E Utrecht, states that *overmacht* is divided into psychological coercion (*psychische drang*, also called *overmacht in engere zin*) and necessity (*noodtoestand*). Simons states that psychological coercion (*overmacht*) is an excusatory defence, while an emergency is a justificatory defence.[30]

B. Terms and Definitions

Article 48 of the Criminal Code uses the term *overmacht*. In Indonesian criminal law literature, there are also authors who still use the term *overmacht*, such as Soesilo,[31] R Tresna,[32] and Satochid Kartanegara.[33] MH Tirta Amidjadja instead uses the terms 'forced cause' for *overmacht* and 'forced circumstances' for *noodtoestandt*,[34] while PAF Lamintang and Fransiscus Theojunior Lamintang use the term 'necessity' for *overmacht*.[35] Meanwhile, Utrecht uses a unique term that is rarely used by other authors: 'opposing weight'.[36] Most common, though, is 'duress', which is used among others by Moeljatno,[37] Kanter and Sianturi,[38] and Eddy OS Hiariej.[39] I myself often use the term 'duress' for *overmacht*, primarily because this term is widely used and understood in Indonesia.

As stated above, coercion is divided into two categories: absolute coercion (which cannot be avoided at all) and relative coercion. When we talk about duress, it means we are talking about relative coercion, as in this situation the power that influences one's actions is not absolute. Absolute coercion means people are forced to do something and cannot do anything else. When under *overmacht* or duress, the coercion is not absolute, because the person experiencing duress can still do other things (although doing those things cannot necessarily be expected). For example, a bank teller is forced by someone holding a gun to surrender all the money in the safe. If the bank teller does not comply with the request, he could be shot and killed. However, the person being threatened can still choose whether to hand over the cash or whether to fight, although if he chooses the latter, he could

[30] Utrecht, *Rangkaian Sari Kuliah Hukum Pidana I* (Surabaya, Pustaka Tinta Mas, 1994) 352.

[31] R Soesilo, *Kitab Undang-Undang Hukum Pidana (KUHP) Serta Komentar-Komentarnya Lengkap Pasal demi Pasal* (Bogor, Politeia, 1995) 63–64.

[32] R Tresna, *Azas-Azas Hukum Pidana* (Jakarta, Tiara, 1959) 158–59.

[33] Kartanegara, *Hukum Pidana*(nd) 376–77.

[34] MH Tirta Amidjaja, *Pokok-Pokok Hukum Pidana* (Jakarta, Penerbit Djakarta, 1955) 70–71.

[35] PAF Lamintang and Fransiscus Theojunior Lamintang, *Dasar-Dasar Hukum Pidana di Indonesia* (Jakarta, Sinar Grafika, 2019) 433.

[36] E Utrecht, *Rangkaian Sari Kuliah Hukum Pidana I* (Surabaya, Pustaka Tinta Mas, 1994) 348.

[37] Moeljatno, *KUHP Kitab Undang-Undang Hukum Pidana* (Jakarta, Bumi Aksara, 2016) 23.

[38] Kanter and Sianturi, *Asas-Asas Hukum Pidana di Indonesia dan Penerapannya* (2018) 271.

[39] Eddy OS Hiariej, *Prinsip-Prinsip Hukum Pidana* (Yogyakarta, Cahaya Atma Pustaka, 2016) 262.

be killed. If he chooses to hand over cash to the robber, he will not be punished because he is in a state of *overmacht*. Of course, he could act differently, such as attempting to fight back, but he is not expected to do so, because the consequences could be disastrous.[40]

According to Tresna, not every act of coercion or compulsion can cause *overmacht* as referred to in Article 48 of the Criminal Code. For example, an employer (A) ordered his subordinate (B) to beat another person (C). Even though B did the act of assaulting C under the influence of his employer, he does not escape punishment on the basis of *overmacht*.[41]

Thus, duress, in the narrow sense meant by Article 48, in fact has a special meaning: coercion that comes from someone who directs or forces someone to commit a crime, where coercion itself is relative and not absolute. Absolute coercion is not called duress and is not regulated by Article 48. Meanwhile, if 'coercion' comes from circumstances or nature (not from a person) and the person himself chooses to commit an unlawful act (not determined or chosen by someone), then it is not 'duress' but 'necessity'.

III. Excessive Self-Defence

A. Legal Grounds

The legal ground for excluding criminal responsibility in the form of a forced defence exceeding the limit (in short: excessive self-defence) is Article 49 paragraph (2) of the Criminal Code which originally read: '*Niet strafbaar is de overschrijding van de grenzen van noodzakelijke verdediging, indien zij het onmiddellijk gevolg is gewest van hevige gemoedsbeweging, door de aanranding veroorzaakt*.' This formulation is exactly the same as the formulation of Article 41 of the Dutch Criminal Code.

Moeljatno translates Article 49 paragraph (2) as: 'An excessive self-defence, which is directly caused by a great mental shock due to the attack or threat of attack, is not punished.'[42] A slightly different translation is given in the Criminal Code published by Balai Pustaka, with the phrase 'because of hot-heartedness or dark eyes',[43] while Moeljatno uses the term 'by a great agitation of the soul'. Dali Mutiara's transation is similar to that of Balai Pustaka, with Mutiara also using the phrase 'because he is very hot-hearted'.[44] Satochid calls it 'a great mental stress'.[45] Finally, Soesilo translates Article 49 paragraph (2) as: 'Exceeding necessary defence

[40] Tresna, *Azas-Azas Hukum Pidana* (1959) 158–59.
[41] Ibid 159.
[42] Moeljatno, *KUHP Kitab Undang-Undang Hukum Pidana* (2016) 23–24.
[43] *Kitab Oendang2 Hoekoeman Bagi Hindia Belanda* (Batavia, Balai Poestaka, 1940) 41.
[44] Mutiara, *KUHP Kitab Undang2* (1951) 38.
[45] Kartanegara, *Hukum Pidana* (nd) 405.

limit, if the act is suddenly carried out because the feeling is disturbed immediately at that time, it should not be punished.'[46]

B. Terms and Definitions

Based on the discussion of Article 49 paragraph (2) above, we find an important term that is also often used to refer to the grounds for excluding criminal responsibility under this article: 'A forced defence that exceeds the limit.' In Dutch, this is called *noodweer-exces*,[47] and almost all Indonesian legal experts use the term 'excessive self-defence' or something similar. Remmelink states that in cases of *noodweer-exces* there is an excess of defence (*excessief* or excessive) or, at least, the defendant has used drastic efforts to defend himself.[48]

Where experts differ is the term *hevige gemoedsbeweging*. Moeljatno translates this as 'a great agitation of the soul'; others describe this as 'very hot-hearted', 'dark eyes', 'a feeling of being shaken', and 'great mental stress'. Tirta Amidjaja uses the term 'great impulse'.[49] Meanwhile, the draft Criminal Code Bill uses the term 'severe mental shock' (Article 43). The terms in the Criminal Code Bill are the same as the terms used by Moeljatno. Do all these terms refer to the same thing? Let us look at the following description first.

According to Satochid, 'great mental stress' – which in Dutch is *hevige gemoedsbeweging* – was originally to be described as *vrees en radeloosheid* (afraid and confused). However, the Dutch Parliament considered the term too narrow, and settled on the term *hevige gemoedsbeweging* instead to use in the draft Dutch Criminal Code. As stated above, this term is translated by Satochid as 'severe mental stress'. Thus with the change in terms (from *vrees en radeloosheid* to *hevige gemoedsbeweging*), the article also includes a mental state of intense anger, as well as fear and confusion.[50]

Unlike self-defence, which as regulated in Article 49 paragraph (1) of the Criminal Code is a justificatory defence, Article 49 paragraph (2)'s excessive self-defence is an excusatory defence.[51] Thus, defence that exceeds the limit is not justified by law; in other words, the act remains against the law, but the perpetrators are not to be punished because their mistakes were negated using an excusatory defence. Of course, this is only if the conditions of Article 49 paragraph (2) are met. This means that not all excessive self-defence is not punishable by law, but rather only excessive self-defence that meets the requirements of Article 49 paragraph (2).

[46] Soesilo, *Kitab Undang-Undang Hukum Pidana* (1995) 64.

[47] See Remmelink, *Hukum Pidana* (2003) 246. See also Tirta Amidjaja, *Pokok-Pokok Hukum Pidana*(1955) 64. See also Soesilo, *Kitab Undang-Undang Hukum Pidana* (1995) 66.

[48] Remmelink, *Hukum Pidana* (2003) 247.

[49] Tirta Amidjaja, *Pokok-Pokok Hukum Pidana* (1955) 64–65.

[50] Kartanegara, *Hukum Pidana* (nd) 405–06.

[51] Ibid 406.

As with self-defence, for the excuse of excessive self-defence, it is required that there must be an attack or threat of attack. An example of excessive self-defence is if an individual defends himself by shooting a gun, even though defending himself with a wooden bat would be sufficient. Exceeding these limits by law is permitted as long as it is caused by a feeling of intense shock arising from an attack or threat of attack.[52]

Soesilo gives another example of an excessive self-defence as follows. A police officer witnessed his wife being raped. He pulled out the gun he was carrying and fired several times at the rapist. Here, the police officer's defence went beyond what was needed, because without shooting him multiple times, the rapist would have stopped what he was doing and fled. If it could be proven at trial that the excessive defence was 'forced', due to the police officer's extreme anger as a result of seeing his wife being raped, then the police officer will not be punished for his actions.[53] In other words, his self-defence did not meet the requirements in Article 49 paragraph (1) of the Criminal Code because it had exceeded the limit, meaning his act of shooting the rapist was still against the law, but his fault was negated based on Article 49 paragraph (2) due to the immense shock of what happened.

In my opinion, when we look at the *noodweer-exces* of Article 49 paragraph (2), we can see it in three parts. The first part is the word 'self-defence; the second is the word 'excessive', and the third is the phrase 'caused directly by a great mental agitation by the attack or threat of the attack'. All three of these parts must be fulfilled in order for the defendant to avoid punishment.

Let us talk about element one, 'self-defence', first. As stated above, in the case *of noodweer-exces*, there must also be the same conditions as in the case of *noodweer*: (1) there is an attack, where the attack must be threatened at that time (*ogenblijkkelijke*) or there is a fear that it will happen soon (*onmiddelijke dreigen*); (2) the attack must be against the law (*wederechtelijk*); and (3) that which is defended is limited to the honour (in a sexual sense) of oneself or others, or one's own or other people's property. According to Remmelink, for the existence of *noodweer-exces*, there must be a *noodweersituatie*; that is, a situation that requires the perpetrator to carry out self-defence.[54]

The second element is 'excessive'. This refers to the existence of conditions that are not met, namely not *geboden* (required) and not *noodzakelijk* (indispensable / forced). It could also be said that the defence was excessive because the defence did not fulfil the principles of subsidiarity and proportionality. The principle of subsidiarity means that there is no other way for those affected by the attack to ward off the attack at that time. The act committed must be forced as a means of defence, and this defence must be absolutely necessary, with no other options. This means that if there is still the possibility to do something else to avoid an attack, the defence cannot be said to be forced (*noodzakelijk*). Meanwhile, the principle of proportionality means

[52] Soesilo, *Kitab Undang-Undang Hukum Pidana* (1995) 66.
[53] Ibid 66.
[54] Remmelink, *Hukum Pidana* (2003) 248.

that the defence is a necessity (*geboden*). This necessity is driven by the attack. There must be a balance between the legal interest threatened by the attack and the legal interest violated by the defence. The legal interests being defended must be more important or at least equal in value to the legal interests that are prohibited.[55]

Thus it is clear that in the case of excessive self-defence, the defendant must fulfil the three conditions for *noodweer*: there is an attack, where the attack is threatened at that time or feared to happen soon (threat of attack); the attack is unlawful; and that which is defended is either the honour (in a sexual sense) of oneself or others, or the property of oneself or others. However, cases of excessive self-defence do not meet the condition: 'there is a defence that is required and it is indispensable/forced'. In other words, the defence is not required and absolutely necessary (ie forced). This is where the 'excessive' lies, in exceeding the limits of what is required and the necessity to do so.

Now, let us discuss the third element. The explanation above is related to excessive self-defence. It is not enough to end here, otherwise the perpetrator will still be punished. The third part of *noodweer-exces* – ie 'which is directly caused by a mental shock due to an attack or threat of the attack' – must also be met in order for the defendant to avoid punishment.

Here, there are two elements: (1) there is a shock of the soul (very hot-tempered, dark eyes, feeling shaken), and (2) mental shock (very hot-tempered, dark eyes, feeling shaken) because of an attack or threat of attack. According to Remmelink, in this case there is 'double causality'. By this, Remmelink means there are two causalities (cause and effect): (1) excessive self-defence is a direct result of mental shock and (2) mental shock caused by an attack.[56]

Thus, it must be proven that the excessive self-defence is directly caused by a shock to the soul, and it must also be proven that the mental shock is due to the attack or threat of attack (and not for any other reason). There must be a causal relationship between the attack or the threat of attack with the mental shock.[57]

For example, A had trouble at work and as a result he was fired from his job. Arriving home that day, he found a thief (B) who was stealing his motorbike. A, who was enraged because he had lost his job earlier, took an iron rod from his house and beat B until B died. Here, the three requirements of *noodweer* have been met, but A has not fulfilled the condition that the defence is required (*geboden*) and indispensable/forced (*noodzakelijk*).

In such a case, the defendant can still be convicted because the requirements of Article 49 paragraph (1) of the Criminal Code are not met. The perpetrator is not punished (the fault is negated) only if the condition 'there is a required defence (*geboden*) and it is indispensable/forced (*noodzakelijk*)' is directly caused by the mental shock (due to an attack or threat of an attack. Not for any other reason.

[55] See JM van Bemmelen, *Hukum Pidana 1, Hukum Pidana Material Bagian Umum*, translated by Hasnan (Bandung, Binacipta, 1987) 190. See also Kartanegara, *Hukum Pidana* (nd) 393–95.

[56] Remmelink, *Hukum Pidana* (2003) 246–47.

[57] Kartanegara, *Hukum Pidana* (nd) 405.

A different reason for perpetrating excessive self-defence could be the character or nature of the perpetrator himself. As Remmelink states, the emotional agitation must be caused by an attack, not because of the character of the perpetrator himself or his emotional sensitivity.[58] In such a case, the perpetrator could still be punished because the excessive self-defence was not caused by the attack itself.

Thus, the description of excessive self-defence above when explained with a chart, will look like this:

(1) self-defence[59]
(2) that exceeds beyond the limits (excessive)
(3) which is directly caused by a severe mental shock (very hot-tempered, dark eyes, feeling shaken) due to attack or threat of an attack.

Now the question is, what are the forms of agitated soul (or very hot-tempered, dark eyes, shaken feeling)? As explained by Satochid, the condition covers extreme anger as well as fear and confusion. This includes a wide array of emotions, including anxiety, helplessness (desperation), rage, and irritation.[60]

Next, why are these conditions able to negate the perpetrator's fault, even though the act committed is still against the law? Jacob Maarten van Bemmelen argues that an attack on oneself, one's honour, morals, or property will cause intense emotions in the person being attacked. Because of these emotions, it is impossible, or at least very difficult, to consider objectively whether the attack could have been defended in any other way. If therefore the person who was attacked exceeds the limits of self-defence because of the mental shock caused by the attack, he can be forgiven and not be punished.[61]

IV. Acting on an Unauthorised Official Order, but in Good Faith

A. Legal Grounds

The legal basis for excluding criminal responsibility is Article 51 paragraph (2) of the Criminal Code:

> Een onbevoegd gegeven amtelijk bevel heft de strafbaarheid niet op, tenzij het door den ondergeschikte te goeder trouw als bevoegd gegeven werd beschouwd en de nakoming daarvan binnen den kring zijner ondergeshiktheid was gelegen.
>
> [An official order given by an unauthorised authority does not exempt from punishment, unless the employee under it sincerely thinks that the authority has the right to

[58] Remmelink, *Hukum Pidana* (2003) 247.
[59] In my opinion, this is what Remmelink means by a situation that requires the perpetrator to carry out self-defence (*noodweersituatie*), as discussed above.
[60] See Remmelink, *Hukum Pidana* (2003) 247–48.
[61] Van Bemmelen, *Hukum Pidana 1* (1987) 193.

> give the order and carrying out the order becomes the obligation of the employee under the order.][62]

Article 51 paragraph (2) is an excusatory defence. This is in contrast to Article 51 paragraph (1), which is a justificatory defence. So, a person who commits an act that is prohibited and is threatened with punishment by laws and regulations for carrying out an unauthorised official order is still punished because his act is against the law. This is different from Article 51 paragraph (1), where a person commits an act that is prohibited and threatened with punishment by the laws and regulations, but the act is done because of a legitimate official order, then the nature of the act being against the law is negated. Therefore, Article 51 paragraph (1) is a justification because it negates the unlawful nature of the act committed.

On the other hand, Article 51 paragraph (2) does not negate the unlawful nature of acts committed due to carrying out an unauthorised official order. However, the law protects a person who carries out an unauthorised official order if he honestly believes that the order given is a legitimate official order. After all, there are other conditions that will be discussed below. If it meets the requirements in Article 51 paragraph (2) of the Criminal Code, the fault of the perpetrator is negated by the excusatory defence.

B. Terms and Definitions

Article 51 paragraph (1) is often referred to as '*ambtelijk bevel*' (carrying out official orders), from one of the phrases contained in the article. Meanwhile, Article 51 paragraph (2) contains the term '*een onbevoegd gegeven amtelijk bevel*' (an unauthorised official order). It is difficult to summarise this clearly, because after that phrase, there are still other important elements that must also be fulfilled. Therefore, I summarise this as 'acting on an unauthorised official order, but in good faith'.

As briefly mentioned above, based on Article 51 paragraph (2), a person who has committed a crime, because he was acting on an official order that has been given by a superior who does not have the authority, can still be punished.[63] This makes certain situations challenging for many people, especially those in subordinate positions who must obey orders from their superiors. If they carry out an order and it turns out that the order was not valid, or was given by a superior who did not have the authority to do so, they can be punished. On the other hand, if they do not carry out orders from their superiors, they will be considered to have rejected the orders or to have been negligent or even disobedient, which can also have negative personal consequences for subordinate employees.[64]

[62] *Kitab Oendang2 Hoekoeman Bagi Hindia Belanda* (Batavia, Balai Poestaka, 1940) 42.
[63] Remmelink, *Hukum Pidana* (2003) 255. See also Lamintang and Lamintang, *Dasar-Dasar Hukum Pidana di Indonesia* (2019) 537.
[64] Lamintang and Lamintang, *Dasar-Dasar Hukum Pidana di Indonesia* (2019) 538.

Thus, employees must always observe and examine whether the superior who gave the order really has the authority to issue such an order. In doing so, the employee may find that he judged the situation correctly, meaning he successfully avoided punishment by not carrying out an unauthorised order. However, he could also find that his judgement was wrong, so he is sanctioned with a criminal offence for committing a crime (albeit on the orders of his superior). Because of this difficult situation for subordinates, lawmakers realise that a subordinate does not always have the ability to judge the correctness of orders he has received from his superiors. The lawmakers thus provide rules regarding the grounds for excluding criminal responsibility for people who carry out unauthorised official orders, but who in good faith considered the orders to be legitimate official orders[65] as regulated in Article 51 paragraph (2) of the Criminal Code.

Just as in discussing the excessive self-defence of Article 49 paragraph (2) above, in discussing the conditions of Article 51 paragraph (2), it can be divided into three parts, as follows:

(1) order of office given by an unauthorised authority;
(2) the one being ordered, in good faith, thinks that the order is given with legitimate authority;
(3) its implementation is included in the work environment / scope of work.

In relation to the first element, it is important to remember an authorised official order (or an order given by an authorised official), according to Remmelink, is not only about the competence of the person who gave the order but also the validity of the order itself. Thus, an unauthorised order, even if given by a legitimate official, must be considered to be an order given illegally.[66] The example above is also relevant: a police official who has the authority to investigate criminal acts, and is also authorised to give orders to his subordinates to carry out investigations and make arrests, orders his subordinates to arrest someone who actually has nothing to do with an alleged criminal act. This is an unauthorised official order. In such a case, the first part of Article 51 paragraph (2) of the Criminal Code is fulfilled.

Regarding the second part of Article 51 paragraph (2), we must ask: should the order be given by a superior to his subordinates? Some experts refer to the term 'an employee who ranks below', while Moeljatno uses the term 'the one being ordered'. I agree with Moeljatno's usage.

The word *ondergeschikte* ('subordinate', or what Moeljatno calls 'the one being ordered') can be applied to both civil servants and non-civil servants. In this context, 'subordinate' does not mean the relationship remains as superior and subordinate. Rather, the relationship is public law ('*publiekrechterlijk*'). This is reinforced by the opinion of Simons, Pompe, GA van Hamel, and WFC van Hattum, as well as the opinion of the Dutch Hoge Raad, which essentially states that the order does not need to be given to the subordinates of the one who gave the order.

[65] Ibid.

[66] Jan Remmelink, *Komentar atas Pasal- Pasal Terpenting dari Kitab Undang-Undang Hukum Pidana Belanda dan Padanannya dalam Kitab Undang-Undang Hukum Pidana Indonesia* (Jakarta, Gramedia Pustaka Utama, 2003) 255.

Simons states that the order does not need to be given to a subordinate – it can also be given to other people, as long as such an order has been given by law. In line with that, Pompe states that what is meant by the word *ondergeschikte* is everyone to whom the order is given. These persons do not need to be in a permanent relationship as subordinate to the person giving the orders, nor do they need to be civil servants. However, the relationship between the person carrying out the order and the person giving the order must be in the context of public law. Still in line with the views of Simons and Pompe above, van Hamel states that the law requires that the order must be *ambtelijk*, or given based on an *ambt* or a 'position' to subordinates, namely to civil servants and to other people.[67]

Finally, the opinion of van Hattum aligns with and complements all the opinions above. Van Hattum states that the orders can also be given to people who are not subordinates. The word *ondergeschikte* should not be interpreted too narrowly, so it must be interpreted to include everyone to whom an order can be given.[68] Thus, it is clear why in my opinion the term used by Moeljatno for Article 51 paragraph (2) of the Criminal Code – that is, 'the one being ordered' – is more appropriate than the term 'an employee who ranks below'.

On to the third part of the requirements, the recipient of the order must be in the scope of work in such a way that the giver of the order is authorised to give certain tasks to the recipient of the order. In this way, lawmakers seek to reduce the overuse of the excuse that a defendant 'in good faith' mistook the order for an authorised order. Therefore, this excuse is limited so that 'the implementation is included in the environment / scope of work'.

Blind obedience – even when thinking an order is an authorised official order – does not absolve a person from guilt.[69] One must also have a critical attitude when receiving orders. Hazewinkel-Suringa states that '*blinde gehoorzaamheid disculpert dus niet*', meaning 'blind obedience does not negate fault from an unlawful act'. The law requires that only orders that have been given by a superior who is authorised to issue those orders must be obeyed, and therefore people who do not obey an unauthorised order are not punished.[70]

Remmelink provides a great example of this. A police commissioner orders his men to beat up a troublesome prisoner. If then his subordinates carry out the order, the police officer cannot use the ground for excluding criminal responsibility in Article 51 paragraph (2) of the Criminal Code, so he is sentenced for battery. This is because he undeniably knew that the police were allowed to make arrests, but were not allowed to beat prisoners. So, he could not justify having good faith in thinking that the order from the police commissioner was a legitimate official order.[71]

[67] Lamintang and Lamintang, *Dasar-Dasar Hukum Pidana di Indonesia* (2019) 535–40.
[68] Ibid 535–40.
[69] Remmelink, *Hukum Pidana* (2003) 255–56.
[70] Lamintang and Lamintang, *Dasar-Dasar Hukum Pidana di Indonesia* (2019) 540–41.
[71] Remmelink, *Hukum Pidana* (2003) 256.

V. Excusatory Defences in the New Criminal Code

In the New Criminal Code, excusatory defences are regulated in Book 1, Chapter II, Part Two, Paragraph Two. In regard to excusatory defences, although there are many similarities between the current Criminal Code and the New Criminal Code, there are also some differences. This can be seen in the comparison in Table 8.1.

Table 8.1 Excusatory Defences in the Criminal Code and the New Criminal Code

Excusatory Defences			
No	**Categories**	**In the Criminal Code**	**In the New Criminal Code**
1	Insanity / Incompetency	Article 44 paragraph (1) Whoever does an act, which cannot be accounted for because of his imperfect mind or because of illness that alters mental capacity, should not be punished.	Insanity is not included in the section on grounds for exclusion of criminal responsibility, but is regulated separately in the section on criminal responsibility in Articles 38 and 39. Article 38 Any person who at the time of committing a crime suffers from a mental disability and/or intellectual disability, his criminal offense can be reduced and subject to action.[72] Article 39 Any person who at the time of committing a crime suffers from a mental disability which is in an acute relapse and is accompanied by psychotic features and/or moderate or severe intellectual disability, cannot be punished, but may be subject to action.

(continued)

[72] Elucidation of Article 38 of the New Criminal Code: 'In this provision, in order to explain incompetency from a medical perspective, it is necessary to present an expert so that the perpetrator of a crime is seen or judged as incapable of being responsible. What is meant by "mental disability" is a disturbance in the function of thought, emotion, and behaviour, among others: (a) psychosocial including schizophrenia, bipolar, depression, anxiety, and personality disorders; and (b) developmental disabilities that affect social interaction skills include autism and hyperactivity. What is meant by "intellectual disability" is a disturbance in the function of thought due to a below average level of intelligence, including slow learning, mental disabilities, and Down syndrome. Offenders who suffer from mental disabilities and/or intellectual disabilities are considered incapable of realising the unlawful nature of the actions committed or to act based on awareness that can be punished.'

Table 8.1 ***(Continued)***

Excusatory Defences			
No	**Categories**	**In the Criminal Code**	**In the New Criminal Code**
2	Duress	Article 48 A person who commits an act because he is forced by a duress that cannot be resisted cannot be punished.	Article 42[73] Not punishable by law, anyone who commits a crime because: a. forced by a duress that cannot be resisted;[74] or b. forced by an unavoidable threat, pressure, or force.[75]
3	Excessive Self-Defence	Article 49 paragraph (2) An excessive self-defence, which is directly caused by a great mental shock due to the attack or threat of attack, is not punished.	Article 43 Anyone who commits excessive self-defence, which is directly caused by a severe mental shock due to an attack or threat of immediate attack against the law, shall not be punished.[76]
4	Acting on an Unauthorised Official Order, but in Good Faith	Article 51 paragraph (2) An official order given by an unauthorised authority does not exempt from punishment, unless the employee under it sincerely thinks that the authority has the right to give the order and carrying out the order becomes the obligation of the employee under the order.	Article 44 An official order given without authority does not result in the exclusion of criminal responsibility, unless whomever being ordered in good faith thinks that the order is given with authority and its implementation is included in the scope of his work.

(continued)

[73] Elucidation of Article 42 of the New Criminal Code: 'This provision relates to coercion which is divided into absolute coercion and relative coercion.'

[74] Elucidation of Article 42 letter a of the New Criminal Code: 'What is meant by "coerced by an irresistible force" or absolute coercion is a condition that causes the perpetrator to have no other choice, except to commit the act. Because of the circumstances that exist in the perpetrator, it is impossible for him to resist or choose when doing the act.'

[75] Elucidation of Article 42 Letter b of the New Criminal Code: 'What is meant by "forced by an unavoidable threat, pressure, or force" or relative coercion are: (a) the threat, pressure, or force according to common sense cannot be expected that he can put up a fight; and (b) if the interests sacrificed are equal to or slightly more than the interests saved. Psychological pressure from outside is the main requirement. It is also possible for someone to experience mental stress, but not because of something that comes from outside, but because of pressure based on the considerations of his own mind. This is not an excusatory defence that can negate the criminal responsibility.'

[76] Elucidation of Article 43 of the New Criminal Code: 'This provision regulates excessive self-defence, provided that: (a) self-defence exceeds limit or is disproportionate to attack or threat of immediate attack; and (b) caused by severe mental shock due to an attack or the threat of an prompt attack.'

Table 8.1 ***(Continued)***

Excusatory Defences			
No	**Categories**	**In the Criminal Code**	**In the New Criminal Code**
5	Children under 12 years old	In the Criminal Code, there is no provision for criminal responsibility for children under 12 years of age. This is discussed in the doctrine.	Article 40 Criminal responsibility cannot be imposed on children who at the time of committing a crime have not yet reached the age of 12 (twelve) years old.[77]

[77] Elucidation of Article 40 of the New Criminal Code: 'This provision regulates the minimum age limit to be criminally responsible for children who commit crimes. Determination of the age limit of 12 (twelve) years is based on psychological considerations, namely the emotional, intellectual, and mental maturity of the child. Children under the age of 12 (twelve) years cannot be held criminally responsible and therefore the case handling is carried out in accordance with the provisions of the laws and regulations governing the juvenile criminal justice system.'

Article 41 of the New Criminal Code states: 'In the event that a child who is not yet 12 (twelve) years old commits or is suspected of committing a crime, investigators, community advisers, and professional social workers make decisions to: (a) hand them back to the parent/guardian; or (b) participate in education, coaching, and mentoring programs in government agencies or Social Welfare Organizing Institutions in agencies dealing with social welfare, both at the central and regional levels, for a maximum of 6 (six) months.'

9

Attempts

I. Definition

Attempts are regulated in only two articles in the Criminal Code: Articles 53 and 54.

Article 53 is the primary reference for attempted crimes. It states '*Poging tot* ***Misdrijf*** *is strafbaar*', meaning an attempt to commit *a felony* is punishable (emphasis added). Note that it refers strictly to serious offences only, leading us to conclude, with reverse interpretation, that attempting to commit a violation (minor offence) is not punishable.

Article 54 affirms this, stating: '*Poging tot overtredingen is niet strafbaar*', meaning that attempting to commit a minor offence is not punishable. However, there is actually another reason why Article 54 explains this. According to Jacob Maarten van Bemmelen, lawmakers deemed it necessary to explain, once again, and firmly, that attempting to commit a minor offence is not criminal in nature, because lawmakers wanted to ensure that regional lawmakers and regulations do not deviate from this determination.[1]

Article 53, paragraph (2) states 'The maximum principal penalty for the crime is reduced by one third in the case of attempt'. Meanwhile, paragraph (3) of the article stipulates that 'If the crime can be punished with the death penalty or life imprisonment, then the maximum imprisonment of 15 years is imposed'. Even so, an attempt to commit a crime is not a reason for mitigating the punishment. This is because punishment is only applicable to a criminal offence that has been completed, while this attempt is precisely about an inchoate offence (incomplete offence).[2]

[1] JM van Bemmelen, *Hukum Pidana 1, Hukum Pidana Material Bagian Umum* (Ons Strafrecht 1, Het Materiele Strafrecht Algemeeen Deel) (Bandung, Binacipta, 1987) 238. See also JE Jonkers, *Buku Pedoman Hukum Pidana Hindia Belanda* [*Handboek Van Het Nederlandsch-Indische Strafrecht*], translated by Tim Penerjemah Bina Aksara (Jakarta, PT Bina Aksara, 1987) 155–56, and D Schaffmeister, N Keijzer, and E PH Sutorius, *Hukum Pidana* (2007) 210.

[2] See also Jan Remmelink, *Hukum Pidana, Komentar atas Pasal-Pasal Terpenting dari Kitab Undang-Undang hukum Pidana Belanda dan Padanannya dalam Kitab Undang-Undang Hukum Pidana Indonesia* (Jakarta, Gramedia Pustaka Utama, 2003) 285. See also Hazewinkel-Suringan as quoted by Eddy OS Hiariej in *Prinsip-Prinsip Hukum Pidana*, revised edn (Yogyakarta, Cahaya Atma Pustaka, 2016) 324.

Let us discuss the definition of *poging* (attempt). Article 53 of the Criminal Code reads in full:

> *Poging tot misdrijf is strabaar, wanneer het vornemen des daders zich door een begin van uitvoering heft geopenbaard en de uitvoering allen ten gevolge van omstandigheden van zijnen wil onafhankelijk, niet is voltooid.*
>
> [Attempts to commit a felony can be punished, if the intention to commit the criminal act is evident, with the commencement of the performance of the offence and the non-completion of the performance only for reasons that are independent of one's own will.]

JE Jonkers argues that the law does not provide a definition of attempt, but rather a designation of when an attempt can be punished.[3] Thus the Criminal Code only outlines the conditions under which a perpetrator can be convicted.

Linguistically, *poging* does not have a special legal meaning itself, such as attempted felony. Instead, if we are referring to an attempt to commit a felony, then the Dutch term is *poging tot misdrij*. There are many definitions of *poging*, including: effort / effort made, endeavour, try/trial, intention, request, difficulty, and struggling without success.[4] Meanwhile, *attempt*, which is the English translation of *poging*, is defined as 'the act of trying to do something, especially something difficult'.[5]

According to Van Bemmelen, citing the opinions of GE Langemeijer, WPJ Pompe, and Willem Zevenbergen, in the case of an attempt, we are dealing with an offender who did not complete a crime but did intend to carry it out. From the perspective of the offender, an attempt is an 'effort without success', while from the point of view of an act, an attempt is a 'partial implementation of the formulation of the offence'. An attempt is 'the realisation of some action', and because the perpetrator was not successful in his efforts, the legislators reduce the maximum principal penalty for the crime.[6]

What is the reason the legislator sanctions a person who commits a crime but does not finish the crime? According to JE Jonkers, Van Bemmelen, and other legal experts, there are two theories that try to answer the question above: subjective theory and objective theory, the latter of which includes formal objective theory and substantive objective theory.[7] Meanwhile, according to Barda Nawawi Arief and Eddy OS Hiariej, who quotes the opinion of Nyoman Sarikat Putrajaya, there is also a third theory called mixed theory.[8]

[3] Jonkers, *Buku Pedoman Hukum Pidana Hindia Belanda* (1987) 155.

[4] https://nl.glosbe.com/nl/id/poging; https://www.woorden.org/woord/poging, accessed 25 February 2022.

[5] https://dictionary.cambridge.org/dictionary/english/attempt.

[6] Van Bemmelen, *Hukum Pidana 1* (1987) 241–42.

[7] Jonkers, *Buku Pedoman Hukum Pidana Hindia Belanda* (1987) 155. See also Van Bemmelen, *Hukum Pidana 1* (1987) 240.

[8] Barda Nawawi Arief, *Sari Kuliah Hukum Pidana II* (Semarang, Badan Penyediaan Bahan Kuliah Fakultas Hukum Universitas Diponegoro, 1993) 4. See also Hiariej, *Prinsip-Prinsip Hukum Pidana* (2016) 329.

The subjective theory states that the perpetrator of a criminal offence deserves to be punished because of his malicious intention in committing a crime, after the crime has begun. Subjective theory views that attempts can be punished because the behaviour is contrary to noble norms and has malicious and harmful intentions. Meanwhile, objective theory sees that with the offender having attempted a criminal offence, there are already harmful consequences. This act has jeopardised the interests of the law. Therefore, for this theory, malicious intent alone is not enough to determine the need for criminal punishment.[9]

In fact, as Van Bemmelen says, the Explanatory Memorandum (MvT) of the Dutch WvS (Criminal Code) confirms the two theories, both subjective and objective. Likewise, jurists argue that both the subjective and objective theories should be used and that judges must consider both approaches. Sometimes, a judge must decide whether the attempt is punishable due to the dangers of the perpetrator's conduct, and/or because of their malicious intent.[10] Remmelink argues that punishing an attempt with criminal sanctions stems from the view of the legislators who linked criminal sanctions not only to the fulfillment of all elements of a crime but also to the performance of some of the elements.[11]

What type of attempted criminal offence can be punished? In general, it is said that an attempt is only punishable by law if it is a serious offence. Attempted minor offences, such as minor battery, are not punishable by law.[12] Interestingly, even among serious offences, not all attempts can be punished. These include Article 184 paragraph (5) of the Criminal Code, which covers an attempt to conduct a duel between two people; Article 302 paragraph (4) of the Criminal Code, referring to an attempt to carry out minor battery against an animal; Article 351 paragraph (5) of the Criminal Code, which is an attempt to commit battery; and Article 352 paragraph (2) of the Criminal Code, which is an attempt to carry out minor battery.[13]

As to whether an attempt is (1) an extension of the formulation of the offence, or (2) the basis for implementing punishment, this is primarily a theoretical or academic debate. In practice, this is not a significant problem. According to Derkje Hazewinkel-Suringa, in general, Dutch criminal law experts,[14] as well as most Indonesian criminal law experts (such as Oemar Seno Adjie), take the view that an attempt is not an extension of the formulation of the offence, but rather an extension of punishment for the perpetrator.[15] Jan Remmelink, for example, states that in the context of an attempt, what happened was a narrowing of the scope of the offence formulation because certain elements did not need to be fulfilled, as

[9] Jonkers, *Buku Pedoman Hukum Pidana Hindia Belanda* (1987) 155. See also Van Bemmelen, *Hukum Pidana 1* (1987) 240. See also Leden Marpaung, *Asas-Teori-Praktik Hukum Pidana* (Jakarta, Sinar Grafika, 2014) 94.

[10] Van Bemmelen, *Hukum Pidana 1* (1987) 240–41.

[11] Remmelink, *Hukum Pidana* (2003) 285.

[12] Jonkers, *Buku Pedoman Hukum Pidana Hindia Belanda* (Jakarta, Bina Aksara, 1987) 156.

[13] Marpaung, *Asas-Teori-Praktik Hukum Pidana* (2014) 97.

[14] Hiariej, *Prinsip-Prinsip Hukum Pidana* (2016) 325.

[15] Arief, *Sari Kuliah Hukum Pidana II* (1993) 2.

well as an expansion of the radius of the imposition of a criminal offence.[16] So, the attempt is not seen as a *delictum sui generis* (a stand-alone offence) but is seen as an imperfect offence (*onvolkomen delicsvorm*).[17]

Meanwhile in Indonesia, there are also some legal experts who clearly view that the attempt is not an extension of the punishment of offenders, but an extension of the formulation of the offence. Moeljatno, Andi Zainal Abidin, and Andi Hamzah take this view. According to Moeljatno, an attempt is a complete and independent offence. The attempt itself is seen as the basis for expanding the criminality of the act. Thus, the attempt is a *delictum sui generis*, but with a special form. The above-mentioned experts also agree on the existence of an attempt offence; in other words, the attempt is an offence in itself, regardless of whether it is completed successfully.[18] According to Moeljatno, attempts are special offences, whereas according to Dutch legal experts, attempts are not special offences that stand alone.[19] Like most other criminal law experts, I hold the view that an attempt is not a separate offence nor an extension of the formulation of the offence, but that an attempt is an extension of an offender's punishment. For me, an attempted offence is not a criminal offence but rather an incomplete offence, therefore it is wrong to call it an attempted offence, such as 'attempted murder' or 'attempted theft'. In my opinion, it is called an offence only if the offence has been completed and/or has fulfilled all the formulations of the offence.

The effect of the existence of an attempt is to widen the scope of who may be regarded as a perpetrator, not to expand the formulation of the offence. This is because if the scope of punishment is not expanded, only those who have completed the offence can be convicted. Meanwhile, if there is an incomplete offence but the offender is punished as the offender of the completed offence, this is only an exception. The existence of provisions regarding attempts (ie Article 53 of the Criminal Code) also makes the Criminal Code and other criminal legislation more efficient, otherwise every article would need to include criminal sanctions for cases where offences are not completed (ie only attempts at the offence have been made). Of course, this would be very inefficient.

In customary criminal law, the concept of 'attempts' does not exist. Conduct that would be categorised as an attempt under Dutch and Indonesian criminal law, according to the Customary Criminal Law would be seen as a particular completed offence.[20] This, as described above, is one of Moeljatno's arguments, where an attempt is an extension of a criminal act and therefore is seen as a separate offence. Personally, I think there is a difference, as according to the Customary Criminal Law there is no attempted offence, but there is an offence itself that

[16] Remmelink, *Hukum Pidana* (2003) 285.

[17] Hiariej, *Prinsip-Prinsip Hukum Pidana* 2016) 325.

[18] Ibid.

[19] Moeljatno, *Hukum Pidana Delik-Delik Percobaan Delik-Delik Penyertaan* (Jakarta, Bina Aksara, 1985) 9–10.

[20] Karni, *Ringkasan Tentang Hukum Pidana* (Jakarta, Balai Buku Indonesia, 1950) 93.

has been completed. Meanwhile, according to Moeljatno, there is a stand-alone attempted offence.

Let us look at an example from 1939. An article from Willem Frans Lublink Weddik refers to a case that occurred in Palembang, where a man named Abusamah held (hugged) a woman named Hudaia with the intention of trying to have sexual intercourse with her in order to force her to marry him. Hudaia managed to escape from Abusamah, and Abusamah fled. Abusamah was convicted of 'capturing the girl's body' and required to pay compensation to the woman family due to *tekap malu* (compensation for shame).[21] According to the Criminal Code, such an incident may be subject to Article 285 (rape or threat of rape) in conjunction with Article 53 on attempted serious offences.

II. Attempt Requirements in Article 53 of the Criminal Code

As explained above, Article 53 of the Criminal Code does not define what constitutes an attempt. Instead, it provides conditions or elements of an attempt that can be punished. These are:

(1) intention;
(2) commencement of performance; and
(3) the performance is not completed only because of circumstances beyond the will of the offender.

The formulation of Article 53 of the Indonesian Criminal Code itself is different to the Dutch Criminal Code, especially since the amendment to the Dutch Criminal Code on 1 April 1994, where the third requirement was removed.[22] In the Dutch Criminal Code, Article 45 (1) in English reads: 'An attempt to commit a serious offence shall be punishable if the intention of the offender has revealed itself by a commencement of the performance of the criminal act.'[23] From that formulation, we see that there are only two conditions for the attempt: (1) intention and (2) what has materialised in the commencement of the performance. However, in Article 46b of the Dutch Criminal Code, there is a provision: 'Neither preparation nor an attempt shall exist if the serious offence has not been completed due to circumstances dependent on the will of the offender.'[24]

[21] Ibid.
[22] See Remmelink, *Hukum Pidana* (2003) 288.
[23] The original text reads: '*Poging tot misdrijf is strafbaar, wanneer het voornemen van de dader zich door een begin van uitvoering heeft geopenbaard.*'
[24] The original text reads: '*Voorbereiding noch poging bestaat indien het misdrijf niet is voltooid tengevolge van omstandigheden van de wil van de dader afhankelijk.*'

A. Intention

The first condition of *poging* (attempt) is '*voornemen*'. In Article 53 of the Criminal Code, this is called '*het voornemen des daders*' (the intention of the offender). Intention must exist for an attempt to be penalised. However, intention is something that is subjective in nature, as it is an element that lies within the offender.

There are two important issues in the discussion around intention. They are:

(1) Is *voornemen* (intention) the same as *opzet* (intentionality)?
(2) If *voornemen* is the same as the *opzet*, is the *opzet* to be understood as the first category, *opzet als oogmerk* (intentionality as an intent / purpose), only? Or can it be in the second category (intentionality with awareness of certainty) and/or intentionally in the third category (intentionality with awareness of possibility)?

On the first question, there are two views. The first is that the *voornemen* and *opzet* are indeed the same. This view is followed by almost all Dutch legal scholars (eg WFC van Hattum) and Indonesian legal scholars (eg Satochid Kartanegara). The second view is that *voornemen* is closely related to *opzet* but not exactly the same. This view is shared by Dutch legal scholar Pompe and Indonesian legal scholar Moeljatno as well as Eddy OS Hiariej.[25] According to Moeljatno, in the event that the attempt is fulfilled (and becomes *voltooid poging* or a completed attempt), then intention is the same as intentionality. However, in the case of a delayed or incomplete attempt (*geschorste poging*), then intention is not the same as intentionality.[26]

For those who argue that *voornemen* (intention) is the same as *opzet* (intentionality), there are three different perspectives:

(1) *Voornemen* is the same as *opzet* and purposefully includes all categories: *opzet als oogmerk* (intentionality as an intent/purpose), *opzet met zekerheidsbewutzijn* (intentionality with awareness of certainty), and *voorwaardelijk opzet/dolus eventualis* (intentionality with awareness of possibility). This view is shared by Remmelink, D Simons, GA van Hamel, Van Dijck, Van Hattum, among others. Moeljatno is also included in this first opinion, ie that the intention has turned into intentionality.[27] Indonesian legal scholars generally also accept this teaching, for example EY Kanter and SR Sianturi.[28]
(2) *Voornemen* is the same as *opzet* but is limited to the first category of intentionality (intentionality as an intent/purpose). This view is held by HB Vos.

[25] Hiariej, *Prinsip-Prinsip Hukum Pidana* (2016) 336–37.
[26] See Arief, *Sari Kuliah Hukum Pidana II* (1993) 5–6. See also Moeljatno, *Hukum Pidana* (1985) 16–20.
[27] See Arief, *Sari Kuliah Hukum Pidana II* (1993) 7.
[28] EY Kanter and SR Sianturi, *Asas-Asas Hukum Pidana di Indonesia dan Penerapannya* (Jakarta, Storia Grafika, 2018) 317.

(3) *Voornemen* is the same as *opzet* in the sense of the three categories of *opzet* but not to the fullest extent. Especially for the third catergory – *dolus eventualis* (intentionality with awareness of possibility) – it is necessary to have restrictions, primarily if the possibility is not so great or the defendant can influence it to avoid the possible consequences. This view is held by Noyon and Langemijer.[29]

As mentioned, Jan Remmelink falls into the first group. In his opinion, there is not a sufficient basis to support a narrow interpretation (intention as the first category of intentionality, ie as an intent/purpose).[30] Meanwhile, Jonkers states that Vos' view is incomprehensible where the intent is only seen as intentionality in a narrow sense (as an intent/purpose). According to Jonkers, an attempt can occur at all levels of intentionality (intentionality as an intent/purpose, intentionality with awareness of certainty, and intentionality with awareness of possibility). As an illustration, B aims to kill A and so places poison in the water storage container in A's house, from which it is known that A and his family drink. If A's entire family drink the water and die, B is guilty of murdering A and his family. If several people drink the poisoned water but do not die as a result, then A is still guilty of attempting to kill them.[31]

The jurisprudence of the Dutch Supreme Court seems to be in accordance with the first view where *voornement* (intention) includes all three kinds of *opzet* (intentionality). In the Arrest (Decision) of the Hoge Raad (Supreme Court) dated 12 March 1943, a person who was standing on the *bordes* (boarding steps) of a train kicked an officer in the leg as the officer was checking his goods. If the officer had not quickly grabbed the iron pole of the train, he would have fallen out and died. In this case, the Dutch Supreme Court stated that attempted homicide had taken place. Likewise, the Arrest of Hoge Raad on 6 February 1951 involved an officer investigating a traffic violation. The officer signalled for a motorised vehicle to stop, but the driver did not obey. Instead, he kept on driving. Fortunately, the officer managed to get out of the path of the vehicle. If he had not, he would have been hit and likely killed. In this case, the Hoge Raad also stated that there was an attempted homicide.[32]

In both cases, it is clear that the offender's intentionality was not the intention (*als oogmerk*) to kill the officer, but rather intentionality with the awareness of the possibility. However, the Dutch Supreme Court nevertheless accepted that in both cases there was an attempted homicide. This means that the intention in the case

[29] Moeljatno, *Hukum Pidana* (1985) 16–18. See also Hieariej, *Prinsip-Prinsip Hukum Pidana* (2016) 335–37. See also Arief, *Sari Kuliah Hukum Pidana II* (1993) 5.

[30] Remmelink, *Hukum Pidana* (2003) 288–89.

[31] Jonkers, *Buku Pedoman Hukum Pidana Hindia Belanda* (1987) 157.

[32] Arief, *Sari Kuliah Hukum Pidana II* (1993) 5. This arrest of HR dated 6 February 1951 is also discussed in Remmelink, *Hukum Pidana* (2003) 288–89.

of an attempt is interpreted in the same way as the third category of intentionality, and is not limited to intentionality as an intention.[33]

With reference to the decisions above, which in my opinion are very in line with a sense of justice – where people must be responsible for actions that cause other consequences (even if they do not want them) but they are aware that they will or may happen – then I agree with the view that *voornemen* (intention) can be equated with *opzet* (intentionality) in all three categories (as intent, with awareness of certainty, and with awareness of possibility).

B. Commencement of the Performance of the Criminal Act

In order to be able to convict the perpetrator of an attempt, it requires *begin van uitvoering* (commencement of the performance). According to D Schaffmeister, N Keijzer, and E PH Sutorius, it seems that the legislators meant that the preparation for an act was not to be punishable; preparation was only considered if the act committed was seen as an act of performance. The boundary between the preparatory act which cannot be punished and that which can be punished has only been determined abstractly in Article 53 (1) of the Criminal Code, but in doctrine and practice, it must be drawn concretely.[34] The act of preparation itself cannot be punished, except for certain offences where the preparation alone can be punished.

In relation to the *begin van uitvoering* (commencement of performance) requirement, the main question of this requirement is: what exactly is meant by *begin van uitvoering*? Is it the commencement of performance of the intention? Or the commencement of performance of the crime? What is the difference between the commencement of performance of the intention and of the crime? The commencement of performance of the intention refers to the subjective aspect of the offender (ie the intention of the offender), while the commencement of performance of the crime refers to the objective aspect (ie the act of the crime). As a result, in criminal law literature, there are two schools of thought on this: subjective teaching and objective teaching.

First, subjective teaching (*subjectieve pogingsleer*) interprets the 'commencement of performance' in Article 53 (1) of the Criminal Code as the commencement of the performance of intentions. This is based on the mental attitude of the offender. For this teaching, the act of performance is any action that shows that the offender is psychologically capable of committing the crime. In Van Dijk's opinion,[35] there is an act of performance if the offender is confronted with the time and place where the crime will be committed, proving that he is capable of carrying out the actions needed to complete it.[36] According to Van Hamel, if viewed

[33] Arief, *Sari Kuliah Hukum Pidana II* (1993) 5.
[34] Schaffmeister, Keijzer, and Sutorius, *Hukum Pidana* (2007) 211–12.
[35] Professor in Amsterdam, The Netherlands (1922–1927).
[36] Schaffmeister, Keijzer, and Sutorius, *Hukum Pidana* (2007) 212.

from the point of view of the offender's intention, it is said that there was an act of performance if from what has been done it turns out that there is certainty of the intention to commit the crime.[37]

Second, objective teaching (*objectieve pogingsleer*) interprets the term 'commencement of performance' in Article 53 of the Criminal Code as the commencement of performance of a crime. This is based on the dangerousness of the act for the rule of law. According to this teaching, the act of performance is any act that endangers the interests of the law. In Zevenbergen's opinion,[38] an offence is the embodiment of a legal phenomenon. Attempts are part of that which only exists when at least one of the elements in the formulation of the offence has been initiated.[39]

Adherents to other objective teachings, such as Simons,[40] argues that the purpose of criminal law is to protect the interests of individuals and the state as recognised by law (*rechtsgoed*). These interests must not be violated nor jeopardised. An attempt is therefore a danger to the *rechtsgoed*. Thus, in order to be sentenced, the attempt must have gone so far that, from an objective point of view, there is a risk to these interests. The nature of whether an act is harmful or not is measured by what usually happens as a result of the act, so the only question is, whether from the act itself there can be consequences that are detrimental to legal interests (*rechtsgoed*)? If the answer is 'yes', then the act has a dangerous nature.[41]

Still according to Simons, in crimes with a formal formulation, there are attempts that can be punished if an act prohibited by law is initiated. Meanwhile, for crimes with a substantive formulation, there is a commencement of performance if according to its nature it can immediately lead to results that are not desired by the law, which, without further action, could cause those results.[42]

Barda Nawawi Arief argues that the objective flow was divided into two: the substantive objective (adopted by Simons) and the formal objective (adopted by Willem Duynstee and Willem Zevenbergen). According to Duynstee,[43] each formulation of the offence in the law prohibits the existence of a certain behaviour that is part of a series of behaviours that are all prohibited offences. Thus, what is forbidden is not only the end but the whole series of behaviours from the first to the last. If one behaviour in the series has been carried out, it means that there has been an injury to the legal system, and although it is not yet a completed injury, it has endangered the legal system. This is used as an indicator to determine the commencement of performance.[44] Therefore, the attempt can be punished, not

[37] Moeljatno, *Hukum Pidana* (1985) 22.
[38] Professor in Amsterdam, The Netherlands (1920–1925).
[39] Schaffmeister, Keijzer, and Sutorius, *Hukum Pidana* (2007) 212–13.
[40] Professor in Utrecht, The Netherlands (1897–1928).
[41] Moeljatno, *Hukum Pidana* (1985) 23.
[42] Schaffmeister, Keijzer, and Sutorius, *Hukum Pidana* (2007) 212–13.
[43] Professor in Nijmegen, The Netherlands.
[44] Arief, *Sari Kuliah Hukum Pidana II* (1993) 9–10

because of the danger of the attempt (as Simons argues), but from the conflict between the act and the *rechtsorde* (legal order).[45]

According to Moeljatno, both in the *Memorie van Toelichting* (Explanatory Memorandum – MvT) of the Dutch Criminal Code and the opinion of the Code's authors, there is no doubt that what is meant is 'the commencement of performance of a crime'. In the MvT, it is explained that a distinction must be made between preparatory actions (*voorbereidingshandelingen*) and performance actions (*uitvoeringshandelingen*). In reality, it is not always easy to distinguish the two, or whether there has been a performance act or just a preparatory act. It is left to the discretion of the judges to determine this.[46] A clear boundary between the preparatory act and the act of performance, in general, cannot be drawn. It is therefore not possible to formulate it explicitly in an article of the law. Thus, this problem can only be solved on a case-by-case basis, by collecting and assessing all possible incident factors.[47] At the time the Dutch WvS was written, the Dutch Minister of Justice firmly left the choice between objective and subjective teachings to legal scholars and the judiciary because both were deemed more capable of finding the right path than lawmakers.[48]

The decisions of the Dutch Supreme Court (Hoge Raad) and the Indonesian Supreme Court are in line with objective teachings, wherein the characteristics of *begin van uitvoering* (commencement of implementation) are determined in the presence of a direct relationship (*rechtstreeks verband, noodzakelijk en onmiddelijk verband*) between the act and the crime intended by the offender.[49]

i. Relevant Decisions

Relevant decisions include:[50]

a. HR Decision 11 January 1904, W 8015:[51]

This case is about rape (in Article 285 of the Criminal Code). A man had embraced and kissed a woman, then forced her to lie on the ground and gagged her mouth so she would not scream. The woman put up a fight and was helped two men who were passing by, preventing the completion of the rape. In this case, the Hoge Raad decided there had been a start of performance, so the offender was found guilty of attempted rape.

[45] Moeljatno, *Hukum Pidana* (1985) 24.

[46] Ibid 21.

[47] Kanter and Sianturi, *Asas-Asas Hukum Pidana* (2018) 319.

[48] Schaffmeister, Keijzer, and Sutorius, *Hukum Pidana* (2007) 215.

[49] Simons as quoted by EY Kanter and SR Sianturi in *Asas-Asas Hukum Pidana di Indonesia dan Penerapannya* (Jakarta, Storia Grafika, 2018) 320.

[50] Kanter and Sianturi in *Asas-Asas Hukum Pidana* (2018) 320–21.

[51] Ibid 320.

b. Decision HR 28 July 1911, W 9225 and 27 June 1932, W 12520:[52]

This case is about the crime of theft with violence (in Article 365 of the Criminal Code). The offender committed violence against the target of the theft, intending to prepare and facilitate the theft. In this case, the Supreme Court stated that there had been a start of violent theft, so the offender was sentenced to attempted theft with violence.

c. HR Decision 21 May 1951:[53]

A man (A) had a love affair with a woman (B), who was married to (C). A and B agreed to end C's life by hitting C on the head with a hammer while he was sleeping until C became unconscious. After that, C was to be dragged into the kitchen and the gas line opened until C died of gas poisoning. On a predetermined night, A was given the key to the house by B, then A entered the bedroom and began to carry out his plan. However, when C was hit with a hammer, he did not lose consciousness due to a slight miss. C fought against A and A hit him several times, before running. According to the Supreme Court, in this case, if someone with mature and calm considerations previously had the intention to knock out another person and then kill him by gas poisoning, then there is *begin van uitvoering* (commencement of performance) of the crime of premeditated murder, namely when he deliberately hit the victim's head with the hammer he was carrying. He had manifested by taking the lives of others in two stages. The first stage was assaulting the victim by hitting his head with a hammer, then the second stage was to open the gas line faucet so that the defenceless victim was killed. So, when stage one was carried out by the defendant, but the crime was not completed because the victim resisted and A could not carry out the second stage, there was still the beginning of the crime of premeditated murder.

d. Arrest HR 19 March 1934, W 12731:[54]

Suspects A and B had intended to burn a house in Eindhoven City, with the consent of the owner who was travelling, with the intention of dividing the insurance payment between the three of them. In some of the rooms, incendiary materials had been installed and in the kitchen above the gas stove, a gas gun had been placed, so that, if a single flame were to escape, the whole house would burn down. The trigger of the gas gun was tied with a piece of rope and stretched through the walls of the house to the outside. The next action planned by A and B was that, when it got dark, they would go back to the house to get some packages,

[52] Ibid.

[53] Schaffmeister, Keijzer,and Sutorius, *Hukum Pidana* (2007) 217–18.

[54] Ibid 216–17. See also Kanter and Sianturi, *Asas-Asas Hukum Pidana di Indonesia dan Penerapannya* (2018) 320.

and then pull the end of the stretched rope and the house would burn down. This last part of the plan could not be implemented because many people had gathered around the house after smelling gasoline. In this case, the Hoge Raad stated that there was no *begin van uitvoering* because none of the actions of the offenders were close enough to the end result of arson that they could be considered as the start of performance.

e. A Case of Attempted Theft in Medan:[55]

Kanter and Sianturi recount a case that was decided by the Supreme Court of the Republic of Indonesia, which tends to be in accordance with objective teachings. In this case, there was a post office employee in Medan who wanted to steal valuables from the post office. Before the post office closed for the day, the employee hid in the restroom, with the intention that after all the other employees went home, he would carry out his theft. However, before he could carry out his intent, he was caught by the postmaster who suddenly returned to the office to pick up some letters. The employee admitted his intention to steal from the postmaster. In the first court decision and appeal, the defendant was found guilty of attempted theft. However, the Supreme Court acquitted the defendant because the act of concealing himself could not be considered as the commencement of performance. After all, it could not be considered as endangering the interests of the law.[56]

ii. Discussion

In my opinion, cases a (HR Decision of 1904), b (Decision of HR of 1911, 1932), and c (HR Decision of 1951) are in line with both subjective and objective teachings. This is not so for case d (HR Decision of 1934 in the Netherlands or case e (in Medan), as according to subjective teachings in those cases there must have been a *begin van uitvoering* (commencement of performance) because the defendants' actions have shown the commencement of performance of their malicious intent. Meanwhile, according to objective teachings, the Hoge Raad decision in case c and the Supreme Court's decision case d were correct because there was no *uitvoeringshandeling* (performance act); there was only *voorbereidingshandelingen* (preparatory action), so the defendants could not be convicted.

C. Involuntary Abandonment of the Attempt

The third condition or element of an attempted crime that can be punished in Article 53 paragraph (1) of the Criminal Code is: the performance is not completed

[55] Kanter and Sianturi did not state the name or case number. See Kanter and Sianturi, *Asas-Asas Hukum Pidana* (2018) 321–22.

[56] Ibid.

solely due to circumstances beyond the will of the offender. This confirms that attempting to commit a crime is different from a completed crime (*voltooid*). In a completed crime, all elements have been fulfilled – for example, in a formal offence, the act which is the formulation of a criminal act has been carried out – while in a substantive offence, the results have occurred or arisen. In an attempt to commit a crime, the act which is the element of the offence has not been completed, or the result which is the element of the offence has not yet arisen. The third condition or element is thus not fulfilled if the implementation is not completed because of the actions or decisions of the person who started the attempt.

In criminal literature, the action of a person who had the intention of committing an offence and started the act of performance, which then becomes incomplete because of his own will is called *vrijwillig terugtred* or *vrijwillig terugtreden* (to resign his intention voluntarily). Such people are guaranteed not to be punished. We can see this from the Memorandum of Elucidation of the Dutch Criminal Code at the time of the formation of Article 53 (1) of the Criminal Code, where it is stated: (1) if the offender can prove that at the right time he still had the desire to withdraw his malicious intent and (2) because such a guarantee is the surest means to be able to stop the commission of an ongoing crime.[57]

The phrase 'The execution was not completed only because of circumstances beyond the will of the offender' is an element of an attempted offence and is not a reason for an excuse of punishment (*strafsluitingsgronden*).[58] Therefore, if the public prosecutor arraigns a defendant as having attempted a criminal act (eg attempted murder as referred to in Article 340 in conjunction with Article 53 of the Criminal Code), the public prosecutor must include all elements in Article 340 and elements in Article 53 (1) in the arraignment, including the element 'The performance is not completed only because of circumstances beyond the will of the offender'. The prosecutor must also prove this element. If it is not proven, the defendant is acquitted (*vrijspraak*). According to Prodjodikoro, the absence of voluntary resignation is an additional requirement for a criminal offence (*bijkomende voorwaarde van de strafbaarheid*), not a reason to eliminate the nature of the crime (*strafsluitings gronden*).[59]

If the defendant declares that the offence was not completed because of his will to withdraw voluntarily, or that he took precautions to ensure that the objectives were not achieved or so that results did not arise, he must prove it. If it can be proven that the defendant fulfills the *vrijwillig terugtred/vrijwillig terugtreden* (resigning his intention voluntarily) or prevented the achievement of the objective or result, then he will not be punished. However, as mentioned above, this element must be included in the arraignment and must also be proven by the prosecutor.

[57] Van Hattum in PAF Lamintang and Fransiscus Theojunior Lamintang, *Dasar-Dasar Hukum Pidana di Indonesia* (Jakarta, Sinar Grafika, 2019) 581–82.

[58] Lamintang and Lamintang, *Dasar-Dasar Hukum Pidana di Indonesia* (2019) 582. See also E Utrecht, *Rangkaian Sari Kuliah Hukum Pidana I* (Surabaya, Pustaka Tinta Mas, 1994) 405–06.

[59] Wirjono Prodjodikoro, *Asas-Asas Hukum Pidana di Indonesia* (Bandung, Refika Aditama, 2003) 114.

How do we judge what is solely the will of the offender and what is not? What is the limit or measure? This is not easy. Judges must review case by case or *in concreto* because the nature of each crime is different. The decision of the Hoge Raad dated 22 November 1915, NJ 1916 needs further scrutiny. Here, the Hoge Raad states:

> … it does not matter whether the problems that cause the completion of a crime to be stopped are due to the intent of the offender who has caused it directly or indirectly. However, what is important is that the resignation of the intention to complete the crime was not caused by the problems that forced him to do so, so that he could not be convicted.[60]

Examples of incomplete performance solely because of a perpetrator's own will were put forward by Van Hattum. Examples include a person who, after commencing the performance of a crime, then regrets his action; a person, who after commencing a crime, takes pity on his victim; or a person who does not complete the performance of his crime because he does not have the ability to do so. On the other hand, an example of incompletion of the performance not solely because of his own will is where someone is caught red-handed while committing a crime; the crime was not completed because the victim resisted; because the offender's shot did not hit the target; or because the victim did not die (eg the victim was successfully rescued).[61]

III. Types of Attempts

We have already discussed the rules of *poging tot misdrijf* (attempt to commit a crime) according to Article 53 of the Criminal Code. The attempt in that article is an attempt that can be punished (*starfbare poging*). There are no other types of attempts in the Criminal Code.[62] But in legal doctrines, several types of attempts are recognised. Types of attempts that are very well known are: (1) perfect attempts;[63] (2) deferred or delayed attempts; and (3) imperfect attempts.[64]

A. Perfect Attempt (*Voleindigde Poging*)

A person has the intention of committing a crime and has begun to carry out the initial performance, but the offence is not completed for some reason.

[60] Lamintang and Lamintang, *Dasar-Dasar Hukum Pidana di Indonesia* (2019) 584–85.

[61] Ibid 585.

[62] Satochid Kartanegara, *Hukum Pidana Kumpulan Kuliah Prof Satochid Kartanegara dan Pendapat Para Ahli Hukum Terkemuka* (Jakarta, Balai Lektur Mahasiswa, nd) 327.

[63] Barda Nawawi Arief uses the term '*percobaan mampu*' or 'adequate attempt'. See Arief, *Sari Kuliah Hukum Pidana II* (1993) 18–19.

[64] Barda Nawawi Arief uses the term '*percobaan tidak mampu*' or 'inadequate attempt'. See Arief, *Sari Kuliah Hukum Pidana II* (1993) 18–19.

For example, X wanted to kill Y and attempted to do this by shooting him in the stomach. Y then was rushed to the hospital, operated on, and was successfully saved. Here, all the conditions/elements of attempts that can be punished in Article 53 (1) of the Criminal Code have been fulfilled. This perfect attempt can be punished according to the subjective theory or objective theory. This attempt, according to Satochid, is called *voleindeigde poging* (a fully completed attempt).[65]

B. Deferred or Delayed Attempt (*Geschorste Poging*)

A person who has the intention of committing a crime who has committed one or more acts to carry out his crime, but, even though it would only take one more action to complete the offence, for some reason the offence is not completed. The attempt is determined to be deferred or delayed.

For example, M wanted to kill N by shooting him. M had loaded a gun with bullets and pointed his gun at N's head. However, when he was about to pull the trigger, another person hit M's hand and the assassination attempt failed. This deferred attempt can be punished according to the subjective theory because it has shown the offender's malicious intent, while according to the objective theory, it can also be punished because there is already a legal interest that is being jeopardised.

C. An Imperfect Attempt (*Ondeugdelijk Poging*)

A person has the intention of committing a crime and has done everything necessary to finish the offence but the offence is not completed. The completion of the offence or the absence of prohibited consequences can be caused by (1) the imperfection of the object (target) or (2) the imperfection of the tools (means) used. This imperfection can be absolute (*absoluut ondeugdelijk)* or relative (*relatief ondeugdelijk*).

i. Imperfect Object (Target)

The imperfection of this object (target) can be relatively imperfect or absolutely imperfect. An example of an absolute imperfect object: Person A wanted to kill B using snake venom. It turns out that the object (target) of the crime, B, is a snake charmer who is immune to snake venom. Another example would be where a woman wanted to terminate her pregnancy, but actually she was not pregnant.[66] Satochid gives an example where A intended to kill B. A then carried out his intention against B, but turns out that, before A's action, B had already died.[67]

[65] Kartanegara, *Hukum Pidana Kumpulan Kuliah* (nd) 326.

[66] Karni in Arief, *Sari Kuliah Hukum Pidana II* (1993) 26.

[67] Kartanegara, *Hukum Pidana Kumpulan Kuliah* (nd) 328–29. Wirjono also gave this example in Prodjodikoro, *Asas-Asas Hukum Pidana di Indonesia* (2003) 112.

Meanwhile, an example of a relatively imperfect object: P wanted to kill Q with a knife. P stabbed a knife into Q's stomach. After being stabbed Q fell and was rushed to hospital. It turned out that the knife did not penetrate deeply, because Q was wearing very thick clothes and Q survives the attack. Wirjono provides an example: stealing a wallet but the wallet is empty and of no value at all.[68]

ii. Imperfect Tool (Means)

Imperfections can also be found in the tools (means) used to commit crimes. Imperfect tools can be absolute or relative. For example, the absolutely imperfect tool: C wanted to kill D by mixing poison into his coffee. D drank the coffee, but he did not die, because what was mixed with the coffee was not poison as C had thought, but vitamins. Another example given by Wirjono: shooting a rifle that has no bullets loaded.[69]

Meanwhile, an example of a relatively imperfect tool: D wanted to kill E by mixing poison into his dinner. After dinner, E vomited, but this did not seriously harm him, and he recovered immediately after taking some medicine. It turned out that D only used one third of the amount of poison needed. According to objective theory, this relatively imperfect tool could be punished because there was a legal interest that was jeopardised, even if the damage was not too severe.

Can an absolutely imperfect and relatively imperfect tool (means) and object (target) be penalised for this type of attempt? I have described above both the subjective and objective perspectives. However, we can also follow Wirjono's opinion as follows: (1) it is usually considered that an attempt with a tool or object that is absolutely inaccurate (imperfect) is not an attempt that can be subject to criminal sanctions; (2) it may be possible to convict the perpetrator under another article of criminal law; and (3) usually it is also considered that attempts with relatively imperfect tools or objects can be subject to criminal sanctions (*strafbaar*).[70]

iii. Several Forms Similar to Attempts

There are two forms of conduct that are similar to attempts: (1) putative offences and (2) *Mangel am Tatbestand*.

a. *Putatieve Delict* (Putative Offence)

According to Utrecht, in the case of a putative offence, there is '*rechtsdwaling*' or an error related to the law.[71] For example, an Indonesian citizen goes to another

[68] Prodjodikoro, *Asas-Asas Hukum Pidana di Indonesia* (2003) 112–13.
[69] Ibid 112.
[70] Prodjodikoro, *Asas-Asas Hukum Pidana di Indonesia* (2003) 113.
[71] Utrecht as quoted by Barda Nawawi Arief in Arief, *Sari Kuliah Hukum Pidana II* (1993) 26.

country and obtains an abortion. She believes that she has committed the crime of abortion in that country, even though the country does not criminalise abortion. Alternatively, someone comes to Indonesia and carries out the act (X) in Indonesia. He believes he has committed a crime, even though X is not a crime in Indonesia.

b. *Mangel am Tatbestand*[72]

This, in Utrecht's opinion, is a '*feitelijke dwaling*' or error regarding the facts.[73] In German criminal law, this is called *Mangel am Tatbestand*, derived from the words *mangel* (deficiency) and *tatbestand* (a correct/perfect condition or matching the formulation of the offence).[74] Here, the crime is not completed because a certain element of the criminal act does not exist.[75] In the case of theft (Article 362 of the Criminal Code), for example, the element of 'goods that are wholly or partly owned by another person' may not exist. Consider a situation where A comes to B's house and takes a motorcycle parked in front of B's house, before selling it. A believes he has stolen the motorcycle, but it turns out that it was actually A's own property, because the previous day B had bought the motorcycle as a gift for A, but A did not know because he had been out of town and had not spoken to B. So, there is no crime of theft here.

*iv. Qualified Attempt (*Gekwalificeerde Poging*)*

Sometimes, in an incident, there is a criminal act that is not completed because the offender resigns voluntarily, yet at the same time, a separate crime has occurred. Utrecht uses the following formulation: 'This can happen if what he has done if viewed separately (*indie op zich zelfbeschouwd*), is a crime.' This is usually called a qualified attempt or *gekwalificeerde poging*.[76] For example, A intended to commit a violent theft against B and he had already begun by shooting B's hand. But afterwards A did not take the bag that B was holding because he felt sorry to see B injured. A then took B to the hospital to get help.

In the illustration of the case, the theft has not been completed; there has only been an act of violence. This is what is meant by a 'qualified attempts'. The offence is not finished but an act of violence has been committed and is a separate offence; in this case, battery (Article 351, Article 353, or Article 354 of the Criminal Code). Thus, in such a case, A is still charged with battery.

[72] *Mangel am Tatbestand* in Dutch is *Ontoreikende delictsinhoud*. Utrecht, *Rangkaian Sari Kuliah Hukum Pidana I* (1994) 408.

[73] Barda Nawawi Arief, *Sari Kuliah Hukum Pidana II* (Semarang, Badan Penyediaan Bahan Kuliah Fakultas Hukum Universitas Diponegoro, 1993) 26.

[74] Ibid. 25.

[75] Utrecht, *Rangkaian Sari Kuliah Hukum Pidana I* (1994) 408–09.

[76] Ibid 408.

IV. Attempts in the New Criminal Code

In the new Criminal Code, attempts are regulated in the Criminal Offence section, with three articles: Article 17, Article 18, and Article 19. There are some differences between the conditions of attempt in Article 53 (1) of the Criminal Code and Article 17 (1) of the new Criminal Code. In the Code, a criminal offence in which an attempt is not punished is no longer a minor offence but is a criminal offence with a certain category, regulated in Article 19. Article 19 states: 'Attempts to commit a crime that is only punishable by a maximum fine of category II are not punished.'[77]

Article 17 paragraph (2) of the Criminal Code explains implementation, stating that the commencement of performance occurs if: (a) the act committed was intended or aimed at the occurrence of a criminal offence; and (b) the action taken has the potential to give rise directly to the intended crime. Article 53 (1) existing Criminal Code submits the meaning of 'commencement of performance' to the opinion of experts or practice, while Article 17 (2) of the New Criminal Code provides a limitation on the meaning of 'commencement of performance' in Article 17 (1).

The New Criminal Code includes the types of attempts contained in the doctrine: (1) attempts that do not achieve results and (2) attempts that do not cause prohibited results. Both are also included in attempts that can be punished (ie not only 'incomplete performance'). The attempt condition (the failure of the attempt was not solely due to his own change of heart') is maintained.

With regards to criminal sanctions, as mentioned above, there is no principal difference between attempts in the current Criminal Code and the new Criminal Code. Article 53 paragraph (2) of the Criminal Code uses the formula 'the maximum principal penalty for which the crime is threatened is reduced by one third in the case of attempt', while Article 17 paragraph (3) of the New Criminal Code states that 'The penalty for attempting to commit a crime is a maximum of 2/3 (two-thirds) of the maximum principal penalty for the crime in question'. Therefore, there is no difference, except for how it is formulated. Likewise, if a crime is punishable by the death penalty or life imprisonment, both Article 53 paragraph (3) of the Criminal Code and Article 17 paragraph (4) of the New Criminal Code sanction the offender with a maximum imprisonment of 15 years. There are also similarities in terms of additional penalties, namely the same as the crime in question (Article 53 paragraph (4) of the Criminal Code and Article 17 paragraph (5) of the Criminal Code Bill).

Article 18 of the New Criminal Code confirms that if a person has fulfilled some of the requirements (intention and an initial performance), but after he has

[77] Category II is IDR10 million (USD671).

started the performance he voluntarily decides not to complete his act, he will not be punished. In my opinion, this provision actually confirms by means of a reverse interpretation the provisions in Article 17 paragraph (1), which includes the condition 'but the performance is incomplete, does not achieve the objective, or does not cause prohibited results, not because of their own will'. That is, if the person wishes the performance to succeed but despite this it is not completed, does not achieve the objective, or does not cause the result, then he fulfils the attempt of a criminal offence and thus can be punished. On the other hand, if it is not completed, does not achieve the objective, or does not cause the results, but this is due to a decision of the person himself, or he prevents completion or ensures that the prohibited results do not arise, then he cannot be punished. Perhaps it is more appropriate that the provisions of Article 18 of the New Criminal Code are referred to as the reasons for the special excuse of punishment for attempted criminal offences.

10

Participation

I. Definition

In Book 1 Chapter V of the Indonesian Criminal Code, we find the term '*deelneming*'. According to Wirjono Prodjodikoro, *deelneming* here means the participation of one or more people when another person commits a crime.[1] Meanwhile, according to EY Kanter and SR Sianturi, participation is when there are two or more people who commit a crime; in other words, there are two or more people taking part in a criminal offence.[2] According to Moeljatno, 'it can be said that there is participation if not only one person is involved in the occurrence of a criminal offence, but several people'.[3] However, not everyone involved in a criminal offence can be named a participant in the meaning of Articles 55 and 56 of the Criminal Code. For that, the participant must meet the requirements mentioned in those articles, as will be discussed below.[4]

There are two views regarding the nature of participation. First, participation as *strafausdehnungsgrund*, which is the basis for extending the punishment for people, and, second, participation as *tatbestandausdehnungsgrund*, which is the basis for expanding the criminality of the act. The first view is shared by, among others, D Simons, WFC van Hattum, Derkje Hazewinkel-Suringa, and most Dutch criminal law experts.[5] In Indonesia, Eddy OS Hiariej holds this view.[6] The second view, meanwhile, is supported in the Netherlands by WPJ Pompe and in Indonesia by Moeljatno,[7] Roeslan Saleh,[8] AZ Abidin, and Andi Hamzah.[9]

[1] Wirjono Prodjodikoro, *Asas-Asas Hukum Pidana di Indonesia*, 32nd edn (Bandung, Refika Aditama, 2003) 117.

[2] EY Kanter and SR Sianturi, *Asas-Asas Hukum Pidana di Indonesia dan Penerapannya* (Jakarta, Storia Grafika, 2018) 336.

[3] Moeljatno, *Hukum Pidana, Delik-Delik Percobaan Delik-Delik Penyertaan* (Jakarta, Bina Aksara, 2017) 63.

[4] Ibid 63–64.

[5] Barda Nawawi Arief, *Sari Kuliah Hukum Pidana II* (Semarang, Badan Penyediaan Bahan Kuliah Fakultas Hukum Universitas Diponegoro, 1993) 28.

[6] Eddy OS Hiariej, *Prinsip-Prinsip Hukum Pidana*, revised edn (Yogyakarta, Cahaya Atma Pustaka, 2016) 350.

[7] Moeljatno, *Hukum Pidana* (2017) 64.

[8] Arief, *Sari Kuliah Hukum Pidana II* (1993) 28.

[9] AZ Abidin and Andi Hamzah, *Pengantar Dalam Hukum Pidana Indonesia* (Jakarta, Yarsif Watampone, 2010) 425.

According to the first view (participation as *strafausdehnungsgrund*), participation is an extension of which perpetrators can be held criminally responsible. Thus, it is not a stand-alone crime.[10] According to Hiariej, participation is about who can be held criminally responsible; therefore, participation here is focused on the perpetrator(s) and not the action. This is reinforced by the fact that the provisions regarding participation are regulated in Book 1 of the Criminal Code, which regulates general provisions, and not in Book 2 or 3, which regulate criminal acts. In addition, in the arraignment of the public prosecutor, articles concerning participation must be combined with other articles related to criminal acts.[11]

According to the second view (participation as *tatbestandausdehnungsgrund*), participation is an extension of the norms contained in the law, thus participation is an extension of actions that can be punished. Participation is a special form of a crime.[12] Participation is a stand-alone and special offence, or *delicta sui generis*.[13]

I prefer the first argument, where participation is not a stand-alone crime, but rather a provision that expands the criminality of a person involved in a criminal act, where that person may be the initiator of the crime but does not commit the crime himself (*doen pleger* and *uitlokker*). It is also possible that the person participated in a crime where he did not fulfill all the elements of the crime (*medepleger*), or he only helped prior to or when someone else committed a crime (*medeplichtige*). Thus, I do not agree with the term 'criminal offence of participation'. In my opinion, there is no criminal offence of participation; there is only participation in a criminal offence. For example, participation in committing the criminal offence of corruption (not a crime of engaging in corruption), or participation in committing the crime of theft (not a crime of participating in theft). So, in the case of premeditated murder using a hired killer, then the initiator of the premeditated murder (eg someone who gave money to another person to commit the murder) is not punished for committing the crime of participating in premeditated murder but is punished for having participated in the crime of premeditated murder.

II. Participation in Articles 55 and 56 of the Criminal Code

Article 55 paragraph (1) of the Criminal Code reads as follows:

> Punishable as perpetrators of criminal offences:
>
> 1st the person who does, orders to do, or participates in doing the act;
>
> 2nd the person who by giving, promising, abusing power or influence, violence, threatening, or fraud, or by providing opportunities, means, or information, intentionally abets in committing an act.

[10] Hiariej, *Prinsip-Prinsip Hukum Pidana* (2016) 350.
[11] Ibid 350.
[12] Pompe in Hiariej, *Prinsip-Prinsip Hukum Pidana* (2016) 350.
[13] Moeljatno in Hiariej, *Prinsip-Prinsip Hukum Pidana* (2016) 350.

Article 55 paragraph (2) of the Criminal Code reads as follows:

> Against the abettor, only acts that are intentionally abetted are taken into account, along with their consequences.

Article 56 of the Criminal Code reads as follows:

> Punishable as accessories of criminal offences:
>
> 1st those who intentionally provide assistance when the crime is committed;
>
> 2nd those who intentionally provide opportunities, means, or information to commit crimes.

Participation comes into the discussion if, other than the perpetrator of a crime, other people are also involved. The latter person is heavily involved in the occurrence of the crime and plays an important role in the chain of causes and effects leading to the occurrence of the crime, to the extent that he must also be considered responsible, either as the offender or as an accessory to the crime, even though he himself only carries out part of the crime.[14]

We also talk about participation if there are several people in a certain relationship, where together they perform the crime, even though each person only carries out part (one or more of the elements) of the crime. However, with their respective roles fulfilling some of the elements of a crime, this leads to the completion of the crime, with all elements of the crime fulfilled.[15]

However, the status of the individuals participating sparks a question. In Article 55 of the Criminal Code, are they perpetrators (*dader*) or are the participants not perpetrators but are nevertheless punished as perpetrators? There are two different views on this question.

The first opinion states that the participants referred to in Article 55 of the Criminal Code are indeed perpetrators (*dader*). This first view is shared by Hazewinkel-Suringa and Pompe. The second opinion states that the individuals are not perpetrators (*dader*) because their actions do not contain all the elements of a criminal offence, but they can be considered as perpetrators for the purposes of punishment. This second view is shared by Jonkers and Taverne.[16]

Initially, the first opinion was held by the Dutch Hoge Raad. In a decision dated 21 April 1913, the Hoge Raad stated that 'participants are not perpetrators'. The meaning of Article 55 of the Criminal Code is simply that 'the maximum penalty that can be imposed on a participant is the same as the maximum penalty that can be imposed on the perpetrator (*dader*)'.[17]

[14] D Schaffmeister, N Keijzer, and E PH Sutorius, in JE Sahetapy and Agustinus Pohan (eds), *Hukum Pidana* (2007) 245–46.

[15] Ibid 246.

[16] E Utrecht, *Rangkaian Sari Kuliah Hukum Pidana II* (Bandung, Penerbitan Universitas, 1962) 10–12.

[17] This Hoge Raad Decision dated 21 April 1913 can be found in Nederlandse Jurisprudentie 1913, 961, Weekblad van Het Recht Br 9501, from Van Bemmelen, *Burgersdijk Arresten over strafrecht* (1949) 170–78 as quoted by Utrecht, *Rangkaian Sari Kuliah Hukum Pidana II* (1962) 10.

In 1932, there was a change in the opinion of the Dutch Hoge Raad. Through a decision dated 27 August 1932, participants were now also perpetrators. Thus, since 1932, the Hoge Raad has followed the first opinion regarding participation.[18] This is also the opinion of Pompe, who states that those who should be seen as perpetrators are all the people mentioned in Article 47 of the Dutch Criminal Code (or Article 55 of the Indonesian Criminal Code). This has been confirmed by the Explanatory Memorandum of the Criminal Code, which states that all the people mentioned in Article 55 are perpetrators.[19]

I agree with this first opinion, that the participants referred to in Article 55 of the Criminal Code – all people who order someone to do, who participate in doing, or who abet – are perpetrators (*dader*), in line with the 1932 Hoge Raad opinion. The words in Article 55 – '*als daders … worden gestraft*' ('as the perpetrator … is convicted') – are distinguished from the words in Article 56 – '*als medeplichtigen … worden gestraft*' ('as an accessory … is sentenced').

In other words, in Articles 55 and 56 of the Criminal Code, there are two kinds of parties: *dader* (perpetrators) in Article 55 and *medeplichtige* (accessory/accessories) in Article 56. That is, all those mentioned in Article 55 are perpetrators of criminal offences, and there is no question over whether the person's actions contain the entire or only some elements of the crime concerned. Meanwhile, Article 56 refers to a person who assists in carrying out a criminal act.[20]

Regarding the different forms of participation in criminal offences, then in Articles 55, 56, and 57 of the Criminal Code there are four types: *doen plegen*, *medeplegen*, *uitlokking* (these first three are contained in Article 55), and *medeplichtig* (contained in Articles 56 and 57). The difference is that this participation is carried out by *doen pleger* (people who order another to do something), *medepleger* (people who participate in doing), and *uitlokker* (people who abet) are convicted as *dader* (perpetrators), so the maximum criminal sanction is as a perpetrator. Meanwhile, *medeplichtig* (accessories) attract a different criminal sanction from the perpetrator, with their sanction reduced by one third, or, if sanctioned with the death sentence or sentenced to life imprisonment, a maximum jail time of 15 years. Therefore, in terms of participation, the Criminal Code provides details on how perpetrators (*dader*) are to be punished and how accessories (*medeplichtige*) are to be punished. Participants in Article 55 of the Criminal Code shall be punished as perpetrators, while those in Article 56 shall be punished as accessories for committing a crime.[21]

[18] Utrecht, *Rangkaian Sari Kuliah Hukum Pidana II* (1962) 11.

[19] PAF Lamintang and Fransiscus Theojunior Lamintang, *Dasar-Dasar Hukum Pidana di Indonesia* (Jakarta, Sinar Grafika, 2019) 606.

[20] Utrecht, *Rangkaian Sari Kuliah Hukum Pidana II* (1962) 11–13. See also Arief, *Sari Kuliah Hukum Pidana II* (1993) 29.

[21] Satochid Kartanegara, *Hukum Pidana Kumpulan Kuliah Prof Satochid Kartanegara dan Pendapat2 Para Ahli Hukum Terkemuka, Bagian Satu* (Jakarta, Balai Lektur Mahasiswa, nd) 2. See also Arief, *Sari Kuliah Hukum Pidana II* (1993) 29.

In Articles 55 and 56, as I have discussed above, there is indeed a mention of a person 'who commits' (*pleger*), but this cannot be interpreted as requiring that there is participation in the form of 'doing', because without any rules regarding participation, if a person acts alone to commit a crime, he will be punished. A perpetrator, who has alone manifested all elements of the offence, is not considered to be a participant. The discussion about the forms of participation cannot be separated from the discussion about the perpetrator, because in every participation, there must be a perpetrator (*pleger*).[22]

The forms of *deelneming* (participation) according to Article 55 of the Criminal Code are: (1) ordering (*doen plegen*);[23] (2) participating in doing (*medeplegen*); and (3) abetting (*uitlokking*). Meanwhile, the form of participation according to Articles 56 and 57 of the Criminal Code is to assist a criminal offence (*medeplichtigheid*).[24] It should be emphasised here that, although Article 55 mentions the word *plegen* (who does), *plegen* is not a form of participation. People performing the three forms of participation recognised in Article 55 are to be convicted as *dader* (perpetrators). On the other hand, Articles 56 and 57 list just one form of participation: assisting criminal offences. Thus, there are four forms of participation in the Criminal Code. These four forms of participation have existed since the original WvS of the Netherlands of 1881, and have persisted in the *WvS voor Nederlandsch-Indie* (in effect from 1918) and the current Criminal Code, without change.

III. *Plegen* and *Dader* (Direct Perpetration)

To review Article 55 of the Criminal Code, let us start with the original formulation of that article in the *WvS voor Nederlandsch-Indie*, which reads as follows: '*Als daders van een strafbaarfeit worden gestraft*'. This can be translated as: 'Convicted as a perpetrator of criminal offence'. The word *dader* comes from the word *daad*, meaning 'deed', 'action', or 'act'."[25] In the Dutch dictionary, the word *daad* is synonymous with the words *actie* and *handeling*,[26] with *actie* also having the specific meaning of 'an action with a specific purpose'.[27]

[22] Surastini Fitriasih, *Penerapan Ajaran Penyertaan dalam Peradilan Pidana Indonesia (Studi terhadap Putusan Pengadilan)*, Dissertation (Depok, Faculty of Law University of Indonesia, 2006) 105.

[23] According to Van Bemmelen, this is also called 'indirect perpetrator'. See JM van Bemmelen, *Hukum Pidana 1, Hukum Pidana Material Bagian Umum*, translated by Hasnan (Bandung, Binacipta, 1987) 264.

[24] See Van Bemmelen, *Hukum Pidana 1* (1987) 264; Lamintang and Lamintang, *Dasar-Dasar Hukum Pidana di Indonesia* (2019) 613; and Fitriasih, *Penerapan Ajaran Penyertaan* (2006) 105.

[25] Lamintang and Lamintang, *Dasar-Dasar Hukum Pidana di Indonesia* (2019) 596.

[26] Nederlands Woordenboek, *daad*, woorden.org/woord/daad.

[27] Nederlands Woordenboek, *actie*, woorden.org/woord/actie.

The person who commits a *daad* is called a *dader*; *dader* is thus defined as 'perpetrator'.[28] What is meant by perpetrator? It must be discussed in the context of different types of crimes, such as formal offences and material/substantive offences. Formal offences, or offences that are formally formulated, are criminal offences that can be considered complete (*voltooid)* immediately after the perpetrator commits an action prohibited by law or immediately after the perpetrator does not do something that is required by law. In order to find out who the perpetrators of this formal type of crime are, we must identify who has violated the prohibition or neglected the obligation. Dirk van Eck states that one can determine who should be viewed as a perpetrator by reading the formulation of the crime in question.[29] Meanwhile, material or substantive offences, or offences that are formulated substantially, are criminal offences that are complete (*voltooid*) due to the occurrence of results prohibited by law. Substantive offences are not finished with the completion of the action. To be able to determine who should be seen as the perpetrator of a substantive offence, one must first be able to ascertain whether an action can be seen as a cause of the results that have arisen.[30]

According to Simons, the perpetrator of a crime is a person who commits the crime in question, either with intent (*opzet*) or as an error (in relation to an act required by law), causing an undesirable effect, or who has taken an action that is prohibited by law or neglected an action required by law. Therefore, *dader* is a person who fulfills all the elements of a criminal offence determined by law, whether they are subjective or objective elements, regardless of whether the decision to commit the crime arises from that person himself or from being driven to do so by a third party.[31]

According to Van Hattum, a perpetrator is a person who fulfills a formulation of a criminal offence, a person who fulfills all elements of the formulation of a criminal offence, or who has fulfilled all elements of a criminal offence completely.[32] In his opinion, we cannot replace the term *dader* with the term *pleger*, as has been suggested by other experts such as Hazewinkel-Suringa.[33]

Jacob Maarten van Bemmelen agrees, and argues that the word *dader* has a broader meaning than *pleger* ('a person who does something'). The word *dader* here has the meaning of '*de aansprakelijk dader*' – an actor who must be responsible. Thus, according to Van Bemmelen, *dader* is a person who has fulfilled the elements of a criminal offence, or a person who has fulfilled all the conditions specified in a criminal offence formulation.[34]

[28] Lamintang and Lamintang, *Dasar-Dasar Hukum Pidana di Indonesia* (2019) 596.
[29] Ibid 601.
[30] Ibid 601–03.
[31] Simons as quoted by Lamintang and Lamintang, *Dasar-Dasar Hukum Pidana di Indonesia* (2019) 605–06.
[32] Van Hattum as quoted by Lamintang and Lamintang, *Dasar-Dasar Hukum Pidana di Indonesia* (2019) 609.
[33] Lamintang and Lamintang, *Dasar-Dasar Hukum Pidana di Indonesia* (2019) 608–09.
[34] Van Bemmelen as quoted by Lamintang and Lamintang, *Dasar-Dasar Hukum Pidana di Indonesia* (2019) 610.

According to Satochid Kartanegara, *pleger* or 'person who commits' in Article 55 of the Indonesian Criminal Code means anyone who commits *by himself* an act that is prohibited by law, or anyone who commits *by himself* an act that causes a result that is prohibited by law.[35] In a criminal act with a formal formulation, the perpetrator is therefore anyone who fulfills the formulation of the crime. On the other hand, in a criminal act with a substantive formulation, the perpetrator is whoever causes a prohibited result. Meanwhile, in criminal acts that have elements of a certain position or quality, the perpetrator is anyone who has the elements of position or quality as determined. For example, in the case of public official crimes, only state officials can commit the crime. Thus, according to Kartanegara, it can be concluded that the perpetrator is 'anyone who fulfills all the elements contained in the formulation of a crime'.[36]

In line with Kartanegara's view, Moeljatno states that for a formal offence, which is formally prepared, *pleger* is the person who commits the behaviour as stated in the formulation of the offence. As for the formulation of a material offence which is prepared substantively, *pleger* is anyone who causes the consequences as stated in the formulation of the offence, as determined by causality.[37]

Importantly, according to Hazewinkel-Suringa, a *pleger* is not a participant (*deelnemer*). In Article 55 of the Criminal Code, people who commit (*pleger*) an act, in addition to others who participate in performing the crime, are punished as perpetrators (*dader*).[38] A *pleger* is anyone who fulfills the core part (*bestanddelen*) of a criminal act, including in an attempt to commit a crime.[39] As previously explained, *bestandelen* are parts of a criminal act that are expressly contained in the description of a criminal offence formulated in an article of law.

Perpetrators are those who carry out their own actions that manifest offences, with these offences not occurring due to deception or misdirection of others, or due to violence committed by another against them so that they are helpless, act unintentionally or in *culpa lata* (negligence), or are not capable of being responsible.[40] Abidin and Hamzah emphasise that, in the case of ordering to commit a crime, the person who ordered it is not a perpetrator.

IV. Doen Plegen

The term *doen plegen* is found in Article 55 paragraph (1). It reads: 'Sentenced as perpetrators of criminal acts: 1st. person who commits (*plegen*), who orders to do (*doen plegen*), or participates in committing acts (*medeplegen*).'

[35] Kartanegara, *Hukum Pidana* (nd) 421.
[36] Ibid.
[37] Moeljatno, *Hukum Pidana* (2017) 105.
[38] AZ Abidin and Andi Hamzah, *Hukum Pidana Indonesia* (Jakarta, Yarsif Watampone, 2010) 451.
[39] Ibid 451.
[40] Ibid 462.

Interestingly, Abidin and Hamzah state that the literal meaning of *doen pleger* is 'a doer perpetrator' or 'a person who makes others do'. They argue that the translation of *doer plegen* as telling someone to do something is incorrect. *Doen* means 'to make' and *plegen* means 'to do'. In their opinion, an accurate translation would be 'to make someone else commit the offence', or more accurately, 'to make someone else (who cannot be convicted) perform the offence'.[41]

Then, what is the accurate meaning of *doen plegen*? Let us summarise several expert opinions. According to Jan Remmelink, the legal form of ordering to do has changed significantly over time, and now it can be formulated as a deliberate effort from someone to ensure that a criminal act is committed by another person who, for one reason or another, cannot be penalised.[42] According to Jonkers, *doen pleger* is not *dader*, but someone who is sentenced as a *dader*. A *doen pleger* is different from a perpetrator, and because a *doen pleger* is not a *pleger*, he is not required to fulfill the legally required position or status of perpetrator, for example being a civil servant.[43]

According to D Schaffmeister, N Keijzer and E PH Sutorius, the person who ordered the act (*doen pleger*) takes his own initiative, using as intermediaries other people who cannot be punished, in order to achieve his goals. The other person ordered to do something is used by the *doen pleger* as an 'unwilling tool'.[44]

According to Kartanegara, *doen pleger* is a person who wishes to do an act but does not do it himself and instead orders someone else to do it. However, at the same time, the act must meet the requirement that the person ordered must be a person who cannot be held accountable under criminal law.[45]

According to Moeljatno, the form of participation in *doen plegen* (ordering to do) occurs before the act is carried out. That is, the person orders the act to be performed through the intercession of another person. *Doen plegen* is also called '*middelijk dadershap*', which refers to when someone wishes to carry out a criminal act but does not want to do it himself, so tells someone else to do it. The person ordered must be a person who cannot be convicted of the crime.[46]

From the understanding given by the criminal law experts above, in my opinion, *doen plegen*, or ordering to commit a crime, is a form of participation that occurs before the occurrence of a crime. The person who wishes to commit a crime does so indirectly, namely by ordering another person or other people to commit the crime. Crucially, the person ordered to commit the crime cannot be held accountable according to criminal law.

[41] Ibid 460.

[42] Jan Remmelink, *Hukum Pidana, Komentar atas Pasal-Pasal Terpenting dari Kitab Undang-Undang hukum Pidana Belanda dan Padanannya dalam Kitab Undang-Undang Hukum Pidana Indonesia* (Jakarta, Gramedia Pustaka Utama, 2003) 311.

[43] JE Jonkers, *Buku Pedoman Hukum Pidana Hindia Belanda* [*Handboek Van Het Nederlandsch-Indische Strafrecht*], translated by Tim Penerjemah Bina Aksara (Jakarta, PT Bina Aksara, 1987) 188–89.

[44] Schaffmeister, Keijzer, and Sutorius, in Sahetapy and Pohan (eds), *Hukum Pidana* (2007) 252.

[45] Kartanegara, *Hukum Pidana* (nd) 4–5.

[46] Moeljatno, *Hukum Pidana* (2017) 123.

To be able to say that there is participation in the form of ordering to do, there are several conditions. These conditions are not regulated in Article 55 of the Criminal Code, but they can be identified based on the notion of participation as discussed above. In my opinion, the conditions for participation are:

(1) there is a person (principal) who wishes to commit a crime;
(2) the principal commits a criminal act indirectly, namely by ordering another person or other people to commit the crime;
(3) the effort of the principal in ordering other people is not specified in the law; the important thing is that the person being ordered (direct perpetrator / material actor)[47] does what he is told;
(4) the direct perpetrator / material actor commits the criminal act ordered by the principal;
(5) the direct perpetrator / material actor cannot be held accountable according to criminal law.

If all the above conditions are met, there is a form of participation ordering to do. If the conditions are not met, then there is no order to do it, or it may fall into other forms of participation. For example, if the fourth condition is not fulfilled, because the person did not commit the crime as ordered, then there is no crime. As another example, the fifth condition, that is 'if the direct perpetrator cannot be accounted for according to criminal law', because it turns out that the direct perpetrator can be held criminally accountable, then there is no form of ordering to do, but rather of abetting (*uitlokking*).

Does the *doen pleger* have to fulfill or meet the required qualifications as a perpetrator of the criminal act committed? On this question, there are two views: (1) the *doen pleger* must meet or have the qualifications or qualities required as a perpetrator of the criminal act committed, and (2) the *doen pleger* does not have to fulfil or have the required qualifications as a perpetrator of the criminal act committed.

According to the first opinion, which states that *doen pleger* must have the qualities of a perpetrator, it is impossible for someone to order someone else to do something that the *doen pleger* himself cannot do. This opinion is held by Simons and GA Van Hamel. For example, A is not a civil servant, so he cannot commit a 'public official' offence, as only civil servants can commit this type of offence. In such a case, A cannot be a direct perpetrator (actor), therefore A also cannot be an indirect perpetrator (actor). So, even though B (whom A ordered to do the crime) is a civil servant, there is no order to commit a crime, as the crime is one that A could not commit even if acting through B.[48] However, Simons states that there is an order to do something if the person who is ordered to commit a criminal act

[47] The term 'substantive perpetrator' in the context of participation in ordering to do (*doen plegen*) is also used by Fitriasih, *Penerapan Ajaran Penyertaan* (2006) 40.
[48] Arief, *Sari Kuliah Hukum Pidana II* (1993) 32.

has in good faith carried out an official order, even though the order was given by a superior who is not in fact authorised to give such an order.[49]

According to Van Hamel, the act of ordering was the act of the *dader*, so the person who ordered him to do it must have all the qualities that a *dader* possesses.[50] E Utretcht draws on several hypothetical scenarios posed by Van Hamel: can a woman make a mentally ill man rape another woman? Article 285 of the Criminal Code requires that the perpetrator of rape must be a man. Can a non-civil servant commit a criminal act of extortion? Article 425 of the Criminal Code, which is included in Article 12 of Law No 31 of 1999 concerning the Eradication of Corruption Crimes as amended by Law No 20 of 2001, states that only civil servants can commit the act of extortion. According to Van Hamel, the answer to such questions is no.[51]

The second opinion states that *doen pleger* does not need to have the qualities of a perpetrator. This view is shared by Pompe, Hazewinkel-Suringa, GE Langemeijer, HB Vos, and JE Jonkers. Decisions of the Dutch Hoge Raad also favour this view. Pompe states that an order to do a public office offence exists not only if the substantive actor (perpetrator) is a public official and the one who ordered the act is not a public official, but also *vice versa*: that is, if the substantive perpetrator is not an official but the one who orders it is an official.[52]

In the *Reispas-arest* (Decision on the Reispas [Passport]) case,[53] the Dutch Hoge Raad was of the opinion that there is participation in the form of ordering to do, even if an employee (who is not an official) instructs another person in a criminal act that requires the perpetrator to be an official. In the *Reispas-arest* case, the defendant was the mayor of Zaandam, who wrote a letter to the *Commissaris der Koningin* (Governor of Noord Holland Province), regarding an individual's plan) to travel to Russia. In that letter, the mayor intentionally, and contrary to the truth, stated that the individual's age was 21, even though he was only 17, so that the Governor would issue the requested travel permit. Here, the act of issuing the travel document was incorrect, because the person mentioned in the travel document was only 17 years old, but the document said 21 years. In this case, the *Hoge Raad* was of the opinion that there was participation in the form of ordering someone to commit a crime, even though the principal (in this case, the mayor) did not have the qualifications required to be the perpetrator of the crime (a Governor).[54]

Langemeijer states that it is possible for a civil servant to be ordered by someone who is not a civil servant to commit a crime of office, provided that what the civil servant has done can result in a crime that can only be committed by a civil servant. For example, crimes in Articles 414 and 416 (regarding counterfeiting),

[49] Lamintang and Lamintang, *Dasar-Dasar Hukum Pidana di Indonesia* (2019) 623.
[50] Utrecht, *Rangkaian Sari Kuliah Hukum Pidana II* (1962) 28.
[51] Abidin and Hamzah, *Hukum Pidana Indonesia* (2010) 464.
[52] Arief, *Sari Kuliah Hukum Pidana II* (1993) 32.
[53] HR 21 April 1913, W 9501, NJ 1913, p 961, as quoted in Remmelink, *Hukum Pidana* (2003) 311.
[54] Remmelink, *Hukum Pidana* (2003) 311.

426 (regarding discharge), 431, 432, and 433.[55] Specifically, Article 414 (1) of the Criminal Code reads:

> An official who deliberately asks for assistance from the Armed Forces to oppose the implementation of the provisions of the law, orders the general authority according to law, decision or court order, shall be punished by a maximum imprisonment of seven years.

According to Jonkers and Vos, it is possible for a non-civil servant to order a civil servant to commit a crime of office. The purpose of every criminal provision is to protect legal interests, therefore it is appropriate for those who violate those legal interests to be punished.[56] In order words, if they are not punished, then any person who orders a civil servant to commit a crime of office cannot be punished, and this is certainly contrary to the intent of upholding the rule of law.

The element of intentionality is also important to examine. If a criminal act contains an element of intentionally, how does this relate to the *doen plegen*? According to Remmelink, the intention of the person who orders to do should at least be directed at ensuring the perpetrator carries out what he is told to do. Regarding criminal acts that must be committed intentionally (*dolus* offence / *opzetdelict*), the consequences of these actions and other conditions related to the crime in question must also be clearly desired by the principal. This is because the word '*doen*' ('ordering') includes the meaning that the person making the order wants to make someone else do something which is a criminal act.[57]

According to Langemeijer, in the case of ordering someone to commit the crime of theft, according to Article 362 of the Criminal Code, the person who orders the theft must have the *oogmerk* (intention) to possess the stolen goods by the person being ordered to act against the law.[58] The *oogmerk* (intention) or *opzet* (intentionality) of the principal can be in one of two forms: (1) the intention or intentionality to possess the stolen goods; or (2) the intention or intentionality to instruct the perpetrator to commit the theft.[59]

In my opinion, the stance of the Dutch Hoge Raad in *Reispas-arest*, as well as the positions of Pompe, Hazewinkel-Suringa, Langemeijer, Vos, and Jonkers is the more appropriate one. It protects the interests of the law and does not allow the principal to escape from criminal charges just because he does not have the qualities of the perpetrator of the crime as determined in the formulation of the law.

According to Simons, an order can also occur if the person who is ordered to commit a crime does not have a *hoedanigheid* ('a certain trait'), as required by law. This refers to a trait that must be possessed by the perpetrator himself.[60]

[55] Lamintang and Lamintang, *Dasar-Dasar Hukum Pidana di Indonesia* (2019) 623–24.

[56] Utrecht, *Rangkaian Sari Kuliah Hukum Pidana II* (1962) 29–30.

[57] Remmelink, *Hukum Pidana* (2003) 312.

[58] Of course, as a condition of having an order to do something, the direct/substantive perpetrator is a person who cannot be held accountable according to criminal law.

[59] Langemeijer in Lamintang and Lamintang, *Dasar-Dasar Hukum Pidana di Indonesia* (2019) 625.

[60] Lamintang and Lamintang, *Dasar-Dasar Hukum Pidana di Indonesia* (2019) 623.

The decision of the Dutch Supreme Court dated 19 December 1910, W Nr 9122 states that:

> based on Article 47 of the Criminal Code (Dutch), a person who orders another person to commit a criminal act is a perpetrator responsible for this crime if the accessory (the person who is ordered) does not meet the requirements to be held accountable as a perpetrator for the crime committed by him, even if he (the person who is ordered) knows that he has done a forbidden act, which the person who gave the order is not allowed to do.[61]

This is because the person who is ordered to commit the act does not have certain qualities (*persoonlijke vereischte*), and these qualities must be fulfilled or met, according to the relevant criminal provisions. In this case, the person who is ordered to do something is called a *doleus werktuig* (a 'knowing tool'). Even though the person does the criminal act knowingly and on purpose, according to the Dutch Supreme Court, the person cannot be convicted.[62]

What about cases when direct/substantive perpetrators cannot be punished according to criminal law? The inability to convict the substantive perpetrator is a consequence of that person not being able to be held accountable by criminal law for his actions. According to Utrecht, there are two reasons which mean that a person who is ordered to do something cannot be punished: (1) the person does not commit a crime at all, or the act he commits does not qualify as a criminal incident, or (2) the person does indeed commit a criminal incident, but he cannot be convicted for one or more reasons which excuse the guilt (*schulduitsluitingsgronden*).[63]

According to Vos, the person who is ordered to do something cannot be punished because of the reasons that excuse guilt in the following situations:

(1) The act committed cannot be accounted for by the person who is ordered (the direct perpetrator) because of his diminished capacity or because of insanity (Article 44 of the Criminal Code). This is also called '*ontoerekeningsvatbaarheid*' ('inability to be responsible').
(2) The person who is ordered to commit the act is threatened or in a state of coercion (Article 48 of the Criminal Code);
(3) The person who is ordered to commit the act carries out an official order given by a person who has no right to give the order but in good faith he thinks that the order is given by a person who is authorised to give the order (Article 51 paragraph 2 of the Criminal Code).
(4) The person ordered to commit the act is not guilty at all (*afwezigheid van alle schuld/AVAS*).
(5) The person ordered to commit the act is a minor.[64]

[61] This Decision is quoted from Utrecht, *Rangkaian Sari Kuliah Hukum Pidana II* (1962) 23.
[62] Utrecht, *Rangkaian Sari Kuliah Hukum Pidana II* (962) 23.
[63] Ibid 20.
[64] Utrecht, *Rangkaian Sari Kuliah Hukum Pidana II* (1962) 26.

Utretcht notes that the final point – on age – is problematic. In the event that the direct perpetrator is a child, the question arises: can the order be given? In my opinion, it depends on the age of the child, in line with Law no 11/2012 concerning the Juvenile Criminal Justice System. If the child being ordered to commit an act is not yet 12 years old, it is considered that the order exists, because the child cannot be sentenced due to his age. Thus, the person who orders him to commit the act is considered an indirect perpetrator, or a *manus domina*, and is sentenced as a *dader* (perpetrator). The child is a tool of the perpetrator, or is a *manus ministra*, and cannot be punished. However, if the child is 12 years old or over, then there is no order to commit a criminal act, but rather an act of abetting *(uitlokking)*, where the child can be subject to action or be punished (although the criminal threat is lighter than for a perpetrator who is aged over 18). In Law no 11/2012, Article 1 point 3 uses the term 'child in conflict with law', which refers to any minor who is 12 years old, but not yet 18 years old, who is suspected of committing a crime. Article 12 paragraph (1) of the Law clarifies what is to be done: in the event a minor who is aged 12 or over commits or is suspected of committing a crime, investigators, community advisers, and professional social workers make decisions to: (1) return them back to their parents/guardians or (2) have them undertake education, coaching, and mentoring programs at government agencies or a juvenile rehabilitation centre at a social welfare agencies, either at the central or regional level, for a maximum of six months.

According to Barda Nawawi Arief, there may be an order to commit a criminal act of *culpa* offence, such as in a case where the person ordered to commit the act is indeed aware of potential negative consequences but assumes the person ordering the act has already acted to prevent such outcomes. For example, A orders B (a worker) to throw a heavy object from the roof of the house they are working on, regardless of whether the object may fall on someone who is passing by. B throws the object, thinking that A has put in place the necessary safeguards to make sure that nobody will be hit by the thrown object. In this case, A can be prosecuted for ordering someone to commit a criminal act, as regulated in Article 359 of the Criminal Code.[65]

V. *Medeplegen* (Co-perpetratorship)

Participating in the committing of a crime is not an easy thing, both at the conceptual level and in practice. Surastini Fitriasih in her dissertation research found that in practice: (1) cooperation is only seen in terms of physical cooperation; (2) the different treatment of the participants (as if each had committed his own offence); and (3) the concept of participation is not properly applied by the courts.

[65] Arief, *Sari Kuliah Hukum Pidana II* (1993) 33.

According to Fitriasih, there is an illogical narrative obtained from the conclusions, specifically because physical cooperation should result in the same qualifications for each participant, because they worked together.[66]

According to Pompe, participating in committing a crime has three possibilities:

(1) Each participant fulfils all the elements in the formulation of a crime. For example, two people work together to steal from a rice warehouse.
(2) One person fulfils all the elements of a criminal act, while the other does not. For example, two pickpockets (A and B) cooperate with each other; A hits the target person while B takes their wallet.
(3) No one fulfils the elements of a criminal act entirely,[67] but together they realise the crime. For example, in theft by damaging property (Article 363 paragraph 1–5 of the Criminal Code), A digs a hole in the ground to create a tunnel into the victim's house, then B enters the house and steals the victim's goods, giving them to A.[68]

Article 55 paragraph (1) point 1 of the Criminal Code mentions very briefly the word '*medeplegen*', which is widely translated by Indonesian legal experts as 'taking part in doing' or 'participating in doing'. Neither the Indonesian Criminal Code nor the MvT (the Explanatory Memorandum of the Dutch Criminal Code) explain the meaning of *medeplegen*.[69] Precisely because the word is very short and there is no explanation whatsoever provided, this has resulted in significant debate and difference of opinion among Dutch legal experts. Even today, the word has not been changed in the Netherlands nor Indonesia.

If even among criminal law experts there is a debate about the meaning and requirements of *medeplegen*, then of course it has consequences in its application in criminal prosecution. Additionally, when translated into Indonesian ('*turut serta melakukan*', or 'join in doing') it is still not very clear what it means, who is involved, how they are responsible, whether all of them must have qualifications in accordance with the qualifications of the perpetrator (*dader*) as determined in respect of a criminal act, how this is different from helping to commit a crime, and so on.

A summary of various opinions about participating in criminal acts is as follows: According to Hoge Raad, with *medeplegen* there can be 'full' perpetrators (who fulfil all the elements of a criminal act), but there can also be perpetrators whose actions only fulfil some elements of a crime. To say that there is *medeplegen*, this requires that there is proof of a conscious collaboration, which is the intentional act of cooperating. There are two kinds of intentionality here: (1) intentionality to cause the result of a criminal act and (2) intentionality to cooperate.

[66] Surastini Fitriasih, *Penerapan Ajaran Penyertaan* (2006) 100–01.

[67] The possible meaning is: each participating in actions that only fulfil part of the elements of the crime, but by each committing some of the elements of the crime, the criminal act is completed in accordance with the formulation of the crime in the Criminal Code.

[68] Arief, *Sari Kuliah Hukum Pidana II* (1993) 33.

[69] Abidin and Hamzah, *Hukum Pidana Indonesia* (2010) 477.

Plans or agreements do not need to be made in advance; what must be proven is that there is mutual understanding between fellow perpetrators, and, when the actions are executed, each perpetrator cooperates to achieve a common goal. Intentions between fellow perpetrators do not have to be the same.[70]

According to the Hoge Raad, *medeplegen* can apply if one of the cooperating perpetrators does not have the personal qualities required by the formulation of a criminal act. A non-public official can participate in committing a crime that can only be carried out by a public official. A non-sailor can participate in committing a shipping crime. Thus, *medeplegen* can apply in terms of: (1) creating and attaching accountability to people who are involved in criminal acts but who cannot be qualified as perpetrators (*pleger*), given the fact that the latter does not meet the factors of criminal acts that constitutive in nature; and (2) expanding the accountability of people who are involved in criminal acts, who in addition to being responsible as perpetrators (*pleger*), must also be responsible for what they do in conscious cooperation with other parties.[71]

It is also possible that someone participated in the activity without the presence of one of the participating perpetrators (*medepleger*) at the place where the crime was committed. This often happens in the case of the import of narcotics, which may involve the use of transport such as aeroplanes. Often people who live in different places agree to participate in achieving a common goal in which they share the results. One example is the Hoge Raad decision of 17 November 1981, commonly known as the *Container Diefstal Arrest*. Although the *megepleger* was not at the scene of the crime, he had an important role in the organisation of the theft.

According to Van Hamel, *medeplegen* can be matched with the presence of a number of people who together become perpetrators of criminal acts. To fulfill the category of *medepleger*, each person must fulfill all the elements of the crime concerned.[72] *Mededaderschap* (actions of participants as perpetrators) and 'participating in doing' are the same.[73]

Meanwhile, according to Simons, those who participate in doing (*medepleger*) are *dader* (perpetrators). Therefore, those who participate in committing the crime must possess in themselves all the qualities possessed by a *dader* of the crime in question. If they do not have the quality of being a *dader*, they cannot be qualified as *medepleger*.[74] Like Van Hamel, according to Simons, *mededaderschap* and 'taking part in doing' are the same.[75]

[70] Hoge Raad in its Decision HR dated 21 June, 1926, NJ 1926, P 955, W 11541, in Remmelink, *Hukum Pidana* (2003) 314.

[71] Hoge Raad in its Decision HR dated 21 June, 1926, NJ 1926, 995, W 11541, in Remmelink, *Hukum Pidana* (2003) 313–14.

[72] Van Hamel as quoted in Remmelink, *Hukum Pidana* (2003) 313–14. See also Utrecht, *Rangkaian Sari Kuliah Hukum Pidana II* (1962) 32.

[73] Utrecht, *Rangkaian Sari Kuliah Hukum Pidana II* (1962) 34.

[74] Ibid 32–33.

[75] Ibid 34.

In TJ Noyon's view,[76] there is a principal difference between *mededaderschap* and 'participating in doing'.[77] *Mededaderschap* is the *daderschap* of several participants. Each participant is a full *dader*. Thus, there are several perpetrators of a crime. According to Noyon, this has no meaning according to criminal law, because a *dader* can already be convicted, even without provisions regarding participation. In this interpretation, *mededarschap* is *daderschap* so it does not require the use of teachings on 'participation'.[78] On the other hand, 'participating in doing' is a separate and special form, as those who participate in doing do not have one of the required qualities[79] that can make them a perpetrator. They are therefore referred to as 'participating in' the crime, not the perpetrators of the crime. So, they are not real perpetrators (*dader*), and only punished as 'perpetrators'.[80]

If there are two people who commit a crime, and both fulfill all the elements of a crime as specified in the law, then both are deemed to have committed the crime (*plegen*). On participation, because they do the crime together, according to Article 55 of the Criminal Code, this constitutes 'taking part in the perpetration' or 'participating in doing' (*medeplegen*). According to Jonkers, in this case, because both fulfil all the elements, they are 'friends of the perpetrator' (*mededader*), not *medepleger*.

On the other hand, if there are two people who commit a crime, but only one fulfils all the elements as specified in the law, with the other person fulfilling part of the elements, then the person who fulfills all the elements is the one who commits the crime (*pleger*). The other person is referred to as *medepleger*. However, according to Article 55, both those who fulfil all the elements of a criminal act (*plegen/pleger*), as well as those who fulfil part of the elements, are considered to be perpetrators (*dader*) and should be punished as such.

Participation cannot be understood simply as a group of perpetrators. Not every person who is qualified to participate in committing the crime has to fulfill all the elements of the crime. There can be a division of tasks with responsibilities assigned to different people, as a *medepleger* is not required to completely fulfil all the elements of a crime. Along the same lines, the implementation of a criminal act does not have to be completely executed by the participating perpetrator (*medepleger*).[81] Referring to the Decision of the Dutch Hoge Raad dated 9 February 1914, NJ 1914, 648, W 9620, Remmelink argues that there is no participation if perpetrators' intentions differ, such as if one perpetrator wants to torture while the other perpetrator actually wants to kill. Their intention must be the

[76] His own opinion (before he co-authored a book with Langemijer).

[77] In Utrecht's book, it is called 'participating in doing'. Utrecht *Rangkaian Sari Kuliah Hukum Pidana II* (1962) 34.

[78] In Utrecht's book, it is called 'participation'. Ibid 34.

[79] The term used by Utrecht is 'qualities'. Ibid 34.

[80] See Moeljatno, *Kitab Undang-Undang Hukum Pidana* (2016) 104. See also Dali Mutiara, *KUHP (Wetboek van Strafrecht voor Indonesie yang telah dibaharui dengan penjelasannya)* (Jakarta, Suar Bookstore, 1951) 145; see also Soesilo, *Kitab Undang-Undang Hukum Pidana* (1995) 208.

[81] Remmelink, *Hukum Pidana* (2003) 317–18.

same as the actions referred to in the law. It is not necessary for every actor who cooperates to carry out the entire series of implementation actions, nor do they need to fulfil all the characteristics of a perpetrator, for example as a public official. However, people working together cannot differ in their intentions (one person is trying to do something completely different from the other person). Thus, it is unacceptable to convict someone as a *medepleger* in a murder when in fact he only intended to torture (even though the other person may indeed have intended to kill).[82]

According to Remmelink, with reference to the above HR decision, to say that there is a *medeplegen*, it is required that: (1) there is a conscious collaboration (intention to cooperate); and (2) joint execution.[83] Remmelink also refers to the HR Decision of 17 November 1981, NJ 1983, 84 (participating in the theft of container transport trucks in Dordrecht and Mijnsheerenland) where there were *medepleger* – ie *medeorganisator* (who participated in managing) while they were in Rotterdam. Physical presence at the time of collection is not required.[84]

Several experts state that the conditions for the existence of *medepleger* are: (1) there is conscious cooperation (*bewuste samenwerking*) and (2) there is the joint execution of criminal acts jointly, specifically physical cooperation (*gezamenlijke uitvoring / physieke samenwerking*).[85] In Pompe's view, in participation and taking part, there are two kinds of intentionality: (1) intentionality to cooperate in the context of executing a criminal act among the perpetrators; and (2) real cooperation in executing the crime.[86] Remmelink states the same.[87]

Both conditions for participation must be proven in court.[88] But exactly what do these two conditions mean?

First of all, there is conscious cooperation (*bewuste samenwerking*). The existence of this conscious cooperation does not mean that there is an agreement beforehand. It is sufficient if there is an understanding between the participants, at the time the action is carried out, that they aim to achieve the same result.[89] What is important is that there must be a will to cooperate and that will is aimed at achieving something that is prohibited by law (in other words, a crime). As stated above, there is no participation if, for example, one person (A) only wants to torture someone (C), while his friend (B) wants C's death.[90]

According to Van Hattum, for *medeplegen* there must be intentional cooperation between the participants. Cooperation that is not realised by the people who work together is not actually cooperation; the participants must be aware that

[82] Ibid 315.
[83] Ibid 314–15.
[84] Ibid 316.
[85] See for example Utrecht, *Rangkaian Sari Kuliah Hukum Pidana II* (1962) 37. See also Arief, *Sari Kuliah Hukum Pidana II* (1993) 34.
[86] Pompe as quoted in Hiariej, *Prinsip-Prinsip Hukum Pidana* (2016) 370.
[87] Remmelink, *Hukum Pidana* (2003) 314–15.
[88] Pompe as quoted in Hiariej, *Prinsip-Prinsip Hukum Pidana* (2016) 370–71.
[89] See eg Arief, *Sari Kuliah Hukum Pidana II* (1993) 34.
[90] Ibid.

they are working together. Therefore, cooperation due to negligence is not possible, so there is no possibility of collaboration due to negligence. What is possible is that two people intentionally cooperate, but there is a *culpa* offence. For example: A and B deliberately work together to throw a heavy object from a high place, and the object falls and hits a person below, killing him.[91]

According to the Dutch Hoge Raad, *medeplegen* requires conscious collaboration to be proven. As mentioned above, conscious collaboration prior to the event is not necessary. What needs to be proven is that there is mutual understanding between fellow perpetrators and when the act is executed, each perpetrator cooperates to achieve a common goal. Each perpetrator who cooperates does not need to fulfill all the characteristics of a perpetrator (eg public officials, people who control objects, etc).[92]

Secondly, there is the joint execution of a criminal act (*gezamenlijke uitvoring*) and physical cooperation ((*physieke samenwerking*). What is meant here is that the manifestation of the criminal act is a direct result of the actions of the participants, and not in the manner specified in Article 56 of the Criminal Code. For example, if A acts to dismantle a safe and B takes the money, this is an act that directly manifests the crime of theft. It doesn't matter who (A or B) completes the execution of the crime. Another example: a murder was carried out by C and D together and it is not clear whose blow caused the death of the victim. This remains a form of participation, as long as there is prior conscious cooperation. What is important is that a crime has occurred, and that each participant perpetrator directly took part. This is contained in the Decision of the Dutch Supreme Court dated 28 August 1933.[93]

The form of participating in committing a crime must be marked by an act of execution (*uitvoering handeling*). If a participant takes part in the execution, then he is a participant perpetrator, but if a person has just arrived at the stage of preparation for execution (*voorbereidings handling*) then he is an assistant to committing the crime (*medeplichtig*).[94]

In this regard, we must not forget the discussion on the issue of criminal attempts, as discussed earlier. We have examined the difference between preparatory action (*voorbereidings handeling*) and implementation action *(uitvoering handeling*). In accordance with Article 53 (1) of the Criminal Code, the second condition of an attempt that can be punished is an implementation action, not a preparatory action. So, in the context of participating in committing a criminal act, if one person has just arrived at the preparatory action, he is not classified as participating in a criminal act, because he has not carried out the implementation of the offence. However, he can be classified as an assistant to committing a crime,

[91] Moeljatno, *Hukum Pidana Delik-Delik Percobaan Delik-Delik Penyertaan* (Jakarta, Bina Aksara, 1985) 118.
[92] Remmelink, *Hukum Pidana* (2003) 314–15.
[93] Kanter and Sianturi, *Asas-asas Hukum Pidana* (2018) 348–49.
[94] Ibid 349.

which we will discuss later, as he is not included in Article 55 of the Criminal Code but is referred to in Article 56. It is also important to note, as Remmelink states, that physical cooperation does not require the participants to be in the same place at the same time, even in the context of fulfilling the second condition (implementation action).[95]

VI. *Uitlokking* (Abetting)

As a reminder, Article 55 paragraph (1) of the Criminal Code in the original text of *WvS voor Nederlandsch-Indie* reads as follows:

> Art. 55. (1) Als daders van een strafbaarfeit worden gestraft:
>
> 1^0 zij die het plegen, doen plegen of medeplegen;
>
> 2^0 zij die door giften, beloften, misbruik van gezag of van aanzien, geweld, bedreiging of misleiding of door het verschaffen van gelegenheid, middelen of inlichtingen het feit opzettelijk uitlokken.

Which, if translated, is as follows:

> Article 55. (1) Sentenced as perpetrators of criminal acts:
>
> 1st the person who does, orders to do, or participates in doing the act;
>
> 2nd the person who by giving, promising, abusing power or influence, violence, threatening, or fraud, or by providing opportunities, means, or information, intentionally abets in committing an act.

In the original formulation, we find the terms '*uitlokken*' and '*uitlokking*'. A person who does this act is called an *uitlokker*. R Tresna uses the term 'persuasion', with the person referred to as a 'persuader',[96] while Barda Nawawi Arief translates *uitlokker* as 'adviser'[97] and 'abetter'.[98] Moeljatno, and Kanter and Sianturi also use the term 'abetting' for *uitlokking*.[99]

Other terms are also in use. Lamintang and Lamintang state that *uitlokker* or abettor is also referred to by other terms, such as 'provocateur', 'agent provocateur', or '*lokbeamte*' ('trap officer').[100] Meanwhile, Tirta Amidjaja offers '*auctor intellectualis*' ('intellectual actor').[101] However, it should be noted here that agent provocateurs, infiltrators, undercover agents, and *lokbeamte* who take action to

[95] Jan Remmelink, *Hukum Pidana – Komentar atas Pasal-Pasal Terpenting dari Kitab Undang-Undang Hukum Pidana Belanda dan Padanannya dalam Kitab Undang-Undang Hukum Pidana Indonesia* (2003) 316.

[96] R Tresna, *Azas-azas Hukum Pidana* (Jakarta, Tiara, 1959) 92.

[97] Arief, *Sari Kuliah Hukum Pidana II* (1993) 36.

[98] Ibid 36.

[99] See Moeljatno, *Hukum Pidana* (1985) 125. See also Kanter and Sianturi, *Asas-asas Hukum Pidana* (2018) 350.

[100] See Lamintang and Lamintang, *Dasar-Dasar Hukum Pidana di Indonesia* (2019) 648.

[101] MH Tirta Amidjaja, *Pokok-Pokok Hukum Pidana* (Jakarta, Penerbit Djakarta, 1955) 99.

encourage other people to carry out criminal acts (eg anti-narcotics agents trying to trap narcotics traffickers) are not punishable.[102]

I prefer to use the term 'abetting' for the act and the term 'abettor' for the person. This is because, in my opinion, the act of abetting is broader than persuasion, incitement, and suggestion, and relies heavily on the efforts made, such as by giving, promising, abusing power or influence, committing violence, threatening, misleading, or providing opportunities, means, or information. The term 'abetting' seems to fit all the types of efforts that are being made. 'Persuasion' or 'suggestion' may be more suitable if the method is by giving or promising, or by providing opportunities, means, or information, while 'incitement' may be appropriate if the method is deception. However, in this book, other terms are also used for the same act (*uitlokkeuitlokking*) and perpetrator (*uitlokker*), because of the array of terminology in use in Indonesia, including in legal documents such as indictments, arraignments, and decisions. I will now summarise how Dutch and Indonesian legal experts understand 'abetting' and similar terms.

(1) Schaffmeister, Keijzer, and Sutorius state that in the case of *uitlokking*, the abettor tries to gain access to other people for his own purposes or plans in order to ensure that the other person commits the crime desired by the abettor. The abettor uses one of the means or powers of abetting listed in the law (such as gifts, promises, abuse of power, violence, threats, deceit, opportunities, means, or information). The person who is abetted (*uitgelokte*) is fully responsible for his actions, while the abettor has moved him towards the action but without being involved in any physical implementation. In other words, the abettor does not participate in the execution of the deed.[103]

(2) Barda Nawawi Arief understands *uitlokker* to mean an adviser. Specifically, he describes them as a person who advises other people to commit a crime by using the means determined by law.[104]

(3) Tresna states that a person who persuades another person to do a prohibited act is called an '*intellectuele dader*' ('perpetrator-planner'). This is a person who deliberately induces another person to commit a criminal act, by giving gifts, promises, abusing authority or dignity, coercion, threats, or deception, or by providing opportunities, means, or information.[105]

(4) Kanter and Sianturi argue that, in abetting, the initiative lies in the abettor. In other words, a crime will not occur (in this form) if the initiative is not with the abettor. Therefore, the abettor must be considered as an actor and must be punished commensurate with the perpetrator who physically commits (*auctores physici*) the criminal act that was abetted. It does not matter whether the abettors have or have not previously held a certain willingness to commit the crime. In essence, the criminal act that was abetted has materialised.[106]

[102] Remmelink, *Hukum Pidana* (2003) 338.
[103] Schaffmeister, Keijzer, and Sutorius, in Sahetapy and Pohan (eds), *Hukum Pidana* (2007) 249.
[104] Arief, *Sari Kuliah Hukum Pidana II* (1993) 36.
[105] Tresna, *Azas-azas Hukum Pidana* (1959) 92.
[106] Kanter and Sianturi, *Asas-asas Hukum Pidana* (2018) 350.

(5) Tirta Amidjaja[107] is of the opinion that a persuader is a person who persuades another person to commit a criminal offence by using the ways which have been determined by law. The initiative to commit the crime came from the persuader.[108]

There is a question about this abetting: does the abettor need to meet the qualifications for a criminal offender? There are several criminal acts where the perpetrator of the crime must be a person with certain qualifications, such as a civil servant, an official, a captain, or a mother. Can A (not a civil servant) be sentenced to act as an abettor (*uitlokker*) to B (a civil servant) for committing the crime of embezzlement in office (Article 415 of the Criminal Code), which can only be committed by civil servants? Can C (a man) be punished for abetting D (a pregnant woman) to kill her child as soon as it is born (Article 342 of the Criminal Code)? The law is clear: yes. Therefore, a person who does not have the qualifications required as the subject of a criminal act can still be an abettor for other people, as long as those other people meet the qualifications.[109]

Article 55 paragraph (2) of the original *WvS voor Nederlandsch-Indie* reads as follows: '*Ten aanzien der laatsten komen alleen die handelingen in aanmerking die zij opzettelijk hebben* ***uitgelokt****, benevens hare gevolgen*' (emphasis added). This is translated as: 'Against *the abettor*, only the act which is deliberately abetted is taken into account, along with the consequences' (emphasis added) Based on these provisions, we can see the limit of the responsibility of the person abetting people to commit a criminal act, which is only limited to 'deeds that are deliberately abetted' and 'the consequences' (referring to, of course, the consequences of the actions that are abetted). Thus, the abettor is not responsible for actions that he does not intentionally abet, and nor is he responsible for the consequences that occur because of actions that he does not abet.

The criminal limitation for the abettor is because the abetting has an *accesoir* ('accessory') nature. As a result, the abettor has no greater responsibility for what is done than the physical perpetrator of the crime (the person he persuaded). Moreover, according to Article 55 paragraph (2) of the Criminal Code, the responsibilities of the abettor do not exceed what he deliberately abetted and the consequences of that abetting.[110] For example, A abets B to physically harm C in exchange for a mobile phone. It turns out that B has a grudge against C and actually intends to kill C, so B beats C until C dies. In this case, A is not responsible for C's death. A is only responsible for inciting the battery. Meanwhile, B is responsible for the death of C. Another example: if in the above case, B did not have the intention of killing C, but B carried out the battery of C as prompted by A and, as a result of his injuries, C died, A is responsible for instigating battery resulting in

[107] Justice of the Republic of Indonesia Supreme Court in the 1950s.
[108] Amidjaja, *Pokok-Pokok Hukum Pidana* (1955) 99.
[109] Schaffmeister, Keijzer, and Sutorius in Sahetapy and Pohan (eds), *Hukum Pidana* (2007) 249–51.
[110] Amidjaja, *Pokok-Pokok Hukum Pidana* (1955) 100–01. See also Moeljatno, *Hukum Pidana* (1985) 126–27. See also Van Bemmelen, *Hukum Pidana 1* (1987) 291–92.

death under Article 351 paragraph (3) of the Criminal Code in conjunction with Article 55 paragraph (1) point 2. A third example: D abets E to steal from F's house. E agrees, and, at night, steals from F's house. However, in addition to stealing, E also abuses F, who turns out to be his old enemy. In this case, D is responsible for inducing theft by aggravation under Article 363 paragraph (1) to 3 of the Criminal Code in conjunction with Article 55 paragraph (1) point 2, but D is not responsible for E's assault of F. Thus, E can be sentenced for theft and battery.

In other words, the responsibility of an abettor is limited. He is only accountable for the actions that he requested from the person he persuaded (the physical perpetrator). In addition to being limited, the responsibility of an abettor is also expanded. That is, the abettor is also responsible for the consequences which arise from the actions he deliberately abets. That is, if A only abets B to harm C, but B's battery of C results in C's death, then A is responsible for instigating the battery resulting in death[111] under Article 351 paragraph (3) in conjunction with Article 55 paragraph (1) point 2 of the Criminal Code.

Perhaps the following question will arise: if the abettor (A) abetted B to harm C, but in fact B actually killed C, or B stole C's property, can A be punished? If yes, based on what? The short answer is A can be punished, but not under Article 55 paragraph (1) point 2 of the Criminal Code (participation). Instead, he can be punished under Article 163 bis of the Criminal Code. This is called *mislukte uitlokking* and will be discussed in more detail in the next chapter.

Criminal law experts describe Article 55 paragraph (1) of the Criminal Code in the form of *uitlokking* (abetting) in several conditions. This means that if these conditions are met, then there is abetting that can be punished according to that provision. Listed below are the conditions for abetting that can be punished, as stated by Indonesian and Dutch legal experts. Broadly speaking, there is no significant difference in interpretation.

According to Moeljatno, there are four conditions for the existence of abetting: (1) there must be someone who has the intention to commit a criminal act by encouraging others; (2) there must be another person who can perform the act that is intentionally recommended; (3) the method of recommending must be by means of one of the methods or efforts specified in Article 55 paragraph (1) point 2 of the Criminal Code; and (4) the recommended person must actually commit the criminal act as desired by the person recommending it.[112]

According to Tirta Amidjaja, there are also four conditions for abetting, although they are slightly different from Moeljatno's. Amidjaja's four conditions are: (1) the persuaded person must intentionally commit the crime requested by the persuader; (2) the persuader must persuade that person to commit a criminal act by using the means established by law; (3) the person who is persuaded by the methods used must genuinely have been persuaded to commit the crime; and

[111] Kartanegara, *Hukum Pidana* (nd) 25–26.
[112] Moeljatno, *Hukum Pidana* (1985) 125–26.

(4) the person being persuaded must have actually committed the crime, or at least have attempted a criminal offence for which he may be sentenced.[113]

Kanter and Sianturi's opinion is very similar to Amidjaja's. They also list four conditions: (1) the intentional abettor intends that a certain action is carried out by the actor who is driven; (2) the effort to abet is certain as formulated in the law; (3) there are people who are abetted, and who have taken an action because of that effort; and (4) the perpetrator who was abetted must have committed the crime that was abetted, or at least attempted the crime.[114]

Lamintang and Lamintang provide a shorter interpretation, with just two objective conditions for the act of abetting: (1) the act that has been abetted to be carried out by another person must result in a *voltooid delict* (completed offence) or *strafbare poging* (an attempt which can be punished); and (2) a criminal act that has been committed by a person is caused because that person has been abetted by an *uitlokking* carried out by another person using one of the methods mentioned in Article 55 paragraph (1) 2 of the Criminal Code.[115]

Remmelink puts forward four conditions of abetting that can be punished, but his views are clearer and more detailed. Remmelink identifies four conditions for abetting: (1) the intentional act of abetting another person to take an action prohibited by law with the help of means as stipulated by law; (2) the decision of the will of the other party (the person who is abetted) to commit a criminal act must be raised, with a mental causality (*psychische causaliteit*) relationship in existence (between the act of abetting of the abettor and the will of the other party/person being abetted); (3) the person who is abetted achieves the plan intended by the abettor to commit a criminal act or at least carry out an attempted criminal act – the act of bad faith alone is not enough, and his efforts must be manifested in action; and (4) the person who is abetted to commit the crime must be able to be held criminally responsible; if he cannot, then there is no abetting (*uitlokking*) but rather an order to commit the crime (*doen plegen*).[116]

According to Barda Nawawi Arief, conditions in which persuasion can be punished are: (1) there is an intentional act to induce another person to commit a prohibited act; (2) the act is abetted by using the measures stated in the law (limitative in nature); (3) the decision of the will of the substantive perpetrator is caused by the above points, meaning there is a *psychische causaliteit*; (4) the substantive perpetrator commits or attempts to commit the recommended crime; and (5) the substantive perpetrator must be accountable in criminal law. Conditions 1 and 2 are conditions for the persuader/abetter, while conditions 3, 4, and 5 are conditions attached to the person who is persuaded/abetted (substantive perpetrator).[117] Efforts of abetting are determined in a limited manner as regulated

[113] MH Tirta Amidjaja, *Pokok-Pokok Hukum Pidana* (Jakarta, Penerbit Djakarta, 1955) 99–100.
[114] Kanter and Sianturi, *Asas-asas Hukum Pidana* (2018) 351.
[115] Lamintang and Lamintang, *Dasar-Dasar Hukum Pidana di Indonesia* (2019) 652.
[116] Remmelink, *Hukum Pidana* (2003) 328.
[117] Arief, *Sari Kuliah Hukum Pidana II* (1993) 36.

in Article 55 paragraph (1) point 2 of the Criminal Code, whereby because of his efforts, a person abets another person to commit a crime. It is said that there is an act of abetting if the physical perpetrator, prior to the abetting efforts made by the abettor, did not have the intention of committing the criminal act. Through the act of abetting, the abettor – by using the efforts mentioned in Article 55 paragraph (1) point 2 of the Criminal Code – persaudes/abets the other person, who then does what the abettor recommended.

This is very different from assisting in committing an offence, in which the perpetrator already intended to commit a crime prior to gaining the help or recommendations of other people. In terms of assistance, the same efforts can be used as in abetting, namely in terms of providing opportunities, means, and information.

However, there is a difference between abetting and assisting. Abetting only occurs if it is carried out under the conditions mentioned in Article 55 paragraph (1) point 2 only. Influencing others to commit a criminal act by using other means, such as giving counsel, by 'exhibiting people who have committed such acts as examples', or by 'imagining the benefits that can be achieved from the act', according to Tresna, does not qualify as abetting as intended in the Criminal Code because abetting by way of exhibiting or exemplifying is not contained in Article 55 (1) point 2.[118]

Specifically with regard to efforts in the form of abuse of influence, according to Kartanegara, this is not contained in the Dutch Criminal Code, because this form is unique to Indonesia. For example, a village head or other prominent community figure who has a respected position in his area and who abuses his influence.[119] What Kartanegara claims is true: Article 47 paragraph (1) 2 of the Dutch Criminal Code reads: '*zij die door giften, beloften, misbruik van gezag, geweld, bedreiging, of misleiding of door het verschaffen van gelegenheid, middelen of inlichtingen het feit opzettelijk uitlokken*.' There is only *misbruik van gezag* (abuse of power) and no *van aanzien* (abuse of influence).

Specifically, regarding participation efforts in the form of 'providing opportunities, means, or information', as contained in Article 55 paragraph (1) point 2 of the Criminal Code, these efforts are additional, because there were no such efforts listed in the Dutch WvS of 1886. These efforts were initially only listed for cases of assistance (Article 56 point 2), in which assistance is provided before a crime is committed. This addition of participation (or being an accessory during the fact) was only made in the 1924 amendment to the Indonesian Criminal Code.[120]

In addition, we must distinguish between abetting in Article 55 paragraph (1) point 2 and incitement, which is a separate offence and regulated in Article 160. Article 160 explains that incitement occurs when someone in public, verbally or in writing, incites others to commit a crime, commits violence against the general

[118] Tresna, *Azas-azas Hukum Pidana* (1959) 93.
[119] Kartanegara, *Hukum Pidana* (nd) 22–23.
[120] JM van Bemmelen, *Hukum Pidana 1, Hukum Pidana Material Bagian Umum*, Hasnan's Translation (Bandung, Binacipta, 1987) 279–80.

authorities, or does not comply with the provisions of the law or the order of office given under the provisions of the law. This incitement offence has the nature of *uitlokking* (abetting), because in incitement there are people who abet other people to commit a crime. However, there are differences: (1) *uitlokking* (abetting) must be carried out using to the efforts/methods listed in Article 55 paragraph (1) point 2 of the Criminal Code; and (2) for incitement, the conditions for effort are not specified as in Article 55 paragraph (1) point 2 of the Criminal Code, but must be carried out verbally or in writing and must be done in public.[121]

VII. Assisting in Committing a Criminal Act

Assisting in committing a criminal act is regulated in Articles 56, 57, and 60 of the Criminal Code. In the original WvS voor Nederlandsch-Indie, Article 56 reads as follows:

> Article 56. Als medeplichtigen aan een misdrijf worden gestraft:
>
> 1^0 zij die opzettelijk behulpzaam zijn bij het plegen van het misdrijf;
>
> 2^0 zij die opzettelijk gelegenheid, middelen of inlichtingen verschaffen tot het plegen van het misdrijf.
>
> Convicted of being an assistant to a crime:
>
> (1) those who intentionally provide assistance at the time the crime is committed;
> (2) those who intentionally provide opportunities, means, or information to commit crimes.

The term used in Article 56 is '*medeplichtigen*' which all Indonesian legal experts translate as '*membantu*' ('assisting/aiding'). There is almost no difference of opinion regarding the translation of '*membantu*' ('assisting/aiding') and '*pembantuan*' ('assistance') in Indonesian criminal law. These relate to two Dutch terms on assistance: '*medeplichtighe/medeplichgtigen*' ('assistant') and '*medeplichtigheid*' ('assistance'). These terms are used interchangeably according to the context. This is different from the Dutch terms *medeplegen* and *uitlokking*, which have different translations among Indonesian legal experts, as discussed above.

Article 56 point 1 of the Criminal Code covers the first category of assistance, referring to people who intentionally provide assistance to the perpetrator when a crime is committed. This article makes it clear that the assistance is only for offences that are felonies, not violations. If assistance is given for the commitment of a violation, there is legally no assistance in this case. This is in contrast to other types of participation (ordering to do, participating in committing, and abetting criminal acts), all of which can occur in both felonies or violations. That assistance does not apply to violations is reaffirmed in Article 60 of the Criminal Code.[122]

[121] Kartanegara, *Hukum Pidana*, Second Part (nd) 23–24.
[122] Article 60 of the Criminal Code reads: 'Assisting in committing violations is not punishable by law.'

Assisting to commit violations, either in the Criminal Code and outside the Criminal Code (in laws or regional regulations), cannot be punished.

From the formulation of Article 56 point 1, we know that the 'assistant' is not that person who committed the crime. Someone else committed the crime, with the assistant only providing assistance. It should be noted that the subjective element of an assistant is 'intentionally' (*opzettelijk*). If it is due to negligence/omission or because that person does not know that someone else has committed a crime, then there is no assistance. 'Intentionally' has been discussed at length in the previous chapters, pointing out elements of 'knowing' (*wettens*) and 'wanting' (*willens*). So, in the assistance in Article 56 point 1 of the Criminal Code, the person who assists a crime intentionally provides assistance at the time of the crime, as he both knew and wanted the other person to commit a crime.

Some examples are as follows. A intends to steal goods from B's warehouse. At night, A manages to enter the warehouse, but it is difficult for him to carry the stolen goods from the warehouse. Then, using a cell phone, A calls his old friend, C, who lives near the warehouse. He tells C that he intends to steal some goods but is having a hard time carrying them, so C arrives at the warehouse with a vehicle and helps A lift the items. This case is in accordance with the formulation in Article 56 point 1 of the Criminal Code: 'those who intentionally provide assistance when a crime is committed.'

Article 56 point 2 covers the second category of assistance: people who intentionally provide opportunities, means, or information to commit crimes. In detail, Article 56 point 2 covers (1) the provision of opportunities (*verschaffen van gelegenheid*); (2) the provision of the means (*verschaffen van middelen*); and (3) the provision of information (*verschaffen van inlichtingen*). In this case, the assistant gives assistance to the main perpetrator (by providing opportunities, means, or information) prior to the crime being committed (*uitvoering handeling*). This is different from the assistance in Article 56 point 1, which involves assistance given at the time the offence is committed.

These three provisions are identical to those covered in *uitlokking* (abetting) formula regulated in Article 55 paragraph (1) point 2. This raises the question: what is the difference? (1) In terms of abetting, the provision of opportunities, means, or information is carried out before the person being abetted has the intention, purpose, or plan to commit a criminal act. The abettor has the will to commit a crime but he does not wish to do it himself, therefore he abets another person to do the crime by providing opportunities, means, or information. Thus, the perpetrator only develops the intention to commit the offence is after he has been abetted. (2) In terms of assistance, the provision of opportunities, means, or information is carried out when the main perpetrator already has the intention, purpose, or plan to commit a criminal act. In other words, the intentionality of the two efforts is different. In abetting, the abettor intentionally abets another person to commit a crime by providing opportunities, means, or information. In terms of assistance, the assistant intentionally assists another person who is about to commit a crime, by providing opportunities, means, and information.

Therefore, we can also conclude that there are only two times for assistance: before a crime, or during a crime. There can be no assistance to commit a crime after the crime has already been committed. In fact, there is also no other participation (such as participating in committing a crime, ordering to commit a crime, and abetting a criminal act) after the crime has been committed. However, this does not mean that people who help other people after a crime is committed are free from the sanction of criminal law.

However, there are several criminal acts that involve the provision of assistance to others after committing a crime, such as Article 480 and Article 221 of the Criminal Code.[123] With punishment for a maximum of four years in prison, Article 480 sanctions whoever buys, offers, exchanges, accepts pledges, accepts gifts, withdraws profits, sells, rents out, exchanges, pledges, transports, stores, or hides an object, which he knows or reasonably or suspects has been obtained from a crime. This is known as 'handling stolen goods' or 'conspiracy' ('*heling*' in Dutch). In other words, this crime is a kind of assistance provided to someone after that person has committed a crime. For example, A steals B's motorcycle (which has a market price of IDR15 million), and C buys the motorcycle from A for only IDR3 million. Here C can be blamed for handling stolen goods, if he either knows A sold him a stolen motorbike or should have suspected it was obtained from theft (or some other crime).

Meanwhile, Article 221 of the Criminal Code threatens maximum imprisonment of nine months for anyone who intentionally hides people who commit crimes or are being prosecuted for crimes, or anyone who provides assistance to avoid investigation or detainment, or with the intention to cover a crime up, or to hinder or complicate the investigation or prosecution, destroy, eliminate, hide objects against which or with which a crime was committed, or covering up traces of other crimes, and so on.[124] Clearly, this crime occurs after other crimes have been committed by other people. For example, G commits battery and later becomes a fugitive from the police. H, who is a friend of G, suggests G should stay at his house to hide so he can avoid being caught by the police, and G agrees. When the police arrive, H states that he has not seen G.

To clarify, then, when *medeplictigheid* (assistance) occurs: there must be a perpetrator (*dader*) and an assistant (*medeplichtige*). The perpetrator is the person who fulfills all the elements of a crime. In a criminal act with a formal formulation, the perpetrator is the person who commits the prohibited act; while in a criminal act with a substantive formulation, the perpetrator is the person who causes the prohibited result. The assistant himself does not fulfill the elements of a criminal act.

Regarding the limits of criminal liability, the prevailing system in Indonesia depends on the form of participation. For those who are classified as *dader*, which is regulated in Article 55 of the Criminal Code (ordering to do, participate in, and

[123] See Soesilo, *Kitab Undang-Undang Hukum Pidana* (1991) 75–76.

[124] See complete formulation in Article 221 of the Criminal Code.

abetting), then the criminal threat is also as *dader* according to the sanctions the perpetrators in each criminal act. So, for example, in a case of ordering to commit theft (Article 362 of the Criminal Code), the *dader* is sanctioned with a maximum of five years in prison, as both participating in theft and abetting theft are punishable by a maximum of five years.

Then there are those who are sentenced as assistants, for providing assistance either before or at the time the offence is committed, in the form of providing opportunities, means, or information. The criminal sanction for an assistant is lower than that given to the perpetrator. This is regulated in Article 57, which states that for assistance, the maximum principal punishment for crimes is reduced by one third (paragraph 1). If the crime is punishable by death or life imprisonment, a maximum imprisonment of 15 years is imposed (paragraph 2). As for additional punishment, the assistance is the same as the crime itself (paragraph 3). For example: P helps Q commit a criminal act as regulated in Article 283 paragraph (1) of the Criminal Code with a maximum penalty of nine months in prison. So, the punishment for P is six months' imprisonment (nine months minus one-third [9 – (9/3) = 9 – 3 = 6 months]). Another example: R helps S commit premeditated murder as regulated in Article 340 of the Criminal Code, which carries the threat of capital punishment or life imprisonment or a maximum of 20 years. Thus, the criminal penalty for R is imprisonment for a maximum of 15 years.

Article 56 paragraph (4) of the Criminal Code limits the liability of the assistant. It states that: 'In terms of determining the punishment for the assistant, what is taken into account is only actions that are deliberately facilitated or facilitated by him, along with their consequences.' So, for example, A helps B carry out premeditated aggravated battery against C (Article 355 paragraph (1) of the Criminal Code). The criminal sanction for B is a maximum imprisonment of 12 years. Meanwhile, A, who assists the offence, is punishable by 12 years minus one-third (12 – (12/3) = 12 – 4 = a maximum of 8 years in prison). If as a result of the battery, C dies, then A is also responsible. The criminal sanction for B is imprisonment for a maximum of 15 years, so the criminal punishment for A is 15 years imprisonment minus one-third (15 – (15/3) = 15 – 5 = 10 years' imprisonment at most).[125]

VIII. 'Participation' in the New Criminal Code

In the New Criminal Code, participation is regulated in Articles 20 and 21. Article 22 of the New Code also regulates the provisions of Article 58 of the current Criminal Code. Article 20 of the new Criminal Code is similar (but not the same) as Article 55 of the current Criminal Code which regulates anyone who does, orders, participates, and abets in committing a criminal act

[125] See further in Van Bemmelen, *Hukum Pidana 1* (1987) 291–92.

The new Article 20 reads:

Anyone shall be punished as a perpetrator of a criminal offence for:

(a) committing a crime himself;
(b) committing a crime by means of a tool or ordering other people who cannot be accounted for;
(c) participating in committing a crime; or
(d) abetting other people to commit a crime by giving or promising something, abusing power or dignity, committing violence, using threats of violence, committing misdirection, or by providing opportunities, means, or information.

Meanwhile, Article 21 of the new Code is similar to Article 56 of the current Criminal Code. The new Article 21 reads:

(1) Anyone shall be punished as an assistant to a criminal act if he intentionally:
   (a) provides an opportunity, means, or information to commit a crime; or
   (b) provide assistance when a crime is committed.
(2) The provisions as referred to in paragraph (1) do not apply to assistance for criminal acts which are only sanctioned with a fine of category II at most.
(3) The punishment for assisting a criminal act is at most 2/3 (two-thirds) of the maximum principal punishment for the crime in question.
(4) Assistance in committing a crime punishable by death or life imprisonment shall be punished with a maximum imprisonment of 15 (fifteen) years.
(5) Additional punishment for assisting in committing a crime is the same as additional punishment for the crime concerned.

Article 20 letter a of the new Code emphasises the phrase 'do it himself'. This is the same as the meaning of *plegen* (he who committed the crime, or the substantive/physical perpetrator). Article 20 letter b has two forms: (1) doing it by means of a tool and (2) ordering people who cannot be accounted for.

First, people who commit crimes 'by means of tools'. This formulation is similar to the terms 'inanimate agent' and 'inanimate object' in common law countries, such as the United States. It covers entities that are not human (eg animals or robots) but can cause criminal acts because they are used by a person.[126] For example, a person orders a monkey to steal someone else's mobile phone, orders a dog to bite another person, or arranges for a robot to take someone else's belongings.

Second, people who order other people who cannot be held accountable to carry out criminal acts. Here, the meaning is the same as *doen plegen* (ordered to do). For example, ordering people with severe mental illness to throw stones at other people and injure them, or asking people to sign fake papers while threatening to shoot and kill them if they do not sign.

The formulation of Article 20 letter c of the new Code is the same as the formulation of the current Article 55 paragraph (1) point 1. Here, the meaning

[126] See eg Edward Eldefonso and Alan R Coffey, *Criminal Law: History, Philosophy, Enforcement* (New York, Harper & Row Publishers, 1981) 47.

is *medeplegen*, but this article clearly uses the term 'participating in doing'. This eradicates the need for terms such as 'participating', 'participating perpetrator', and 'participating to do' as a translation of *medeplegen*.

The formulation of Article 20 letter d of the new Code is almost the same as the formulation of the current Article 55 paragraph (1) point 2. Both indicate the participation form of *uitlokking/uitlokken*. The formulation is almost the same, but the new Code strictly uses the term 'abetting' instead of 'persuading', 'counselling', or 'inciting'.

For the new Article 21, the difference is that the element 'if it is done intentionally' in Article 21 (1) takes precedence. Additionally, the current Article 56 of the Criminal Code clearly mentions assisting felonies, while Article 21 (1) of the new Code only mentions assisting criminal offence. This is because, as mentioned earlier, the new Code does not differentiate between felonies and violations. There is only a criminal offence.

For the two types of assistance, the formula is almost the same, only the order is reversed. In the new Code, assisting when a crime is committed is listed second, while assisting by providing opportunities, means, or information is listed first. In Article 56 of the current Criminal Code, this formulation does not exist, because the current version only refers to 'assisting felonies'. Article 21 (2) of the new Code stipulates that assisting a criminal offence that is punishable by a fine in category II is not penalised.

11

Sentencing

I. Definition

The term 'punishment' is very broad in its meaning. This is because punishment can also fall outside of criminal sanctions: there are also administrative penalties, civil sanctions, disciplinary penalties, social penalties, and so on. As Terance D Miethe and Hong Lu put it:

> Punishment is the universal response to crime and deviance in all societies. As such, it takes various forms. Criminal sanctions like imprisonment and death sentences are allocated and dispensed by state authorities. Other formal punishments involve civil lawsuits and administrative decrees to either reconcile or restore relations among the parties, compensate for personal injuries, and/or prevent further wrongful conduct through restrictions of ongoing practices. Punishment may also involve various types of informal sanctions by family, peers, and extralegal groups like vigilante committees and paramilitary organizations to promote their own interest.[1]

Satochid Kartanagara states that sanctions in criminal law are in the form of threats with punishment that cause suffering and torment. Why torment? Because punishment is intended as retribution for violations committed by a person against legal interests protected by criminal law. The legal interests (*rechsbelang*) that are protected are: life, body, honour, freedom, and property rights.[2]

A similar view is expressed by D Simons, a Dutch legal expert, who states that punishment is a form of suffering that is sentenced by a judge against a guilty person according to criminal law relating to the violation of norms. That view is very similar to what is put forward by GA Van Hamel, who states that punishment is a special suffering imposed by the competent authority in charge of public law order against an offender because he has violated legal regulations that must be enforced by the state.[3]

[1] Terance D Miethe and Hong Lu, *Punishment A Comparative Historical Perspective* (Cambridge, Cambridge University Press, 2005) 1.

[2] Satochid Kartanegara, *Hukum Pidana, Kumpulan Kuliah Prof Satochid Kartanegara dan Pendapat2 Para Ahli Hukum Terkemuka, Bagian Dua* (Jakarta, Balai Lektur Mahasiswa, nd) 49.

[3] Eddy OS Hiariej, *Prinsip-Prinsip Hukum Pidana*, revised edn (Yogyakarta, Cahaya Atma Pustaka, 2016) 36.

Considering the development of criminal law, including the philosophy or purpose of sentencing as well as the subject (ie the perpetrator of the crime, and not limited only to natural persons), in my view the punishment is a formal reaction from the state through the judge's decision against any person or corporation who violates the norms protected by criminal sanctions in laws and regulations, where the consequences for the perpetrators involve deprivation of freedom, property, or other consequences specified in the legislation. With this understanding, the consequences do not have to be in the form of suffering, misery, or torment for those who are found guilty, as alternative philosophies of punishment take a different approach.

II. The Philosophy of Punishment

In this section, I discuss different punishment philosophies: absolute, relative, and combined (meaning a combination of absolute and relative). This division into three penal philosophies is a common division we find in the criminal law literature in Indonesia as well as in the Netherlands.

Criminal sanctions are severe sanctions. In comparison with other legal sanctions, criminal sanctions can, in fact, be very severe. It is said that there is a paradox in this regard. On one hand, the state must protect the security of its people, make its people prosperous, ensure the tranquillity of its people, and guarantee the freedom and independence of its people, but on the other hand, the state is also the one who imposes punishment on its people if they violate criminal law. Thus, the state may punish a person, impose a prison sentence on a person (thus depriving him of his freedom), or impose a fine on a person (thus seizing his property). Such a paradox leads to the question: what are the reasons that can justify imposition of a criminal sentence by the state?[4]

A. Absolute/Retributive

As Jacob Maarten van Bemmelen argues, the absolute theory has been accepted for centuries. This theory is closely related to human experience, with every attack by a person provoking retribution from the attacked party.[5]

Absolute theory proposes that punishment is released from any purpose. In other words, sentencing does not need to have any purpose other than simply the implementation of punishment. Since it is forbidden to commit a crime, both according to morality and law, crime should not happen; therefore, if someone

[4] E Utrecht, *Rangkaian Sari Kuliah Hukum Pidana I* (Surabaya, Pustaka Tinta Mas, 1994) 157–58.

[5] JM van Bemmelen, *Hukum Pidana 1, Hukum Pidana Material Bagian Umum*, translated by Hasnan (Bandung, Binacipta, 1987) 25.

commits a crime, they deserve to be punished. Thus, the punishment is a form of retribution for committing a crime. Punishment is carried out to avenge the actions of the offenders, and there is no other purpose.[6]

In other words, there is no practical purpose to punishment, according to the theory of retribution. This means alternative sentences such as rehabilitation of criminal offenders serve no purpose, as it is the crime itself that contains the elements to be punished. The crime is absolute because the crime was committed. In this theory, whether there are benefits or goals that can be achieved by imposing a punishment is not taken into account. Every crime must result in the imposition of a sentence on those who have violated the law. Therefore, this theory is called the absolute punishment theory because punishment is an absolute demand – a necessity. The essence of punishment is retribution.[7]

From the description above, in my view, this theory of punishment rests on the reasoning that punishment is imposed on the offender in order to avenge the crime – to retaliate without intending to exceed the actions of the offender. There is no other purpose of the punishment (not even to act as a deterrent), meaning the sentencing only looks to the past (backward looking), rather than looking to the future (forward looking).

B. Relative / Utilitarian / Purposive

Of course, the absolute or retributive theory discussed above is not accepted by all experts. This is because according to this theory punishment is imposed for no other purpose other than retribution for the offender's actions. Proponents of the relative theory criticise this approach. They argue that punishment should not be imposed solely as a response to a crime that has already been committed (backward looking), but that sentencing must also look to the future (forward looking). Relative theorists state that punishment must have a purpose: there must be benefits for the offender, the victim, or the community. As such, this approach is also sometimes referred to as the 'theory of goals'.

Another term used for this philosophy is the 'utilitarian theory of punishment'. The utilitarian philosophy is advocated by Jeremy Bentham and has been very influential on ways of thinking about crime and sentencing. It is referred to as 'utilitarian' because what is sought is the greatest benefit for the most people. The punishment imposed is not just for criminal purposes (in comparison to absolute/retributive philosophy), but to achieve certain benefits or goals. There must be a reason for the punishment, and there cannot be punishment solely for the sake of punishment.

[6] Ibid.
[7] Andi Hamzah, *Asas-Asas Hukum Pidana* (Jakarta, Yarsif Watampone, 2005) 31.

With this background, and using literature from Indonesia, the Netherlands, and common law jurisdictions such as the United States and the United Kingdom, I will discuss the relative theory through eight sub-theories: (1) general deterrence / general prevention; (2) specific deterrence / specific prevention; (3) rehabilitation / education / medical; (4) social protection; (5) incapacitation; (6) isolation; (7) reintegration; and (8) restitution.

*i. General Deterrence (*Generale Preventie*)*

The terms 'general deterrence' and 'general prevention' are interchangeable (Dutch: *generale preventie*). According to the United States Department of Justice, 'Deterrence is designed to demonstrate the certainty and severity of punishment to discourage future crime by the offender and by others'.[8]

The basic idea of the theory or philosophy of general deterrence or general prevention is that punishment is imposed on the perpetrator as a lesson for other people (the wider community), to encourage others not to imitate or follow the perpetrator in committing the crime. In other words, if the criminal act is emulated by other people, the same result will be experienced: they will be punished in the same way as the offender, who was sentenced.[9]

In general deterrence, the purpose of general criminal law or a certain punishment is to discourage, restrict, or prevent people from committing a crime.[10] A relevant legal maxim says '*ut poena ad paucos, metus ad omnes perveniat*', or 'so that punishment afflicts few, (and) fear affects all'.[11]

In this context, the main purpose of sentencing is prevention. Prevention is aimed at the wider community and encourages people not to take actions that violate public order.[12] Scholars who support general prevention argue that governments have the authority to impose penalties to prevent the general public from committing criminal acts. General prevention thus has three functions: upholding the authority of the government, enforcing norms, and forming norms.[13]

According to HB Vos, the longest form of general prevention theory is in the form of a punishment that contains a significant or terrifying deterrent. This discourages other community members from committing the same crime as those who are currently serving said punishment. The public implementation of that punishment is considered as something that must be done (*noodzakelijk*) in order to maintain public order.[14]

[8] G Larry Mays and L Thomas Winfree Jr, and Rick Ruddel, *Contemporary Corrections: A Critical Thinking Approach* (Belmont, Thomson/Wadsworth, 2005) 3.

[9] Ibid 4.

[10] Bryan A Garner (ed), *A Handbook of Criminal Law Terms* (St Paul, Minnesota, West Group, 2000) 199–200.

[11] Ibid 751.

[12] Bambang Poernomo, *Asas-Asas Hukum Pidana* (Jakarta, Ghalia Indonesia, 1992) 29.

[13] Van Bemmelen, *Hukum Pidana 1* (1987) 27–28.

[14] Poernomo, *Asas-Asas Hukum Pidana* (1992) 29.

Is the theory of general deterrence accepted in Indonesia? E Utrecht refers to a decision by the Jakarta High Court on 7 June 1951, in which the concept was accepted and taken into consideration, with the panel of judges stating:

> … especially against an offender like this defendant, who has shown that he does not pay attention to the punishments that have been sentenced on acts of smuggling … but on the other hand argues that both from the point of view of *speciale preventie* and from the point of view of *generale preventie* to terrify the defendant in the future and to prevent other people from committing acts like the defendant …[15]

According to the judges' consideration in the decision, it appears that judges in Indonesia also have insight into the deterrence/preventive argument (both specific and general) as to why a sentence is imposed on a criminal offender. This is clear from the panel's use of the phrase 'to prevent others from committing acts like the defendant', indicating that the judges sentenced the defendant in order to set an example for the community not to do the same thing, because they would be punished in the same way as the defendant. Thus, from the view of general prevention, crime also has an element of 'educating' the public. The question is thus: can the public be educated through learning about the punishment imposed on perpetrators? Utrecht argues that, as the 'terrifying' or deterrent element, the educational element is a relative path.[16]

ii. *Specific Deterrence/Special Prevention*

The term specific deterrence, or special prevention, refers to the philosophy that assumes that sentencing an offender can prevent future crimes. The basic idea behind the special deterrence theory is that punishment is imposed on the offender as a deterrent so that the convicted offender does not commit that crime again. If he does, then he will be punished again.[17] In fact, we can also see that there are regulations that increase punishment for those who repeat crimes ('recidivism rules') in the Indonesian Criminal Code.

According to the special prevention theory, the purpose of the crime is to restrain the bad intentions of the offender (*dader*). This means holding back the offender from repeating his actions. People who support this theory include Van Hamel in the Netherlands and Franz Von Liszt in Germany. According to Van Hamel, lawmakers – when determining a threat of punishment – can only imagine a threat to individuals, not to society. Van Hamel states that there must be the following elements: (1) punishment must contain a frightening element in order to specifically restrain or ward someone off from committing bad intentions; (2) punishment must contain an element that corrects the convicted person; (3) punishment must contain an element of destruction for the criminal which is

[15] Utrecht, *Rangkaian Sari Kuliah Hukum Pidana I* (1994) 184.
[16] Ibid 184–85.
[17] See further in Mays, Winfree, and Ruddel, *Contemporary Corrections* (2005) 4.

completely irreparable; and (4) the sole purpose of punishment is to maintain the rule of law.[18]

One of the reasons for sentencing is that punishment is considered to help to prevent violations of criminal law. However, the relationship between punishment and deterrence has always been hotly debated, both with a philosophical approach and by presenting empirical data from research results. Humans are seen as rational beings and, within certain limits, are free to choose whether to violate criminal law or not. Only through punishment can humans be forced not to violate the law. This is known as the concept of free will (freedom of choice), and this rationalism sits as the rationale for deterrence theories both general deterrence and specific deterrence. Empirical data from research on recidivism is also used to prove the benefits of punishment as deterrence, although what may be proven is only specific deterrence.[19]

a. Rehabilitation / Reformation / Education / Medical Model

Rehabilitation is a process that seeks to improve the character of offenders and their future so that they can function in society without committing other crimes. Rehabilitation is one of the philosophies of punishment, and in Dutch it is known as '*verbetering van de dader*' or 'correcting the offender'.[20] According to rehabilitation theory, the purpose of punishment is to rehabilitate criminal offenders so that they become good human beings. Serving a sentence must be accompanied by rehabilitation, which can be in the form of training in a skill.[21]

At correctional institutions across Indonesia, many education and skills programmes are implemented by the Director General of Corrections. There is an emphasis on moral and religious education, as well as skills in making souvenirs or items needed by the community, which are then sold. On certain occasions, public exhibitions of the products made by the residents of correctional facilities are also held.

Sometimes, rehabilitation is seen as contradictory, in that offenders are sentenced to a certain punishment but also undergo rehabilitation. Nevertheless, according to this philosophy, the primary aim is to rehabilitate the offender. The ultimate goal of rehabilitation is to restore a convicted person to a constructive place in society through a combination of action, education, and training. This rehabilitation philosophy is reflected in the use of terms such as 'correctional facilities', 'reformatories', and 'therapeutic communities' instead of 'detention' and 'prison'.[22]

[18] Utrecht, *Rangkaian Sari Kuliah Hukum Pidana I* (1994) 184–85. See also Poernomo, *Asas-Asas Hukum Pidana* (1992) 30.

[19] Mardjono Reksodiputro, *Kriminologi dan Sistem Peradilan Pidana* (Jakarta, Universitas Indonesia, 1994) 149–50. See also Topo Santoso, 'Suatu Tinjauan atas Efektivitas Pemidanaan' and Martin Moerings, 'Apakah Pidana Penjara Efektif' in Agustinus Pohan, Topo Santoso, and Martin Moerings (eds.), *Hukum Pidana dalam Perspektif* (Denpasar, Pustaka Larasan, 2012) 209–50.

[20] Garner (ed), *A Handbook of Criminal Law Terms* (2000) 581.

[21] Poernomo, *Asas-Asas Hukum Pidana* (1992) 30.

[22] Miethe and Lu, *Punishment: A Comparative Historical Perspective* (2004) 22.

However, in Indonesia, research on whether the rehabilitation, coaching, and correctional programmes carried out in correctional institutions have been running well and have had a positive impact on the lives of individuals remains limited, with more work needed.

b. Isolation

Isolation is a very old philosophy of punishment that has been used historically to fulfil two purposes. First, isolation solely as punishment, namely removing the offender to a tower or very remote place that stops him from being able to communicate with other human beings. Second, as a 'rotten apple' response, removing offenders from broader society to avoid their bad influence on others. For this reason, experts in penology view the function of punishment as providing a social environment that is free from crime ('social sanitation'). Correctional institutions thus become holding places for people who are not wanted by society, because they are seen as dangerous or make the community uncomfortable.[23]

Efforts to isolate offenders may take various forms, not just imprisoning the offenders so that they are removed from society and unable to commit crimes. In the past, efforts to isolate the offenders of crimes was sometimes carried out by means of exile or expulsion to a remote location, where the offenders could not contact their families or former communities. This might be, for example, by sending the offenders to an island, which is strictly guarded so that offenders cannot escape.

c. Incapacitation

A variant version of isolation is incapacitation, sometimes known as 'selective incapacitation'. The theory here aims to separate criminals from society to reduce their chances of committing further crimes while they are serving their sentences in correctional institutions. Incapacitation is a utilitarian form of punishment which involves a variety of actions designed to reduce the physical capacity of the offender to commit a crime or other deviant behaviour as much as possible. The principle of incapacitation focuses on the 'elimination' of individuals' opportunities to commit crimes and violations through various kinds of physical restrictions on their actions.[24]

Most studies on incapacitation refer to research from Marvin Wolfgang and colleagues from the University of Pennsylvania. Their research, called the Philadelphia Birth Cohort Studies, identified a group of high-risk and high-level offenders, who were later dubbed 'career criminals'. The model of selective incapacitation was developed to answer the problems posed by this particular group.[25]

[23] Mays, Winfree, and Ruddel, *Contemporary Corrections* (2005) 5–6.
[24] Miethe and Lu, *Punishment* (2004) 17–18.
[25] Mays, Winfree, and Ruddel. *Contemporary Corrections* (2005) 6.

At the heart of selective incapacitation is the assumption that career criminals can be identified early on, perhaps from a young age as a child or teenager. Once these career criminals are identified, law enforcement officers in the criminal justice system will be able to continue to follow and monitor their activities. This philosophy reflects the desire of policy makers to ensure that career criminals are caught, tried, proven guilty, and sentenced to sufficiently long terms in prison. The expected result of this approach is a significant reduction in the total crime rate. This is because most recidivists will have spent time behind bars, thus rendered incapable of committing crimes in the community during that time.[26]

d. Reintegration

Beginning in the late 1970s and early 1980s, professionals in the corrections field began to emphasise the value of reintegration as a philosophy of punishment. Reintegration relates to the fact that the vast majority of prison inmates will eventually complete their sentence and be released from prison. Once they leave, many former inmates often experience difficulties in their relationships and social interactions. They must readjust to their families and attempt to return to work. Since most are already considered to be 'ex-convicts', they will not get a warm welcome from the community. Therefore, something must be done to help them in their transition from life in prison to becoming free members of society.[27]

Reintegration is very important for several reasons. First, most recidivists resume committing crimes within just months of being released from prison. Second, the longer offenders are locked up in prison, the more difficult the transition back into society will be. Therefore, the correctional system must help them during this transition. If not, there is a high risk of recidivism and reimprisonment.[28]

In 2003, Harkristuti Harkrisnowo stated that in the context of the legal system in Indonesia, although the philosophy of punishment was not formulated, the country's criminal and punishment system was not always without a philosophy of punishment. Various ancient law books as well as customary law practices from various regions have implied the purpose of a tailor-made response in the event of violations of common rules.[29] More recently, Law No 12 of 1995 concerning Corrections encourages the concept of 're-integration to the community', which is very much in line with principles of reintegration outlined above. The definition of 'corrections' in this law is 'activities to provide guidance to Correctional Inmates based on the system, institution and method of development which are the final

[26] Ibid 6.

[27] Ibid 6–7.

[28] Mays, Winfree, and Ruddel. *Contemporary Corrections* (2005) 7.

[29] Harkristuti Harkrisnowo, 'Rekonstruksi Konsep Pemidanaan Suatu Gugatan Terhadap Proses Legislasi dan Pemidanaan di Indonesia', speech at the Inauguration of Tenured Professor in Criminal Law, University of Indonesia, 8 March 2003, 13.

part of the criminal justice system in the criminal justice system'.[30] The direction of the correctional system is also clear from Article 1:

> The Correctional System is an arrangement regarding the direction and boundaries as well as the method of rehabilitating Correctional Inmates based on Pancasila which is carried out in an integrated manner between the coaches, those who are rehabilitated, and the community to improve the quality of Correctional Inmates so that they are aware of their mistakes, improve themselves, and do not repeat criminal acts *so that they can be returned and accepted by the community*, can play an active role in development, and can live normally as good and responsible citizens.[31] [emphasis added]

The goals of the correctional system in Indonesia are thus clear. They aim to have offenders returned to and accepted by their communities. This is further confirmed in Article 2:

> The correctional system is held in order to shape Correctional Inmates so that they become fully human, realize mistakes, improve themselves, and do not repeat criminal acts so that they *can be accepted back by the social environment*, can play an active role in the development, and can live normally as good and responsible citizens.[32] [emphasis added]

C. Combination

In addition to the two major groups of theories discussed above (absolute and relative), there is also a third philosophy referred to as 'combination theories'. Combination theories state that punishment is imposed on the basis of retribution while at the same time maintaining social order. Combination theories come in an array of different forms, combining elements of theories of retribution with elements of relative punishment. According to Utrecht, combination theories can be divided into three groups:[33]

(1) combination theories that focus on retribution, while noting that retribution should not exceed what is necessary and sufficient to maintain social order;
(2) combination theories that emphasise the defence of public order, but emphasising the punishment may not be more severe than the act committed by the convict;
(3) combination theories of the two above elements (retribution and defence of public order) but with the same level of emphasis on each.

According to Andi Hamzah, one of the experts who adheres to combination theories is WPJ Pompe, who states that people should not turn a blind eye to

[30] Article 1 number 1 of Law No 12 of 1995.
[31] Article 1 number 2 of Law No 12 of 1995.
[32] Article 2 of Law No 12 of 1995.
[33] See further in Utrecht, *Rangkaian Sari Kuliah Hukum Pidana II* (1994) 186.

retribution. Criminal sanctions can be distinguished from other sanctions. It cannot be understated that punishment is a sanction and is thus bound with the objectives of the sanction. Therefore, it will only be applied if it benefits the fulfilment of the rules and is useful for the public interest. Hamzah also refers to Hugo Grotius, who emphasises absolute justice, which is manifested in retribution but is also useful for society. The basis of each crime is suffering, the severity of which is in accordance with the severity of the actions committed by the convict. However, the extent to which the severity of the crime and the severity of the actions committed by the convict can be measured is determined by what is useful to society.[34]

Other experts also adhere to the combination theories, such as Jacob Maarten van Bemmelen, who states that the purpose of punishment is to avenge mistakes and protect society. All actions intend to secure and maintain the goal, so the crime and the punishment both aim to prepare the convict to return to public life.

III. Types of Punishment

A. Basic Punishment

In Indonesia, punishments are regulated in Chapter II Book 1 of the Criminal Code, titled 'Punishment'. Article 10 lists the types of punishment:

a. basic punishments:
   1. death penalty
   2. imprisonment
   3. light [short-term] imprisonment[35]
   4. fine
   5. jail (*tutupan*).

b. additional punishments:
   1. revocation of certain rights
   2. confiscation of certain goods
   3. announcement of the judge's decision.

In imposing a punishment, the judge is bound to only impose basic or additional punishments as stipulated in Article 10 of the Criminal Code.[36] In Supreme Court

[34] Hamzah, *Asas-Asas Hukum Pidana* (2005) 36.

[35] Imprisonment: 1 day up to 15 years / 20 years/for life. Normally imposed for felony. May be located in or outside the city where the crime is committed.

Light imprisonment / short-term imprisonment: 1 day up to 1 year. Normally imposed for violation. Located in the city where the crime is committed.

[36] PAF Lamintang, *Hukum Penitensier Indonesia* (Bandung, CV Armico, 1984) 59.

Decision No 59 K./Kr./1969, the Supreme Court affirmed that adding to the types of punishment specified in Article 10 is prohibited.[37] Furthermore, in Supreme Court Dccision No 61 K./Kr./1973, the Supreme Court revoked an additional punishment that had been imposed by a district court, because in its decision, the district court had also sentenced the defendant to pay a certain amount of money for the losses suffered by the state.[38] This form of punishment is not listed in Article 10 and therefore cannot be imposed.

Can we surmise that the Supreme Court decision above is relevant only to certain cases, handled by the Supreme Court itself at the cassation level? What if a new type of punishment differs from Article 10 of the Criminal Code but is contained in another law? In fact, there have been several additions regarding different types of crimes in Indonesian legislation.

One development that should be mentioned is Law No 11 of 2006 concerning the Government of Aceh.[39] This law states that criminal acts are divided into two: (1) *jinayah* (regulated in the Qanun [Islamic criminal canon], with cases falling under the jurisdiction of the Aceh Shariah Court) and (2) criminal acts regulated in the Indonesian Criminal Code or criminal provisions outside the Criminal Code (which are handled by the District Court).[40] Article 241 paragraph (4) of Law No 11 of 2006 states that 'the qanun regarding *jinayah* (criminal law) is excluded from the criminal sanctions regulated in the previous paragraphs'. One otherwise excluded form is regulated in the Qanun: 'whipping punishment', which is in Article 4 of the Qanun of the Province of Nanggroe Aceh Darussalam No 6 of 2014 concerning *Jinayat* Law.[41]

There are also other provisions regulated by Indonesian law, such as Law No 11 of 2012 concerning the Criminal Justice System.[42] Article 71 (1) states that the main punishments for juvenile offenders consist of: (1) a warning; (2) punishment with the following conditions: coaching outside the institution, community service, or supervision; (3) work training; (4) coaching within the institution; and (5) imprisonment. Article 71 paragraph (2) also states that additional punishments consist of: (1) confiscation of profits derived from criminal acts; or (2) fulfilment of customary obligations. From this provision, we see a number of types of punishment that are not contained in Article 10 of the Criminal Code: warnings, supervision, community service, and fulfilment of customary obligations.

[37] Decision of the Supreme Court of the Republic of Indonesia No 59 K./Kr./1969 dated 11 March 1970. This is contained in Lamintang, *Hukum Penitensier Indonesia* (1984) 59.

[38] Decision of the Supreme Court of the Republic of Indonesia No 61 K./Kr./1973 dated 13 August 1974. This is contained in Lamintang, *Hukum Penitensier Indonesia* (1984) 59.

[39] State Gazette of the Republic of Indonesia Year 2006 Number 62.

[40] See Article 128 and Article 129 of Law No 11 of 2006.

[41] Aceh Gazette of 2014 Number 7. This Qanun No 6 of 2014 revokes previous qanuns which also contained caning, namely the Qanun of the Province of Nanggroe Aceh Darussalam Number 12 of 2003 concerning alcoholic beverages, Qanun of the Province of Nanggroe Aceh Darussalam Number 13 of 2003 concerning *maisir* (gambling), and the Qanun of the Province of Nanggroe Aceh Darussalam Number 14 of 2003 concerning *khalwat* (close proximity).

[42] State Gazette of the Republic of Indonesia Year 2012 Number 153.

i. Death Penalty

In Article 10, letter a, of the Criminal Code, the death penalty sits at the top of the list of basic punishments. As mentioned in previous chapter, the Criminal Code used in Indonesia originated from the Dutch *Wetboek van Strafrecht* of the colonial era (WvS 1881), which was adopted in the Dutch East Indies as *Wetboek van Strafrecht voor Nederlands-Indie* in 1915, coming into force on 1 January 1918.[43] Interestingly, at the point, the Netherlands itself was no longer implementing the death penalty: it had been abolished in 1870 through a law introduced in September 1870 (Staatsblad 1870 Number 182). The main reason was that, in practice, the death penalty was rarely carried out, because death row inmates almost always received a pardon or clemency from the King of the Netherlands. It was only in the Military Criminal Code that the death penalty was maintained at that time.[44]

In contrast, the death penalty was still implemented in the Dutch East Indies during the colonial period. It remains in use today. So why, under the WvS applicable in the Dutch East Indies, was the death penalty maintained? Kartanagara puts forward several reasons: (1) The Dutch East Indies consisted of a wide variety of ethnic groups, leading to inter-ethnic conflict, so to avoid this conflict and all its consequences, the death penalty was still needed; (2) the Dutch East Indies consisted of many islands with few government tools and imperfect means of communication; and (3) for a colony, absolute power is needed to maintain public order.[45] According to JE Jonkers,[46] these conditions were different from conditions in the Netherlands, thus it was not appropriate to abolish the death penalty altogether. This death penalty also applies to both Europeans and the natives. The Dutch Minister of Justice at the time, Anthony Modderman, in his explanation to the Dutch Parliament regarding the Criminal Code that would apply in the Dutch East Indies, stated that the state has the right to carry out all of these penalties, without which the state cannot fulfil its obligations, especially to ensure law and order.[47]

In the context of how to carry out the death penalty in Indonesia, Article 11 of the Criminal Code explains that the method was to be by hanging. It reads:

[43] Read more about the history of the enactment of this Criminal Code in Topo Santoso, *Hukum Pidana, Suatu Pengantar* (Jakarta, Rajawali Press, 2020).

[44] Lamintang, *Hukum Penitensier Indonesia* (1984) 62. Kartanagara mentions several other reasons besides those mentioned by Lamintang, such as that the sentence cannot be corrected; it is against humanity; it is against decency, with the imposition of the death penalty; efforts to reform the convict are not possible; and it does not achieve the goal and instead, leads to pity from the community. For these various reasons, in practice, the concept of the death penalty has no value anymore so it has been abolished. Kartanegara, *Hukum Pidana* (nd) 269–71.

[45] Kartanegara, *Hukum Pidana* (nd) 271–72.

[46] JE Jonkers was a judge in Sulawesi during the Dutch East Indies period and later became a professor in the Netherlands.

[47] JE Jonkers, *Buku Pedoman Hukum Pidana Hindia Belanda [Handboek Van Het Nederlandsch-Indische Strafrecht]*, translated by Tim Penerjemah Bina Aksara (Jakarta, PT Bina Aksara, 1987) 293.

'The death penalty is carried out by the executioner by hanging, by using a noose around the neck of the convicted person and tightening the noose to the hanger and dropping the board on which the man was standing.' This is a rather primitive form of execution.[48]

In 1964, the method of execution for the death penalty was changed from hanging to firing squad.[49] This was because of the issuance of Law No 2/Pnps/1964, namely Presidential Decree No 2 of 1964 (State Gazette 1964 Number 38), which was enacted through Law No 5 of 1969.

In Indonesia, the death penalty is not to be carried out in public and is to be done in the simplest way possible, except if otherwise determined by the president.[50] The law requires regional police chiefs to form firing squads from the police mobile brigade (*brimob*), consisting of a non-commissioned officer and 12 enlisted men, under the leadership of an officer. Specifically to carry out this task, the members of the firing squad do not use their own weapons. This firing squad is under the orders of the high prosecutor, who is responsible for the implementation of the death penalty until the execution is complete.[51]

There are several criminal acts in the Criminal Code that are punishable by death. These include Article 104 on 'treason with the intent to kill, or to seize independence, or to negate the ability of the President or Vice President to govern', Article 110 (1) on 'evil conspiracy to committing crimes according to articles 104, 106, 107, and 108 are threatened with criminal sanctions in those articles', Article 124 (1) on 'in times of war, intentionally providing assistance to the enemy or harming the state for the benefit of the enemy', and Article 340 on 'Whoever by intention and with premeditation taking the lives of others, is punishable due to premeditated murder', among others.

Chapter I of Book 2 of the Criminal Code on Crimes against State Security contains the majority of death penalty provisions. The death penalty is always sanctioned as an alternative form of punishment: 'sanctioned with the death penalty or life imprisonment or a temporary imprisonment of twenty years'.

Several other laws outside the Criminal Code also regulate the death penalty. They include:

(1) Military Criminal Code. Article 6 states that the basic punishments are death penalty, imprisonment, light imprisonment, and jail. There are several

[48] Kartanegara, *Hukum Pidana* (nd) 273.

[49] The definition of death adopted by Indonesia is the one declared by the Indonesian Doctors Association, which is also in accordance with that adopted by the other world, with only slight differences. There are two definitions of death: first, classic, namely the cessation of spontaneous function of breathing and circulation which is definite or in other words irreversible – the classical definition is the same throughout the world. Second, if a person experiences brain stem death, that person is declared dead even it his heart still beats, and his kidneys, liver, and lungs are still throbbing. Regarding this second issue, in other countries there are those who adhere to brain death, meaning that they wait for all the brain to die before the person is declared dead. See Constitutional Court Decision Number 21/PUU-VI/2008, p. 14.

[50] Article 9 of Law No. 2/Pnps/1964.

[51] Article 10 of Law No. 2/Pnps/1964.

mentions of the death penalty in the Military Criminal Code. The death penalty is sanctioned, among others, in Article 64 concerning military personnel who in time of war intentionally provide assistance to the enemy or harm the state on behalf of the enemy, and military personnel who in time of war hold an evil conspiracy to commit military betrayal.

(2) Emergency Law No 7 of 1955 concerning Economic Crimes in conjunction with Government Regulation in Lieu of Law No 21 of 1959.[52] Article I paragraph (2) states that if the criminal act committed can cause economic chaos in the community, the offender is sentenced to death, life imprisonment, or a temporary imprisonment sentence of up to 20 years.

(3) Law No 15 of 2003 in conjunction with Law No 5 of 2018 on the Eradication of Criminal Acts of Terrorism. Several articles regulate the use of the death penalty, including Article 6 on intentionally using violence or threats of violence to create an atmosphere of terror or fear in people widely, causing mass casualties by depriving people of their independence or causing people to lose their lives and property, or causing damage or destruction to strategic vital objects, the environment or public facilities or international facilities.

As with the provisions in the Criminal Code, in all articles in the Law outside the Criminal Code, the death penalty is always sanctioned as an alternative through the phrasing 'the death penalty or life imprisonment or a maximum temporary imprisonment sentence of 20 years'. The exception is Law No 31 of 1964, which offers the death penalty, life imprisonment, or maximum imprisonment of 15 years.

The Constitutional Court of the Republic of Indonesia is of the opinion that the death penalty is not contrary to the 1945 Constitution. This can be seen from Constitutional Court Decisions Number 2/PUU-V/2007, Number 3/PUU-V/2007, and Number 15/PUU-X/2012. In these three decisions, the petitioners put forward the same proposal: the death penalty is against the right to life guaranteed by the Constitution. If the death penalty is related to the right to life, which cannot be reduced under any circumstances (a non-derogable right), and which is guaranteed in Article 28 I paragraph (1) of the 1945 Constitution, the Constitutional Court concludes:

> that viewed from the perspective of the original intent of the formation of the 1945 Constitution, all human rights listed in Chapter XA of the 1945 Constitution can be limited in their validity. The original intent of the formation of the 1945 Constitution which stated that human rights could be limited was also strengthened by the placement of Article 28J as the closing article of all the provisions governing human rights in Chapter XA of the 1945 Constitution … the provisions of human rights in the 1945 Constitution is systematically in accordance with the provisions in the Universal Declaration of Human Rights which also places an article on the limitation of human rights as a closing article, namely Article 29 paragraph (2) which reads, 'In the exercise

[52] State Gazette of the Republic of Indonesia 1959 Number 130.

> of his rights and freedoms, everyone shall be subject only to such limitations as are determined by law solely for the purpose of securing due recognition and respect for the rights and freedoms of others and of meeting the just requirements of morality, public order and the general welfare in a democratic society'.[53]

Thus, according to the Constitutional Court, the death penalty as a form of limitation of human rights is justified constitutionally, because it does not conflict with the right to life as guaranteed in Article 28 paragraph (1) of the 1945 Constitution, and is in accordance with the Universal Declaration of Human Rights.

The Constitutional Court has also decided on the constitutionality of the implementation of the death penalty. As discussed above, the method of implementing the death penalty in Indonesia is by firing squad, in accordance with Law No 2/Pnps/1964. In its decision, the Constitutional Court stated that 'the method of implementing the death penalty must take into account the dignity of the death row convict. The death penalty which is carried out with the right shot can cause a quick death while maintaining the dignity of the death row convict.'[54]

ii. Imprisonment

Imprisonment is a form of punishment that restricts the movement of a convicted criminal offender. It is carried out by locking up the individual in a correctional institution, and requiring that person to obey all the rules and regulations that apply in the correctional institution, which is associated with disciplinary action for those who have violated these regulations.[55] In English, the word 'imprisonment' comes from the French '*emprisonne*' ('imprisonment', 'jail', 'incarceration'), which itself comes from the Latin '*prensio*' ('seize', 'take hold of'). Imprisonment is an action based on a court decision that imposes a punishment by separating a convict from the outside community and locking them up in a correctional institution (also referred to as prison or jail). Correctional institutions are designed as facilities for those who violated the law and were sentenced to prison, where they are kept away from society. Inmates serve their sentence for a certain period of time and have little freedom during their time in prison.

a. Imprisonment in the Criminal Code and Correctional Law

Imprisonment is listed second in Article 10, letter a, of the Criminal Code, under the death penalty. This shows that the severity of a prison sentence is considered less severe than the death penalty. In Chapter II of the Criminal Code, there are many articles that regulate imprisonment, in contrast to the death penalty, which is only regulated in one article (Article 11). Specifically, imprisonment is regulated

[53] See the decision of the Constitutional Court Number 15/PUU-X/2012, p 20.
[54] Constitutional Court Decision Number 21/PUU-VI/2008, p 73–74.
[55] Lamintang, *Hukum Penitensier Indonesia* (1984) 69.

in Articles 12 to 17, with Article 12 stipulating that imprisonment (*gevangenisstraf*) can be of two kinds: (1) life imprisonment (*levenslang*) and (2) temporary imprisonment (*tijdelijk*).

Temporary imprisonment is for a minimum of one day and a maximum of 15 years. However, imprisonment can be up to a maximum of 20 years in the following circumstances: (1) there is an alternative punishment for a criminal offence that is punishable by death or life imprisonment or 20 years; (2) the addition of criminal sanctions due to concurrent criminal offences; (3) due to aggravating reasons in the form of recidivism of the crime; and (4) due to the provisions for aggravating reasons in Article 52 of the Criminal Code.[56] According to Article 27, the length of imprisonment for a certain time and light imprisonment in the judge's decision is stated in days, weeks, months, and years, not in fractions.

Outside the Criminal Code, other laws tend to set specific minimum criminal sanctions as well as the more commonly-used special maximums. This is because the Criminal Code otherwise allows a minimum imprisonment of just one day. For example, in Law No 44 of 2008[57] concerning Pornography, there are several specific minimum sanctions, such as imprisonment for a minimum of six months and/or a fine of at least IDR250 million (in Article 29), imprisonment for a minimum of four years (Article 31), and imprisonment for a minimum of one year (Article 35). On the other hand, there are also laws that only contain a special maximum penalty and no special minimum penalty, such as Law No 8 of 2010 concerning the Prevention and Eradication of the Crime of Money Laundering.[58] Articles 3, 4, 5, and 7 only mention maximum criminal sanctions. Nevertheless, it can be said that, in recent years, the pattern of a special maximum penalty and a special minimum penalty has been widely used in new Indonesian criminal laws.

b. Conditional Imprisonment (Probation)

Article 14a paragraph (1) of the Criminal Code states that if the judge imposes a maximum sentence of one year or light imprisonment, not including substitute imprisonment, in the decision the judge may also order that the sentence should not be served, unless later there is a judge's decision that determines otherwise. This can occur when the individual commits a crime before the probationary period specified in the abovementioned order expires, or because during the probation period the individual does not meet the special conditions that may be specified otherwise in the order.

[56] The term of imprisonment may not exceed 20 years. See Article 12 paragraph (4) of the Criminal Code.

[57] State Gazette of the Republic of Indonesia of 2008 No 181.

[58] State Gazette of the Republic of Indonesia of 2010 No 122.

c. Prisoners' Rights

As in other countries, Indonesian law also guarantees the rights of prisoners. The Correctional Law regulates guarantees for the rights of prisoners, including the rights to: (1) perform worship according to their religion or belief; (2) receive treatment, both spiritual and physical care; (3) obtain education and teaching; (4) obtain health services and proper food; (5) submit a complaint; (6) obtain reading materials and participate in other mass media broadcasts that are not prohibited; (7) obtain wages or premiums for their work done; (8) receive visits from family, legal counsel, or certain other persons; (9) obtain a reduction in the sentence period (remission); (10) obtain opportunities to assimilate including time off to visit family; (11) obtain parole; (12) obtain leave of absence before being released; and (13) obtain other rights in accordance with the applicable laws and regulations.[59]

All adult and juvenile inmates, except for civilian children, are entitled to parole once they have served at least two-thirds of their sentence period, with the provision that the two-thirds of the sentence period must be at least nine months. In addition, they must behave well during at least the nine months prior to the date when they have served two-thirds of their sentence period. Conditional release for a child under state custody is given after undergoing training for at least one year.[60]

Every inmate and child under state custody may also be given leave before being released if he has fulfilled the requirements and has served at least two-thirds of the sentence period, provided that two-thirds of the sentence period is not less than nine months, he has behaved well while serving a sentence period of at least the last nine months.[61]

iii. Light Imprisonment

Light imprisonment (or 'short-term imprisonment') is sanctioned for several crimes in Book 2 of the Criminal Code and for almost all crimes in Book 3. For crimes regulated in provincial and district/city regional regulations, only light imprisonment and fines are permitted. There is no imprisonment sanction in provincial and district/city regulations. This is in accordance with the provisions of Law No 12 of 2011 concerning the Establishment of Legislation[62] as amended by Law No 15 of 2019[63] and Law No 23 of 2014 concerning Regional Government.[64]

[59] Article 14 of Law No 12 of 1995.

[60] Article 43, Article 44, Article 45, Article 46, and Article 47 of PP No 32/1999 as last amended by Government Regulation No 99 of 2012.

[61] Article 42A paragraphs (1) and (2) Government Regulation No 32 of 1999 as last amended by Government Regulation No 99 of 2012.

[62] State Gazette of the Republic of Indonesia of 2011 Number 82.

[63] State Gazette of the Republic of Indonesia of 2019 Number 183.

[64] State Gazette of the Republic of Indonesia of 2014 Number 244.

According to Article 15 paragraphs (1) and (2) of Law No 12 of 2011, criminal provisions contained in provincial and district/city regulations are in the form of a maximum imprisonment of six months or a maximum fine of IDR50,000,000. Article 15 paragraph (3) adds that provincial and district/city regulations may contain sanctions of light imprisonment or fines other than those referred to in paragraph (2) in accordance with what is stipulated in other laws and regulations.

Similar provisions are contained in Article 238 paragraph (2) of Law No 23 of 2014, which states that a regional regulation can implement maximum light imprisonment of six months or a maximum fine of IDR50,000,000. Paragraph (3) also permits light imprisonment or a fine other than as referred to in paragraph (2) in accordance with the provisions of the legislation.

Light imprisonment is a minimum of one day and a maximum of one year.[65] If there is a crime caused by concurrent crimes or recidivism, or because of the provisions of article 52, light imprisonment can be increased to one year and four months, which is the absolute maximum.[66] A person sentenced to light imprisonment is obliged to carry out the work assigned to him, in accordance with the implementing rules of Article 29.[67] He will be assigned a lighter job than a person sentenced to imprisonment.[68]

A judge who imposes an imprisonment sentence or a maximum light imprisonment of one month may determine that the prosecutor may allow the inmate to move freely outside the prison after working time.[69] If the inmate who is granted freedom does not arrive at the time and place determined in order to carry out the work assigned to him, then he must undergo his sentence as usual, unless his absence is not of his own free will.[70]

In contrast to imprisonment, a light imprisonment sentence must be served in an area where the inmate resides at the time the judge's decision is executed, or if he does not have a place of residence, in the area where he is located, unless the Minister of Justice (at the request of the inmate) allows him to serve his sentence in another area.[71]

In contrast to imprisonment, people who are sentenced to light imprisonment at their own expense, may only lighten their fate according to the rules that will be stipulated by law.[72] This is called the *pistole* right. This means they have the right to take care of their own food and bedding, but at their own expense.[73]

[65] Article 18 paragraph (1) of the Criminal Code.
[66] Article 18 paragraph (2) and (3) of the Criminal Code.
[67] Article 19 paragraph (1) of the Criminal Code.
[68] Article 19 paragraph (2) of the Criminal Code.
[69] Article 20 paragraph (1) of the Criminal Code. The provision in paragraph (1) is not applied to the convict if at the time of committing a crime there have not been two years since the convict has finished serving a prison sentence or confinement (Article 20 paragraph 3 of the Criminal Code).
[70] Article 20 paragraph (2) of the Criminal Code.
[71] Article 21 of the Criminal Code.
[72] Article 23 of the Criminal Code.
[73] EY Kanter and SR Sianturi, *Asas-Asas Hukum Pidana di Indonesia dan Penerapannya* (Jakarta, Storia Grafika, 2018) 471.

Persons sentenced to imprisonment or light imprisonment may be required to work inside or outside the walls of the correctional facility.[74] However, some people cannot be assigned work outside: people who are sentenced to life imprisonment, women, and people who, according to a doctor's examination, are not allowed to carry out such work.[75] If considering the condition of the inmate himself or the community, the judge considers there is a reasonable excuse, then in the decision it may be determined that the inmate may not be obliged to work outside the walls of the correctional facility.[76]

iv. Fines

Fines are a form of punishment that are widely used in addition to imprisonment. In the Netherlands and other developed countries, the short sentence of deprivation of liberty has been eliminated and replaced with fines. This is also being proposed in Indonesia, with the draft Criminal Code Bill abolishing light imprisonment sentences. The Bill also offers alternatives to imprisonment, such as supervision, community service, or punishment with a probationary period.

Although they are a less severe punishment than imprisonment or light imprisonment, fines are not without preventive and deterrent power. Remmelink refers specifically to fines as a form of general prevention.[77] It is understandable, as if the public knows that committing a certain crime carries a penalty of IDR one billion, which for the members of that community is a very large sum, it may be hoped that no one will try to commit the crime.

In my opinion, fines also have a special prevention purpose. Imagine if someone's monthly income is IDR five million, and that person is sentenced to pay a fine of IDR five million. This is then equal to his monthly income. This is a form of special deterrence, where the fine is imposed in the hope that the individual will not repeat his actions.

Another advantage of a fine, compared to imprisonment or light imprisonment, is from the state's perspective. With a fine, the state does not incur the costs associated with individuals serving prison sentences.[78]

However, there are also objections to fines, namely that rich people benefit because they can easily pay fines while poor people will struggle. Therefore, the severity of a fine penalty must take into account a person's financial capacity.[79] This is a concern in the Criminal Code Bill, specifically in Article 80 of the Criminal Code Bill, which will be discussed below.

[74] Article 24 of the Criminal Code.
[75] Article 25 of the Criminal Code.
[76] Article 26 of the Criminal Code.
[77] Jan Remmelink, *Hukum Pidana, Komentar atas Pasal-Pasal Terpenting dari Kitab Undang-Undang hukum Pidana Belanda dan Padanannya dalam Kitab Undang-Undang Hukum Pidana Indonesia* (Jakarta, Gramedia Pustaka Utama, 2003) 485.
[78] Ibid 485.
[79] Ibid.

In 1960, Government Regulation in Lieu of Law No 18 of 1960[80] amended the amount to be paid as fines in the current Criminal Code, multiplying the original amounts by 15. Likewise, there was a change in the value for violation (petty theft, light embezzlement, and minor fraud as regulated in Articles 364, 373, 379, 384, and 407 paragraph 1): the fine increased from IDR25 to IDR250.[81]

However, since 1960, the financial penalties stated in the Criminal Code have not been readjusted.[82] This is despite the fact that since 1960, the value of the rupiah has decreased significantly (by about 10,000 times compared to the price of gold at that time).[83] Therefore, it is necessary to make changes to values and violation in the Criminal Code.[84] This change should be a matter of legal substance, but of course changes to the law generally take quite a long time, even while relevant cases continue to go to court. Therefore, the Supreme Court took the initiative to issue Supreme Court Regulation No 02 of 2012 to adjust the value of the rupiah in the current Criminal Code. This Supreme Court Regulation is not an amendment to the Criminal Code; it only adjusts the value of money in the Code, which was not in accordance with current conditions.[85]

In Article 1, Supreme Court Regulation No 02 of 2012 states that: 'The words "two hundred and fifty rupiahs" in Articles 364, 373, 379, 384, 407 and Article 482 of the Criminal Code are read as Rp. 2,500,000.00 (two million five hundred thousand rupiah).' With regard to fines, Article 3 also states that 'Every maximum amount for fines sanctioned in the Criminal Code, except Article 303 paragraph 1 and paragraph 2, 303 bis paragraph 1 and paragraph 2, is multiplied by 1,000 (one thousand) times.'

The original Article 30 paragraph (1) of the Criminal Code states that the maximum fine is three rupiah and seventy-five cents.[86] Paragraph (2) then states that if the fine is not paid, it is replaced with light imprisonment of a minimum of one day and a maximum of six months.[87]

If there is an increase in the criminal fine due to concurrent crimes or recidivism, or because of the provisions of Article 52,[88] the substitute light imprisonment

[80] Government Regulation in Lieu of Law No. 18 of 1960 concerning Changes in the Amount of Fines in the Criminal Code and in other Criminal Provisions issued before 17 August 1945.

[81] State Gazette of the Republic of Indonesia of 1960 Number 50.

[82] This has implications for the use of the ordinary theft article as regulated in Article 362 of the Criminal Code for the crime of petty theft as regulated in Article 364 of the Criminal Code.

[83] See the General Elucidation on the Regulation of the Supreme Court of the Republic of Indonesia No 02 of 2012 concerning Adjustment of the Limits of Minor Crimes and the Amount of Fines in the Criminal Code.

[84] Except for Articles 303 and 303bis, because these two articles have been adapted to Law No 7/1974 on Gambling Control.

[85] Consideration on the Regulation of the Supreme Court of the Republic of Indonesia Number 02 of 2012 concerning Adjustment of the Limits of Minor Crimes and the Amount of Fines in the Criminal Code.

[86] Rp 3.75 x 1000 = Rp 3750.

[87] Article 30 paragraph (3) of the Criminal Code.

[88] Article 52 of the Criminal Code states that if an official when committing a criminal act violates a special obligation from his position, or when committing a criminal act uses the power, opportunity or means given to him because of his position, the punishment can be increased by one-third.

is a maximum of eight months.[89] Substitute light imprisonment may not exceed eight months.[90]

Article 31 paragraph (1) states that the convict can serve substitute light imprisonment without waiting for the deadline for paying the fine, with paragraph (2) noting that the individual is always authorised to free himself from substitute light imprisonment by paying the fine.

*v. Undisclosed Penitentiary (*Hukuman Tutupan*)*

'Undisclosed penitentiary' (*Hukuman Tutupan*) was not originally included as a form of punishment in Article 10 of the Criminal Code. It only became an option with the enactment of Law No 20 of 1946.[91] Outside the Criminal Code, we do not find crimes that are punishable by jail, for example in the phrase, 'Whoever commits a criminal offence … will be subject to jail punishment'. This is because a jail sentence is actually a substitute for imprisonment; what is stated in Indonesian law is, in fact, the term 'imprisonment'. If a crime meets the conditions as stipulated in Law No 20 of 1946, namely that 'the crime was committed with an intention that deserves to be punished', then the judge can impose a jail sentence for the convict, not imprisonment.[92]

Arrangements for jail is regulated by Government Regulation No 8 of 1948, so we can compare it with imprisonment. The provisions for jail include, among other things, that persons serving jail time may not be employed outside the walls of the jail facility;[93] the assignment of work to each person who is sentenced to jail must take into account the physical and spiritual condition of that person;[94] on Sundays and holidays, inmates may not be employed, but may work at their own discretion, and in cases that are absolutely necessary at the discretion of the Minister of Defence;[95] in the facility, a doctor should be employed;[96] in the facility it is permitted to provide appropriate modest entertainment;[97] and inmates are allowed to bring books, magazines or newspapers into the facility and buy/subscribe to books, newspapers, and magazines with their own money, with the amount to be determined by the head of the facility.[98]

Articles 1 and 2 of Law No 20 of 1946 state that, in addition to the basic punishment stated in Article 10 letter a of the current Criminal Code and Article 6 letter a of the Military Criminal Code, is the new basic punishment of *Hukuman*

[89] Article 30 paragraph (5) of the Criminal Code.
[90] Article 30 paragraph (6) of the Criminal Code.
[91] Official Gazette of the Republic of Indonesia of 1946 No II.
[92] Lamintang, *Hukum Penitensier Indonesia* (1984) 147.
[93] Article 14 paragraph (2) of the Government Regulation No 8 of 1948.
[94] Article 15 paragraph (2) of the Government Regulation No 8 of 1948.
[95] Article 18 paragraph (1) of the Government Regulation No 8 of 1948.
[96] Article 29 paragraph (1) of the Government Regulation No 8 of 1948.
[97] Article 44 paragraph (1) of the Government Regulation No 8 of 1948.
[98] Article 46 paragraph (1) of the Government Regulation No 8 of 1948.

Tutupan. The judge may impose a sentence of *Hukuman Tutupan*, replacing the sentence of imprisonment, where someone has committed a crime that is punishable by imprisonment which was motivated by an intention that deserves respect. The regulation does not apply if the act which constitutes a crime, or the method of committing the act, is the result of the aforementioned act, so that the judge is of the opinion that imprisonment is more appropriate. The phrase 'an intention that deserves respect' is not explained, however, so it is left to the judge to interpret this.[99]

B. Additional Punishment

The imposition of additional punishment is facultative in nature, in the sense that the judge does not always have to impose additional punishment at the time he imposes the basic sentence on a defendant. The judge has full authority to decide whether an additional punishment will be imposed. However, in imposing the basic or additional punishment, the judge is restrained to the types of punishment that have been determined in Article 10 of the Criminal Code.[100]

In Indonesia, there is the possibility of imposing additional criminal punishments without imposing the basic criminal offence, both in the Criminal Code and in other laws. In the Criminal Code, this is found in Article 39 paragraph (3) in conjunction with Articles 45 and 46.[101] Articles 45 and 46 relate to children under 16 years of age committing criminal offences. Based on these articles, if the defendant is found guilty, but because the defendant cannot be sentenced on the grounds of being a minor and is therefore handed over to the government, then any confiscated goods can be forfeited. However, these were declared no longer in effect by Law No 3 of 1997 concerning Juvenile Court, which was later replaced by Law No 11 of 2012 concerning the Juvenile Criminal Justice System.

Another Criminal Code provision is Article 40, which states that if a person under the age of 16 possesses, imports, or transports goods in violation of the rules regarding shipping control in certain parts of Indonesia, or the rules regarding the prohibition of entering, issuing, and continuing to transport the goods, the judge may confiscate the goods as punishment, even if the person found guilty is returned to his parents, guardian, or foster parent without any punishment.

Outside the Criminal Code, additional punishment can be found in Law No 31 of 1999 concerning the Eradication of Criminal Acts of Corruption as amended by Law No 20 of 2001. In Article 38 paragraph (5), it is stated that in the event that

[99] Lamintang, *Hukum Penitensier Indonesia* (1984) 147.

[100] Ibid 58–59. See also AZ=. Abidin and Andi Hamzah, *Pengantar Dalam Hukum Pidana Indonesia* (Jakarta, Yarsif Watampone, 2010) 247.

[101] The provisions of Articles 45 and 46 of the Criminal Code have been declared no longer in effect by Law No 3 of 1997 concerning Juvenile Court. Meanwhile, the Juvenile Court Law is no longer in effect with the issuance of Law No 11 of 2012 concerning the Juvenile Criminal Justice System.

the defendant passes away before sentencing and there is strong evidence that the defendant had committed a criminal act of corruption, the judge on the request of the public prosecutor can determine the seizure of the confiscated goods.

However, the cases above occur under atypical circumstances; under normal circumstances, additional punishment cannot be imposed without imposing the basic punishment.

Finally, there is Article 361 of the Criminal Code, which mentions additional punishment. Specifically, it mentions the deprivation of the right to carry out a livelihood and the announcement of the judge's decision. This is an example of an article that clearly states that some offenders may be subject to additional punishments, with the additional punishment also clearly stated. Many other articles do not clearly state what additional punishment can be imposed. However, the judge may impose additional punishment according to the case at hand. For example, recently there have been several decisions in corruption cases where judges imposed additional punishments in the form of the revocation of the right to be elected as a public official in general elections for several years. These decisions can be found in Supreme Court Decision Number 537K/Pid.Sus/2014 and Decision Number 1195K/Pid.Sus/2014.[102]

i. Revocation of Certain Rights

Article 35 paragraph (1) of the Criminal Code stipulates that certain rights of convicted individuals can be deprived by judges, but only in matters specified in the law. These rights include: (1) the right to hold office in general or a certain position; (2) the right to serve with the armed forces; (3) the right to vote and be elected in elections held based on general rules; (4) the right to become a legal adviser or administrator upon court order; the right to become a guardian, co-guardian, curator or co-curator over other children than his own; (5) the right to exercise paternal authority, guardianship, and curatorship over one's own children; and (6) the right to exercise certain professions. However, it must be noted that the judge is not authorised to discharge an official from his position if, in special rules, another authority has determined the dismissal.[103]

The right to hold an office in general, to hold a certain position, and to serve with the armed forces, except in the cases described in Book 2, can be removed in the case of punishment for a crime of office or a crime that violates the special obligations of a position, or for using the power, opportunity, or means given to the convict because of his position.[104]

[102] See the discussion of these two decisions in Warih Anjari, 'Pencabutan Hak Politik Terpidana Korupsi dalam Perspektif Hak Asasi Manusia' (2015) 8(1) *Jurnal Yudisial* 23–44.

[103] Article 35 paragraph (2) of the Criminal Code.

[104] Article 36 of the Criminal Code.

Paternal authority, guardianship, and curatorship over one's own children, both over one's own child or over another person, can be deprived in cases of: (1) parents or guardians who intentionally commit a crime together with a minor who is under their control; and (2) parents or guardians of minors who, under their control, commit crimes mentioned in chapters XIII, XIV, XV, XVIII, XIX, and XX of Book 2.[105] Such revocation may not be carried out by a criminal judge against persons for whom civil laws concerning the revocation of parental, guardian, and guardian authority have been applied.[106]

If a right is revoked, the judge determines the duration of the revocation as follows. First, in the case of a death penalty or life imprisonment, the duration of the revocation is life; second, in the case of imprisonment for a certain time or imprisonment, the duration of revocation is a minimum of two years and a maximum of five years longer than the basic punishment; and third, in the case of a fine, the duration of the revocation is a minimum of two years and a maximum of five years.[107] The revocation of rights takes effect on the day the judge's decision can be executed.[108]

ii. Revocation of Permits

Additional punishment in the form of revocation of permits is imposed on offenders and accessories to criminal offences who commit crimes related to those permits.[109] The revocation of permits is carried out by taking into account the circumstances accompanying the crime committed; the circumstances accompanying the offenders and accessory to the crime; and the correlation of permit ownership with the business or activity carried out.[110] In the case of being sentenced to imprisonment, *Hukuman Tutupan* (undisclosed penitentiary), or supervision for a certain time, the permit revocation is carried out for a minimum of two years and a maximum of five years longer than the basic sentence imposed.[111] In the event that a fine is imposed, the permit is revoked for a minimum of one year and a maximum of five years.[112] The revocation comes into force on the date when the court's decision obtains permanent legal force.[113] The last provision is slightly different from the provisions in the Criminal Code, which stipulates that the revocation of rights will take effect on the day the judge's decision can be executed.[114]

[105] Article 37 paragraph (1) of the Criminal Code.
[106] Article 37 paragraph (2) of the Criminal Code.
[107] Article 38 paragraph (1) of the Criminal Code.
[108] Article 38 paragraph (2) of the Criminal Code.
[109] Article 95 paragraph (1) of the New Criminal Code.
[110] Article 95 paragraph (2) of the New Criminal Code.
[111] Article 95 paragraph (3) of the New Criminal Code.
[112] Article 95 paragraph (4) of the New Criminal Code.
[113] Article 95 paragraph (5) of the New Criminal Code.
[114] Article 38 paragraph (2) of the Criminal Code.

iii. Forfeiture of Certain Goods

Properties obtained through crime or which are intentionally used to commit a crime can be forfeited.[115] In the case of a conviction for a crime that was not committed intentionally or because of a violation, a decision on forfeiture may also be imposed based on matters specified in the law.[116] Forfeiture can be carried out against a convict that is handed over to the government (such as a minor), but only on goods that have been confiscated.[117]

If a person under the age of 16 owns, enters, or transports goods in violation of the rules regarding shipping control in certain parts of Indonesia, or the rules regarding the prohibition on the entry, exit, and continued transportation of goods, then the judge can impose a criminal forfeiture of the goods, this also applies if the person found guilty is returned to his parents, guardian or foster carer, without punishment.[118]

iv. Announcement of Judge's Decision

Only Article 43 regulates the announcement of this judge's decision in the Criminal Code. This article states that: 'In cases where the judge by virtue of this code or another general regulation orders the publication of his verdict, he shall at the same time determine the manner in which the order shall be executed at the expenses of the sentenced person.' In the draft Criminal Code Bill, there is also only one article that regulates announcements (Article 93), which states that if court decision orders that the decision be announced, it must be determined that the method of carrying out the announcement is at the expense of the convict.[119] If the expense of announcement is not paid by the convict, a fine is applied as a substitute punishment provision.[120]

v. Additional Punishment Outside the Criminal Code

Outside the Criminal Code, we can find many provisions regarding additional punishment, such as Law No 31 of 1999 concerning the Eradication of Criminal Acts of Corruption[121] as amended by Law No 20 of 2001.[122] In Article 17, it is stated:

> In addition to being subject to a criminal sentence as referred to in Article 2, Article 3, Article 5 to Article 14, the defendant may be sentenced to additional punishment as referred to in Article 18.

[115] Article 39 paragraph (1) of the Criminal Code.
[116] Article 39 paragraph (2) of the Criminal Code.
[117] Article 39 paragraph (3) of the Criminal Code.
[118] Article 40 of the Criminal Code.
[119] Article 93 paragraph (1) of the Criminal Code Bill.
[120] Article 93 paragraph (2) of the Criminal Code Bill.
[121] State Gazette of the Republic of Indonesia of 1999 No 140.
[122] State Gazette of the Republic of Indonesia of 2001 No 134.

Article 18 paragraph (1) of the Law stipulates the following:

> (1) In addition to additional punishments as referred to in the Criminal Code, additional punishments are:
>
> 1. forfeiture of tangible or intangible movable goods or immovable goods used for or obtained from criminal acts of corruption, including companies belonging to the convict where the corruption is committed, as well as from the goods that replace the goods;
> 2. payment of substitute money in the maximum amount equal to the property obtained from the criminal act of corruption.
> 3. closure of all or part of the company for a maximum period of 1 (one) year;
> 4. revocation of all or part of certain rights or elimination of all or part of certain benefits, which have been or may be granted by the Government to the convict.

Another example can be seen in Law No 3 of 2011 concerning Fund Transfers.[123] Article 88 of this Law states:

> In addition to the basic punishment, the criminal acts as referred to in Article 80 paragraph (2), Article 81, Article 83 paragraph (2), or Article 85 may also be subject to the obligation to return the proceeds of a criminal act as well as services, interest, or compensation to the injured party.

C. Measures

i. Regulation of Measures within the Criminal Code

In the sections above, punishments in Indonesian criminal law have been discussed. Now let us turn to measures. Since the end of the nineteenth century, in addition to threatening criminal acts with consequences that cause suffering, lawmakers have introduced measures to respond to certain events that meet the requirements specified by law, especially for children and people with mental disabilities or disorders.[124]

Kartanagara states that according to the theory of retribution, punishment has the nature and essence of torture or suffering, which is imposed through criminal law on a person who violates a legal norm determined by the criminal law, and that torture or suffering is imposed upon the guilty defendant by the judge's decision. Torture and suffering are imposed because the actions taken by that person constituted a violation against legal interests protected by criminal law (human soul and body, honour, morality, personal liberty, property/wealth). However, a new school of criminal law has emerged which suggested that punishment should no longer be a form of suffering, but should instead be aimed at measures to protect or improve society itself. Therefore, in addition to punishment (*straf*), there must be

[123] State Gazette of the Republic of Indonesia of 2011 No 39.
[124] Van Bemmelen, *Hukum Pidana 1* (1987) 19.

what is called an appropriate measure (*maatregel*). The measure is taken to protect the community and improve the perpetrator himself.[125]

The purpose of measures is not to increase suffering, but rather to protect the community from the actions of the perpetrator, as well as to treat, repair, and educate people who violate the law. If the measures still cause suffering, it is not intended. With the expansion of these measures, according to van Bemmelen, criminal law is growing closer to other laws, because measures are also contained in state administrative law as well as civil law.[126]

Regulations regarding measures are found in several articles in Chapter III Book 1 of the Criminal Code. Chapter III regulates matters that negate, mitigate or aggravate punishment. Article 44 centres on people who are unable to take responsibility. Article 44 paragraph (1) states:

> Anyone who commits an act that cannot be accounted for by him because of his mental capacity (*zijner verstandelijke vermogens*) is disabled in growth or is disturbed due to illness, will not be punished.

Meanwhile paragraph (2) states:

> If it turns out that the act cannot be held responsible against the perpetrator because his mental growth is disabled or disturbed due to illness, then the judge may order that the person be admitted to a mental hospital for a maximum of one year as a probationary period.

Therefore, the measure is found in paragraph (2) of Article 44: 'the judge ordered that the person be admitted to a mental hospital'.

Measures for juvenile offenders are regulated in Articles 45, 46, and 47. As mentioned earlier, these provisions were later abolished in 1997 with a new law. Meanwhile, measures against people with mental disabilities or suffering from mental disorders are regulated in Article 44 of the Criminal Code. From the provisions of Article 45, we find measures in the phrases 'ordering that the guilty be returned to their parents, guardians, or foster parents' and 'taken into state custody'. These are the options from which the judge can choose, separate from or in addition to punishment. The judge can also determine that the defendant should be taken into state custody. This can happen, for example, in the event that it is impossible or inappropriate to return the child to their parents, guardians, or foster parents.

With regard to giving the state responsibility for individuals, this is regulated in Article 46 paragraph (1) of the Criminal Code, although this is no longer in effect according to Law No 3 of 1997 on Juvenile Court. The Criminal Code states that those who are guilty are to be educated in a state rehabilitation facility, or be handed over to a certain person who resides in Indonesia or to a legal entity,

[125] Kartanegara, *Hukum Pidana* (nd) 252.
[126] Van Bemmelen, *Hukum Pidana 1* (1987) 19–20.

foundation, or charitable institution in Indonesia to provide education, or at a later date, at the expense of the government, in other ways; in all cases, at most until the guilty person reaches the age of 18.

ii. Arrangements for Measures Outside the Criminal Code

Let us now discuss provisions regarding measures regulated outside the Criminal Code. Our discussion will focus on four laws: the Juvenile Criminal Justice System Law, the Narcotics Law, the Environmental Law, and the Government Regulation in Lieu of Law on Castration. In Law No 11 of 2012 concerning the Juvenile Criminal Justice System,[127] measures that may be imposed on a juvenile include: (1) return to parent/guardian; (2) surrender to someone; (3) treatment in a mental hospital; (d) care in a Social Welfare Institution; (e) the obligation to attend formal education and/or training held by the government or private agencies; (f) revocation of a driving licence; and/or (g) reparation for the impact of the crime.[128] The measure of surrendering the child to someone is carried out for the benefit of the child concerned, while[129] any treatment measures for the child are intended to assist the parent/guardian in educating and providing guidance to the child concerned.[130]

In Law No 35 of 2009 concerning Narcotics,[131] narcotics addicts and victims of narcotics abuse are required to undergo medical rehabilitation and social rehabilitation. Parents or guardians of narcotics addicts who are underage are required to report them to the public health centre, hospital, and/or medical and social rehabilitation institution appointed by the government to receive medication and/or treatment.[132] Narcotics addicts who are adults are required to report themselves, or be reported by their families, to a public health centre, hospital, and/or medical and social rehabilitation institution appointed by the government to receive medication and/or treatment.[133]

In Law No 32 of 2009 concerning the Protection and Management of the Environment,[134] Article 119 states that in addition to the punishments referred to in this law, business entities may be subject to additional punishments or disciplinary measures in the form of: (1) deprivation of profits derived from criminal acts; (2) closure of all or part of the place of business and/or activity; (3) repairs due to criminal acts; (4) the obligation to do what is neglected; and/or placing the company under supervision for a maximum of three years.

[127] State Gazette of the Republic of Indonesia of 2012 No 153
[128] Article 82 paragraph (1) Law No 11 of 2012.
[129] Article 83 paragraph (1) Law No 11 of 2012.
[130] Article 83 paragraph (2) Law No 11 of 2012.
[131] State Gazette of the Republic of Indonesia of 2009 No 143.
[132] Article 54 paragraph (1) Law No 35 of 2009.
[133] Article 54 paragraph (2) Law No 35 of 2009.
[134] State Gazette of the Republic of Indonesia of 2009 No 140.

In Law No 23 of 2002 concerning Child Protection, which was last amended by Government Regulation in Lieu of Law No 1 of 2016 then stipulated by Law No 17 of 2016 to become law,[135] Article 81 paragraph (6) states that perpetrators, as referred to in paragraphs (4) and (5),[136] may be subject to measures in the form of chemical castration and installation of electronic monitoring devices. The measure to be implemented is decided together with the basic punishment by specifying the period of execution of the measure.[137] Chemical castration and electronic monitoring device usage can be imposed for a maximum period of two years and are carried out after the convict has served the basic punishment.[138] Implementation of chemical castration is accompanied by rehabilitation,[139] with the procedure for implementing the measure and rehabilitation is regulated by a Government Regulation.[140] Additional punishments and measures are excluded for juvenile offenders.[141]

IV. Purpose and Types of Punishment in the New Criminal Code

A. Purpose of Punishment

In the New Criminal Code, the purpose of punishment is described in Article 51, which states that the purpose is to prevent criminal acts from being committed by enforcing legal norms for the protection and security of society; reintegrating ex-convicts by conducting coaching and guidance to help them become good and useful people; resolving conflicts caused by criminal acts, restoring balance, and bringing a sense of security and peace in society; and cultivating ex-convicts' senses of remorse and release their guilt.

[135] State Gazette of the Republic of Indonesia of 2016 No 99.
[136] Article 81 paragraph (3) of the Child Protection Law states that: 'In the event that the criminal acts as referred to in paragraph (1) are committed by parents, guardians, people who have family relationships, child caretakers, educators, education personnel, government officials, which handles child protection, or is carried out by more than one person together, the punishment is added by 1/3 (one-third) of the criminal sanction as referred to in paragraph (1).' Article 81 paragraph (4) of this Law states that in addition to the perpetrators as referred to in paragraph (3), the addition of 1/3 (one-third) of the criminal sanction is also imposed on perpetrators who have been convicted of committing a crime as referred to in Article 76D. Article 81 paragraph (5) states that in the event that the criminal act as referred to in Article 76D results in more than 1 (one) person being killed, causing serious injury, mental disorders, infectious diseases, disruption or loss of reproductive function, and/or the victim dies, the offender is sentenced to death, life imprisonment, or imprisonment for a minimum of 10 (ten) years and a maximum of 20 (twenty) years.
[137] Article 81 paragraph (8) Child Protection Law.
[138] Article 81A paragraph (1) Child Protection Law.
[139] Article 81A paragraph (3) Child Protection Law.
[140] Article 81A paragraph (4) Child Protection Law.
[141] Article 81 paragraph (9) Child Protection Law.

B. Types of Punishment

In the New Criminal Code, the basic punishments are outlined in Article 64 letter a, and consist of imprisonment; *tutupan* (undisclosed penitentiary); supervision; fines; and community service.[142]

There are also additional punishments (Article 64 letter b) and special punishments for certain crimes as stipulated in the Law (Article 64 letter c). Notably, the New Criminal Code no longer lists the death penalty first in the list of basic types of punishment. Substantive punishment is now to be contained in a new category, regulated in Article 64 letter c, with the death penalty regulated in Article 67 which states: 'Punishment of a special nature as referred to in Article 64 letter c is the death penalty which is always threatened alternatively.'

According to the Elucidation of Article 67, in this provision, criminal acts that can be threatened with special punishments are very serious or extraordinary crimes, including narcotics crimes, terrorism crimes, corruption crimes, and serious crimes against human rights. For this reason, the death penalty is included in a separate section to show that this type of punishment is truly special. When compared with other types of punishment, the death penalty is the most severe type of punishment. Therefore, it must always be threatened as an alternative to other types of punishments, namely life imprisonment or a maximum imprisonment of 20 years.

What differs between the existing Criminal Code and the New Code is the type of punishment permitted. In addition to rearranging the death penalty, there are two new types of punishment (supervision and community service) while light imprisonment has been removed. These changes will be discussed in further detail below.

i. Death Penalty in the New Criminal Code

As mentioned, Article 65 no long ranks the death penalty first among the main types of punishment. The death penalty is threatened only as an alternative and a last resort to prevent criminal acts and protect the community.[143] Importantly, the death penalty can only be carried out if the president rejects the convicted person's request for clemency.[144] If the request for clemency of the death row convict is rejected and the death penalty is not carried out for 10 years after that date, and not because the convict has fled, the death penalty can be changed to life imprisonment by presidential decree.[145]

[142] Criminal Code as a result of discussion in 24 November 2022.
[143] Article 98 of the New Criminal Code.
[144] Article 99 of the New Criminal Code.
[145] Article 100 of the New Criminal Code.

Regarding the implementation of the death penalty, the New Criminal Code stipulates that the death penalty is not carried out in public.[146] It is carried out by execution by firing squad or other methods specified in the law.[147] Shooting is the chosen method as it is considered to be the most humane. If in the future there are other, more humane methods available, the implementation of the death penalty is to be adjusted to these developments.[148]

The execution of the death penalty against pregnant women, women who are breastfeeding their babies, or people who are mentally ill, is to be postponed until the woman gives birth, the woman is no longer breastfeeding, or the mentally ill person recovers.[149] Pregnant women are not to be executed until after both giving birth and finishing breastfeeding, so that the implementation of the death penalty does not kill two people and guarantees the human rights of the baby.[150]

There is one new provision regarding the death penalty in the New Code, which is a probation period for death row convicts. The judge can impose the death penalty with a probationary period of 10 years if the defendant shows remorse and there is hope for improvement, if the role of the defendant in the crime is not crucial to the crime, or there are mitigating reasons.[151] The death penalty with probation must be included in the court's decision.[152] The 10-year probationary period begins one day after the court's decision has permanent legal force.[153] If during the probationary period, the convict shows commendable attitudes and actions, the death penalty can be changed to life imprisonment by a presidential decision after receiving consideration from the Supreme Court.[154] However, if the convict does not show commendable attitudes and actions and there is no hope for improvement, the death penalty can be carried out by order of the Attorney General.[155]

ii. Imprisonment

In the New Criminal Code, the provisions state that imprisonment is imposed for life or for a certain period of time.[156] Imprisonment for a certain period of time is imposed for a maximum of 15 consecutive years or a minimum of one day, unless

[146] Article 99 paragraph (2) of the New Criminal Code. This provision is the same as Article 9 of Law No 2/Pnps/1964.
[147] Article 99 paragraph (3) of the New Criminal Code.
[148] Elucidation of Article 99 paragraph (3) of the New Criminal Code.
[149] Article 99 paragraph (4) of the New Criminal Code.
[150] Elucidation of Article 99 paragraph (4) of the New Criminal Code.
[151] Article 100 paragraph (1) of the New Criminal Code.
[152] Article 100 paragraph (2) of the New Criminal Code.
[153] Article 100 paragraph (3) of the New Criminal Code.
[154] Article 100 paragraph (4) of the New Criminal Code.
[155] Article 100 paragraph (6) of the New Criminal Code.
[156] Article 68 paragraph (1) of the New Criminal Code.

a different minimum is specified for certain crimes.[157] Imprisonment for a certain period of time may not be imposed for more than 20 years.[158] This provision is almost the same as the provisions in the current Criminal Code, except for the phrase 'unless a special minimum is specified'.

If an inmate serving life imprisonment has served a minimum term of 15 years, the life imprisonment may be changed to 20 years in prison by Presidential Decree after obtaining consideration from the Supreme Court.[159]

The New Criminal Code stipulates that imprisonment as far as possible should not be imposed if the following conditions are found: the defendant is a minor; the defendant is over 75 years old; the defendant has committed a crime for the first time; the loss and suffering of the victim is not too great; the defendant has paid restitution to the victim; the defendant does not realise that the criminal act committed will cause a large loss; the crime occurred because of a very strong incitement from another person; the victim of a crime encourages or abets the occurrence of the crime; the crime is the result of a situation that cannot be repeated; the personality and behaviour of the defendant ensures that the defendant will not commit another crime; imprisonment will cause great suffering to the defendant or the defendant's family; guidance outside the correctional institution is expected to be successful for the defendant; the imposition of a lighter sentence will not reduce the serious nature of the crime committed by the defendant; the crime occurred in the family; and/or the criminal acts occurred due to negligence.[160]

These provisions do not apply to criminal acts that are punishable by imprisonment of five years or more, crimes that are punishable by a special minimum sentence, or certain crimes that are very dangerous or detrimental to the community or financially or detrimental to the country's economy.[161]

If a person commits a crime which is only punishable by a prison sentence of less than five years, but the judge is of the opinion that it is not necessary to impose a prison sentence after considering the purpose of punishment and the sentencing guidelines as referred to in Articles 52 and 54,[162] that person may be subject

[157] Article 68 paragraph (2) of the New Criminal Code.
[158] Article 68 paragraph (4) of the New Criminal Code.
[159] Article 69 paragraph (1) of the New Criminal Code.
[160] Article 70 paragraph (1) of the New Criminal Code.
[161] Article 70 paragraph (2) of the New Criminal Code.
[162] Sentencing is not intended to demean human dignity (Article 52) while Article 54 paragraph (1) obliges judges to consider the following when sentencing: 'a. the form of the fault of the offender of the Crime; b. the motive and purpose of committing the Crime; c. the inner attitude of the perpetrator of the Crime; d. Crime is committed with premeditation or unpremeditation; e. means to commit a Crime; f. the attitude and actions of the offender after committing the Crime; g. personal history, social condition, and economic condition of the offender of the Crime; h. influence of the Crime on the future of the offender of the Crime; i. influence of the Crime on the Victim or the Victim's family; j. forgiveness from the Victim and/or his family; and/or k. values of law and justice that live in society.' Article 54 paragraph (2) states: 'The lightness of the act, the personal condition of the perpetrator, or the circumstances at the time the crime was committed and what happened afterwards can be used as a basis for consideration not to impose a crime or not to impose a measure by taking into account the aspects of justice and humanity.'

instead to a fine.[163] The fine can only be imposed if the crime has no victims, the victim is not concerned, or the crime was not a case of recidivism.[164] The fines are the maximum fines according to category V and the minimum fines according to category III.[165] Such provisions do not appear in the current Criminal Code.

iii. Parole (Conditional Release)

In terms of parole, Article 72 of the New Criminal Code is very similar to the provisions in the Criminal Code and Law No 12 of 1995, where it is stated that inmates who have served at least two-thirds of their prison sentence, provided that the two-thirds of sentence served is not less than nine months, may be granted parole.[166] If a convict has served several imprisonments in a row, this is considered to be one sentence.[167] In granting parole, a probationary period and any conditions that must be met during the probationary period are determined.[168] The probationary period is the same as the remaining period of imprisonment that has not been served, plus one year.[169] If inmates are detained as suspects or defendants in another case this is not counted as time of incarceration as a probationary period.[170]

The conditions that must be met during the probationary period consist of general conditions in the form of convicts not committing a crime and special conditions in the form of convicts having to do or not do certain acts, without prejudice to freedom of religion and politics, unless determined otherwise by the judge.[171] The special conditions can be changed or revoked, or new conditions made if they are solely for the purpose of guiding convicts.[172] Convicts who violate these conditions may have their parole revoked.[173] Parole cannot be revoked if only three months remain of the probationary period, unless during that three months the convict is prosecuted for committing a crime during the probationary period.[174]

[163] Article 71 paragraph (1) of the New Criminal Code.
[164] Article 71 paragraph (2) of the New Criminal Code. The provisions as referred to in paragraph (2) letter c (not repetition of criminal acts) do not apply to people who have been sentenced to imprisonment for crimes committed before the age of 18 years (Article 71 paragraph (4) of the Criminal Code.
[165] Article 71 paragraph (3) of the New Criminal Code. According to Article 79 (1) Criminal Code Bill, the fine is category III, IDR50,000,000 (fifty million rupiah) and category V, IDR500,000,000 (five hundred million rupiah).
[166] Article 72 paragraph (1) of the New Criminal Code.
[167] Article 72 paragraph (2) of the New Criminal Code.
[168] Article 72 paragraph (3) of the New Criminal Code.
[169] Article 72 paragraph (4) of the New Criminal Code.
[170] Article 72 paragraph (5) of the New Criminal Code.
[171] Article 73 paragraph (1) of the New Criminal Code.
[172] Article 73 paragraph (2) of the New Criminal Code.
[173] Article 73 paragraph (3) of the New Criminal Code.
[174] Article 73 paragraph (4) of the New Criminal Code.

iv. Tutupan *(Undisclosed Penitentiary)*

The regulation of *Tutupan* (undisclosed penitentiary) is only briefly mentioned in the New Criminal Code. Article 74 states that people who commit criminal acts punishable by imprisonment, due to personal circumstances and their actions, can be subject instead to undisclosed penitentiary (a lighter sentence than imprisonment).[175] A undisclosed penitentiary sentence can be imposed on a defendant who commits a crime motivated by respectful reason.[176] This provision does not apply if the method of committing the crime or the consequences of the crime are such that the defendant is more likely to be sentenced to imprisonment.[177] The provisions in Article 74 of the New Criminal Code are almost the same as the current provisions in Law No 20 of 1946 concerning the undisclosed penitentiary punishment.

v. Light Imprisonment (Short-term Imprisonment)

The sentence of 'light imprisonment' ('short-term imprisonment) has been omitted from the New Criminal Code. The provisions of Articles 64 to 66 no longer mentions light imprisonment as a punishment, whether as a basic, additional, or special punishment. It seems that the drafters of the New Criminal Code are of the view that the options of imprisonment or fines are sufficient. This can be seen from the provisions of Article 619 of the New Criminal Code, which states that when this law comes into force, light imprisonment in other laws (other than this law and regional regulations) is replaced with a fine with the following provisions: (1) light imprisonment for less than six months is replaced with a maximum fine of category I;[178] and (2) light imprisonment of six months or more is replaced with a maximum fine of category II.[179] (2) In the event that a fine that is threatened alternatively with light imprisonment as referred to in paragraph (1) exceeds category II, the provisions in the legislation still apply.

vi. Fines

There are eight categories of fines in the New Criminal Code, with Category I the lightest and Category VIII the heaviest. A fine is a sum of money that must be paid by the convict based on a court decision.[180] If no specific minimum is specified,

[175] Article 74 paragraph (1) of the New Criminal Code.
[176] Article 74 paragraph (2) of the New Criminal Code.
[177] Article 74 paragraph (3) of the New Criminal Code.
[178] According to Article 79 paragraph (1) letter a New Criminal Code Category I is IDR1,000,000 (one million rupiah).
[179] According to Article 79 paragraph (1) letter b New Criminal Code Category II is IDR10,000,000 (ten million rupiah).
[180] Article 78 paragraph (1) of the New Criminal Code.

the fine is set at a minimum of IDR50,000 (USD3.33 in mid-2022).[181] The categories of fines are regulated in Article 79 of the New Criminal Code as follows:

(1) The maximum fines are determined based on:
- category I, Rp 1,000,000.00 (one million rupiah);
- category II, Rp 10,000,000.00 (ten million rupiah);
- category III, Rp 50,000,000.00 (fifty million rupiah);
- category IV, Rp 200,000,000.00 (two hundred million rupiah);
- category V, Rp 500,000,000 (five hundred million rupiah);
- category VI, Rp 2,000,000,000.00 (two billion rupiah);
- category VII, Rp 5,000,000,000.00 (five billion rupiah); and
- category VIII, Rp 50,000,000,000.00 (fifty billion rupiah).

(2) In the event of a change in the value of money, the provisions for the size of fines shall be stipulated by a Government Regulation.

The provisions of Article 79 paragraph (2) are important because they permit changes to the size of fines if the value of the Rupiah shifts. Changes can be made quickly through the issuing of government regulations. This is expected to avoid lengthy delays associated with altering the Criminal Code itself, even though the value of the Rupiah has changed considerably. This is the current situation Indonesia finds itself in: since 1960, there has been no change in the fines and values of violation (petty crimes) in the Criminal Code, despite significant changes in the value of the Rupiah. Supreme Court Regulations instead have been used to make alterations.

In imposing a fine, the judge must consider the ability of the defendant to pay the fine, by taking into account the actual income and expenses of the defendant.[182] This provision does not reduce the application of the specific minimum penalty imposed.[183] Fines must be paid within a certain period of time, as stated in the court's decision, although the court may also permit payment in instalments.[184] If the criminal fine is not paid within the required period of time, the wealth or income of the convict can be confiscated and auctioned by the prosecutor to pay off the unpaid fine.[185]

If the confiscation and auction of the assets or income are insufficient to pay off the fine, or are impossible to carry out, the unpaid fines are replaced with imprisonment, supervision, or community service, provided that the fines do not exceed category II fines.[186] The substitute sentence includes: for a substitute

[181] Article 78 paragraph (2) of the New Criminal Code.
[182] Article 80 paragraph (1) of the New Criminal Code.
[183] Article 80 paragraph (2) of the New Criminal Code.
[184] Article 81 paragraphs (1) and (2) of the New Criminal Code.
[185] Article 81 paragraph (3) of the New Criminal Code. If the confiscation and auction of assets or income as referred to in Article 81 paragraph (3) cannot be carried out, the unpaid fines above category II are replaced with imprisonment for a minimum of 1 (one) year and a maximum as stated in the Criminal Code for the crime concerned. (Article 83 paragraph 1).
[186] Article 82 paragraph (1) of the New Criminal Code.

imprisonment, a minimum of one month and a maximum of one year, which can be aggravated by a maximum of one year and four months if there is a concurrent increase in the fines; for a substitute supervision punishment, a minimum of one month and a maximum of one year, and the conditions as referred to in Article 76 paragraphs (2) and (3) apply; or for substitute community service, a minimum of eight hours and a maximum of 240 hours.[187] If at the time of serving a substitute sentence, the fine is partially paid, the length of the substitute sentence is reduced according to the appropriate value.[188] The calculation of the length of the substitute sentence is based on the size of the fine, with each IDR50,000 (or less) equivalent to one hour of community service or one day of supervision or imprisonment.[189]

vii. Supervision

Supervision as a form of punishment is not regulated in the current Criminal Code. However, Article 65 of the New Criminal Code list supervision after imprisonment and *tutupan* (undisclosed penitentiary). This means that, while there are only two main types of punishment (imprisonment and fines), supervision (in addition to jail time and community service) is offered by the New Code as an alternative model of criminal punishment.

The New Code states in Article 75 that for a criminal act that carries a maximum imprisonment of five years, the judge can impose supervision against the defendant, of course with due regard to the provisions in Article 52 (ie sentencing is not intended to degrade human dignity). Supervision is imposed for a maximum period similar to imprisonment (not more than three years in prison).[190] In the court's order on supervision, general conditions are determined, primarily that the convict does not commit another crime.[191] In addition, the decision may specify special conditions stating that (1) the convict, within a certain period of time, which is shorter than the supervision period, must replace all or part of the losses incurred as a result of the crime committed; and/or (2) the convict must do or not do something, without reducing the convit's religious and political freedom.[192]

viii. Community Service

In the Netherlands, community service (*dienstverlening*) has been implemented as a form of punishment since 1 December 1989, with the enactment of the Law

[187] Article 82 paragraph (2) of the New Criminal Code.
[188] Article 82 paragraph (3) of the New Criminal Code.
[189] Article 82 paragraph (4) of the New Criminal Code.
[190] Article 76 paragraph (1) of the New Criminal Code.
[191] Article 76 paragraph (2) of the New Criminal Code.
[192] Article 76 paragraph (3) of the New Criminal Code.

on 25 October 1989, stb 1989, 482.[193] This law regulates criminal acts in the form of unpaid community service.[194] In the Netherlands, community service is not given as an alternative to conditional punishment, fines, or light imprisonment, because community service is a heavier punishment than conditional punishment or probation. Likewise, if the fine is replaced with a community service, it is considered more severe.[195]

Only work carried out in the interest of public service can be classified as a community service. This includes work with institutions in the fields of public health, environment, culture, protection of nature conservation, and other social forms of assistance. It is considered more appropriate that judges attempt to ensure that the nature of the community service carried out is in accordance with the crime committed by the convict. For example, those who are guilty of destroying public facilities can be punished by carrying out community service with the cleaning and landscaping office. The judge can only impose a community service sentence if it is confirmed that there are people or institutions that are willing to give the short-term job to the convict. If an appropriate placement cannot found, the judge will impose an imprisonment sentence.[196]

Article 85 of the New Criminal Code states that community service can be imposed on defendants who commit crimes punishable by imprisonment of less than five years, upon whom the judge imposes a maximum imprisonment of six months or a maximum fine of category II.[197] In imposing the community service as referred to in paragraph (1), the judge is obliged to consider the following: the defendant's confession of the crime committed; the ability of the defendant to work; the defendant's approval after explaining the objectives and all matters relating to community service; social history of the defendant; protection of the defendant's work safety; the defendant's religious and political beliefs; and the ability of the defendant to pay the fine.[198] The implementation of community service should not be commercialised.[199] Community service punishment is imposed for a minimum of eight hours and a maximum of 240 hours.[200] Community service punishment is carried out for a maximum of eight hours in one day and can be performed in instalments over a maximum of six months, by taking into account the activities of the convict in carrying out his livelihood and/or other 'useful' activities.[201]

[193] This law has been amended and added through the Law dated 7 September 2000, Stb 2000.
[194] Remmelink, *Hukum Pidana* (2003) 478.
[195] Ibid 479.
[196] Ibid 480.
[197] Article 85 paragraph (1) of the New Criminal Code. According to Article 79 category II is IRD10,000,000 (ten million rupiah).
[198] Article 85 paragraph (2) of the New Criminal Code.
[199] Article 85 paragraph (3) of the New Criminal Code.
[200] Article 85 paragraph (4) of the New Criminal Code.
[201] Article 85 paragraph (5) of the New Criminal Code.

ix. Regulation of Measures in the New Criminal Code

Sentencing in the New Code adheres to a double-track system. That is, in addition to the type of punishments, the type of measures is also regulated. In this case, the judge can impose measures on those who commit criminal acts but are not able to account for their actions because of mental and/or intellectual disabilities. In addition to being punished in certain cases, the convict can also be subject to measures with the intention of providing protection to the community and upholding social order.[202]

The term 'measures' appears several times in the New Criminal Code. Article 12 paragraph (1) of New Code states that 'Criminal acts are acts which are threatened by criminal sanctions and/or *measures* by laws and regulations' (emphasis added). Meanwhile, paragraph (2) of this Article explains that to be declared a criminal act, an act that is threatened with criminal sanctions and/or *measures* by laws and regulations must be against the law or contrary to the law that lives in society.

In addition, Article 38 states that 'Every person who at the time of committing a crime suffers from a mental disability and/or intellectual disability, his criminal offence can be reduced and subject to measures'. Article 39 adds that any person who at the time of committing a crime suffers from a mental disability which is in an acute exacerbation state and is accompanied by psychotic features and/or moderate or severe intellectual disability cannot be sentenced but may be subject to measures.

Finally, the most complete and detailed arrangement is set out in Chapter III of the New Code, entitled Sentencing, Punishment, and Measures. The arrangement on measures is set out in paragraph 2 with the title Measures. Article 103 paragraph (1) states that the measures that can be imposed together with basic punishment are: counselling; rehabilitation; work training; treatment in an institution; and/or reparation for the impact of the crime. These can be said to be common types of measures, which can be imposed on every criminal offender. Meanwhile, measures for offenders who suffer from mental or intellectual disabilities are regulated in paragraph (2) of this Article. As mentioned earlier, more forms of measures are listed here than in the existing Criminal Code. The current Code offers only treatment in institutions, while the New Code also provides for counselling, rehabilitation, job training, and reparation for the impact of the crime.

Specifically related to juvenile offenders, the types of measures are regulated in Article 113 paragraph (1). It states that every child can be subject to measures in the form of: return to parents/guardians; give right to certain person to take care of the child; treatment in a mental hospital; care in a social welfare institution; obligation to attend formal education and/or training held by the government or private agencies; revocation of driving licence; and/or reparation for the impact of the crime.[203] Such measures, especially care in a social welfare institution,

[202] General elucidation of number 8 of the New Criminal Code.
[203] Article 113 paragraph (1) of the New Criminal Code.

obligation to attend formal education and/or training, and revocation of driving licence, are imposed for a maximum of one year. Meanwhile, paragraph (3) of this Article states that a minor under the age of 14 years cannot be sentenced to punishment and can only be subject to measures.

Specifically for corporations, measures are regulated in Article 123. According to this Article, measures that may be imposed on corporations are: takeover of the corporation; financing of job training; placement under supervision; and/or placing the corporation under guardianship/ custody.

V. Increases and Reductions of Sentences

A. Increases and Reductions of Sentences in the Criminal Code

Chapter III of the Criminal Code regulates the reasons for excluding criminal responsibility, reasons for mitigating criminal responsibility, and aggravating criminal responsibility. Only two aggravating reasons are regulated in this chapter, specifically in Articles 52 and 52a letter e. Article 52 reads:

> If an official, due to committing a criminal offence, violates a special obligation from his position or when committing a criminal offence uses the power, opportunity or means given to him because of his position, the punishment can be increased by one-third.

So, for example, if an official who because of his position is given a vehicle and then uses the vehicle to commit a crime, the punishment can be increased by one-third.

However, it must be remembered that the provisions of Article 52 do not apply to criminal acts regulated in Chapter XXVIII, which regulates offences of office. This is because the punishments in that chapter have been calculated separately, so that there is no need to carry out further punishment if an offender commits a crime by violating a special obligation of his position or using the power, opportunity, or means given to him because of his position.

Meanwhile, Article 52a reads: 'If at the time of committing a crime, the national flag of the Republic of Indonesia is used, the punishment for the crime may be increased by one-third.' This article was added in 1958. It is not explained in this article how the national flag might be used when committing a crime, but it seems that the intention is to prevent offenders from using the national flag to make it appear as if the actions they have committed (eg fraud) are official or legal.

Other provisions regarding recidivism regulated in Articles 486, 487, and 488 of the Criminal Code are also considered as reasons for aggravating criminal responsibility.

The provisions regarding recidivism in the Criminal Code are divided into two. The first is the *tussen stelsel* (intermediate/middle system), regulated in Articles 487, 488, and 489. They are called this because the provisions in Articles 486, 487, and 488 are neither general recidivism nor special recidivism. General recidivism is when someone who has committed a crime and has been sentenced by a judge, then commits another crime. The repetition can be any type of crime, not just the same as the first crime. The second provision in the Criminal Code is special recidivism, which is contained in several articles, and is therefore applicable only to certain crimes, not to all crimes. Special recidivism is also a crime that an offender commits again, but the type of crime must be the same as the offender's previous crime. The Criminal Code does not use general recidivism, but does use special recidivism for several criminal acts, and intermediate recidivism systems as regulated in Articles 486, 487, and 488, which regulate crimes relating to property, human life and body, and insults and defamation. In these three articles, it is determined that a person's punishment can be one-third if (1) they repeat a crime in the same group (ie within the same article); and (2) the second crime (which is committed again) is committed within five years since the perpetrator finished serving all or part of his previous sentence.

Regarding the reasons for mitigating criminal responsibility in the Criminal Code, only Articles 45, 46, and 47 regulate this. These articles regulate criminal acts committed by juvenile offenders under the age of 16 years. They essentially stipulate that those who commit a crime under the age of 16 have two options: (1) to be returned to their parents, guardians, or foster parents or to be taken into state custody (education institution/certain person/organisation) without any punishment; or (2) be sentenced but with the maximum basic punishment for the act reduced by one-third, or, if is a crime which could be punishable by death or life imprisonment, a maximum of 15 years.

Special aggravating and mitigating reasons in the Criminal Code are provisions in certain articles that will either increase or reduce the punishment for criminal acts formulated in those articles. This is known as a 'qualified offence'. For example, theft in Article 362 is punishable by five years' imprisonment. However, Article 363 increases the criminal sanction to a maximum of seven years if the theft is committed against animals or when there is a fire or flood. Meanwhile, the mitigating reasons include Article 364, which applies if the value of the stolen item is less than IDR2,500,000, meaning the maximum sanction is three months' imprisonment.

B. Increases and Reductions of Sentences Outside the Criminal Code

It should be emphasised that, since 1997, with the enactment of the Juvenile Court Law, Articles 45, 46, and 47 of the Criminal Code are no longer valid.[204] In this law, the age range for juveniles who commit criminal acts (referred

[204] Article 67 of Law No 3 of 1997.

to as 'juvenile delinquency') is defined in Article 1 as from eight to 18 years of age. However, the minimum age was later increased in 2010 to 12 years by Constitutional Court Decision No 1/PUU-VIII/2010. Article 26 of the Law states that if a juvenile commits a crime, the penalty will be reduced by one half of the maximum adult sentence. This is different from the old provisions in Article 47 of the Criminal Code which is reduced by one third (from the sanction of adult punishment).

In 2012, the 1997 Juvenile Court Law was replaced by Law No 11 of 2012 concerning the Juvenile Criminal Justice System, meaning the 1997 law is no longer in effect. The term to be used is no longer 'juvenile delinquency' but 'child in conflict with the law',[205] but the age limit remains the same (12 to 18 years). Importantly, Article 69 states that children who are not yet 14 years old can only be subject to measures. The law made many changes to the previous version, including in terms of types of punishments (warning, probation, job training, and coaching in institutions); protection of rights; a restorative justice approach in all stages of the judiciary; and special arrangements for all parties who handle juvenile cases (investigators, public prosecutors, judges, correctional officers, etc). If a juvenile is sentenced to a punishment, Article 79 states that the sanction is the same as a maximum of half of the maximum punishment for adults; this is the same as in the 1997 law.

Meanwhile, as to reasons for aggravating criminal responsibility outside the Criminal Code, individual laws regulate their respective reasons. For example, this is seen in Article 2 paragraph (2) of Law No 31 of 1999 as amended by Law No 20 of 2001. Article 2 paragraph (1) of this Law states:

> Everyone who unlawfully commits an act of enriching himself or another person or a corporation that is detrimental to state finances or the state's economy, shall be sentenced to life imprisonment or a minimum of 4 (four) years and a maximum of 20 (twenty) years and a minimum fine of Rp 200 million and a maximum of Rp 1 billion.

Article 2 paragraph (2) provides the aggravating reason:

> In the event that the criminal act of corruption as referred to in paragraph (1) is committed under certain circumstances, the death penalty may be imposed.

What is meant by 'under certain circumstances' here is:

> Circumstances that can be used as a reason for aggravating criminal responsibility for perpetrators of criminal acts of corruption, namely if the crime is committed against funds designated for the prevention of dangerous conditions, national natural disasters, mitigation of social unrest caused by widespread, overcoming the economic and monetary crisis, and the repetition of corruption.

[205] Article 1 number 3 of Law No 11 of 2012.

C. Increases and Reductions of Sentences in the New Criminal Code

In the New Criminal Code, Article 58 states that the factors that aggravate punishment include:

(1) officials who commit criminal acts so that they violate special position obligations or commit criminal acts by abusing authority, opportunity, or facilities given to them because of their position;
(2) the use of the national flag, the national anthem, or the symbol of the Indonesian state when committing a crime; or
(3) repetition of a crime.

Article 59 states that punishment for the reason of aggravating criminal responsibility as referred to in Article 58 can be increased by a maximum of one-third of the maximum criminal punishment. This is the same as in the current Criminal Code.

In the New Criminal Code, criminal acts committed by and measures imposed on juveniles are no longer referred to as reasons for mitigating criminal responsibility. This is regulated in detail in the section on punishments and measures for juveniles (Part IV, Book 1). The provisions are similar to those in Law No 11 of 2012 concerning the Juvenile Criminal Justice System.

VI. Concurrence of Criminal Offences in the Criminal Code

In criminal law literature, there are three types of concurrence: (1) *Eendaadse Samenloop* (concurrence with one action); (2) *Meerdaadse Samenloop* (concurrence with several actions); and (3) *Voorgezette Handeling* (concurrence in the form of continuing actions).[206] What do these three types of concurrence mean? They will be discussed one by one below.

A. Concurrence of Criminal Offences in the Form of One Action

According to Simons, *eendaadse samenloop* (concurrence with one action) is if the defendant only commits one prohibited action, but, by committing that action, this action turns out to have fulfilled the formulations of several criminal provisions. In other words, if by committing one act, the defendant is found to have in

[206] Wirjono Prodjodikoro, *Asas-Asas Hukum Pidana di Indonesia* (Bandung, Refika Aditama, 2003) 142.

fact committed several criminal acts.[207] Kartanagara agrees with this definition, stating that *eendaadse samenloop* exists when a person commits an act and, by committing that one act, violates several rules of criminal law, thus committing several offences.[208]

According to Hazewinkel-Suringa, there is an *eendaadse samenloop* (*concursus idealis*) if an act has fulfilled a formulation of the offence, but inevitably it also includes other criminal regulations. For example, a rape that is perpetrated on a public road is included under rape (Article 285 of the Criminal Code) and under violations of public decency (Article 281 of the Criminal Code). According to Pompe, in this situation, there occurs a *concursus idealis*: that is, if a person commits a concrete act directed to a single goal, but it is the object of (another) legal rule. For example, sexual relations with one's own child who is not yet 15 years old. This act is included in Article 294 of the Criminal Code (obscene acts with one's own child who is underage) and Article 287 of the Criminal Code (premarital sexual intercourse with a woman who is under 15 years old). According to Bernardus Maria Taverne, there is a *concursus idealis*: when viewed from the point of view of criminal law, there are two or more acts, and these actions cannot be considered separately. Therefore, a *concursus idealis* does not occur in the case of an intoxicated person driving a car without lights at night. Here 'driving a car while being intoxicated' describes the act of the person, while 'driving a car at night without lights' describes the state of the car.[209]

Let us examine another example of this *eendaadse samenloop* (*concursus idealis*). A man on a public street physically sexually assaults a woman. In this incident, the man perpetrated one act of sexual assault (one *daad*). However, because it was carried out on a public street, this behaviour has fulfilled the formulation of two different criminal provisions: (1) physical sexual harassment as regulated in Article 4 paragraph (1) in conjunction with Article 6 of Law No 12 of 2022 on Criminal Acts of Sexual Violence with a sanction of imprisonment of four years and/or a fine of IDR50 million and; (2) ruining public decency, as regulated in Article 281 of the Criminal Code, with a sanction of imprisonment of two years and 8 months.[210]

Eendaadse samenloop is regulated in Article 63 of the Criminal Code, which reads:

> (1) Valt een feit in meer dan eene strafbepaling, dan wordt slechts eene dier bepalingen toegepast, bij verschil die waarbij de zwaarste hoofdstraft is gesteld.
> (2) Indien voor een feit dat in eene algemeene strafbepaling valt, eene bijzondere strafbepaling bestaat, komt deze alleen in aanmerking.

[207] PAF Lamintang and Fransiscus Theojunior Lamintang, *Dasar-Dasar Hukum Pidana di Indonesia* (Jakarta, Sinar Grafika, 2019) 688.

[208] Kartanegara, *Hukum Pidana Kumpulan Kuliah* (nd) 140.

[209] Barda Nawawi Arief, *Sari Kuliah Hukum Pidana II* (Semarang, Badan Penyediaan Bahan Kuliah Fakultas Hukum Universitas Diponegoro, 1993) 50–51.

[210] Article 281 of the Criminal Code contains the formulation of the offence: (1) Deliberately violating decency in public; (2) Deliberately violating decency in front of other people whose presence there is not of their own volition.

[(1) If an act falls under more than one criminal law, only one of these rules will apply, if different, the one that is imposed contains the most severe basic punishment.
(2) If an act, which is included in a general criminal code, is also regulated in a special criminal rule, then only the specific one will be imposed.]

We can see there is a division between Article 63 paragraph (1) and paragraph (2). Paragraph (1) states if there is *een feit* (one behaviour) that falls under more than one criminal rule (*strafbepaling*), and the relevant punishments vary in severity, what applies is the provision that contains a more severe criminal sanction.

An example of an incident that meets the formulation of Article 63 paragraph (1) is as follows: A shoots at B who is behind a glass door. B dies, and the glass in front of him shatters. Here, there are two provisions that are violated: homicide, as regulated in Article 338 of the Criminal Code, with a maximum penalty of 15 years in prison, and damage to other people's property, as regulated in Article 406 of the Criminal Code, with a maximum penalty of two years and 8 months in prison. In this case, the provision on homicide (15 years in prison) will be used, as it is more severe.

However, Article 63 paragraph (2) is different. It deems that if there is *een feit* (one behaviour) which is included in more than one criminal rule, and those include both *algemeene strafbepaling* (general criminal rules) and *bijzondere strafbepaling* (specific criminal rules), then specific provisions are used (no matter whether the relevant sanctions are heavier or lighter). So, Article 63 paragraph (2) of the Criminal Code applies the principle of *lex specialis derogate legi generali*.[211]

An example of an incident that is in accordance with the formulation of Article 63 paragraph (2) would be this: in order to nominate himself as a candidate for the X Provincial House of Representatives, A submits a counterfeit diploma to fulfil one of the requirements to stand for election to the General Election Commission of Province X. Here, one act is committed (using a counterfeit diploma), but it violates two provisions: (1) Article 263 paragraph (2) of the Criminal Code with a penalty of six years, which is a general provision; and (2) Article 520 of Law No 7 of 2017 concerning General Elections, specifically 'intentionally using counterfeit letters or documents to become candidates for members of the House of Representatives, Regional Representative Council, Provincial House of Representatives, Regency/City House of Representatives', with a maximum imprisonment of six years and a maximum fine of IDR72 million. In an incident like this, A should therefore be subject to the latter article (ie Article 520 of Law No 7 of 2017), as it is a special provision.

Let us look at another example of the provisions in Article 63 (2) of the Criminal Code, in a situation where both the criminal acts committed are regulated in the Criminal Code. For example, A steals cattle belonging to B. Here A's action fulfils two articles in the Criminal Code: Article 362 regarding theft

[211] Lamintang and Lamintang, *Dasar-Dasar Hukum Pidana* (2019) 177.

('Any person who takes property, wholly or partially belonging to another') and Article 363 paragraph (1), specifically on theft of cattle. The theft of cattle fulfils all the formulations of Article 362 but because the stolen element is cattle, Article 363 paragraph (1) is used because it is a special provision while Article 362 is a general provision.

Overall, the system used in Article 63 of the Criminal Code is absorption (pure absorption).[212] This can be seen from the Article's use of the phrase 'only one of the rules is imposed'. The definition of a pure absorption system is that if a person commits an act that constitutes several criminal acts, each of which is sanctioned with various kinds of punishment, then that person is only sentenced to one punishment, and the punishment is as if it includes other punishment which are subject to these crimes.[213]

Therefore, there are several provisions that must be applied, but only one is actually applied. In the event that some of these provisions use more severe criminal sanctions, then the provisions with the heavier punishment are used. If some of the provisions are general and some are specific, then special provisions are applied, no matter whether the relevant punishment is lighter or heavier. This is a pure absorption arrangement.

B. Concurrence of Criminal Offences in the Form of a Continued Action

According to Remmelink, *voorgezette handeling* (continued action) originates from Germany. In a continued action, there is more than one action and one action is related to another and forms unity. The connection must meet two conditions: (1) it is the embodiment of a forbidden will and decision; and (2) the act must be of the same kind. That is, the act falls under the same criminal provisions.[214]

R Soesilo describes a continued action as several actions that are related to one another. To be considered as a continued action, the following conditions must be met: (1) the actions must arise from an intention, will, or decision; (2) the actions must be the same or the same kind; and (3) the time between one action and the next should not be too long.[215]

In Indonesia, examples of *voorgezette handeling* are often found in corruption cases. For example, A intends to commit corruption in the form of embezzlement in office, with the fraud amounting to IDR100 billion. However, A did not do this all at once, because it would be very noticeable and suspicious. So, he perpetrated

[212] See D Schaffmeister, N Keijzer, and E PH Sutorius, *Hukum Pidana* (Bandung, Citra Aditya Bakti, 2007) 176–77. See also Arief, *Sari Kuliah Hukum Pidana II* (1993) 51–52.
[213] Kartanegara, *Hukum Pidana Kumpulan Kuliah* (nd) 137.
[214] Hiariej, *Prinsip-Prinsip Hukum Pidana* (2016) 408–09.
[215] R Soesilo, *Kitab Undang-Undang Hukum Pidana (KUHP) Serta Komentar-Komentarnya Lengkap Pasal Demi Pasal* (Bogor, Politeia, 1995) 81–82.

several embezzlements in his position every few months, until after one year, he had embezzled the IDR100 billion as intended. Another example: A intended to deceive B to obtain IDR100 million. He does not do it all at once. One day, A cheated B into giving him IDR10 million. A week later, he did it again, and so on, until A had obtained IDR100 million from B.

The arrangement for *voorgezette handeling* in the Criminal Code is contained in Article 64. This article consists of three paragraphs, with the first paragraph containing the conditions for *voorgezette handeling*. The second and third paragraphs provide special provisions or exceptions from paragraph one, specifically for the crimes of counterfeiting and using counterfeit money (second paragraph), and several violation/petty crimes (third paragraph). The full text of Article 64 (1) of the Criminal Code is as follows:

> If between several acts, even though each of them is a felony or violation, there is a relationship in such a way that it must be considered as one continuous act (*voorgezette handeling*), then only one criminal law is imposed; if they are different, the one imposed which contains the most severe basic punishment.

Article 64 paragraph (1) regulates the conditions for *vorgezette handeling* as well as the punishment system. The conditions for *voorgezette handeling* are: (1) there are several actions; (2) each of these acts is a felony or each is a violation; (3) the actions are related in such a way that they must be considered as continuing actions.

The statement that actions are 'related in such a way' in the doctrine is explained that three things must be fulfilled, as mentioned above: (1) must arise from an intention, or will or decision; (2) the actions must be the same or the same kind; and (3) the time between one action and the next should not be too long.[216] What does 'not be too long' mean? It is unclear: is it one hour, one day, one week? It must be assessed by judges on a case by case basis as to whether these conditions are met.

C. Concurrence of Criminal Offences in the Form of Several Actions

According to D Schaffmeister, N Keijzer, and E PH Sutorius, in cases of *meerdaadse samenloop* (concurrence through several actions), there are several different criminal acts that must be brought to court to be tried.[217] According to Simons, *meerdaadse samenloop* occurs when the defendant has committed more than one prohibited behaviour, and by carrying out these behaviours, the defendant has committed more than one crime.[218] Meanwhile, according to Kartanagara,

[216] Soesilo, *Kitab Undang-Undang Hukum* (1995) 81–82.
[217] Schaffmeister, Keijzer, and Sutorius, *Hukum Pidana* (2007) 177.
[218] Lamintang and Lamintang, *Dasar-Dasar Hukum Pidana* (2019) 689.

meerdaadse samenloop exists when a person commits several *feit* (actions) which are considered as individual acts, each of which being a criminal act, and none of these acts has been sanctioned with punishment.[219]

Here is an example of *meerdaadse samenloop*.

Action 1: A committed a burglary at B's house on 10 January 2020. Action 2: On 12 January 2020, A committed battery against C. Action 3: On 15 January 2020, A insulted D.

A was caught on 21 February 2020 and put on trial on 30 March 2020. In this case, there was *meerdaadse samenloop*, because he committed theft on 10 January, battery two days later, and insult three days after that. The judge, in imposing a sentence on A, must therefore refer to the concurrence rules in the Criminal Code.

Meerdaadse samenloop is regulated in Articles 65 to 71 of the Criminal Code. Among those articles (particularly Articles 65, 66, and 70) there is a division, namely the combination of several behaviours consisting of: (1) a felony that is punishable by a similar basic punishment (Article 65); (2) a felony that is punishable by a different basic punishment (Article 66); (3) felony with violation (Article 70); and (4) violation with violation (Article 70). For Articles 65 and 66, the cumulative system applies, which is limited in nature.[220] This can be seen from the phrasing used in Article 65: 'The maximum sentence imposed is the maximum amount of punishment that is sanctioned for that act, but the amount may not exceed the maximum heaviest punishment plus one-third.'[221] For Article 70, however, the system used is cumulative (unlimited/pure).[222]

VII. Concurrence of Criminal Offences in the New Criminal Code

The regulation of concurrent criminal acts in the New Criminal Code is almost the same as that in the current Criminal Code. Article 125 paragraph (1) of the New Code is similar to Article 63 paragraph (1) of the current Code, but the new Article 125 paragraph (2) differs from the old Article 63 paragraph (2). Article 63 (2) of the current Code states that if general provisions clash with special provisions, then special ones apply. Article 125 (2) of the New Code states the

[219] Kartanegara, *Hukum Pidana Kumpulan Kuliah* (nd) 173.

[220] The sentencing system regulated in Article 65 of the Criminal Code is cumulative (limited). Simons and Pompe disagree with Remmelink. According to Simons and Pompe, Article 65 of the Criminal Code contains an absorption system (which is sharpened). See Remmelink, *Hukum Pidana* (2003) 574.

[221] While the phrase in Article 66 of the Criminal Code reads: '… a criminal offence is imposed for each crime, but the amount may not exceed the maximum heaviest punishment plus one-third'.

[222] Schaffmeister, Keijzer, and Sutorius, *Hukum Pidana* (2007) 177. The meaning of this system of unlimited (pure) accumulation is that if a person commits several acts which are punishable by separate punishments, then all the punishments for all the crimes committed by that person are imposed on that person.

same, but adds 'unless the Law provides otherwise'. Overall, however, the norms are the same.

The norms of Articles 127 and 128 of the new Criminal Code are also essentially the same as the norms in Articles 65 and 66 of the current Criminal Code, with several editorial changes to make them clearer and more detailed. The essence remains: (1) there is a concurrent form of *meerdaadse samenloop* (*concursus realis*); and (2) there is a cumulative (limited) sentencing system.

Article 129 of the New Criminal Code and Article 67 of the current Criminal Code also have the same essence: if in a case of concurrence, an offender is sentenced to death or life imprisonment, the individual may not be sentenced to other punishment, except for additional punishment. Article 130 of the new Bill is almost the same as Article 68 of the current Code, only the editorial differences are clearer. Likewise, with regard to 'lagging offences', the rules in the new Article 131 are similar to the current Article 71. However, in Article 131 paragraph (2) of the new Criminal Code, there are clearer guidelines for judges, stating: If the sentence imposed as referred to in paragraph (1) has reached the maximum punishment, the judge simply declares that the defendant is guilty without imposing criminal sanction.'

BIBLIOGRAPHY

Abidin, Andi Zainal, *Hukum Pidana I* (Jakarta, Sinar Grafika, 1883).

Abidin, AZ and Hamzah, Andi, *Pengantar Dalam Hukum Pidana Indonesia* (Jakarta, Yarsif Watampone, 2010).

Adams, Wahiduddin, 'Perbandingan dan Hierarki Qanun, Perdasi, Perdasus dan Perda dalam Sistem Hukum Nasional' (2004) 1(2) *Jurnal Legislasi Indonesia* 32–33.

Agusman, Damos Dumoli, 'Self-Executing and Non-Self Executing Treaties: What Does it Mean' (2014) 11 *Jurnal Hukum Internasional* 320–44.

Allen, Michael, *Textbook on Criminal Law* (New York, Oxford University Press, 2007).

Amidjaja, MH Tirta, *Pokok-Pokok Hukum Pidana* (Jakarta, Penerbit Djakarta, 1955).

Anindyajati, Titis, Rachman, Irfan Nur, and Onita, Anak Agung Dian, 'Konstitusionalitas Norma Sanksi Pidana sebagai Ultimum Remedium dalam Pembentukan Perundang-Undangan' (2016) *Jurnal Konstritusi* 12, 4, 884–85.

Anjari, Warih, 'Pencabutan Hak Politik Terpidana Korupsi dalam Perspektif Hak Asasi Manusia' (2015) 8(1) *Jurnal Yudisial* 23–44.

Arief, Barda Nawawi, *Kapita Selekta Hukum Pidana* (Bandung, Citra Aditya Bakti, 2003).

Arief, Barda Nawawi, *Sari Kuliah Hukum Pidana II* (Semarang, Badan Penyediaan Bahan Kuliah Fakultas Hukum Universitas Diponegoro, 1993).

Committee for the 75th Anniversary of Kasman Singodimedjo, *Hidup itu Berjuang, Kasman Singodimedjo 75 Tahun* (Jakarta, Bulan Bintang, 1982).

Daud Silalahi, M, *Hukum Lingkungan dalam sistem penegakan hukum lingkungan Indonesia* (Bandung, PT Alumni, 2014).

Eldefonso, Edward and Coffey, Alan R, *Criminal Law: History, Philosophy, Enforcement* (New York, Harper & Row Publishers, 1981).

Fitriasih, Surastini, *Penerapan Ajaran Penyertaan* (2006).

Fokkema, DC, Chorus, JMJ, Hondius, EH, and Lisser, E Ch (eds), *Introduction to Dutch Law for Foreign Lawyers* (Deventer, Kluwer, 1978).

Garner, Bryan A (ed), *A Handbook of Criminal Law Terms* (St Paul, Minnesota, West Group, 2000).

Gouda, Frances, *American visions of the Netherlands East Indies/Indonesia: US foreign policy and Indonesian nationalism, 1920–1949* (Amsterdam, Amsterdam University Press, 2002).

Hamzah, Andi, *Asas-Asas Hukum Pidana* (Jakarta, Yarsif Watampone, 2005).

Hamzah, Andi, *Asas-Asas Hukum Pidana*, revised edition (Jakarta, Rineka Cipta, 1994).

Han Bing Siong, *Hukum Pidana 1 (Capita Selecta) Kuliah Mr. Han Bin Siong 1960–1961* (Jakarta, Faculty of Law and Social Sciences, University of Indonesia, 1961).

Hiariej, Eddy OS, *Asas Legalitas & Penemuan Hukum dalam Hukum Pidana* (Jakarta, Erlangga, 2009).

Hiariej, Eddy OS, Paper on the Scientific Discussion on Deferred Prosecution Agreement at the Faculty of Law, University of Indonesia, Depok, 17 February 2020.

Hiariej, Eddy OS, *Pengantar Hukum Pidana Internasional* (Surabaya, Erlangga, 2009).

Hiariej, Eddy OS, *Prinsip-Prinsip Hukum Pidana* (Yogyakarta, Cahaya Atma Pustaka, 2016).

Hiariej, Eddy OS, *Prinsip-Prinsip Hukum Pidana*, revised edn (Yogyakarta, Cahaya Atma Pustaka, 2016).

Huda, Chairul, *Dari 'Tiada Pidana Tanpa Kesalahan' Menuju Kepada Tiada Pertanggungjawaban Pidana Tanpa Kesalahan – Tinjauan Kritis Terhadap Teori Pemisahan Tindak Pidana dan Pertanggungjawaban Pidana*, 6th edn (Jakarta, Kencana, 2015).

Jareborg, Nils, 'Criminalization as Last Resort (Ultima Ratio)' (2005) 2 *Ohio State Journal of Criminal Law* 521, 524–25.
Jonkers, JE, *Buku Pedoman Hukum Pidana Hindia Belanda* [*Handboek Van Het Nederlandsch-Indische Strafrecht*], translated by Tim Penerjemah Bina Aksara (Jakarta, PT Bina Aksara, 1987).
Kanter, EY and Sianturi, SR, *Asas-Asas Hukum Pidana di Indonesia dan Penerapannya* (Jakarta, Storia Grafika, 2018).
Karni, *Ringkasan tentang Hukum Pidana* (Jakarta, Balai Buku Indonesia, 1950).
Kartanegara, Satochid, *Hukum Pidana, Kumpulan Kuliah Prof Satochid Kartanegara* (Jakarta, Balai Lektur Mahasiswa, nd).
Kartanegara, Satochid, *Hukum Pidana Kumpulan Kuliah Prof Satochid Kartanegara dan Pendapat-Pendapat Para Ahli Hukum Terkemuka* (Jakarta, Balai Lektur Mahasiswa, nd).
Kartanegara, Satochid, *Hukum Pidana Kumpulan Kuliah Prof Satochid Kartanegara dan Pendapat Para Ahli Hukum Terkemuka* (Jakarta, Balai Lektur Mahasiswa, nd).
Kartanegara, Satochid, *Hukum Pidana Kumpulan Kuliah Prof Satochid Kartanegara dan Pendapat2 Para Ahli Hukum Terkemuka, Bagian Satu* (Jakarta, Balai Lektur Mahasiswa, nd).
Kartanegara, Satochid, *Hukum Pidana, Kumpulan Kuliah Prof. Satochid Kartanegara, S.H. dan Pendapat-Pendapat Para Ahli Hukum Terkemuka* (Jakarta, Balai Lektur Mahasiswa, nd).
Lamintang, PAF and Lamintang, Fransiscus Theojunior, *Dasar-Dasar Hukum Pidana di Indonesia* (Jakarta, Sinar Grafika, 2019).
Lamintang, PAF, *Hukum Penitensier Indonesia* (Bandung, CV Armico, 1984).
Larry Mays, G, Thomas Winfree Jr, L, and Ruddel, Rick, *Contemporary Corrections: A Critical Thinking Approach* (Belmont, Thomson/Wadsworth, 2005).
Leavens, Arthur, 'A Causation Approach to Criminal Omissions' (1988) *California Law Review* 1.
Machmud, Syahrul, *Problematika Penerapan Delik Formil dalam Perspektif Penegakan Hukum Pidana Lingkungan di Indonesia* (Bandung, CV Mandar Maju, 2012).
Malik, Adam, *Riwayat Proklamasi Kemerdekaan 17 Agustus 1945* (Jakarta, Wijaya, 1962).
Marpaung, Leden, *Asas-Teori-Praktik Hukum Pidana* (Jakarta, Sinar Grafika, 2014).
Mertokusumo, Sudikno, *Mengenal Hukum: Suatu Pengantar* (Yogyakarta, Liberty, 1999).
Mertokusumo, Sudikno, *Mengenal Hukum: Suatu Pengantar* (Yogyakarta, Liberty, 2002).
Miethe, Terance D and Lu, Hong, *Punishment A Comparative Historical Perspective* (Cambridge, Cambridge University Press, 2005).
Moeljatno, *Asas-Asas Hukum Pidana* (Jakarta, Rineka Cipta, 1993).
Moeljatno, *Azas-Azas Hukum Pidana* (Jakarta, Rineka Cipta, 2002).
Moeljatno, *Hukum Pidana Delik-Delik Percobaan Delik-Delik Penyertaan* (Jakarta, Bina Aksara, 1985).
Moeljatno, *Hukum Pidana, Delik-Delik Percobaan Delik-Delik Penyertaan* (Jakarta, Bina Aksara, 2017).
Moeljatno, *Kitab Undang-Undang Hukum Pidana (Indonesian Criminal Code)*, new edition (Jakarta, Bumi Aksara, 2016).
Moerings, Martin, 'Apakah Pidana Penjara Efektif' in Agustinus Pohan, Topo Santoso, and Martin Moerings (eds), *Hukum Pidana dalam Perspektif* (Denpasar, Pustaka Larasan, 2012).
Mutiara, Dali, *Kitab Undang-Undang Hukum Pidana Republik Indonesia* (Jakarta, Bintang Indonesia, 1948).
Mutiara, Dali, *KUHP, Kitab Undang2 Hukum Pidana Republik Indonesia* (Jakarta, Toko Buku 'Suar', 1951).
Mutiara, Dali, *KUHP, Kitab Undang-Undang Hukum Pidana Republik Indonesia (Wetboek van Strafrecht voor Indonesie jang telah dirobah dan dibaharui)* [Books of Criminal Law of the Republic of Indonesia] (Jakarta, Toko Buku 'Suar', 1951).
Poernomo, Bambang, *Asas-Asas Hukum Pidana* (Jakarta, Ghalia Indonesia, 1992).
Poernomo, Bambang, *Asas-Asas Hukum Pidana*, 7th edn (Jakarta, Ghalia Indonesia, 1994).
Prakoso, Abintoro, *Sejarah Hukum* (Yogyakarta, Aswaja Pressindo, 2019).
Prodjodikoro, Wirjono, *Asas-asas Hukum Pidana di Indonesia* (Bandung, Eresco, 1969).
Prodjodikoro, Wirjono, *Asas-Asas Hukum Pidana di Indonesia* (Bandung, Refika Aditama, 2003).
Prodjodikoro, Wirjono, *Asas-Asas Hukum Pidana di Indonesia* (Bandung, Refika Aditama, 2004).
Pustaka, Balai *Kitab Oendang2 Hoekoeman Bagi Hindia Belanda* (Batavia, Balai Poestaka, 1940).

Reksodiputro, Mardjono, *Kriminologi dan Sistem Peradilan Pidana* (Jakarta, Universitas Indonesia, 1994).

Reksodiputro, Mardjono, *Sistem Peradilan Pidana* (Jakarta, Rajagrafindo Persada, 2020).

Remmelink, Jan, *Hukum Pidana – Komentar atas Pasal-Article Terpenting dari Kitab Undang-Undang Hukum Pidana Belanda dan Padanannya dalam Kitab Undang-Undang Hukum Pidana Indonesia*, translated by Tristam Pascal Moeliono (Jakarta, PT Gramedia Pustaka Utama, 2003).

Saleh, Roeslan, *Perbuatan Pidana dan Pertanggungjawaban Pidana: Dua Pengertian Dasar dalam Hukum Pidana* (Jakarta, Aksara Baru, 1983).

Santoso, Topo, 'Suatu Tinjauan atas Efektivitas Pemidanaan' in Agustinus Pohan, Topo Santoso, and Martin Moerings (eds), *Hukum Pidana dalam Perspektif* (Denpasar, Pustaka Larasan, 2012).

Santoso, Topo, *Hukum Pidana, Suatu Pengantar* (Jakarta, Rajawali Pers, 2021).

Sapardjaja, Komariah Emong, *Ajaran Sifat Melawan Hukum Materiil dalam Hukum Pidana Indonesia* (Studi Kasus tentang Penerapan dan Perkembangannya dalam Yurisprudensi) (Bandung, Alumni, 2002).

Schaffmeister, D, Keijzer, N and Sutorius, E PH, *Hukum Pidana* (Bandung, Citra Aditya Bakti, 2007).

Schaffmeister, D, Keizer, N and Sutorius, E PH, *Hukum Pidana* (Yogyakarta, Liberty, 2003).

Sjahdeini, Sutan Remy, *Ajaran Pemidanaan: Tindak Pidana Korporasi & Seluk-Beluknya* (Jakarta, Kencana, 2017).

Soesilo, R, *Kitab Undang-Undang Hukum Pidana (KUHP) Serta Komentar-Komentarnya Lengkap Pasal demi Pasal* (Bogor, Politeia, 1995).

Soesilo, R, *Pokok-Pokok Hukum Pidana Peraturan Umum dan Delik-Delik Khusus* (Bogor, Polietia, 1984).

Sofian, Ahmad, *Ajaran Kausalitas Hukum Pidana* (Jakarta, Kencana, 2020).

Sudarto, *Hukum Pidana I*, revised edn (Semarang, Sudarto Foundation, 2013).

Tresna, R, *Azas-azas Hukum Pidana* ((Jakarta, Tiara, 1959).

Tresna, R, *Azas-azas Hukum Pidana Disertai Pembahasan Beberapa Perbuatan Pidana yang Penting* (Yogyakarta, Tiara Wacana, 1959).

Utrecht, E, *Rangkaian Sari Kuliah Hukum Pidana 1* (Surabaya, Pustaka Tinta Mas, 1994).

Utrecht, E, *Rangkaian Sari Kuliah Hukum Pidana II* (Bandung, Penerbitan Universitas, 1962).

Van Bemmelen, JM, *Hukum Pidana 1, Hukum Pidana Material Bagian Umum*, translated by Hasnan (Bandung, Binacipta, 1987).

INDEX

www.ingramcontent.com/pod-product-compliance
Ingram Content Group UK Ltd.
Pitfield, Milton Keynes, MK11 3LW, UK
UKHW020243290926
15470UKWH00002B/711

9 781509 950928